Shopping Malls and Other Sacred Spaces

PUTTING GOD IN PLACE

JON PAHL

Brazos Press
A Division of Baker Book House Co
Grand Rapids, Michigan 49516

Published by Brazos Press
a division of Baker Book House Company
P.O. Box 6287, Grand Rapids, MI 49516-6287
www.brazospress.com

Printed in the United States of America

Library of Congress Cataloging-in-Publication Data

Pahl, Jon, 1958–
Shopping malls and other sacred spaces : putting God in place / John Pahl.
p. cm.
Includes bibliographical references.
ISBN 1-58743-045-2 (pbk.)
1. Sacred space. 2. Theology. 3. Sacred space—United States. 4. Christianity and culture—United States. I. Title.
BV895.P34 2003
261′.0973—dc21 2003012189

Shopping Malls and Other Sacred Spaces

Contents

Part 2 God's Clothing 139

To Martin E. Marty

With gratitude

Introduction

This book began more than fifteen years ago as a somewhat whimsical slide show for a church education event. The congregation of which I was at the time a member—Ascension Lutheran Church in Riverside, Illinois—was planning a major renovation of the interior space of the building. As chair of the Christian Education Committee, and as an earnest graduate student at the University of Chicago Divinity School, I was asked by my mentor, Martin E. Marty—also a member of Ascension—to prepare "something" for an adult forum presentation on "sacred space." As I look back, I suspect that I was invited to make this presentation in order to help justify the renovation to potentially reluctant congregants. In any event, Marty invited me to use his personal library for books and images on the topic, and I spent several very pleasant hours at his home reading about places and photographing images (this was "back in the day" before scanners). The show eventually gained the ostentatious title: "What in the World Is Sacred Space? From Bethel to the Sacred Shrine of the Mall." Despite its title, the forty-five minute show apparently did its work well. There was little or no resistance to the renovation. The slide show also set me on the scholarly "trajectory," as such things are called, that has culminated in this volume. It is out of gratitude to Marty, as a teacher, mentor, historian, theologian—and himself an author of a series of books on places—that I dedicate this book to him.[1]

Basically, though, the thesis of the book develops an insight of one of Marty's mentors at the University of Chicago—Sidney E. Mead. Mead claimed that "in America space has played the part that time has played in the older cultures of the world."[2] Marty quoted that line often—and it apparently sunk in for me. This book takes that insight seriously and reflects on what it means for Christian theology and American culture. As a reader walks with me through the chapters of the book, we will see that the peculiar spatial character of American theology—especially on the level of popular culture—has both risks and benefits for the public good. Readers might disagree with me about where the risks are, and what the benefits. But I hope that Mead's central point—that it's important in American history, culture, and theology to attend to what people do with places—still comes through clearly.

Over the years, I have had the benefit of many critical readers for most of the book's chapters. Initially at Valparaiso University, where I taught for twelve years, I shared chapter drafts with undergraduates and let them turn the tables on a professor and serve as my editor. Those lively class sessions made for some of my favorite memories of teaching at "Valpo," as readers will discover in the coming pages, where I sometimes allude to how students responded to my work. Since joining the faculty at the Lutheran Theological Seminary at Philadelphia in 2000, two other groups of readers have enriched my thinking and writing. The first were high school students enrolled in the 2001 "Summer Theological Academy" of the Theological Education with Youth program of the seminary. The second were seminary students in a course I offered on the topic of "American Sacred Places" in the spring of 2002. Both of these groups of students were extraordinarily generous and helpful to me, and their critical reading skills resulted in numerous improvements in the work. Finally, some of my colleagues on the seminary faculty gave me feedback on selected chapters—especially Pamela Cooper-White, John Hoffmeyer, Beth Huwiler, Phil Krey, and Timothy Wengert. To all of these readers, I say thanks. Many former students have over the years called or written to me to ask when the book they helped with would be done. I'm glad to be able to say, now, that it is, and I hope that it meets their expectations.

The basic plot hasn't changed over the years, although the work has grown in size. I develop Sidney Mead's insight into three points. Most generally, I suggest that it's up to us to clothe or locate God in ways that promote life, rather than destroy it. Theology is a human project, embedded or revealed in the limits of language, and often operating for good or ill through metaphors of place. Second, I contend that some of the ways we clothe God in America—some of our "sacred places"—can be shown to be pretty destructive. Finally, I try to develop several ways to clothe the divine from within the Christian tradition—fashions for God—into a theology of place that I contend will be life-giving and constructive for the common good.

In part 1, "Discovering God," I engage primarily in cultural critique of ways to clothe God that do more harm than good as "sacred places." Chapter 1, "Does God Wear Clothes?" raises the central question of the work, and links the problem of clothing God to human suffering. In it, I point out that clothing is an important facet of human culture and that fashions for God are both inevitable and always changing. We often clothe God, furthermore, through metaphors of place—although since St. Augustine professional Christian theologians have preferred to clothe God in metaphors of time and event. This fashion for God raises some serious difficulties, however, in the face of human finitude and evil, and often seems to evade the realities of human suffering. The question then becomes how our ways of clothing God can help us to respond to, rather than to hide from, the inevitability of suffering.

Chapter 2, "Seeking Sacred Places," is the most theoretical chapter of the book. After a brief description of the two leading schools of religious interpretation of places, I suggest that both can be used with some modification in a theology of place. I then exemplify the two approaches, and the truth they can bring to bear on understanding places, through a critical introduction to two popular films—*Monty Python and the Holy Grail* and *A River Runs through It*. Finally, I introduce the reader to my own method of approach to places, which seeks to understand places through a threefold process of poetics, politics, and pilgrimage. The latter, in particular, emphasizes that places—even places in nature—are constructed by human beings who visit them, through imagination, language, and more. Places and pilgrims interact, in short, through political and poetic processes that together define the sacred character of a place.

Chapter 3, "The Shopping Mall as 'Stairway to Heaven,' Leading Nowhere," is the first of three case studies of the theological significance of sacred places in America. In it, I begin with the conceptual framework of a "religion of the market," as developed in an influential article by Buddhist Professor David Loy. I then turn to a description of some basic features of mall design, to clarify how they function as "cathedrals" in the religion of the market. Finally, I take the reader along on a "pilgrimage" I made to the Mall of America in Bloomington, Minnesota, with my family in the summer of 2001.

Chapter 4, "Worshiping the Golden Mouse: Walt Disney World and American Civil Religion," develops the construct of "American civil religion" to show how Walt Disney World functions as a sacred place in the lives of many visitors. I attend throughout the chapter especially to the way Walt Disney World invites guests to consider their mortality and then provides them (for a fee) with an "escape" from peril. Most of the chapter analyzes specific attractions at The Magic Kingdom, but in the final section I recapitulate the basic themes by also discussing Disney's Animal Kingdom and EPCOT.

Chapter 5, "Private Possessions: American Domestic Religion and the Suburban Household," borrows from historian of religions Peter Gardella the idea that many people in America—whatever their nominal religion—also follow a "domestic religion" oriented to everyday places and practices. Within this domestic religion, the suburban home is perhaps the preeminent sacred space. Within it, practices of domestic sanitation and lawn care can occupy the time (and/or resources) of people in ways that reveal a somewhat skewed location of the divine in demons I call, respectively, "Tidiness" and "Toro."

Part 1 concludes with chapter 6, "God Naked." In this chapter, I pull together the significance of the three case studies to suggest that devotion to the mall, Mickey, and the green grass of home may be harming human beings and probably isn't doing the environment much good either. Such banal ways to clothe the sacred actually violate authentic human longings for abundant life, comfort, and intimacy, and render individuals beholden to corporations who pretend to care for people but who in fact seek primarily to maximize profit. Such violence has, furthermore, shielded us from the kind of collective action that might lead us to authentic and fulfilling life paths and to remedies for many of the social problems plaguing American culture—such as the crisis of affordable housing.

Part 2, "God's Clothing," turns from cultural critique to theological construction. In each chapter, I highlight how a particular biblical metaphor for God connects people to a place of grace, or to gifts that orient living in a way that can't be bought or sold. Chapter 7, "Living Waters," traces three ways that waters can help humans clothe God. Waters highlight the origins of life, including human birth. Waters also threaten a flood of justice and the dissolution of petty attachments in a flood of change. And, finally, waters baptize a person in clothes of compassion, just as Christians believe God, too, was "baptized" in waters that link all of life from Genesis to the end of time.

Chapter 8, "The Light of the World," is perhaps the most conventional chapter in the book. God has often been clothed with light, sometimes explicitly so in Hebrew and Christian Scriptures. As such, God is revealed to be like energy—a vital force that weaves through everything that is. Scripture also develops the fabric of God as light by identifying God as a refiner. Sometimes, light is present as a place of fire—a heat that purifies in the interest of a more fulfilling future. And finally, God clothed as light is revealed to encompass all the colors of the spectrum; a wisdom as wide and wise as the eye can imagine. Such ways to clothe God as light are commonly reflected in the architecture of Christian churches—which also vary greatly in which colors and hues they seek to emphasize.

Chapter 9, "The Rock of Salvation," explores the many ways God is identified with the properties of places of rock, mountains, and earth. Most obviously, rock endures. This feature of rock as a "permanent gift" can be used to characterize God as well. Rock, however, is also hard—and the challenge and temptation that rock signifies to fragile human beings is not absent from any theology that clothes God in this way. Finally, rocks also reveal the ancient processes of evolution at work—and the wonder of life's surprises that sustain us even in the face of decimations and suffering.

Chapter 10, "The True Vine," turns our attention to growing things as fabrics for God. The first section, "The Tree of Life: God as Life-Bearer," introduces the many ways that God is represented in the Hebrew Bible and the writings about Christ as a giver of life, like a fruitful tree. The second section explores the flip side of this association of God with place, by suggesting that trees reveal a God who is also fragile—trees die. And the third section introduces a conception of the medieval mystic, Hildegard of Bingen, who developed the concept of *viriditas* to describe the "greening power" that is God's gift to all the living.

Chapter 11, "One Body," explores the many associations of "embodiment" as a way to clothe the divine. In the first section, "The *Anima* of Animals," I point out how often Scripture itself uses animal metaphors to describe God, and I then suggest that the everyday experience of living among domesticated animals can give people a pretty clear understanding of God's grace. In the second section, "Limits and Liberation," I explore how both the pain and the pleasure that bodies experience illumine aspects of our relationship with the sacred. Finally, in the last section, "One Body," I explore how this most material and intimate of all metaphors for God is an important one to preserve. To clothe God as "one body" weaves human beings into the fabric of all the living in a way that will lead us to sustain the lives of others—out of thanks and gratitude—as expressed most vividly in the Christian celebration of the Eucharist.

Chapter 12, "Cities of God," concludes the book by engaging at last both the nemesis and inspiration for this entire enterprise—*The City of God* by St. Augustine. In that work, which has set the direction for Christian theology ever since, Augustine intended to rhetorically juxtapose evil and good, and thereby lead people away from temptation and into fulfillment. He did so, however, by juxtaposing human cities to the city of God and thus removed matter from the incarnation. The effects of this juxtaposition have been long lasting and, I suggest, contrary to Augustine's own intentions. For cities are not utterly evil in Scripture, and cities are surely not evil in human experience—as Augustine himself recognized in his better moments. Indeed, the gospel of Christ—the crucifixion and resurrection of God incarnate—had to happen in a city, and the movement that began afterward also had its origins in cities. We have not yet taken seriously what this means and how cities somehow themselves reveal God's intention for us to overcome the dualisms of body and soul, nature and culture, death and life, by finding the freedom that comes from living in relationship.

Now, from reading these brief and highly condensed descriptions of the chapters, I fear I may have dissuaded a reader from slogging through them with me. Nevertheless, I can only assure you that this has been my "fun book" and that it's also been written with the hopes that readers will find it fun to read, while also perhaps learning a little something in the process. I know that sounds arrogant, but I can't help it. I'm taking up an argument with no less than a saint, and suggesting a paradigm shift for a way of doing theology that has been in control of Christian thought for over 1,500 years. Still, I have no idea what significance this work will have in my lifetime, and, frankly, I'm prepared for the worst. The royalties from my first book bought me a quilt rack. Besides, I'm a historian, not a theologian—so I can always plead the status of an amateur if the reviews are bad. Nevertheless, if a reader finds some joy in these pages—a laugh or two, and perhaps a glimmer of grace—I'll be happy. I often share with my students a quote from Julian of Norwich, the fourteenth-century English nun who lived through the plague and still managed to write, pray, preach, teach, and minister to the sick and dying. "The way to fight evil," Julian suggested, "isn't to cudgel the brain, but is to live a life of love and laughter." Or as I paraphrase it for my students: "The way to fight evil isn't to bang your head against the wall. God wants you to live, love, learn, and laugh."

Part 1

Discovering God

1

Does God Wear Clothes?

"One must obtain forgiveness for every essay in theology."

—Jean-Luc Marion, *God without Being*

The title of this chapter is akin to what Zen Buddhists call a koan.[1] A koan is as unique as the teacher who offers it, but the word literally means "a public record." Historically, a koan was the publication of the dialogue between a Buddhist teacher and students. More substantively, however, koans are paradoxical riddles, folk tales, or mind puzzles. "What is the sound of one hand clapping?" is an example often cited. Another is the question: "What is your face before your parents were born?" Koans defy logic and disrupt ordinary rationality. For practitioners of Zen, though, this disruption is salutary. Koans can clear a space for truth. Most people, most of the time, are caught up in the illusion that they control life. We seek this or that goal and calculate how to maximize pleasure and minimize pain. Zen teachers suggest, however, that living a calculated life can actually impede the experience of pleasure and bring its own kind of pain. Koans, by absorbing one's attention and defying reason, can release one from the emotional clutter of constant calculation, freeing one to live fully in the moment as it opens to eternity, where one can find bliss in the most simple act, such as breathing. This experience Buddhists call enlightenment. Enlightenment is the goal-that-is-always-and-never-reached, or the path that leads to infinity. Those "definitions" of enlightenment are themselves, of course, koans.

The title of this chapter is, more specifically, a Christian koan. On one level the answer to the question of whether God wears clothes must be a clear no. God doesn't shop at the Gap. But on another level, if the answer is no, then surely this limits God in some way—and who are we to say that the Almighty must spend eternity running around naked? That doesn't seem right, either. To juxtapose God—the eternal or universal—with clothing—the fabricated or particular—seems absurd. It defies logic.

And yet, for Christians, who affirm that God became incarnate as a human being in Jesus of Nazareth, the possibility that God is garbed becomes not only likely but a matter of historic fact. What kind of clothing, though, could possibly fit the Infinite One? If, then, a koan opens up a place for enlightenment, perhaps our question can open up a place for grace. And indeed, one way to describe the question is to say that it is a form of prayer. It asks a question for which there is no apparent answer. Like every prayer, it begins by giving up, and then goes on. Paradoxically, however, by giving up but going on, we might find remarkable power—personal and political. Prayer admits futility but then brings solidarity. My hope in this chapter, then, and in fact throughout this book, is that the questions contained herein work like koans, or like prayers, to open up or reveal places of grace, truth, and beauty. In the process, alas, we will also discover some ugliness, hatred, violence, and suffering.

The first section of the chapter, "The Fashion System," takes up a question not about God, but about us. Among the animal kingdom to which we belong, we are the only beasts who clothe ourselves. Why do we do it? The answer is more complicated than it might at first seem. Indeed, once our clothing habits come under consideration, it will become apparent that clothing not only is a suitable topic for theological discourse but also calls into play sociology, psychology, anthropology, and politics—not to mention economics. If clothing ourselves has become such complicated business, then what might it mean to imagine clothing the Creator, Redeemer, and Sustainer of the Universe?

With some help from a series of theologians, we will discover in the second section of the chapter that people have been dressing up God in one fashion or another for millennia. From theologians who worship God as Krishna, for example, we can discover that God wears red, or black, or green silks, although Krishna and his consort, Radha, might be dressed in almost any fashion, as they are remembered for their love of music, dance, and each other. From the German Christian theologian Martin Luther, we will learn that clothing God is a matter of boldly fabricating promises that reflect or identify God's trustworthiness in a world that is often frightening and unreliable. And from the contemporary American Methodist theologian Sallie McFague, we will come to see that clothing God may be a matter of considerable consequence for both individuals and society. All three streams of tradition, however, remind us that all we do—for good and ill—is filtered through motives or ethics shaped by language. If we clothe God in language that suggests that we should act in ugly, untrustworthy, and violent ways, then it is quite likely that we will act in ugly, untrustworthy, and violent ways. When we discover such cases, we should also feel free to change them, since language is a matter finally of circumstance and fashion. McFague suggests several such changes, as Luther had suggested changes before her, and devotees of Krishna before both of them. Finally, though, we turn to St. Augustine to explore perhaps the most enduring Christian fashion for God.

From Augustine, we inherited a fashion for clothing God in time and event. Augustine fabricated this fashion in the wake of the sack of Rome by barbarian Goths in 410. After that event, locating "the city of God" in any earthly place seemed inherently wrongheaded, and although time was no more dependable, eternity surely was. With such a "temporally biased" fashion for God we may now be in a good situation to question and to begin to frame alternatives in a theology of place. For also from Augustine—the Doctor of Grace—we learn that our theologies do not save us. That is, gratefully, God's doing. Language, however, and everything that follows from it—notably ethics, culture, politics, and history—is up to us. If eternity is God's theater, history is ours. The earth and its places, as the material substrate of history, are our responsibility to clothe well or to clothe badly. The same, of course, is true of God—whose relation to matter is, at best, controverted. This much is certain: when we do not take care of time, or when we confuse our time-specific clothing for God with the living and eternal God and then try to build on that foundation in some "kingdom" or another, we invariably botch it.

The evidence of that assertion is all around us, or as Reinhold Niebuhr once put it, "original sin is the one empirically verifiable doctrine in Christianity." In the final section of the chapter, then, I turn to the problem of human suffering, which bears a close if dangerous relationship to the old-fashioned concept of sin. The reality of suffering, manifest especially in the fact of death, is the problem of significance that every theology finally needs to answer. What difference does it make if God wears clothes or not? How can we imagine God so that we do not violate others, or ourselves, but act in ways to promote beauty, and goodness, and truth in life? How can we clothe God so that grace can work through us, instead of the ugliness and capacity to cause pain for which the human species seems only too prone? I here introduce an extended passage from and meditation on a classic text by the Nobel Peace Prize Winner Elie Wiesel, who fashions the question of God and human suffering in a vivid way. For Wiesel, the significance and difficulty of clothing or locating God in language is made manifest when we experience something in history that brings us to the point of speechlessness. This experience takes many forms, but in the twentieth century it has often been an encounter with the fear and destructive potential in oneself and in others. Christians call that evil, and in the modern world, it was manifest especially as violence.

The Fashion System

Before we take an initial peek into God's closet, however, perhaps we need to look into our own. Like most "professionals" in American culture, I own a wide variety of apparel. A brief itemized list would include about a dozen suits and two dozen ties, four or five sport coats, fifteen or twenty dress shirts, eight or nine pairs of pants, a half dozen sweaters, jackets, blue jeans, polo shirts, sweatshirts, shoes, sneakers, and one tuxedo. Those are the clothes in the closet. In the chest of drawers are more personal garments. In one drawer are my socks—various pairs of blue and black, two pairs of olive green and brown, a variety of white athletic socks, and about a dozen lonely strays. In another drawer I keep underwear—I'll spare the reader an itemized list. In yet a third drawer I keep my gym shorts, swimsuit, walking shorts, and various odd elastic bandages, hospital scrubs, and sweatpants. Altogether, if I added in the outerwear in our front hall closet, I'd guess my wardrobe extends to well over two hundred items. I realize that this number represents unbelievable affluence to most of the people in the world, but somehow I've convinced myself that I need them all. I "need" them, of course, because clothes mean more than just merchandise. As anyone who has ever worn a uniform knows, we multiply objects of clothing and other accessories because bodily adornment marks status. Clothes "make the man," as the cliché has it.

I learned this lesson the hard way. For most of my childhood, I wore whatever clothing my parents bought or made for me. My easygoing compliance had its consequences. In second grade, for instance, I endured the taunts of other boys at Lincoln Elementary School who called me "Snow White" for the white winter jacket I wore. As an eight-year-old, such insults didn't bother me too much. The approval of my parents mattered more than the preferences of my peers. In junior high, however, things changed. I began to demand a pair of blue denims. Mom and Dad saved up their pennies and eventually brought home a pair of heavy-duty Wrangler stretch jeans, guaranteed never to fade, tear, or lose their permanent creases. I remember vividly the scorn of my seventh-grade peers the first day I wore them to school. I also wanted a pair of black Converse All-Stars, with the Chuck Taylor signature on the side. My parents bought me Keds. I may have been the best point guard in seventh grade, but I was learning that I was a dork.

Low status in the world of teenage fashion bedeviled me in various forms throughout my adolescence. My "official" high school senior photograph, for instance, featured me wearing a red, white, black, and blue plaid tweed sport coat over a red shirt with white cowboy stitching underneath, with a navy blue tie. It was pretty hideous, although students since have compared my attire favorably to the wardrobe of the television "great" Greg Brady. Even in my first year of college, my favorite clothing accessory was a pair of leather moccasins, which I wore most of the time (including in winter), and a metallic pea-green leisure suit that graced my body as I escorted a future homecoming queen to the freshman spring dance. Why she went with me, I'll never understand. I guess it was a favor of some sort, or maybe she was interested in my roommate, who was from a big city and knew how to dress in the latest "disco" styles (maybe I wasn't in such bad shape, after all). All in all, clothes matter.

Among the earliest literary investigations of human sartorial habits is a delightful book by Lawrence Langer entitled *The Importance of Wearing Clothes.* Langer rejects the argument that we wear clothes for utilitarian reasons, noting that clothing is a distinctly human enterprise: "We differ from all the other creatures which inhabit the earth by creating and wearing clothes."[2] Indeed, the ever-expanding range of bodily adornment available to humanity suggested to Langer that there is something important about this distinctively human creation, namely that we wear clothes to *hide* our kinship with the animals. Humans are, in fact, rather poor representatives of the animal kingdom, all things considered. We are hardly the largest beasts around. We don't have particularly strong jaws. We don't run all that fast (compared to cheetahs). And we can't fly (without machines). We also have strange mating habits, not tied to particular periods of heat. We wear clothes, then, to mask or disguise our kinship with the animals and to help keep us from acting like beasts all the time.

These efforts can be more or less successful. In the not-too-distant past, of course, all clothing was homemade. I remember as a child receiving numerous gifts of clothing crafted by my maternal grandparents and from my mom, who is an excellent seamstress. Among these items were some that by today's standards would be considered eccentric. For instance, every Christmas my grandparents would give me a pair of homemade "mukluks," or bedroom slippers. They had leather bottoms, with yarn-sewn tops. I hated them. Now, of course, I wish I had a dozen pair. They were warm, durable, and comfortable—and they would keep my naked human feet, uncovered with suitable hair, warm in the cold Midwestern winter. For another example, in 1973 my mom sewed matching blue and white checked pajamas for the whole family, which we took along on our first big family vacation—to California aboard Amtrak. In what became one of the funnier of our family stories, we met in the train's dining car a photographer who claimed to be doing an article on Amtrak for *Money* magazine. He asked if he could take some photos of the family in our sleeping berth. We agreed and dutifully dressed in our matching blue-and-white checked pj's to greet the photographer when he arrived. He took several photos of Dad holding my youngest brother, David, up to the top bunk, with the rest of us sitting around. As the photographer was leaving, we noticed that my dad had worn his pj bottoms backward, so that the hand-sewn fly was gaping open to reveal more than a little naked buttock when he lifted Dave to the top berth. Needless to say, the photos never made it into *Money*. Our clothes didn't hide our "animality" enough.

By clothing ourselves to hide our kinship with the animals, Langer continues, we also signal to other human beings social status and prestige, and communicate superiority and inferiority. We have no fangs to bare when threatened, and most of us don't have fur on our backs that can bristle when we meet a rival. We can, however, wear a "power" suit and tie, or "dress down" to communicate "accessibility" and "openness." Clothes, in short, not only hide our animal nature, they also function as signs or symbols. In America, the fashion and advertising industries exploit this social function of clothing to create desires for particular styles or pieces of clothing over others. This process is remarkably complex and subtle. French theorist Roland Barthes notes that "there are . . . for any particular object [of clothing] . . . three different structures, one technological, another iconic, the third verbal."[3] In other words, for any piece of clothing there is a product, its function as a sign, and its description in words. These three structures together constitute what Barthes calls the "fashion system," by means of which preferences are communicated through the mass media and through informal means such as peer approval or disapproval. Such preferences can be more or less rigidly enforced, depending upon the hierarchy or relations at stake. In the military, for instance, clothing signs are rigid and unchanging: a misrepresentation of one's status is a serious breach. In everyday life the signs are more flexible and subject to change: conventions of formality, informality, and beauty change and vary from time to time and place to place but still function to exclude and include. Imagine, for instance, the scandal that would occur if someone showed up at a formal occasion in swimwear, even though some formal dresses cover up no more skin than a swimsuit and wrap.

Even flexible conventions, however, carry significance, for they can become tools of social control. Social historian Linda B. Arthur has recently argued, for example, that "dress [is] a vital component of the social control system of cultures."[4] Clothing can communicate boundaries of "right" and "wrong," "insiders" and "outsiders," "success" and "failure." For instance, one day in 1981 when I was a seminary student in Columbus, Ohio, I was having a bad hair day, so I tossed on a fishing hat and wore it to chapel. I kept it on through the entire service. It just so happened that the Gospel reading that day was about how Christians are to be "fishers of people," so I thought the hat was perfectly appropriate. I wore the yellow Zebco piece of haberdashery with pride. In the student lounge afterward, however, one student came up to me and said, standing in my face: "I was offended that you kept your hat on through prayers. That was disrespectful." One verse in the Bible, I had forgotten, suggests that men should not wear hats during worship. I was still reeling from the judgment of my fellow student when a faculty member sought me out seconds later, and put his judgment of my fashion choice more bluntly. "Cloddish," he called it. I was stunned, and my glow at proudly being a "fisher of persons" turned to shame. Historian Philippe Perrot catalogs, more impersonally, the wide range of control messages clothing can convey. He writes that clothing "manifests through symbols or convention . . . seniority, tradition, prerogative, heritage, caste, lineage, ethnic group, generation, religion, geographical origin, marital status, social position, economic role, political belief, and ideological affiliation."[5] Clothing matters, and clothing serves (often unconsciously) to control.

Gender relations, in particular, are carefully prescribed by the clothes we choose. Thus, a group of feminist Christian theologians, led by Mary Stewart Van Leeuwen, has recently argued that

> the Creator did not intend for us to be slaves to culturally mandated, ideal body types, or to live in the tyrannical grip of clothing whose main purpose is to display our wealth (if we are male) and our seductive capacities (if we are female). The frantic pursuit of fashion and physical perfection inhibits us as builders of God's kingdom because it takes undue time and attention and because it reinforces sex and class divisions. It is just another bar in the cage.[6]

This cage contains both men and women, and it is built on the backs of poor laborers around the world.

To support our efforts to hide our animality and assert our success through status-defining clothes, we depend upon the labor of garment workers around the world, who often suffer under working conditions not fit for the lowliest beasts. The economic phenomenon in question, known as the "sweatshop," is familiar in the United States, but few bother to do anything about it, other than to place gleeful blame when a cultural icon like Kathie Lee Gifford or Michael Jordan gets publicly shamed for profiting grossly from exploiting others' labor. But the fashion system implicates us all. Anyone who has ever worn the "countercultural" icon of blue jeans, for only one example, might want to look into how and where they're made, not only for the economic, but also for the environmental, damage done in their production. Cotton for many jeans is grown with heavy use of pesticides, and stonewashing or other dyeing processes similarly pollute earth and water. Various manufacturers are more or less socially responsible. Guess Jeans, for instance, recently was cited by coopamerica.com, a nonprofit monitoring agency, for moving 40 percent of their manufacturing production to Mexico and South America. They did so, according to coopamerica, to escape union organizers and Department of Labor oversight, to pay workers low wages, and to maximize profits. When the Department of Labor then removed Guess from its socially conscious "Trendsetters" list, Guess subsequently ran an advertising campaign that falsely claimed their jeans were "100 percent sweatshop free."[7] Such a story is, of course, only the needle in the haystack of the fashion system. The system implicates us all.

Now, of course, one can take scrupulous attention to the economic origins and environmental consequences of buying clothing too far. If everyone had to research every piece of clothing they wore, little else would get done. Furthermore, antisweatshop crusaders can be self-righteous about this issue while utterly ignoring their complicity with all kinds of other injustices. Yet a little research and thoughtfulness can go a long way. One reader of a draft of this chapter helpfully pointed out that while it is important to critique marketed "fashion" and its exploitation of workers, it also is true that clothing can be used to convey a personal style that might even carry spiritual significance. After all, everybody has to wear something, and clothing can convey and enhance human beauty and personality as well as hide (and reveal) some features of our bodies. Indeed, such personal style may even overlap at points with fashion trends, although by definition it would not be "personal" if it *only* conformed to marketed dictates. We can take pleasure in clothing ourselves, then, enjoying the choices and colors and fabrics while we have them, while also working to see to it that others can experience the same choices—or at least have a warm coat when they need one.

I solve the dilemma of clothing myself in the midst of the fashion system by shopping at resale stores or by wearing the gifts people give me (I am delighted to receive underwear every year from my kids for Christmas). I buy most of my clothes, though, from the Salvation Army, the Presbyterian Resale Store, St. Vincent DePaul, or (most recently) the nearby Swarthmore Goodwill. At such places I have acquired suits, jackets, and pants by Donna Karan, Calvin Klein, Armani, Brooks Brothers, and Ralph Lauren—some of them still with the hefty price tags in the pockets. In the past ten years, I have never paid more than twenty dollars for a suit. Even if I have to spend twice that amount for alterations, I can own a fine-looking, well-tailored suit for about sixty bucks. I'm fortunate to be a relatively average size, I know, and I'm privileged to live in the midst of such affluence. But my strategy does more than get me bargains and fashionable clothes—although those things are nice. By wearing recycled clothing, I undercut sweatshops by purchasing a commodity for what I suspect is close to its "actual" value. I also reduce the environmentally damaging production of even more clothes. Finally, I support a charitable agency that assists the poor in our midst (we also take clothes to Goodwill when we no longer want them, or we give them to friends). The practice isn't perfect. By wearing designer clothes I still portray and legitimize an image of "success." Perhaps I was burned by those "Snow White" taunts of second-graders more than I want to remember. And I could choose to buy new clothes from environmentally and socially conscious companies. By doing so, I would help redistribute wealth by spending a little extra on goods for which people are paid a living wage to produce. But the truth is, I can't afford to pay much more than I do for clothing. I'm still, at age forty-three, paying off student loans. I also have three kids to feed and a mortgage and taxes to pay.

When I tell my students where I shop, though, they look at me strangely. My words undercut the message my "power" clothing is designed to convey, namely, that I'm a "success" with access to the symbols of professional (or is it priestly?) status in the fashion system. Some students even have gone so far as to criticize my use of recycled clothes, suggesting that I'm "stealing" from the poor. I find this accusation hard to understand. The criticism would go away, I suppose, if I simply bought my clothes at the mall. Then the link between the icons I wear and the economic system I support would be seamless, rather than jarring, and my students wouldn't have to think about their own behavior or the economic systems they support. Alternatively, I suppose, I should just shut up. Then our worship of status and "success" could go on unquestioned, as we prefer it here in America. And I suppose it's true that I could afford new clothes from the mall if I sold my car, or lived in a smaller house, or made other "lifestyle changes." But I'm trying, and most of the people who accuse me of doing something "wrong" by shopping at Goodwill don't seem even to want to make that step. It's easier to be a critic of individuals than to work to change the system. Maybe they're jealous, resentful that despite my modest income I can still experience the pleasure of a tasteful suit and display myself in a fashionable style. Underneath their accusation is a subtle assumption that supposes that we'd be closer to God if we were all wearing hair shirts, for one example, or *burqas,* for another. But I think we know where the logic of imposing such ascetic discipline leads, and I for one don't care to go there. I also doubt that my accusatory students would go with me. Finally, I suppose I could be more radical and start wearing dresses. But that's not my style, and besides, it would probably offend the transgendered. The point, finally, is a simple one: understanding the existence and functioning of the fashion system can keep us from being its slaves. At the same time, we have learned that the way we clothe ourselves carries some serious implications. All of that is even more true, of course, of the fashion systems for God.

Fashions for God

Early in my teaching career with undergraduates at Valparaiso University, I occasionally would take classes into Chicago for a visit to the Hare Krishna temple. Krishna is an incarnation of God within Hinduism, and the members of the Hare Krishna movement—officially known as the International Society of Krishna Consciousness—devote themselves to worship and praise of this delightful and beautiful manifestation of the deity. Krishna is present in the temple in the form of a statue (or many statues), and devotees come to the temple to see God through the statue. They also believe that God sees them in return. Seeing and being seen by God is a central act of worship in many religious traditions with roots in India; it is a practice known as *darshán*.[8] Devotees also engage in other practices, known collectively as *puja*, that involve attending to the deity's presence through the image by enwrapping the statue in garlands of flowers, wafting incense before it, and offering the images food and water. My students were always surprised, though, when, on the way downstairs to the delicious vegetarian buffet (called *prasadam*, or "grace"), in which we were invited to share with the temple devotees, we would pass a clothes-washing machine with a bold label on it: "For Deity Use Only." The devotees wash God's clothing; taking such care with the fine silks in which they clothe the deity that they have a separate washing machine set aside specifically for that purpose.

To pay such attention to an image of God and its clothing often appeared silly to many of my students. Some of them called it "superstitious," and a few even used the word "idolatry." In fact, however, clothing God is a rather sophisticated sort of devotion, honed over thousands of years of Indian experience in religion. Such an ancient practice of clothing God recognizes that we "clothe" God in a variety of ways—with language, texts, action, and symbols. Why not, then, with clothing? The clothes with which devotees of Krishna cover a statue are what might be called material prayers. They are offered not for the benefit of the statue but as "gifts" to the God incarnate in the statue and for the benefit of those who gather. As gifts, they represent an attitude of gratitude that ideally extends to all of life. Clothing God in beauty is a way to express one's love of God and delight in the presence of the Lord—who is of course present not only in the statue but in all of life. Thus, along with doing *puja* or solemn devotional acts toward the deity, devotees also chant, pound drums, and dance. They thus experience God through one another and seek to realize the ecstasy of being embraced in God's loving grace that can follow from such intense acts of devotion. Finally, the devotees don't only worship God through the statue and its clothing or through dance and chanting. They also sit to listen to an exposition of "formal" theology, where God is "clothed" through an interpretation and application of a text from the *Bhagavad Gita* or from one of the hundreds of other sacred texts of India.

Furthermore, this idea of God's clothing is also found within Christianity. Some fashions for God have come and gone. Some we still can access through study of history. We know, for instance, that Jesus himself probably clothed God in the language of Aramaic. The earliest accounts about Jesus, by contrast, namely the Epistles of Paul and the Gospels, clothed God in the fabric of Greek words. Within a few centuries, the material had changed again, with Latin now the official language of the Western church. In the East, however, Greek still ruled, and eventually Russian was added to the stock. The fashions multiplied rapidly. Augustinian, monastic, ascetic, mystical, Thomistic, scholastic, nominalist, and many more ways to clothe God emerged. Eventually Martin Luther, reformer of the church in the view of the branch of Christianity that I claim as my own, joined the guild of theological garment workers, initially as an Augustinian friar. Eventually, of course, Luther and his colleagues translated the entire Bible into the German language of their parishioners and wrote lyrics for hymns that borrowed tunes from familiar folk songs. Luther also encouraged woodcuts and other art forms and made widespread use of the relatively new technology of the printing press to make public his theology. Unlike many later Protestants, Luther was not an iconoclast.

And in fact, Luther attended directly to the idea of clothing God. Throughout his writings is a conviction that human beings always experienced God "masked," "veiled," or "clothed."[9] Luther once wrote, for instance, that he hoped his followers would never "be confronted by the unclothed God." What he meant by this phrase is open to interpretation, but on one level, Luther surely believed that the naked truth of the infinite and eternal would probably terrify a finite and temporal individual, if such an encounter did not in fact drive a person to despair. Luther could relate to this terror and despair from his own experience in the monastery, where he spent frantic years in efforts to fabricate the perfect clothes for God. This experience of self-imposed but also socially sanctioned suffering made him all the more persistent and persuasive in his articulation of the problem. So, rather than cling to naked power, Luther encouraged believers to worship a "God who is clothed in . . . promises." It is only God's grace and mercy, Luther believed, that saves us all. Grace—the gift of God's promise to love us despite sin and to save us despite suffering and death—makes the very power of the Creator of the universe accessible to even the most frail and flawed human beings. Thus, Luther went on, as finite beings we invariably relate to God as God is "bound to a specific place. . . . We do not now discuss a vagabond, naked God but rather one who is clothed with definite signs in place."[10]

Luther believed that humans needed some "definite signs in place" to orient devotion, because he was, first and foremost, a pastor. He wanted to guide his parishioners to freedom, where they could experience God's love and hope for human fulfillment, as conveyed in the life, death, and resurrection of Jesus Christ. What Luther saw around him, however, were people being misled and oppressed by wolves dressed in shepherd's clothing. With no clear empirical proof of God's promises, and without access to the Scriptures in their native language, people's hearts and minds were susceptible to the God-tailor with the most persuasive (or most terrifying) fashions. Thus, in his *Large Catechism,* Luther explained:

> A god is that to which we look for all good and in which we find refuge in every time of need. To have a god is nothing else than to trust and believe him with our whole heart. As I have often said, the trust and faith of the heart alone make both God and an idol. If your faith and trust are right, then your God is the true God. On the other hand, if your trust is false and wrong, then you have not the true God. For these two belong together, faith and God. That to which your heart clings and entrusts itself is, I say, really your God.[11]

Luther here was trying to teach people desiring to be Christian that we can, and often do, put our faith in objects or places that fail to satisfy. We can clothe God in ways that are superficial, banal, or tacky, and that provide at best short-term gratification. We can attach ourselves to fabrications that demonstrate and reinforce the desire of humanity to control life rather than the capacity of humanity to love the living. And we can be led to such idolatry not only by our own short-term desires but by collective forces conveyed through powerful institutions with coercive as well as persuasive power. When such idolatries become the leading fashions for God, people mistrust one another and invariably wind up killing.

Thus, Luther himself eventually had to flee the church in which he grew up, taking refuge in the castle of a friendly prince, out of fear for his life. He called the church to stop imposing on people a fashion for God that was "one size fits all." Indeed, his entire protest against the church was an effort to call the church to a way of clothing God that comforted people who were suffering, rather than perpetuated ecclesiastical power. For raising the question of how to clothe God in promises, of course, Luther was excommunicated. He did not, however, stop writing and preaching, and he even left the monastery to marry a nun and to raise children, clothing God in the fabric of family life. Of course this German reformer had his flaws—large ones. But he also understood that clothing God was a matter of considerable significance for human well-being and that clothing God badly led to violence.

Now, of course, the ancient practices of Krishna devotees and the ideas of a sixteenth-century Christian reformer cannot simply be incorporated today without change. Fortunately, many contemporary theologians have been developing the idea that the ways we clothe God cannot be confused with the living God, and the same thinkers have been experimenting with new metaphors, images, or places to locate God's presence.[12] One of the most prominent among them is the recently retired Vanderbilt Divinity School theologian Sallie McFague. Writes McFague:

> All talk of God is indirect: no words or phrases refer directly to God. . . . [A metaphorical theology insists that] our concept of God is precisely that: our concept of God—and not God. . . . How language, any language, applies to God we do not know; what religious and theological language is at most is metaphorical forays attempting to express experiences of relating to God.[13]

Here McFague identifies, without using the name, how idolatry begins. People fixate on certain words (or more concrete images or places for God), and then (often in the interest of power) confuse their language with the living God. Theology becomes theo-LOGY; people worship their words rather than the living God.[14] What follows, invariably, is violence.[15] People devote themselves to some other name than to the "One who is," and in that name claim the "right" or the "calling" or even the "command" to destroy something living. Language that inherently acknowledges the way it "clothes" God, then, is least likely to lead into idolatry, because it will not be easily confused with the reality of the living God.

McFague goes on to suggest a number of powerful and helpful ways to rethink the clothing of God through the fabric of words. She suggests, for instance, that the Trinity might be conceived not only as relation between God as Father, Son, and Spirit but also as relation between God as Mother, Lover, and Friend. Each of these suggestions, while controversial, is arguably as biblically grounded as the more traditional terms and also holds historical and contemporary resonance for many people. Most centrally, however, McFague suggests that we try clothing God through a metaphor that sees the "world as God's body." For McFague, the traditional Christian doctrine that translates the presence of God in Jesus after his death into a few brief appearances here on earth and then has him ascend into heaven is a mythology that no longer makes sense today and that might be dangerous. We know heaven is not "up," yet we continue to imagine that in the ascension God was "beamed" out of the cosmos. This removal of God from the place of the earth may well set the stage, McFague suggests, for our own exploitation and potential destruction of the cosmos in an age of ecological degradation and weapons of mass destruction. McFague thus suggests an alternative to the "beam me up" model of the resurrection-ascension. "What if," she asks, "we were to understand the resurrection [of Jesus] not as the bodily translation of some individuals to another world . . . but as the promise of God to be permanently present, 'bodily' present to us, in all places and times of our world?"[16] What if, indeed, we imagined the "world as God's body?" Wouldn't we then be more careful with the world, exercise more responsibility for it, and therefore avoid both environmental degradation and nuclear decimation—all as logical consequences of our prayerful worship of God?

For McFague, this model of "the world as God's body" has a distinct advantage over the traditional model of God's presence, which she describes as "the monarchical model." In the traditional model, God is only selectively present to us, from on high, in the same way a king is selectively present to his subjects. God is thus distant and selectively benevolent (or harsh). We, conversely, are largely passive subjects who must wait on God's benevolence (or judgment). But, argues McFague, this model is no longer appropriate for our time, for "the power balance has shifted from nature [and God] to us."[17] We can, after all, destroy nature—through nuclear devastation or ecological degradation—and we have, more or less, also destroyed the traditional model of God. People may imagine that they worship a God in the sky, but they don't live like it in their everyday relations. Indeed, attempts to bolster the traditional model of God as king are increasingly frantic and politically embedded. Fundamentalist Christians and militant Islamists here share a similar logic: they seek to bolster the tattered clothing of an image of God as king with various calls for "jihads" or "crusades," as evident most dramatically in the behaviors of Timothy McVeigh and Osama bin Laden. The "king of kings" seems more and more removed from the ordinary course of events; *that* emperor is truly wearing no clothes.[18]

Thus, McFague suggests that we experiment with the metaphor of "the world as God's body" as one way to make tangible God's promise in Christ: "Lo, I am with you always." (Matt. 28:20). In other words, "God acts in and through the incredibly complex physical and historical-cultural evolutionary process that began eons ago."[19] Everything is thus interconnected, by virtue of being intrinsically related to the living God. Writes McFague:

> What this experiment with the world as God's body comes to, finally, is an awareness, both chilling and breathtaking, that we as worldly, bodily beings are in God's presence. It is the basis for a revived sacramentalism that is painfully conscious of the world's vulnerability, its preciousness, its uniqueness. The beauty of the world and its ability to sustain the vast multitude of species it supports is not there for the taking. The world is a body that must be carefully tended, that must be nurtured, protected, guided, loved and befriended as valuable in itself—for like us, it is an expression of God—and as necessary for the continuation of life.[20]

This is a truly beautiful vision of God; a fabric of words for the divine that connects the eternal to the temporal, the finite to the infinite, in profound and gracious ways.

It is not, however, without flaws—as its author is only too ready to admit. I have taught McFague's text on at least an annual basis since its publication in 1987, and I have learned from this repeated use of it with students to find its problems. Most immediately, my students have had trouble understanding that this metaphor of the "world as God's body" *was* a metaphor. They were constantly pulled to make it literal. Thus, they would make jokes such as: "So, Sallie, if 'the world is God's body,' does that mean that if I step on an ant, I've killed God?" I don't think this defensive critique only reflected my students' lack of facility at abstract reasoning. It resulted, rather, from a failure intrinsic to the metaphor. "The world as God's body" overgeneralizes, and thus allows students to turn the metaphor into the absurdity on the brink of which metaphor always teeters. Perhaps we can clarify it this way. The students liked the idea that God was present through each molecule on the planet. They found such intimacy with God comforting. But the problem was in the generalized moralism behind the metaphor. In its stress on God's action, and human action, McFague's work produced a kind of hyper-moral crisis among readers—forcing them to face the abyss of nuclear decimation or ecological degradation. Now, the threats of nuclear decimation and ecological degradation are indeed very real, and I agree that we need to address them, but this naked truth terrifies people and leads them to dismiss the entire argument by worrying about the moral status of ants. In short, the metaphor of the world as God's body is too general to comfort human consciences while also motivating reasonable actions to care for the environment and political processes.

Perhaps, then, we can still draw upon the strength of this metaphorical approach to clothing God by avoiding the danger of literalism associated with generalizations such as "world" and "body" and the moralism of seeing God primarily as an agent. To do so, we can stress instead (in Luther's language) God's promise to be *present* in *place*—including (of course) in the bodies of the world and all its other elements. I hope readers do not underestimate my deep debt to McFague. The generalization of "the world as God's body" is still an illuminating one in its own right, and I will always be grateful to McFague for suggesting it. It saved Christianity as a theological system for me. But the world isn't God's body, because the world itself isn't a body, although it does have some of the elements of a body. And God does not "express" God's self through the world, although surely God works through human agency and language—as Christian doctrines of special revelation have asserted for millennia. But primarily *we* are the ones who express things; human beings are the ones who use language. We have bodies, and we act. By identifying nature and the places of the world with God's body, then, McFague actually pulls back from the metaphorical character her theology recommends, and erodes both human agency and God's divinity. I simply want to take her metaphorical approach another step, both into Scripture and into human experience. For the uniquely *human* feature of our bodies is not that we have them (all animals do), but that we clothe them. Even more, what makes human beings unique is that we can relate to our bodies not only on the basis of our instincts, but also as we decide through our languages and images—through motives, in short. We live, so to speak, after "the fall," when, as the story in Genesis 3 has it, the first humans felt compelled to cover themselves. We not only relate to God through metaphors and images, then; we also do the same with ourselves, with the world, and with its places. We live by fabrications that are as fragile as the most unstable element in our midst. As the poet Wallace Stevens put it, in a line I quote repeatedly to students: "We live in the description of a place, not the place itself."[21]

The usual critique of McFague's theology is that she erodes God's transcendence, and if God is understood primarily as the ultimate moral agent and historical actor, that's probably true. But this preference for moral agency and action in time is not the only way to clothe God. I have been studying theology more or less since birth, from the songs my mom sang to me as she put me to sleep, through Sunday school, confirmation, and youth group, into college and seminary and graduate school, and now as a scholar. Over that span of time, it has gradually dawned on me that almost every fabric I have been given with which to clothe God has been shaped less by the category of space than of time. If space and time interweave in relationship to God, in the *theology* or *talk-about-God* that I grew up with, time dominated space. Like many young Christians, for instance, I learned to locate God in history, in the "mighty acts of God," as it was often put. God worked through events, especially in miraculous acts of supernatural power. God the Father created the world at its beginning, redeemed it through the life, death, and resurrection of Jesus Christ, and sustained it in the ongoing work of the church through the person of the Holy Spirit. God was in control, and God acted in history, in time. When I prayed as a child, consequently, I kept expecting to experience some interruption in the fabric of time. I hoped fervently that God would appear in some dramatic manifestation of God's activity, as I had been led to expect from the ways the stories in the Bible had been interpreted to me by pastors and teachers. But my experience didn't mesh with the expectation. And I have since come to recognize that this bias for time over space is so common as to be all but unquestioned among Christians. Some believers continue well into their adulthood to expect God to interrupt the normal flow of time more or less constantly on their behalf. They also look askance at those of us who don't find God popping into our experience or history on a regular basis. This bias is pernicious and is one of the greatest barriers to Christian witness in the world.

I also believe that this bias toward theologies of time can be traced to one of the great geniuses of all time, Augustine, who was for much of his life Bishop of Hippo in Northern Africa. Augustine lived at the height of the Roman empire, from 354 to 430. He also experienced, however, the sack of Rome by Gothic barbarians in 410. His response to this trauma, the magisterial work called *The City of God*, established the Christian philosophy of history that has prevailed ever since. It is impossible to do the massive work justice in brief. Suffice it to say that shortly into my first reading of the massive text—as a young professor at Valparaiso University—I knew it was the most profound work of theology I had every read. But the essence of Augustine's work was an opposition between the "City of God" and the "City of Man." This move divided space, while it privileged time. It is understandable why the "Doctor of Grace" did this. The fall of Rome was a brutal shock to citizens throughout the empire. Time seemed untrustworthy, but space even more so. By bifurcating the city into temporal and eternal manifestations, Augustine offered real comfort to his followers. He promised them an eternal city, even if their real city was threatened. By making this move, however, Augustine effectively gave up on the real cities of the world. Rome was left to the pagans, or to the barbarians, or to whatever forces happened to prevail within them. God would redeem time in eternity, Augustine offered his Christian followers as solace, but places would suffer. The consequences of this theological move have been with us ever since. Monasticism, asceticism, mandatory celibacy, patriarchy, bodily masochism, supernaturalist superstition, crusades, inquisitions, and all of the rest of the bad fashions for God that have sometimes plagued Christianity were the all-but-inevitable fashions for God to follow. We have lived with the theological consequences of the barbarian sack of Rome long enough.

Furthermore, as I try to show in chapters 7 through 12, the biblical record itself unseats Augustine's one-sided emphasis on time and event. Most of the metaphors that describe God's presence in the Bible are spatial. Thus, God "hovers over the deep waters" in Genesis and "rides through the skies" in Deuteronomy. Jewish devotion to land, temple, and king—not necessarily in that order—coalesced for some Jews in the person of Jesus, whom they understood to incarnate God as "living water," the "light of the world," "the rock of our salvation," and the "true vine." Indeed, Christians themselves are called to be nothing less than "the body of Christ" and citizens of a "heavenly city." Once you start looking, the Bible encourages a surprisingly spatial piety. There are plentiful "cities of God" right here in our midst, and Christians have no cause to despise or abandon them.

Perhaps, then, God's transcendence is not clothed most accurately in acts of moral agency or historical causality. Maybe history is really up to us, and God is a rather (as Luther sometimes intuited) sheer, loving presence available through places clothed in promises of grace. If so, then God's transcendence is available to human beings in some dramatically new ways that do not demand distorting history or experience but that turn us quite directly to the means of grace as clothed in quite specific places. If God's transcendence is best clothed not as action or event, but rather as the taking up of space into a transcendence that includes past, present, and future, and that includes all the living in its scope, then perhaps it truly is up to human beings to clothe God in ways that promote life rather than destroy it. Perhaps the responsibility for this world—for history—truly is ours. If so, then clothing God, as the particular calling of theologians, is a rather important little calling, for which sweatshops probably won't do.

However, if theology is (on this side of eternity) human fabrication, it is not the case that all ways of clothing God are equal. Some direct us to places that we really need and that can provide deep comfort to human beings. Preeminent among them are places in nature—although what follows is anything but a "natural theology." Quite the opposite is true, in fact. For while we experience (when we are honest) the elements of nature as gifts, and while we also happen to need these gifts for life to continue as we know it, we also have to clothe "nature" in language as rich and diverse as the language we use to clothe God. There is no recourse to immediacy in theology, natural or otherwise. All theologies are implicated in the fashion system. A theology that attends to clothing God is first of all a theology of grace—in which natural metaphors and elements can take their rightful place.

That said, however, it is clear that places in nature carry a certain privilege as fabrics to clothe God. That is undeniably true of Holy Scripture itself, as we shall see in chapters 7 through 11, but it is also true from our experience. No human being, for instance, creates his or her own body. Our bodies are given to us as infants, when, we hope, our elders nurture them with care. Even more, the bodies we clothe are humus—made up of and dependent upon the same carbon, hydrogen, oxygen, and nitrogen as all other known forms of life. This life, too, of course, no human has created, but is sheer gift. Finally, human actions also have ripple effects that extend far beyond the limits of our bodies into the beings and bodies of others, whose existence we also can experience as gifts. The energy that animates our bodies, in short, is the energy that also animates all bodies and that comes to us as gift. Such a gift is not ours to possess or own. Such a gift is our temporary responsibility, and some metaphors for God, some ways of clothing God, can make us more likely to care for them. Among these gifts to humanity are also, of course, the various fabrics to clothe God's gifts as given to us by our ancestors.

We have woven together so far a tapestry with three fabrics—Indian, German, and American. But it is, finally, an African thread that holds it all together. If Augustine's work on *The City of God* is the antagonist against which this work is defined, it is also the hidden thread woven throughout. For Augustine saw brilliantly that human efforts to produce "kingdoms" that attempt to mirror in one naïve way or another the power of God usually wind up killing people and leaving cities and the earth bare, ruined, and burned. We have now had plenty of historical evidence since Augustine to demonstrate the truth of his argument, but still people struggle to get the point. All that's at stake with our theologies is how we live, how we are clothed, and how we clothe God. Eternity, God will take care of, as Augustine's constant emphasis on grace sought to remind folk. Our theologies don't save us; thankfully, one might add, possibly with a smile or a chuckle or, as the epigraph to this chapter suggests, a confession. Of course, there is a serious side to theology. Because we live through language, the ways we clothe God will to a large degree determine how God appears to us. But although faith is subjectively fabricated, and no clothes can fit the Infinite, this does not mean that theologies do not have an objective side and cannot be evaluated empirically. Putting it as bluntly as I can: A "good" theology will reduce human suffering and increase political justice, while also responding effectively to suffering and injustice when both inevitably appear. A "bad" theology will increase human suffering and injustice and will avoid facing them or respond poorly when suffering and injustice inevitably come. If, then, we have been living with the intellectual consequences of the barbarian takeover of Rome long enough, we also need more than ever to hear that there's a difference between a city, kingdom, or civilization that clothes God well and one that clothes God badly. So it is to one report from one of these supposed "kingdoms" that we must now turn. That "kingdom" was called the Third Reich, and the theology at its foundation produced a policy called "the Final Solution." Among its victims was a young Jew named Elie Wiesel.

Clothing God and Human Suffering

As should be apparent by now, this book has grown directly out of my teaching. It is a "public record," a koan of conversations I've had with students of various kinds over the past fifteen years. For the most part, the book was shaped by my work with undergraduates at Valparaiso University—a small private school located forty-five miles south of Chicago in northwest Indiana. Among the classes I regularly taught at "Valpo" was "Theology 100: Introduction to Christian Theology." In multiple sections of that course, offered every semester between 1992 and 1997, I asked students to answer the same question in a three-to-five-page paper. "Where," I asked them, "if anywhere, is God?" It was a trick question, actually, and I was always a little glad when every semester some students struggled to come up with "the answer." I had not yet matured as a theologian (this is a relative matter, of course). I thought that people could best understand God if they had to suffer a little bit first, preferably through learning metaphysics and hermeneutics and epistemology. Since I did, however, feel a little guilty about forcing eighteen- and nineteen-year-olds to ponder such a difficult matter as God's presence or absence, I also gave the young people a few clues.

I suggested that they pick three metaphors to exemplify their central point or three "locations" that specified the main place where they located the sacred.

Given this help, the majority of my students (those who didn't want to struggle too much) argued one variant or another on the thesis that "God is everywhere," and then more or less picked the places at random. Just about every semester at least one paper located God in the shower stall of a nearby dormitory. Other students invariably claimed to get in touch with God in the privacy of their bedrooms, but usually spared me most of the details. Other students arguing the "everywhere" thesis preferred more public places to locate God's presence. One intrepid student thus claimed to have spotted God at McDonald's, although he fudged a little and suggested that it might actually have been Elvis. Another found God in the locker room of the university's football team. Yet another claimed to have seen God at Jackson's Bar, a seedy local tavern that smells perpetually of stale beer and smoke but also serves the best cheeseburgers in town. Those papers made fun reading. They were also largely incoherent, rendering the traditional attributes of the First Cause or Prime Mover all but meaningless. Gone were goodness, truth, and beauty, and we were left with God drunk on a barstool. I admired the willingness of these students to consider that God was one of us, but I doubted that they were really serious that the Creator of the universe was quite that much of a slob.

Another smaller set of papers, usually produced by those students more deeply steeped in the Christian tradition, resisted locating the sacred in any place and argued one or another variant on the thesis "God is Spirit." These earnest students could not imagine God located anywhere on earth (apparently having forgotten that Jesus was a human). So they identified God's place as "in heaven," in the believer's "heart," in the human "soul," or in "the Bible." These papers tended to be solidly boring. They spouted clichés or quoted Bible verses thoughtlessly and without reference to context, in the hopes that conventionally pious language might make up for lack of reasoning. The odd thing is that the papers were generally as incoherent as the ones that located God "everywhere." They conveyed no more sense of rational human engagement with a living, life-transforming power of infinite goodwill than did the papers that found God in the bathroom or barroom. They seemed like somebody else's answer to the question.

Finally, a few students—among them both devout and uncommitted souls—were honest enough to admit that they had little clue of God's whereabouts and that most of the time the deity seemed to be oddly missing in action. These were the papers I grew to be quite fond of. They took seriously the possibility that the sacred was nowhere but in the figments of their own fevered imaginations. They were also humble enough to admit that their efforts to clothe God in language may have had very little to do, actually, with how the divine worked or what the Alpha and the Omega intended for their lives. They didn't imagine that they could wrap God up in a pretty package that would then be their private possession. In other words, these students had learned that when it came to locating God we ought to proceed pretty carefully, lest we confuse some image of our own making with the living Reality that was greater than any that could be conceived. Such modesty seems to me highly recommended for the twenty-first century. For in the twentieth, great damage was done, if not in the name of "God," then by people who claimed, at least on Sundays, to be pretty certain they knew where God was.

The students in my classes encountered the question of God's whereabouts not in the abstract, but through reading *Night,* the powerful Holocaust narrative by Nobel Peace Prize Winner Elie Wiesel. The key episode comes near the middle of the book, when Wiesel records the execution of three prisoners by hanging, including a young servant boy accused of conspiring to blow up the power station of the concentration camp Buna:

> One day when we came back from work, we saw three gallows rearing up in the assembly place, three black crows. Roll call. SS all around us, machine guns trained: the traditional ceremony. Three victims in chains—and one of them, the little servant, the sad-eyed angel.
>
> The SS seemed more preoccupied, more disturbed than usual. To hang a young boy in front of thousands of spectators was no light matter. The head of the camp read the verdict. All eyes were on the child. He was lividly pale, almost calm, biting his lips. The gallows threw its shadow over him.
>
> This time the Lagerkapo refused to act as executioner. Three SS replaced him.
>
> The three victims mounted together onto the chairs.
>
> The three necks were placed at the same moment within the nooses.
>
> "Long live liberty!" cried the two adults.
>
> But the child was silent.
>
> "Where is God? Where is He?" someone behind me asked.
>
> At a sign from the head of the camp, the three chairs tipped over.
>
> Total silence throughout the camp. On the horizon, the sun was setting.
>
> "Bare your heads!" yelled the head of the camp. His voice was raucous. We were weeping.
>
> "Cover your heads!"
>
> Then the march past began. The two adults were no longer alive. Their tongues hung swollen, blue-tinged. But the third rope was still moving; being so light, the child was still alive . . .
>
> For more than half an hour he stayed there, struggling between life and death, dying in slow agony under our eyes. And we had to look him full in the face. He was still alive when I passed in front of him. His tongue was red, his eyes were not yet glazed.
>
> Behind me, I heard the same man asking:
>
> "Where is God now?"
>
> And I heard a voice within me answer him:
>
> "Where is He? Here He is—He is hanging here on this gallows . . ."[22]

When I first read this narrative, it simultaneously sickened me because of its honest depiction of human brutality, brought tears to my eyes because of its poignant depiction of human suffering, and clarified the question I first asked myself and then asked my students: Where, if anywhere, is God?

In the context of this narrative, that question cannot be answered effectively with a glib "God is everywhere" or with a pious "God is in heaven." On one level Wiesel intended in *Night* to record a testimony so strong that his readers could never forget the historical genocide of the Shoah. The God he located on a gallows at Buna had covenanted with a specific people—the Jews. But by sharing his story with readers, not all of whom would share the faith with which he grew up, Wiesel clearly intended to bring into question not only the goodness and power of a particular God but the very prospect of the living presence of any God at all. It was that possibility that I wanted students to reckon with. I did so not because I expected them to face extermination by a government for their racial identity. I pushed the students to ponder Wiesel's haunting cry of absence because I was certain that at some point in their lives Wiesel's question would also confront them, not in the context of a novel, but in the context of living.

For, on another level, Wiesel's story is one of lost faith that all people living in the wake of the twentieth century can share. If the question of God's location is always triggered by a specific historical event in time, it is also the case that every human being experiences anomalies, unexplained horrors (or joys) after which a comfortable sense that "everything is in its place" begins to crumble. Early in *Night*, Wiesel describes how he grew up with a pious, even "strong" faith in God's goodness, power, and presence. The entire narrative, of which the above episode is only the most theologically pregnant, documents how the experience of suffering at Buna and other camps stripped his life of meaning and purpose and destroyed his faith. *Night* thus challenges its readers to locate or clothe God—or however we identify the Source that orients and the Goal that gives meaning to our life—in the midst of human suffering. And all of us will, alas, know suffering. Our challenges may not be as immediate or overpowering as the ones faced by Elie Wiesel. They may even be, or seem to be, banal, mundane, or trivial by comparison. That does not, however, make them any less significant as triggers for asking the question of God's presence.[23] Faith can be lost as surely through a thousand simple choices as through one dramatic trauma.

I grew up Lutheran in Appleton, Wisconsin—a town of about fifty thousand at the time. I went to church every Sunday, and throughout my first eighteen years I had little reason to doubt the existence of God, the goodness of people, and that Jesus loved me. My father was the Sunday school superintendent at our church throughout most of my school-aged years, and to me God was "Father," a loving-but-powerful figure who had everything in control and who intervened miraculously to save his people. My faith was simple and naïve—or, less a matter of conscious choice than a matter of assumption and convention. I never recognized that to call God "Father" was a metaphor. I assumed it was a definition. And so, when my father in fact proved to be less than God, as any earthly parent will, I was left with more questions than I was prepared to answer.

That process was accelerated by a good college education—a portion of which took place in the classroom. In college, during the late seventies, God let me make my own choices—and they didn't always turn out well. Most notably, in my senior year I became engaged to marry a woman with whom I was ill suited intellectually and spiritually. We fought more or less constantly and were plagued by jealousy, but we were also powerfully united by our physical attraction. After I broke off the three-month engagement, I felt like a failure: How could I have been so wrong about such a significant decision? Since I had been raised in a devout family, personal questions invariably merged with theological ones for me. Where was God in the midst of the mess I had made of my life? My choices paralyzed me, prayer offered no relief, and I turned to a wide variety of means to tranquilize myself. I joined a fraternity. I sought comfort in other people. I reveled in reason. I played sports and music. None of it seemed to matter: a nagging sense of absence—unarticulated but real—wouldn't go away.

At the height of my identity crisis, a few months after I had barely managed to graduate from college, a friend gave me a copy of Elie Wiesel's book and told me to read it. I did, and Wiesel's narrative crystallized for me the question I needed to be asking and motivated me to change my life. I identified with how Wiesel had lost the familiar and powerful God of his childhood. I knew that my situation was nothing like Wiesel's, but I also felt like I knew what he was asking when he remembered the question of the man by the gallows: "Where is God?" This book is, in some sense, my fifteen-year effort and several more than three-to-five-page answer to the question that he posed for me and that I later posed for my students. Of course, over those fifteen years, the question has also changed from the immediate lamentation and accusation of Wiesel's question into the Christian koan that is now the title of the chapter.

The reasons for that change are complex, and I will explore some of them in the next chapter. Basically, however, I have come to realize that each experience of the absence or presence of God is unique and irreproducible. An answer to the question of where God is, or how to clothe God, has to be personal and particular, specific to a point in time and location in place. All we can do is try to share with each other the pain of absence and the pleasure of presence (or, depending upon the situation, the opposite!) as we experience them, by clothing God in the most beautiful, good, and above all, true questions, statements, and images we can. For Elie Wiesel, as a Jew living in a situation in which not only divinity but even his own humanity was under assault, locating God on a gallows made sense. For me, as a Christian living in a situation in which evil was more banal, the result of my own choices as much as from a political system, locating God on a gallows still seemed to make sense. Somehow, we had found common ground.

And indeed, Wiesel continued to write after *Night,* producing two titles, *Dawn* and *The Accident,* that together form a trilogy of works that reflect his mature understanding of the horror of the Holocaust. I have also continued to write since my own adolescent "Night," and if the traumas I experienced are only in the most tangential ways like the ones Wiesel did, perhaps they nevertheless can illuminate and clarify for other readers some of their experiences, as Wiesel's narrative did for mine. For indeed, anyone living in the United States after September 11, 2001, knows at least something of the fear felt by European Jews from the organized efforts of the Nazis to exterminate their people, to hang God on a gallows. On that date, things changed in the United States, perhaps in much the same way that things changed for Augustine when the barbarians sacked Rome in 410 or for Elie Wiesel when he was forcibly removed from his home by the Nazis. In one day, two powerful symbols of the American nation—one of our technological power, and another of our global market dominance—were brought into devastating contact. Thousands of people died horribly violent deaths. The date and its images will forever be remembered in America as a day of shock and terror, a day when evil was loose in the world, as it surely was, especially because the violence of that day was "justified" by reference to God.

On that day, I first heard of the attacks as I sat in my car in the driveway of our suburban Philadelphia home. I turned my car on, tuned in NPR, and, rather than pulling away from the driveway as usual, just sat there listening to the reports of first one, then another, airplane attack on New York's World Trade Towers. As I sat there, my wife, Lisa, came running out of the house to ask me if I had heard what was happening. I said, simply: "We're at war." I had little doubt that this was a terrorist attack. I hoped the perpetrators would not be Islamic militants, but I knew the odds were likely that such an act was inspired by religion. In fact, I was teaching from a book the next morning that surveyed the connections between religion and violence around the globe and that included prominent mention of Osama bin Laden.[24] More gradually, however, as the day went on, my shock at being attacked gave way to the dawning recognition that this was one of those events when the millstone of time was visibly turning.

Now, I serve on a church committee that meets every couple of months in uptown Manhattan. The first meeting of this committee after the attack was held in December. As the meeting ended, night was falling, and I decided to drive past the site where the World Trade Towers once stood and take the Lincoln Tunnel toward Philadelphia. As I went past, even though it was raining, and three months after the attack, when I rolled down my window and breathed deeply, my senses recoiled. My experience was, I imagine, something that Elie Wiesel might have understood and, perhaps, even that Augustine would have recognized. It was something that I hope my students never experience, and I pray that my children do not have to know. For amidst the smell of burning concrete dust, melted steel, incinerated bodies, smoldering jet fuel, and untold experiences of human suffering, I also sensed what many visitors to the site have since affirmed and what will eventually be confirmed by memorials to be built after long and heated negotiations. The site of the World Trade Towers was a sacred place, even a place where God was present, in, with, and under the death and destruction. To make such an affirmation is not to seek a magical escape from suffering, as if saying the name of God could immediately make pain and loss go away. Rather, such an affirmation is to assert, first, that we must face honestly human evil, violence, and suffering, especially as manifest in oneself and one's midst.

For only when we have shed some dangerous ways of clothing or locating God that bring destruction and despair can we experience being embraced ourselves in God's beautiful and soft clothing as the true comfort it is. And such a possibility is the second assertion contained in any naming of the World Trade Center site as a sacred place. Comfort is possible, even in the wake of horrifying pain and loss. Such comfort is not the sudden appearance of a fantastic fabric that covers up pain. God's clothing is, rather, a real, if fragile, presence that takes seriously a cry of absence and anger like Elie Wiesel's, or the yawning absence that is the abyss at "Ground Zero," and meets it on the common ground of the gifts we share as human beings.

2

Seeking Sacred Places

Events such as the terrorist attacks of September 11, 2001, pose in a jarring way Elie Wiesel's question to theologies of time: "Where is God?" When history seems to spin out of control, the question of God's place often surfaces—as in fact it did shortly after September 11 among some of the people who were closest to the event.[1] But any experience of suffering, even banal adolescent struggle, can trigger a sense of absence. Among the many writers who have sought to bring solace to sufferers is Annie Dillard, especially in one of her early works, *Holy the Firm*. In this brief and powerful book, Dillard tells the story of a seven-year-old child named "Julie," of whom the author was a fond acquaintance. The little girl's face is badly burned in an airplane crash. Dillard dwells on this horrific accident to clarify how all suffering comes together under the millstone of time:

> The pain within the millstone's pitiless turning is real, for our love for each other—for world and all the products of extension—is real, vaulting, insofar as it is love, beyond the plane of the stones' sickening churn and arcing to the realm of spirit bare. And you can get caught holding one end of a love, when your father drops, and your mother; when a land is lost, or a time, and your friend blotted out, gone, your brother's body spoiled, and cold, your infant dead, and you dying: you reel out love's long line alone, stripped like a live wire loosing its sparks to a cloud, like a live wire loosed in space to longing and grief everlasting. . . . The question is, then, whether God touches anything. Is anything firm, or is time on the loose?[2]

This is a brilliant, and beautiful, way to put the question. Less poetically, it comes out like this: If God acted in the burning of little Julie, if God acted at Buna, or if God was in any way behind September 11, then is God a sadist? Alternatively, the question takes yet another form. If God could have acted to prevent any of those events but chose instead to suffer with victims, then God's character appears in a better light, but God's power seems strangely circumscribed. Dillard asserts, "God despises everything, apparently," and then plaintively raises the Christian question: "Did Christ descend once and for all to no purpose?" More bluntly, in my words: Is God a masochist?

Neither God as sadist nor God as masochist is a pleasant option, and neither Dillard nor I will leave it at that. But Dillard's answer, *Holy the Firm,* is one that less poetic seekers across the United States are exploring in practice, if not in theory, as they flock to "sacred places" to fill the void left by failing theologies of time.[3] Such sacred places vary widely—from traditional shrines to more recent inventions, but the turn from time to place in "spirituality" is evident not only in the modern invention of tourism, but also in a resurgence of pilgrimage among diverse peoples around the globe.[4] Now, defining what constitutes a sacred place is no easy matter, as we shall see in the first section of this chapter. For Christians, of course, a sacred place is one where God is, but this definition obscures as much as it clarifies—given the questions with which we began. Among historians of religions, two broad schools of thought exist on how to define a sacred place.[5] One school, generally following Mircea Eliade, poetically emphasizes that sacred places are "revealed" to human beings and that sacred places share some mystical unity with "being" or "reality" that distinguishes them from "ordinary" or "profane" places. The best approach we can take to such places, so this argument goes, is to let them be, which for a scholar means to describe them in ways that allow their "revelation" to be manifest. This essentially romantic attitude toward places is characteristic of many "new age" endeavors.[6] Another approach, generally identified with Jonathan Z. Smith, emphasizes that sacred places are all constructed by historically discernible human agency, especially by the characteristically human activities of ritual. Sacred places are, furthermore, hardly places to "let be," since they are, rather, sites at which complex political, economic, and social issues crucial to a culture are worked out. This school of thought suggests that an attempt to make a place sacred is always an attempt to "take" place for one's own person or tribe. The attitude of many military leaders toward almost any place is a good example of this mentality. We will learn much from both of these ways of defining what makes a place sacred, while also contending—as the examples might suggest—that both have shortcomings.

To clarify the potential and the shortcomings of these two approaches, I will focus attention in the second section of the chapter on the Christian tradition. More specifically, I will draw out the implicit theologies of place in two very different films. The first, *Monty Python and the Holy Grail,* is a hilarious (to me, anyway) satire of how Christian quests to "take" place can cause great damage. In the film, "King Arthur" and several "Knights of the Round Table" seek to acquire the Holy Grail, or the cup Jesus used at the Last Supper. In the process of their quest, however, the good "Christian" knights are revealed on the screen as lusty cowards who lie, maim, and kill. They are, in short, hypocrites whose religious zeal blinds them to the way they do violence to themselves and others. For as the knights perform one absurd test after another and witlessly obliterate any obstacles impeding their quest, they are themselves consumed and possessed in the process. Monty Python exposes Christian efforts to "take" place as death-defying and destructive strategies for living.

The second film is Robert Redford's adaptation of Norman Maclean's memoir, *A River Runs through It*. Here, a Christian theology of place is represented not so much as a destructive strategy to deny death as a hopeful effort to affirm life.[7] In this coming-of-age film, set in 1920s Montana, two brothers, Paul and Norman Maclean, are taught by their Presbyterian pastor father to love fly-fishing, the Big Blackfoot River, their family, and words. Norman, the older brother, eventually leaves Montana to become an English professor. Paul, however, stays in Montana as a journalist. Paul also develops a love for drinking and gambling that leads him to an early and violent death. Long after Paul has died, however, through his memoir Norman lovingly remembers his brother, recognizes the beauty and power of the Big Blackfoot, and celebrates the fragile art of fly-fishing through the medium of words. In short, *A River Runs through It* bridges death in a fragile fabric of words and images that does not defy death's absences, but that does find solace in the grace of remembering the past, celebrating the present, and recognizing the fragility of the future. If both films are in some way "about" Christian approaches to places, then between them they pose the central problem for a theology of place very clearly. The Christian quest for place can be a death-defying and destructive strategy or a life-affirming path to remembering and recognition. Any individual's quest is, usually, a little of both.

Finally, in the last section of this chapter I will sketch the three processes that together constitute the "method of approach" to places that I will use throughout this book. In this section, I argue that the dichotomy between the two leading ways to interpret sacred space is spurious. Both methods bear fruit, just as both methods have problems. A full approach to the study of sacred space, then, must simultaneously respect, critique, and recognize its own place among the poetics, politics, and pilgrims present at any sacred place. This sentence will take some unpacking, but it suggests, in short, that neither an Eliadean poetics nor a Smithean politics of sacred places can take into account fully the pilgrims' presence in this process. People surely make places sacred, but people aren't only poets or politicians. They are also unpredictable—capable of horrible evil, capable of great grace. Readers disinterested in questions of academic method might choose to skip this section, although I hope to communicate what I'm up to in a way that will not be mystifying—as is unfortunately so often the case with academic arguments. I have grown increasingly impatient over the years with scholarship that merely legitimizes the power of the scholar or of the academy.

As we explore the three key terms of my method—poetics, politics, and pilgrims—it will perhaps begin to be apparent to a reader that many of the "sacred places" of modern America may not be particularly good poetically or politically, and may even be harmful to the millions of pilgrims who visit them. Consider, for one brief instance of foreshadowing, a piece of public art I discovered in 1987. It was called *Big Bil-Bored*. This sculpture basically amounted to a triangular wedge—thirty feet high by thirty feet wide by two feet deep—of discarded home appliances and other

commodities, welded and cemented together and plopped on a pedestal in front of a shopping mall and a McDonald's in North Riverside, Illinois. When I first noticed this piece of art I laughed out loud. It was unbelievably ugly, not only because it contained busted toys and car parts and toasters and hair dryers welded and cemented together, but because the pigeons found it a delightful perch and used it as a drive-by outhouse. I found the irony of the artwork delightful. "Here's what a trip to this kind of a 'sacred place,' as advertised in billboards, will get you," I interpreted the artist saying about the mall—a bunch of stuff that breaks and rusts and that you will eventually grow bored with and throw out. The sculpture was designed and built by Nancy Rubins in 1980. After a history of controversy, it was destroyed in 1993. Apparently the satire was no longer appreciated by mall tenants and visitors.

And it is precisely because *Big Bil-Bored* has, apparently, met with its demise that I think it's important to pay serious attention to places, and to differentiate between those that function primarily in a salutary way and those that function in a manner akin to wolves masquerading as shepherds. For it seems to me that *Big Bil-Bored* represented and exposed a pretty systematic symptom of modern life—what I will describe in chapter 6, following René Girard, as "the desire to acquire." This desire has motivated some great things. The abundance of commodities in American culture is a remarkable historic achievement. But the destruction of this sculpture I also take as a symptom of modern life, what I will also describe in chapter 6, following Hannah Arendt, as "the violence of banality." In an effort to locate God, and overcome our fear of time, we collect stuff at the mall or on some other quest. But eventually we grow bored with what we have collected and throw it out or destroy it. If we did this only with commodities, perhaps it would not be such a problem—although the shortage of landfills across the United States is an increasingly troublesome dilemma. But we also grow bored with and discard artwork. We grow bored with and discard places. We grow bored with and discard people, marriages, traditions. It is this latter tendency especially—to be blind to how our desires to acquire cause us to destroy—that is the most troubling aspect of the American turn to a theology of places.[8] Catering to the desire to acquire may bring short-term gratification, but in the long run it brings destruction, and we are left "holding one end of a love," as Dillard put it so well, facing the naked truths of "spirit bare" and "grief everlasting."

This is a harsh judgment, but the evidence of its accuracy as diagnosis is all around us in any sociology of the modern world, in any political reflection on recent history, or in any edition of the American Psychological Association's *Diagnostic and Statistical Manual*. Many citizens living in the world of late modernity, postmodernity, or what I prefer to call "mediated modernity" have come to accept a deep (if dim) sense of absence as "normal." At the same time, we also have learned largely to ignore the all-too-present suffering of our neighbors, while we simultaneously and frantically attach ourselves to places in a passionate effort to deny our own mortality. Such ways of clothing God by hiding the truths of suffering have not been very successful. Human beings have undeniably gone more places and seen more things in the past century alone than in all the millennia before. But at the same time we have come to depend upon awesome technologies that threaten either to consume us in our own waste or to destroy us in an instant's flash. Somewhere between and beyond "letting be" and "taking" place, then, lies a path that will liberate pilgrims not only poetically to enjoy but also to understand politically their experiences of places, so that finally those places themselves will not be destroyed. A way to begin to discover this path is to study how people in the past have, consciously or unconsciously, created sacred places.

Letting Be and Taking Place

For Christians, a sacred place is obviously one where God is, but this definition obscures as much as it clarifies, because everything hinges upon how one identifies "God." It will be good, then, to spend a bit of time assessing several attempts at understanding how people have related to places religiously. The going will be a little rough: heavy on theory, light on example. But the work now will pay dividends later, when we turn directly to examples. The best-known theorist of sacred space, then, is Mircea Eliade, the late historian of religions who taught for many years at the University of Chicago. According to Eliade,

> For religious [people], space is not homogeneous; [they] experience interruptions, breaks in it; some parts of space are qualitatively different from others. . . . There is, then, a sacred space, and hence a strong, significant space; there are other spaces that are not sacred and so are without structure or consistency, amorphous. . . . [This] is not a matter of theoretical speculation, but of a primary religious experience that precedes

> reflection on the world. For it is the break effected in space that allows the world to be constituted, because it reveals the fixed point, the central axis for all future orientation. When the sacred manifests itself in any *hierophany,* there is not only a break in the homogeneity of space; there is also revelation of an absolute reality, opposed to the nonreality of the vast surrounding expanse. The manifestation of the sacred ontologically founds the world. In the homogeneous and infinite expanse, in which no point of reference is possible and hence no *orientation* can be established, the *hierophany* reveals an absolute fixed point, a center.[9]

Here, sacred space is the opposite of profane, ordinary space. Sacred space "appears," in a *hierophany* or "manifestation" of the holy. Such a place becomes an "axis" around which people orient themselves; indeed, around such a place people "found" a world. We will lean heavily upon Eliade's emphasis on the way sacred space provides people with "orientation," but his overall definition (while still widely used) has also come under considerable and accurate critique.

For instance, Jonathan Z. Smith, also of the University of Chicago, has shown that Eliade misinterpreted badly the historical facts surrounding some of the sacred places he studied. Smith also has argued, on the basis of this evidence, that Eliade's definition by its very nature obscures many of the ways sacred places were historically created and functioned. Consequently, Smith has come to favor a definition of sacred space that sets it within the context of ritual action. He writes:

> Ritual is, first and foremost, a mode of paying attention. It is a process for marking interest. . . . [It is not] blind and thoughtless habit. It is this characteristic, as well, that explains the role of place as a fundamental component of ritual: place directs attention. . . . Such a preliminary understanding of ritual and its relation to place is best illustrated by the case of built ritual environments—most especially, crafted constructions such as temples. When one enters a temple, one enters marked-off space . . . in which, at least in principle, nothing is accidental; everything, at least potentially, demands attention. The temple serves as a focusing lens, establishing the possibility of significance by directing attention, by requiring the perception of difference. Within the temple, the ordinary (which to any outside eye or ear remains wholly ordinary) becomes significant, becomes "sacred," simply by being there. A ritual object or action [or place] becomes sacred by having attention focused on it in a highly marked way. From such a point of view, there is nothing that is inherently sacred or profane. These are not substantive categories, but rather situational ones. Sacrality is, above all, a category of emplacement.[10]

If Eliade stressed that sacred places are "revealed" through hierophanies, Smith stresses that they are created through human interpretation, and especially through the action of ritual. Both scholars agree, at least, that sacred space functions to orient people to, or to focus them on, significant cultural values or practices.

Most recently, historians of religion David Chidester and Edward T. Linenthal have edited a collection of essays, *American Sacred Space,* in which their coauthored introduction significantly advances the understanding of the issues at stake between Eliade and Smith. "In the study of religion," Chidester and Linenthal explain,

> two broad lines of definition have been advanced, one substantial, the other situational. In the first instance, some definitions of the sacred presume to have penetrated and reported its essential character . . . [or evoked] certain experiential qualities that can be associated with the sacred. . . . By contrast, however, a situational analysis . . . has located the sacred at the nexus of human practices and social projects . . . [recognizing] that nothing is inherently sacred.[11]

The first approach, of course, is Eliade's. The second belongs to Smith. Chidester and Linenthal go on to agree generally with Smith, and argue that:

> sacred space is inevitably contested space, a site of negotiated contests over legitimated ownership of sacred symbols. . . . Power is asserted and resisted in any production of space, and especially in the production of sacred space. Since no sacred space is merely "given" in the world, its ownership will always be at stake. In this respect, a sacred space is not merely discovered, or founded, or constructed; it is claimed, owned, and operated by people advancing specific interests.[12]

This is a very helpful advance in Smith's corrective to Eliade's view of sacred places. Sacred space is invariably situated in a complex cultural context replete with political, economic, biological, and other factors of influence.

But is it fair to say that no sacred space is ever experienced as "given" in the world? And even more, is ownership "always" at stake in relation to sacred places? I admire Chidester and Linenthal's approach. It clearly highlights the weaknesses of Eliade's romantic imagining that we can simply "let be" or neutrally describe sacred places as "revealed," as if human agency had no role in the process. By highlighting, furthermore, the importance of sacred places in establishing "order" out of chaos, Eliade seems to support a politics that allows power to be granted to the owners or controllers of any place and a politics that values order over participation. These are serious problems. But as my questions above suggest, it also seems to me that Eliade pointed to something intellectually significant that Smith, Chidester, and Linenthal can't, or won't, acknowledge. They reduce sacred places to the struggle for power, prestige, and ownership. Such a reduction is illuminating, but it also misses, on the one hand, how scholars are not without their own interests in proposing such a reduction. Scholars can be as driven as any pilgrim to "take" a place, even if they do so only by claiming for themselves a more "critical" interpretation of it. Smith, Chidester, and Linenthal also miss, on the other hand, that the sacred places and pilgrimages of people around the world seem to have endured scholarly efforts to expose their dastardly political functioning rather successfully over the past few centuries. Indeed, while I am inclined to agree that many, if not most, sacred places have functioned as sites of conflict, it can also be pointed out that a situational approach to sacred places necessitates that the experiment be an open one. There is no reason to believe, if situation truly shapes sacrality, that under some situations a sacred place might not function very differently than as a site of "contestation" over "ownership" or as a prop for a totalitarian politics of order. And indeed, if one listens with any attention at all to the reports from pilgrims at such places, it pretty quickly becomes apparent that those pilgrims think that something other than either a *hierophany* or a "contestation" is going on. There is no reason, then, theoretically or historically, to exclude the possibility that some sacred places might exist (or be created) where something like a poetic appreciation for beauty, a political opening to freedom, or a pilgrim's awe before the eternal, might just make sense. Sacred places might in fact truly be gifts to pilgrims, where they can heal and be healed, grant power and be empowered, or even give and experience love.

Two Films: The Christian Problem

Now, all this theorizing has the typical air of academic abstraction about it, and it imagines that there is something called "religion" or "sacred space" that exists apart from historical traditions, symbol systems, or actual places. Consequently, we need to focus our attention on some examples less driven by abstraction and more focused on the faith of actual folk. We can move a little closer toward this goal by studying briefly two popular films that suggest a range of options for Christians if they seek to clothe God in places. Each film is a splendid piece of art. Neither is a systematic theology, except implicitly. Both take up, however, the question of how Christians might clothe God in places.

The first film is *Monty Python and the Holy Grail,* produced on a very low budget in 1974. The film is a clever and cutting critique of the tendency of Christians to locate God in ludicrous places or to wrap God in clothes that don't fit. Many of my students, both graduate and undergraduate, know this film well, and some can quote entire sections of the dialogue by heart (often complete with bad British accents). However, most of them have never really studied what the movie means. The film is set primarily in "England 932 A.D.," but occasional scenes or narration from "the present" are interspersed throughout. The main character is "King Arthur," who seeks first to recruit "knights" for his court at "Camelot," and who then leads the "knights" on a quest for the Holy Grail.

The farcical quality of the film is announced in its first scene. Arthur appears on the screen, prancing through a forest as if riding a horse and dressed in a white Crusader tunic adorned with a red cross. He is followed by his sidekick, whose name we later learn is "Patsy." Patsy does not prance like Arthur, but hunches over in a submissive posture and clomps together two coconut shells to imitate the sounds of a horse cantering. Within the first four scenes of the film, then, Arthur and Patsy introduce viewers to a world riddled with death and dominated by struggles over power. The two characters first travel to a town beset by the plague, where they observe a young man anxious to kill off his disease-ridden father. The father protests, "I'm not dead yet" and "I feel happy," before getting clubbed over the head and thrown on a pull-cart with other victims of the disease. Arthur and Patsy then engage in conversation with "Dennis the peasant," a young man Arthur mistakes for an old woman. Dennis, who is a member of an "anarcho-syndicalist-commune," excoriates Arthur for his monarchical pretensions. When the king claims that his right to the throne was revealed to him by "The Lady of the Lake," Dennis protests that a vision of "a watery tart" legitimized in a "farcical aquatic ceremony" is clearly not a good foundation for a government. Arthur then assaults Dennis, while Dennis cries out to his partner, who is building castles or bricks (it's unclear) in the mud: "See how he's oppressing me! See the violence inherent in the system! It's the violence inherent in the system!" In the third scene, the "violence inherent in the system" becomes further manifest as Arthur engages "The Black Knight" in a sword fight. One by one, the knight's limbs are severed by the king, accompanied by outrageously gory spurts of theatrical blood, after which Arthur prays to God, of course, in thanks for giving him the victory. Finally, Arthur and Patsy stumble upon the trial of a woman charged with witchcraft. She is inevitably found guilty according to a tortured logic that determines that since witches burn, they must be made of wood, and that since wood floats, a witch must weigh the same as a duck. The scales of justice, of course, are unbalanced. At a critical juncture in the witch's trial, Arthur reveals himself as a man "skilled in the ways of science." This display of knowledge leads the king to success in recruiting the "Knights of the Round Table." Unfortunately, however, when the knights finally arrive at the legendary castle, they are disappointed, despite engaging in a rowdy song-and-dance number. "Camelot," Arthur concludes, is "a silly place."

God then enters the film. The divine one is suitably, for the satire, depicted as a bearded old cartoon-figure king cut out of cardboard. He appears to the knights from a cloud and irascibly claims to be tired of people always groveling before him. "God" nevertheless sets the knights on their mission: to find the Holy Grail. In the twenty scenes that make up the remaining hour or so of the film, the knights then engage in one hypocritical (and hilarious) encounter after another. The chaste "Sir Galahad" succumbs to the peril of sexual temptation in the "Castle Anthrax." The brave "Sir Robin" demonstrates pants-wetting cowardice when sworn to courage. And the bold "Sir Launcelot" kills wantonly in the name of God. Among the victims along the way is a "famous historian," dressed in the English tweeds of a 1970s academic. This historian appears suddenly on the screen as a narrator of the action and functions to connect 932 A.D. to the present. When the historian falls, slain by the sword of one of the knights, a woman (presumably his wife) kneels down to mourn over his body, and then a police investigator briefly appears on the screen.

In the final scenes of the film, the knights first conquer a "killer rabbit" by resorting to the "Holy Hand Grenade of Antioch." This weapon is suitably sanctified by a long ritual process, in a hilarious send-up of the repetition of much liturgy. The knights then pass through the "Cave of Caerbannog," only to arrive at "The Bridge of Death," which crosses over "The Gorge of Eternal Peril." At the bridge, all of the knights are asked three questions—and only some survive. Those who do then come to yet another castle that looks oddly identical to one at the beginning of the film.

The knights now identify this castle as "a sacred place," confident that it is indeed the home of the Holy Grail. Unfortunately, the knights discover that "French" soldiers already inhabit the holy place, and the French soldiers taunt the English knights with what seem to the knights to be blasphemous sacrilege against "the name of the Lord." The knights then marshal an impressive medieval army to prepare for a holy war. The film ends—abruptly—when modern police cars drive up before the army can advance. The police investigator from the earlier scene jumps out, accompanied by the wife of the slain "famous historian." The investigator handcuffs Launcelot and Arthur and loads both of them into a paddy wagon. Other police then disperse the rest of the warriors, and the film is over but for the calliope music at the end.

The giddiness with which this film tramples on religious pretension is truly stunning and undoubtedly calls for a fuller study someday. For now, however, the role of death as the motive behind the knights' madness and violence is the key point. Christians, this comedy troupe suggests, have often sought after sacred places in a frantic effort to cross "the Bridge of Death" and to avoid "the Gorge of Eternal Peril." But in such seeking, "Christians" have violated both themselves and others.[13] Monty Python, in short, takes a situational approach to sacred space, satirically critiquing the contests over power that religious quests often mask. In the situations they depict with such deft humor, the Christian "knights" portrayed by Monty Python do damage because they imagine that by "clothing" (or even simply by naming) God, they have thereby gained for themselves God's apparently arbitrary power to create and destroy. The knights, in short, confuse an image of their own making and the power it promises to bring them with something living. Such confusion leads them to *destroy* something living. This is "the violence inherent in the system."

That this is, of course, also an accurate representation of many episodes in Christian history gives the satire its plausibility and its edge. Christians, most notably in the Crusades, have often sought to defy death through seeking to acquire some sacred places, and such crusaders have often wound up both destroying and being destroyed in the process.[14] But the true edge to this satire is that such confusion of image with reality is hardly only a medieval problem. Modern Christians have been no less violent and hypocritical than the "Knights of the Round Table," as the occasional scenes from the present in the film clearly point out. The film implies, then, a theology of place in which Christians are unable to accept the limits of mortality or the limits imposed by embodied existence, and in an effort to possess or "take" sacred space, they do great damage. The Christian quest for sacred space can be a death-defying strategy that imprisons Christians in a death-dealing system.

Fortunately, however, that is only one side (albeit a large one) of the Christian tradition in its approach to sacred places. Another very different possibility surfaces in *A River Runs through It.* If we laugh at Monty Python's satire, we cry at the pathos of Norman Maclean's memory of his brother, Paul, who was "beautiful," who attained "perfection" in a moment of fly-fishing, but who died a violent death as a young man. The film moves between three central places—nature, the Maclean home, and the church in which the Macleans grew up. The natural setting is the unspoiled

Montana of the 1920s. The Maclean home is a parsonage, for the father of the two boys is a Presbyterian pastor. The church, of course, is the place where the family gathers to hear the father preach, to sing the hymns of the faithful, and to celebrate birth and mourn death.

As with the Monty Python film, *A River Runs through It* deserves a full study in its own right. For now, however, what demands our attention is the way Norman Maclean and director Robert Redford link nature with words and images. Through the story of the film, Maclean focuses readers on, and Redford helps viewers see, the grandeur and grace of nature, even while directing attention to human frailty and fragility. I will say more about the film in chapter 7, but for now two parallel scenes from near its beginning and end can convey the way the movie recognizes the power of nature—including the threat of death—and remembers to celebrate the joys and discoveries of living. The first scene is when the two teenaged Maclean boys, in an effort to "go down in history," as Paul puts it, "shoot the chutes," or ride down a set of very fast rapids on the Big Blackfoot River. To do so, they steal a skiff that was anchored on the river's shore. The soundtrack of the film roars with the rush of the rapids, as the images on the screen show the boys riding in the little wooden boat down the increasingly rough and noisy river. "Jesus, Mary, and Joseph!" exclaims one of the boys, as the boat crashes against the huge rocks at the bottom of the run, sending both boys spinning into the water, where it is unclear for many moments whether they will resurface. When they do—surprising and relieving their friends, who have been watching horrified along the banks—the boys' aquatic rite of passage is complete. They "shot the chutes" and will share the glory of going down in history. But the film then goes on, moving now into the household, to show the boys being chastized by their father for stealing the boat. Paul's dream of glory is dashed upon the rocks of his father's sense of justice.

That scene foreshadows the plot of the entire film. Norman uses the love for words his father conveys to him through his preaching and teaching, first to go to college at Dartmouth, and then toward an academic career at the University of Chicago. Paul, however, seems stuck by his attraction to the rush of the river and professes to Norman, "I'll never leave Montana, brother." The older brother, called "Preach" by his younger sibling, has at best an ambivalent relationship to the institutional church, but he clearly draws sustenance from his father's preaching. Even as a very young child, however, Paul laughs when it is suggested that he might become a preacher. His career as a hard-drinking journalist allows him to tell jokes and stories with language that makes his father laugh. But he will never use words to preach, like Norman, in a way that makes his father proud. The film cascades toward its conclusion like the rush of a great river. In a scene near its end, Paul reenacts his earlier rite of passage when he hooks a huge fish that drags him downstream in the Big Blackfoot for hundreds of yards. Now, however, he is alone, and he has no boat to carry him. As he clings to the fragile filament that connects him to the fish, he completely submerges at times, carried between the boulders, until at last he surfaces, triumphant, having caught a beautiful rainbow trout. Norman, having watched the struggle from the banks of the river, proclaims in a voice-over narration that he was aware, at that moment, that he "was witnessing perfection." His brother's performance at fishing was like a great work of art: a whole symphony, or a perfect poem. "But," the voice-over continues, "life is not a work of art, and the moment could not last." Indeed, no such moment can, and the film ends just a few minutes later. The narration is again a voice-over, recalling the night that Paul was found beaten to death by the butt of a revolver, with all of the bones in his right hand broken.

The last few scenes of the film retrace the boys' coming-of-age in scenes at home, at the church, and at the river. The first scene is years after Paul's death, long years that have passed with mostly silence between father and elder son about the loss of Paul. Standing outside their home, Norman recalls to his father that Paul "was a fine fisherman." His father, whose words still inspire and comfort the elder son, corrects him one last time. "He was more than that," the father offers sharply. "He was beautiful." The scene then changes to the church, where the father is preaching. A voice-over tells us, "Paul was always present in my father's thoughts." The voice of the preacher then proclaims: "Each one of us will see a loved one in need, but what is needed will elude us. . . . It is those we live with and should know, who elude us most of all. We can still love them, even without full understanding." And then the viewer is at the river, where a solitary old man casts his line into the water. He is alone. "All those are dead," the voice-over intones about the other characters in the story, "but I still reach out to them."

Now, it should be clear that *A River Runs through It* depicts a very different understanding of the Christian approach to sacred space than does Monty Python. On one level, the film can be interpreted in a romantic or mystical mode—there are surely elements of Hollywood homage to mystical "being" in the film. But the film does not suppose that any sacred place is "revealed" to the brothers. There are no miraculous appearances or hierophanies of Paul after his death to console his older brother. There is only an affirmation of Paul's beauty by his father in a casual household conversation. There is only a lament over loss and an affirmation of love by a preacher in a sermon. And, of course, there is only a river. Most of all, though, there are fabrics of words and images. The point is profound for our purposes. Through memory, empathy, and imagination, as articulated in words and images, ordinary places become available as sacred places.[15] They do so not primarily as hierophanies, or as sites of "contestation," but as places of grace where death is not denied and where the gifts of life are affirmed. When we "clothe" a place well, in other words, we can put-back-together, or re-member that which was violated or broken in our lives. When we "clothe" a place well, we can empathically re-create our solidarity with all who suffer and all who experience joy. When we "clothe" a place well, we can imagine a world in which we care for everything fragile, and especially goodness and truth, insofar as we are able.[16] All of the above can also be said, of course, of how we clothe God. Through language, this film finally affirms, all places can be places of grace, even though our connection to any specific place might be contingent, distant, and fleeting. These two films have thus brought us to the point where the scholarly disciplines known as the history of religions and theology both touch down. And that point is the matter of method.[17]

Poetics, Politics, and Pilgrims

In a two-year period between Veterans Day 1993 and Veterans Day 1995, I interviewed and surveyed 185 visitors to the Vietnam Veterans Memorial in Washington, D.C. I am not a sociologist, so the survey was undoubtedly flawed as a scientific instrument, the interviews impressionistic. But I undertook the project while in the D.C. area on a semester-long research leave, as part of a larger study of the relationship between religion and violence in the United States.[18] At the time, the memorial was the most frequently visited site on the Mall, and Glenna Goodacre's statue remembering the women who served in Vietnam was just being completed and dedicated. The question that motivated my research was a simple one: does the Vietnam Veterans Memorial, as its builders intended, "heal" a nation of violence?[19] I expected, to be honest, an answer of "no." I was a young child during most of the Vietnam War, and though I grew up in a very patriotic family and sported a "Goldwater for President" bumper sticker on my tricycle, I had learned to be suspicious of almost anything connected with that conflict. I feared that the memorial was likely to be a shrine to American nationalism—a way to mask the violence of the conflict and to obscure the failure of the war as foreign policy under all kinds of patriotic rhetoric and ritual. What I discovered was more complex than I had imagined.

Ninety-two percent of the pilgrims at the Wall agreed with the first question on my survey, which asked them simply whether they thought the memorial was "a sacred place." But as I conducted interviews with and observed the behavior of pilgrims at the Wall, I discovered that what people meant when they affirmed that the memorial was a "sacred place" varied a great deal from person to person and from group to group. I did discover those who wanted to use the Wall to bolster American military might and national pride. In fact, I found several different groups of such folk, all trying to blame or scapegoat different targets for the deaths recorded by the fifty-eight thousand names inscribed on the Wall. Some visitors blamed the government, some blamed Jane Fonda or other antiwar protesters, some blamed the Vietnamese, and some blamed themselves. All in all, there was plenty of blame to go around. But the targets for this blame were diffuse and unfocused, and there were two other features of the memorial that took me by surprise.

The first one was the design of the shrine itself and the history of its construction. The memorial was built only after great "contestation," so to speak. Although the project was initially the inspiration of veteran Jan C. Scruggs, it was designed by architect Maya Lin, whose model of a black granite "wall of names" was chosen in a competition funded in part by financier H. Ross Perot. Perot, however, was so incensed by the winning design—he called it a "black gash of shame"—that he pulled strings to force delays and an eventual compromise to the design, evident now in the "Three Servicemen Statue" and eventually supplemented by the "Vietnam Women's Memorial." Still, I observed that it was the Wall to which most pilgrims gravitated. And it seemed clear to me that the meanings of the Wall could not be erased by any compromise. The fifty-eight thousand names etched in the reflective granite panels simply weren't going anywhere. As pilgrims walked along the pathway that gently descends beside the black panels, they could, on a sunny day, see themselves reflected in the Wall—along with the Washington Monument, in a stunning embedding of a symbol of power in the memorial to those who had died. I imagined that the meaning of the Wall—often described as a tomb—as "sacred place" was that it was a beautiful reminder of the fragility of life. Surely, I thought, it helped people recognize the futility of violence. And even, I supposed, through its ability to "reflect" a viewer in the names, the Wall pointed to the potential complicity of all pilgrims with the misuse of power.

But, of course, not everyone understood the shrine in this way. The second feature of the memorial that surprised me, then, was the tolerance, if not in fact jarring pluralism, embraced, or at least permitted, at the Vietnam Veterans Memorial. Many visitors simply came to "do" the memorial as part of a bus tour, snapped a quick photo, and were on their way to the next stop on their tour in fifteen minutes. But I observed that even these "pilgrims" rarely escaped without some token sense of the meaning of the place. Some of them discovered on the Wall the name of a neighbor, family member, or friend, and left with a "rubbing" of the name on a piece of paper provided for that purpose by a representative from the National Park Service. Others left with a souvenir T-shirt or trinket, or a book or pamphlet sold or given to them by vendors or veterans groups whose booths surrounded the memorial. Of course, many others at the Wall were more intentional about their pilgrimage. They took nothing with them but memories, perhaps; rather, they left gifts of their own to add to the history of the memorial. They did so in many different ways. Some brought music. Some brought prayers. Some made speeches. More concretely, many visitors left objects at the Wall. Letters, photos, cigarettes, medals, beer cans, flags, panties, flowers, crosses, rings, arrows, shoes, and countless other personal items were left at the memorial by pilgrims, only to be collected at night by the National Park Service and sent to a huge warehouse, where they were catalogued and stored. What was going on here?

The clue to unlock that question came when I compared two very different visits I made to the place. The first was when I attended the public Veterans Day celebration on November 11, 1993. This service began with an invocation by Chaplain Alice Farquhar Mayes, a Vietnam veteran. The prayer was, simply, a pacifistic proclamation. It ended by declaring "without equivocation that all war is appalling and abhorrent to You and to each of us here gathered." A long silence settled over the crowd after the chaplain said, "Amen." Then suddenly, the Air Force Band struck up a rendition of "She's a Grand Old Flag," a tune not listed on the program. The juxtaposition of pacifist and patriotic symbols was jarring on one level but also, I came to discover, typical of the paradoxical capacity of the place to embrace the most extreme differences of opinion. No one other than me, apparently, batted an eye at the paradox. This capacity to embrace extremes became further evident when I made a 2 A.M. visit to the Wall on the Saturday night of Veterans Day weekend in 1995. At night, the mood at the memorial changes. It is quiet, usually, reinforcing the characteristic response of visitors to the shrine at all times of day, namely silence. So I went to the Wall this night expecting some silence and hoping for some solitude. But as I approached, I heard a man shouting. Perhaps naively, I kept walking toward the Wall from the direction of the women's statue but slowed and finally stopped near a ring of trees. A solitary man was pacing back and forth at the base of the Wall's apex. He was gesticulating, and from what I could make out of what he was saying, in between epithets and curses, he was a veteran of the conflict with some scores to settle. I was uncertain how to respond but stayed long enough to see a woman who had been sitting on the lawn in front of the Wall walk toward the vet and reach out to console him. The man stopped shouting then, the couple sat down, and the woman cradled the man in her arms. I turned and walked away, ashamed at having observed such raw emotion and certain I had no words to offer from my own experience that could possibly have encompassed his own. In short, what I discovered from those two very different visits to the Vietnam Veterans Memorial is that the range of responses to this "sacred place" was very wide, from pacifism to propaganda, from silence to shouting, from poetry to politics and beyond. In short, the meaning of the place was not fixed and could not be fixed. It would always be open to new interpretations—depending upon the language in which the place was described, the political structures that supported or controlled it, and especially the pilgrims who attended to it. Its future was truly open.

The same is true, of course, of clothing God. Three processes—poetic, political, and personal—need to come together in any theology of place, as they do in any approach to sacred space. A poetics of sacred space, or of a theology of place, then, draws upon the insights of Eliade into the way sacred places are not wholly the result of human interpretation. Places also shape human responses. Places give people something to contest or appreciate. According to Aristotle, poetry is the art that "imitates by language alone."[20] Obviously, for imitation to occur, there must be something previously "given" or "revealed" to imitate. A poetic approach to sacred space thus seeks to imitate in language, in as direct a fashion as possible, what a place gives to those who have visited it. A poetic approach to clothing God similarly seeks to reiterate or clothe "experiences" of God in language. Of course, in the case of God, there may not seem to be the immediacy of encounter available with more material places, but this obviously depends upon how one locates God. A historian of religions drawn to this approach might, for instance, seek to re-create through language the appearance, history, and interactions within a temple, church, or shrine, over a specified period of time. A theologian who undertakes a poetic path to clothing God seeks, similarly, to imitate in language and metaphor his or her own experiences of God, along with those revealed over the history of the tradition. Both scholars might not only visit sacred places, or seek "experiences" of God for themselves, but might in addition—or even rather—study texts about God or places. In any event, a scholar who uses a "poetic" approach seeks primarily to let the place, or to let God, "be." The place, or God, can "speak for itself," so to speak, and the scholar primarily imitates in language how humans "experience" the object of study. A poetics of place, then, whether historical or theological, is primarily an enterprise in phenomenology, or the study of appearances, as filtered through language and imagination.

A politics of sacred space, or a political theology of place, by contrast, draws upon the insights of Smith, Chidester, and Linenthal to assert one's own claim to define the meaning of the place, or to fashion clothing for God. Various scholars do this more or less overtly and consciously. Rather than imitation of appearance in language, *analysis* of social, cultural, and political function (preferably bolstered with charts, tables, diagrams and such) determines this approach. Again turning to Aristotle for definition, politics is the study of human association that aims to create the most just modes of associating. He writes in a famous passage that "the human is a political animal." This animal, he goes on, differs from other animals by the use of speech "to indicate what is useful and what is harmful, and so also what is just and what is unjust." Human beings, the philosopher continues, can be the best of all animals when speech serves to guide human association into paths of justice, but humans can also be the worst of the animals when we misuse language to perpetuate injustice or perpetrate violence.[21] A historian of religions drawn to this process, in short, will, like Smith, Chidester, and Linenthal, assert on the basis of their analyses that sacred places have produced "contestation" or "conflict" in the past and might even point out that such places have propped up oppressive regimes and led to killing. A theologian, of course, might say the same thing about any number of theological fashions of the past millennia, especially if the theologian espousing the fashion in question happens to be a rival or belongs to a competing group. Finally, of course, another historian, possibly even examining the same sacred place as the first, might come along and "prove" that sacred places promote peace, and a theologian, studying the same "fashion" as the first, might demonstrate that in fact this way to clothe God promotes happiness. A politics of place, in other words, is primarily an enterprise in ethics, driven by a commitment to justice, truth, and perhaps other virtues (or perhaps vices) as well.

Obviously, incorporating (in many senses) both poetics and politics are the pilgrims who visit a sacred space, or the people who clothe God in places, including both historians and theologians. This insight is so stunningly simple that its significance is usually missed. Scholars themselves participate in creating the meaning of a place through whatever methods they happen to bring to it.[22] In virtual or real ways, scholars are also pilgrims and have the potential to effect changes in the meaning and significance of any place. More often than not, I've found, scholars imagine that they have more importance than the historical record suggests is true, for scholars have only one voice among many, with a more or less privileged access to truth and a more or less privileged access to power. The fact is that any historically significant sacred place is subject to a collective cacophony of voices claiming to understand it, and the same, quite clearly, is true of God. Finally, then, the pilgrim's role in the approach to sacred places moves beyond the aesthetics of poetry or the ethics of politics to the argumentation of rhetoric. Do you recommend the place, or not? Do you extol an image for God, or not? Do you seek to persuade other pilgrims to join you on the way, or not? Any history of a sacred place, then, as with any theology of place, is finally a rhetorical or personal act of persuasion—more or less overt.

The postmodern theorist Edward Soja has described the difference between these three approaches to space in a helpful way. According to Soja, the approach of historians such as Smith, Chidester, and Linenthal is characteristic of what he calls a "Firstspace" perspective, or "perceived" space. Here, space is "studied as a set of materialized 'spatial practices' that work together to produce and reproduce the concrete forms and specific patternings" connected with any particular location.[23] What one can *perceive* by analysis through the material senses is what matters about any place. This is the politics of place. The approach of theologians and scholars such as Eliade, in contrast, matches what Soja calls a "Secondspace" or "conceptual" space perspective. Here, space is studied less as a set of social practices than as a "mental or ideational field, conceptualized in imagery, reflexive thought, and symbolic representation . . . of the imagination." What one can conceive a place to be, through the poetic imagination, is what matters about a place. Finally, Soja himself suggests and attempts to develop what he calls "Thirdspace." By this he means "lived" space, or "a simultaneously real-and-imagined, actual-and-virtual, locus of structured individual and collective experience and agency." The chief mark of "Thirdspace" is that as a method, it recognizes that "perfect or complete knowledge is impossible. There is too much that lies beneath the surface, unknown and perhaps unknowable. . . . The best we can do is selectively explore, in the most insightful ways we can find, the infinite complexity of life."[24] In other words, this perspective acknowledges that the scholar, too, lives in the space she or he tries to describe and is shaped and changed by it, while also trying to shape it through language.

I hope it becomes clear throughout this book that I agree with Soja that "Thirdspace" is the most promising approach to the study of places. Given this method, however, it is important for a reader to understand something of my lived experience—lest my efforts at persuasion be mistaken as something more insidious or sinister than the modest theology of place that I intend. I will surface five features of my lived experience that seem to me important for a reader to know. I attend to these five features of my experience not because I think my experience is all that interesting or unique, but to help the reader understand both the potential and the limitations of what follows. I hope it will also be apparent that my lived experience has changed me—and continues to do so. First of all, then, I'm a Christian. Even more, I'm a lifelong Lutheran whose ethnic heritage is half-Norwegian, half-German. I joke with those who know something about the history of these Northern European groups in America—and that means primarily with other Lutherans—that such a "divergent" identity has made me very confused, especially when I intend to drink alcohol, which I do socially. If my German side predominates, I can drink all night and maintain reasonable coherence (although I'll let my wife drive). If my Norwegian side prevails, I have one glass of wine and I'm under the table. Of course, for anyone outside the circle of Norwegian and German Americans, this joke might not mean much (Norwegian Lutherans have a history of being teetotalers; Germans like their beer and brandy). As far as most folks can tell, I'm simply a white, Protestant, American male.

Yet the German side of my Lutheran heritage is especially significant in my status as a pilgrim. Most notably, it might make a reader wonder whether I have any right to use Elie Wiesel's narrative from Buna. Many of those who tormented Wiesel—and killed his sister, mother, and father—were baptized as Lutherans, or perhaps as Catholics, with whom Lutherans share much by way of faith. Most certainly, the tormentors of the Wiesel family were Germans or under the influence of German leadership. Even more, the Germanic founder of Lutheranism—Martin Luther, about whom I said such glowing things in chapter 1—also wrote some horrible things about Jews that the Nazis found very convenient for their political purposes. Finally, the church body of which I am a member, the Evangelical Lutheran Church in America, just got around to repudiating and confessing for Luther's anti-Semitism in 1990. This is why, in part, I have reframed the question that Elie Wiesel raised so powerfully in his *Night*. For me to use that question directly, as I did for many years in my teaching, I have to acknowledge that "my people" bear historic responsibility for triggering his powerful experience of absence and the suffering that went with it. I always offered that confession in the classroom, and I offer it here, because to do any less would be to claim the privilege of using Wiesel's story without acknowledging my place, and the place of my tradition, within it.

At the same time, I do not believe that the horrors of the Holocaust are a necessary and logical consequence of Lutheranism, Christianity, or German ethnicity. To be sure, Lutheranism and Christianity played their parts in creating the Nazi ideology. I cannot correct that past. I can, however, remember it (both here and in chapter 6, especially) and do what I can with my own language to prevent Christian anti-Semitism from recurring. To do so, I can honor both the memory of those lost and the integrity of those living, by clothing God in a way that respects Judaism as an ongoing tradition of faith and that honors the Jewish people for the gifts they have so often been in human history. To do any less, of course, would ironically be to deny that the one my tradition calls the Christ was a gift to humanity! After all, even the Gospels and Epistles are largely the arguments of Jews interpreting Jewish writings for each other. In short, the way I clothe God will seek to affirm the historic contexts of the texts in the Bible. The way I clothe God will clearly be a Christian and Lutheran way, but I do not believe those designations need to be made in a way that defines either Christianity or Lutheranism over and against Judaism (or Islam, Buddhism, or Hinduism, for that matter). Rather, a Christian reading of texts can be done in a way that takes its place as one way to understand the larger human problem with which the canonical stories struggle. I even hope that perhaps a Jewish reader could find benefit as a Jew (or a Hindu, as a Hindu) from some of the ways I interpret texts and places. On that point, of course, only a Jewish or Hindu reader can be the judge.[25]

I am a white, male member of the middle class, who has lived his entire life in the United States. These four other designators of my lived experience, then—of my race, gender, class, and culture—have joined with my religious affiliation to connect me to privileges that most people in the world can barely imagine. I lived most of my early life, for instance, with deep racist prejudice. I met my first African American face to face when I was twelve years old. And while I was of course aware of racial difference prior to that encounter, most of my awareness was riddled with stereotypes that I would be ashamed to relate. Because of my privilege as a white male in the United States, however, I have had access to resources that have helped me to move beyond some of those stereotypes and some of my racial blindness. Most notably, I moved first to the Chicago metropolitan area for college, then to Columbus, Ohio, for seminary, and then back to Chicago to complete my Ph.D. In each place, I learned some new things about racial diversity and dynamics. Over the years, I've marched against the KKK, "sat-in" and spoken at protests in support of opportunities for African Americans, and worshiped and worked with black Christians of many denominations. Even before my turn to racial activism, however, I was the beneficiary of an excellent musical education, and the role of music in opening my eyes to the issues of race in America has been inestimable. It is also a sign of how privileged I have been and of the limits I still live with.

Among my earliest childhood memories is sitting on the floor in the living room of my Wisconsin home, listening to Dixieland and dancing with my stuffed animals to rhythms and harmonies drawn from African-American experience. As a child, of course, I had no idea that I was learning harmonies and rhythms alien to my European ancestors. I just knew I liked them. When it came time, then, for me to choose an instrument to play in the sixth-grade band, it was only natural that I would take up the clarinet, no doubt to become the next Pete Fountain, who was the most famous Dixieland woodwind player. By eighth grade, alas, it was apparent that my skills on the clarinet were limited, although I could play a mean "Little Brown Jug."

Fortunately, my eighth-grade band instructor—Rand Skelton—persuaded me to take up the saxophone. Over the past thirty years, I have spent countless hours of delight playing the blues, jazz, and gospel music. Most recently, for instance, I was a regular member of the Valparaiso University Gospel Choir as a saxophone soloist, where I learned to play songs by Kirk Franklin, Donnie McLurkin, Hezekiah Walker, and many others. Today, I proudly display on the wall of my seminary office the plaque and photo that the choir members gave to me, "with much love," when I left to move to Philly. This entrée through music into the most important minority ethnic community in the United States—given the history of slavery—has allowed me insights and experiences that I truly treasure and could not possibly quantify. It has also helped me to research and write about African-American youth in a way that I hope honors them and their communities.[26] Such an entrée, of course, is also directly the result of my experience of privilege, especially the excellent education I received in well-funded and well-supplied schools. Such an entrée also falls far short of understanding the full force of the exclusions and stereotypes that continue to plague America on the matter of race. Now that I am a professor at the seminary in Philadelphia, I have many African-American students. Time and again they have accurately called me to account for the ways some of my fashions for God, and my choices of historical examples, still exclude them—even as they also express appreciation for other choices I make.

Just as I grew up racist and benefited from being white, so too did I experience the privilege of patriarchy. My extended family of origin was deeply defined by an ideology of the separate spheres. Women controlled the house; men controlled the world. These conventional roles were seldom questioned in public, at least as far as I recall, although I'm guessing they were the cause of considerable negotiation in private. As a male child, however, I remember receiving every encouragement to forge a public life-course that would reap personal and economic benefits for me. Indeed, I recall how one female relative proudly said of me, when I was about twelve, that I was becoming a "lady-killer." She meant this as a compliment—that I was growing tall and handsome. I have since, however, come to realize how such a casual phrase suggests a trap for men and a real danger for women. For women *are* killed and abused by men who claim to love them. And men—including batterers—are often blocked by grandiose expectations of public success from experiences of true intimacy. As with my advocacy on issues of racial justice, I have become an activist seeking for gender equality. I think of and describe myself as a feminist. I use inclusive language in all of my preaching, teaching, and writing. And I support gender equity in hiring, salaries, sports, and all social opportunities. My "feminism" has, furthermore, led to some costly personal encounters and to some lost political opportunities. I would even support an equal rights amendment to the U.S. Constitution, were such a prospect not so unlikely to be realized in my lifetime, ruled, as the present cultural ethos is, by a backlash against feminism and the sexual revolution of the sixties. Still, I know that to many feminists, no matter how much I work with them and for them, I come across as a pretty traditional "guy," who is probably more comfortable talking about sports than about my feelings—if I don't in fact come across as an enemy. I will have more to say about gender, including the matter of sexual orientation, in later chapters.

Both my experiences of racial and gender privilege were (and are) reinforced by the fourth characterization of my social location as a pilgrim—namely, that I'm comfortably "middle class." I am the "product," if you will, of an economic and educational system that prepared me for a "profession" in which I can gain access to convenient, if expensive, commodities. I inhabit both the realms of supply and demand in this class system. I commute twenty miles from Swarthmore to Philadelphia to supply students at the seminary with my "expertise" as a historian of religions in the United States. In exchange, I live in a desirable home in an old, wooded, parklike subdivision, just off an expressway and a trolley line, with two shopping malls within five miles of my home. This is a good deal. My life is, by the world's standards, luxurious. I'm tenured and reasonably accomplished as a professional. My life partner has a good-paying profession as well, so I should rest assured that my status as a member of the middle class is more or less secure. Still, I struggle to pay bills on time, and I wake up at night thinking about taxes, about funding college for my children, and about other such matters. The point is simply this: the places I imagine as "sacred" are places that reflect my middle-class mentality, and the ways I clothe God are also undoubtedly shaped by the assumptions of privilege and by the blinders and anxieties that are characteristic of those in my economic situation.

Finally, then, my location as a citizen of the United States is as significant a factor in my pilgrimage through life and in my theological formation as my membership in the church, my race, my gender, and my class location. Simply put, I live in an empire, and I benefit from the military might, industrial prowess, and informational expertise of that regime. This is, honestly, an excellent thing. I rarely have feared for my life because of attack by a hostile enemy, even since September 11. At the same time, I often wonder how my experiences and worldview have been shaped by the violence that is necessary to support and maintain the *pax Americana*. I wonder how I'm complicit with the domination and subordination of others, simply by being a citizen of such a great and powerful nation. And I wonder what I can do to contribute to a more just political life, both here at home and around the globe. I know that many people do not experience the "freedoms" I so often take for granted, much less have their basic needs met. I have tried to make the world a more just and humane place, as a parent, as a teacher, as an activist, and as a writer. But no matter what I do personally or professionally, I know that I have reaped benefits—and continue to do so—from systems of privilege, for no other reason than that I am white, middle class, male, and American. That I can't change. I can, however, try to build some bridges through the stories I tell, the cultural critiques I offer, and finally, the ways I clothe God—although I am all too aware that a bridge made of a fabric of words is a fragile thing indeed.

At the same time that this is a theology that reflects my own changing social location as a pilgrim, then, it also includes some very personal narratives. Some of these stories might make a reader smile or even laugh. I tell stories that I find funny because I like to laugh and because I like to be around people who laugh. I offer them in that spirit, as a way to meet a reader on the common human ground of humor, and even, perhaps, as a way to suggest that God doesn't mind being dressed in some funny outfits. Some of the other personal stories I tell might be emotionally involving for a reader. I have, from time to time, had students who read some of these chapters in draft form tell me that a story brought tears to their eyes. I am always suspicious of such compliments, especially when a grade is on the line. But tears, if they come, I hope reflect honest recognition on the part of a reader, not sentimental manipulation. Finally, a few of the stories I share in the pages to follow disclose matters that some might find scandalous or shameful. I share such stories not out of some exhibitionist impulse or as a way to do therapy in print. Least of all do I include any of these stories because I want a reader to feel sorry for me, as if I were some kind of victim. I am privileged to have a forum to speak from my experiences—and any narration of my experience would not be honest if it did not reveal both suffering I have caused and suffering I have experienced.

I have learned from my feminist and liberationist colleagues to trust very personal stories as a way to clothe God; these colleagues increasingly eschew the illusion of "objective" and "universal" theology because they realize (as I believe) that the personal is political. More accurately, I believe private choices have public implications, just as public policies and practices can badly distort and damage the ability to make wise private choices. Some of the stories I share point to the first problem, some to the second. All of them, however, are consistent with the method I sketched above, and all of them are told because I hope they can help readers find a place, or clothe God, in a way that will be beneficial to them. I also recognize, all too well, that such stories can offend or distance. The personal can be painful. But I take such a risk because otherwise I would be perpetuating the same silencing of suffering and refusal to speak the truth about uncomfortable matters that I see as among the most serious problems in American culture, and especially in the church, today. I am not interested in scandal. I am interested in telling the truth about places, and about God, insofar as I am able. And sometimes the truth appears in places or events where I least expected to find it or even where I wished I hadn't found it.

All of this is, in short, what I mean by entitling this first section of the book "Discovering God." In the next three chapters, I will develop a cultural critique, or a theological disclosing, of three "sacred places" in American culture—the shopping mall, Walt Disney World, and the single-family suburban home. That these places are "sacred" may not be immediately apparent to readers, but I think the evidence I marshal is pretty clear, both that such places function for many millions as sacred places and that such places do damage to them and to others. My first hope, then, is that a reader will come to understand something of the poetics of these places through my descriptions in language of the promises and desires that draw people to them and the practices in which people engage while they are there. Throughout, I will utilize a rhetoric of satire to describe some of the interactive processes that define the mall, Walt

Disney World, and the suburban home. A rhetoric of satire is warranted in relationship to these places because of a stark disparity between the promises that draw people to them and the actual interactive processes that define them. These are some bad poems, in other words, or some places that clothe God in some pretty ugly ways.[27]

Such satire seems to me warranted precisely because of the politics of such places—a second insight I hope readers will take from these next three chapters. I will find, in brief, that the politics of the mall, Walt Disney World, and the suburban home converge on a form of human association that simultaneously rigidly divides *and* horribly confuses public and private, the social and the individual, the political and the personal. Such division, or disorientation, unfortunately, leads rather directly to a politics of control and punishment where individuals (and groups) abdicate their own agency to institutions or collective decision-making bodies that supposedly act on their behalf. Under such a political ethos, furthermore, totalitarian solutions to public order can masquerade as true "justice," and many people can be resigned to silent suffering. A politics of control exploits people's hopes for happiness, or desires for salvation, in efforts to channel their private energies into "public" projects of one kind or another that in fact exist to promote the private welfare of a select few. It is truly a sad irony of our times that to the most thoughtful, enlightened, and entertaining individuals among us—like the members of the Monty Python troupe—the world has been disenchanted and God has seemed absent, if not in fact an "evil" to be avoided. At the same time as the most entertaining folks among us have all but shunned God, some of the most powerful have used God to justify horrific acts of violence and injustice. In the modern age, we have stripped daily life and ordinary places of God's presence, while at the same time we have turned the place we call earth into a harbor for weapons of total destruction and a cesspool for our mushrooming waste. We have moved beyond the need for God, we told ourselves, and turned our trust toward the naked truths of science, technology, human striving, and national self-interest. The by-product of that process was the most violent century in human history. We moderns (even those who call themselves "Christians") have "penetrated" space, "conquered," "colonized," and "developed" it, but in most places, most of the time, we have acted as if God were absent. Perhaps, we have been reluctant to locate God, because then we have been able to do to places what we want. God's "absence" has been a convenient excuse for our own self-assertion. A rhetoric of satire seeks to disclose the contradictions, reversals, false promises, and delusions that emerge when private and public are confused or rigidly divided. In such cases, some interests masquerade as public when they in fact are properly private, and others that would be in the best interest of the public to have realized can be silenced.

Finally, though, I will seek to develop a rhetoric of grace as my contribution to a theology of place, as one pilgrim among many. This rhetoric, which simply is a way of describing the world that holds that life is best lived with gratitude, will emerge especially in part 2, or the last six chapters of the book. I hope also to foreshadow such a rhetoric in the next few chapters in a way that balances their satire and accusations—or else the rhetoric of satire could quickly grow wearisome. For accusation, judgment, and critique alone will not motivate people to change. We need common places of grace to orient ourselves, and nothing can more effectively orient us to gratitude than the common, ordinary places that we often take for granted, but that we all need to live. For Christians, such places of grace can be conveniently summarized by the name of God, who is both their giver and participates with them, as a body wears its clothing. Absent such places of grace, we are left with the specter of a war of all against all in which each tries to grab as much as possible, no matter the means. This dog-eat-dog world of unchecked competition is as gross and inhuman as the metaphor suggests. Even more, there is ample warrant for a piety centered around common places within the Hebrew Bible and writings about Christ.[28] These are the only sacred texts I know with any authority, but from what I know of other traditions, theologies of place and rhetorics of grace can probably be multiplied and developed for all of the world's religious traditions. At the least, the sacred texts of Jews, Christians, and Muslims are replete with love for, even devotion to, places of grace, if only we have eyes to see them, and ears to hear. This rhetoric of grace, then, is in fact also a rhetoric of confession in two senses. It is first a confession of my own complicity with and blindness to the kind of damage that grasping, greed, and a parochial view of the world can bring. And it is a confession from the depths of the *Confessions* of my own tradition. For Lutherans, there is nothing more amazing than grace, and grace is the very power of the eternal God to save us from ourselves and the suffering we both cause and must endure.

But, alas, the places of grace of the sacred Scriptures are not the sacred places of modern America, and they never have been. Our culture, as Gertrude Stein once observed of Oakland, California, is a place where there is "no there, there." We live in a culture largely devoid of its own history and sense of time, and as such we create "sacred places" willy-nilly, places that "orient" us, draw our devotion, and lead us into patterns of living that invariably fail to satisfy. This "lifestyle" would not be so bad if it did not also blind us to the way our consumption consumes us, leaving us exploited by people who claim to exercise power on our behalf but who in fact seek primarily to maximize their own profit. We worship the market, "stars," and conspicuous consumption, in other words, and wonder why we feel alienated, inadequate, and lonely. All the while, of course, we are missing the God whose grace is free, whose love is unconditional, and who hopes we all can get along. Before we can explore in detail such places of "holy the firm," however, we must first attend to some "spirit bare." To do so, we need to meet "a lady who's sure all that glitters is gold, and she's buying a stairway to heaven" that is really an escalator in a shopping mall, leading nowhere.

3

The Shopping Mall as "Stairway to Heaven," Leading Nowhere

I was conditioned at a young age to love shopping malls. My hometown of Appleton, Wisconsin, located in the Fox River Valley, was the site of Valley Fair, one of the first climate-controlled indoor shopping centers in the United States. Valley Fair was built in 1957, or one year before I was born, and I remember from my very early childhood anticipating trips to this place. On each, I could count on a surprise purchase, probably a small toy, but I also remember being drawn to Valley Fair by more than just the promise of an acquired commodity. I took delight in the ambience of this indoor shopping center (no small consideration during Wisconsin winters), where I could toddle along the aisles, ambling into shop after shop of clothes, candies, and other commodities. I remember especially the central foyer of this prototype mall. There, under a skylight and high ceiling, were trees—indoors, with a small fountain and reflecting pool—where I enjoyed playing while my parents sat and rested on nearby benches, in a scene of blissful consumer contentment.[1]

Today, any child living in America can be initiated into such "bliss." There are at present roughly twenty thousand climate-controlled indoor shopping centers in the United States.[2] Over the fifty years of their existence, malls have with good reason taken on considerable homogeneity in their architectural design, in ways that develop and expand upon my experience at Valley Fair. Indeed, just as churches usually have some standard features to accomplish particular tasks and to remind visitors of important values, so do malls. Malls follow these standard architectural patterns because they are more than ordinary buildings. They function, in fact, as sacred places in a religion of the market.

The first section of this chapter takes up this matter of a religion of the market. Following the hypothesis of David Loy, a professor of Buddhist Studies at Bunkyo University in Japan, we will begin to discover the context in which malls developed. Loy has argued that over the past century a new religion—a religion of the market—has emerged to shape practices and values in many cultures, and especially in the United States. According to Loy, the devotion once expended in traditional religious practice has increasingly diffused into activities connected with economic markets. People seek to "save" themselves—whether from disease, or failure, or death does not much matter—through economically driven projects such as work, the goal of an early retirement, or a pilgrimage to the mall. In other words, the hopes and dreams people once sought to realize through systems of traditional religious symbols, and the institutions associated with them, are now sought through economic accumulation and status display and by shopping at the most fashionable malls.

If Loy's hypothesis holds up to critical scrutiny, which I believe a trip to any suburb in the United States would verify, it then becomes possible to see how typical mall architecture has imitated features of religious sanctuaries—the topic of the chapter's second section. Windowless, with no external markers of direction, and lacking the grid pattern American surveyors have imposed upon the land, malls disorient visitors. They do so quite intentionally, in order to reorient pilgrims toward the purveyors of commodities from whom shoppers might acquire an impulsively purchased "bargain." Along with this general organization of space, mall designers have also made shrewd use of water, light, trees, music, and images of the body. These phenomena are all traditional elements in religious symbolism and ritual. They combine with the explicit, if subtle, use of religious language in advertising to make a visit to a mall "more" than an ordinary shopping trip. Indeed, for many, the mall has become, if not a consumer paradise, perhaps a stairway to heaven.[3] Malls are labyrinths of consumer desire

In the last section of this chapter, we will explore our thesis through a narrative account of our family pilgrimage in August 2001 to the Mall of America near Minneapolis, Minnesota. Some years ago the anthropologists Victor and Edith Turner noted that "a pilgrim is half tourist, and a tourist is half pilgrim," and this is manifest in obvious ways in Minneapolis.[4] We were, furthermore, hardly the only visitors on pilgrimage to this behemoth in Bloomington.[5] Throughout the year, often led by enterprising tour guides, people travel from around the globe to this spectacular place. They do so less in the interest of acquiring goods than to "experience" the place itself. The Mall of America is vast and complex, and it works its spirit subtly on all of its visitors—as became patent especially in the experience of my "research associate" and eight-year-old daughter, Rheanne.

Malls, then, have come a long way from their first manifestation as places like Valley Fair, but their function has been consistent. They may be tacky, and exploitative, but I retain a fair amount of empathy for people who are drawn to the only "public" places they can imagine being safe within. Such is the pathos of this new form of pilgrimage. People seek happiness in malls and in the acquisition of commodities not so much because they truly imagine that they will find salvation in this way, but because they have been sold such a "truth" through the advertising, spatial design, and language associated with malls.

In the final analysis, then, it's not simply that malls are horrible places. Malls have lots of cool stuff, and they can be far more pleasant to shop or work in than a typical Wal-Mart. But pilgrims unaware of the function of their visits to the mall can betray a willingness to conform to marketed symbols of "beauty" or marketed commodities as signs of the "good" life. And this conformity blinds us to what might be better ways of living and more expansive (and less expensive) beauty. To point out, at last, that malls cause extensive environmental degradation, both in their construction and in the process of automobile trips to them, is almost beside the point. Their primary damage is to the human heart and mind. But of course these negative features of malls are all masked by their promises of prosperity—by their function as sacred places, as places "more" than ordinary, in the religion of the market.

The Religion of the Market

Writing in the *Journal of the American Academy of Religion*, David R. Loy has argued that

> our present economic system should also be understood as our religion, because it has come to fulfill a religious function for us. The discipline of economics is less a science than the theology of that religion, and its god, the Market, has become a vicious circle of ever-increasing production and consumption by pretending to offer a secular salvation.[6]

Historically speaking, Loy sees the "religion of the market" as a development that renders traditional religions "increasingly irrelevant." Traditional religions have failed to offer a "meaningful challenge to the aggressive proselytizing of market capitalism," Loy contends, "which has already become the most successful religion of all time, winning more converts more quickly than any previous belief system or value-system in human history."[7] Especially since the fall of communism, Loy argues, the religious features of market capitalism have become increasingly apparent.

Now of course this argument is open to objection: haven't religions themselves continued to do rather well in the twentieth century? Indeed they have, at least in the United States, but Loy contends that many so-called houses of prayer in fact have become temples to mammon. This contention that connects traditional religions and capitalism is historically verifiable in any number of ways. For instance, following the sociologist Max Weber, Loy traces the origins of capitalism to Protestantism and argues that "market capitalism began as, and may still be understood as, a form of salvation religion." Consistent with their Protestant forebears of the sixteenth century, people in the modern West were dissatisfied with the world as it was and injected a new promise into it—the promise of ever-increasing production and consumption. Motivated, then, by "faith in the grace of profit and concerned to perpetuate that grace," capitalists developed "a missionary zeal to expand and reorder . . . the economic system." Salvation became prosperity, and heaven became a life on earth filled with economic success.[8]

One need not take Max Weber at his word on this. There are churches, of course, where this process continues more or less overtly. One of the most famous speeches in the history of American religion, in fact, delivered over six thousand times, is Russell H. Conwell's "Acres of Diamonds." In it, Christianity was clearly being tailored to the religion of the market. Conwell, who eventually founded Temple University in Philadelphia, was a Civil War veteran and lawyer who became a Baptist preacher and as such openly promulgated a "Gospel of Wealth."[9] The message was simple and has been repeated in paler forms by many Christian ministers over the years:

> I say that you ought to get rich, and it is your duty to get rich. . . . To make money honestly is to preach the gospel. . . . Let me say here clearly, and say it briefly . . . ninety-eight out of one hundred of the rich men of America are honest. That is why they are rich. . . . Money is power, and you ought to be reasonably ambitious to have it! You ought because you can do more good with it than you could without it. Money printed your Bible, money builds your churches, money sends your missionaries, and money pays your preachers, and you would not have many of them, either, if you did not pay them. . . . I say, then, you ought to have money. . . . It is your Christian and godly duty to do so.[10]

This same gospel now is marketed at some "megachurches" across the United States, whose architecture increasingly mimics mall designs and at smaller churches that are not-so-mega but *are* wanna-bes.

Still other objections to Loy's hypothesis can be raised. Isn't the market a "secular" process? Loy explains that "although we think of the modern world as secularized, its values . . . are not only derived from religious ones, they are largely the same ones." Sixteenth-century Protestants trusted in grace to get them to heaven; modern capitalists trust in the market to get them prosperity. The logic is an identical future-oriented hope. Here, a simple examination of the practices on Wall Street—yet another "sacred place" in the religion of the market—can demonstrate how this system works. Each day on Wall Street begins with a simple liturgy. A "presider," or group of special people, stands at a podium and rings a bell. For the next eight hours, exchanges occur that determine the well-being of the market for that day, that bring either hope or despair to the participants in the ritual. This experience of a bull-market "heaven" or a bear-market "hell" is indistinguishable in effect from revivalist experiences of being "saved" or "damned." A simple economic exchange becomes something "more" than that within the ritual parameters of the Wall Street market. The day ends, of course, exactly as it began: with a ritual ringing of a bell. The stock market is the soul of capitalism, and capitalism is the soul of the nation.

Now, many devotees of this religion of the market might object that their spirituality serves noble purposes. They take care of their families, ensure security for their future, and offer jobs or charity to the less fortunate. Many CEOs and CFOs—the high priests of this religion—no doubt go to church on Sundays to guarantee that their "salvation" is taken care of. But unconsciously, Loy suggests, the everyday behavior of people driven by the market betrays the fact that their economic activities bear ultimate significance for them. They may go to church on Sundays, but on Monday through Saturday the true orientation in their lives—and their true "god," in the sense that we found Martin Luther using the term in chapter 1—becomes apparent. Loy draws out the analytical judgment: "From a *religious* perspective the problem with market capitalism and its values is twofold: greed and delusion."[11]

Greed—understood simply as unlimited desire—can consume a human being. And the market surely encourages greed. Loy points out, for instance, that the average compensation for Fortune 500 CEOs went up 600 percent between 1980 and 1993—to $3.7 million a year—while their corporations cut 4.4 million jobs over the same time span. More recently, abuses of power by executives at Enron, MCI-Worldcom, and other corporations provide ample evidence that greed is alive and well in America. But people don't just wake up one day and decide: "I'm going to be greedy now." The process is subtle, and that's why Loy contends that the religion of the market depends upon a delusion, namely, "the delusion that happiness is to be found" in the acquisition of commodities. People understandably, and quite rightly, seek fulfillment from life. Yet, Loy continues, trying "to find fulfillment through profit, or by making consumption the meaning of one's life, amounts to idolatry, i.e., a demonic perversion of true religion, and any religious institution that makes its peace with the *priority* of such market values does not deserve the name religion."[12] This is a strong assertion, but the evidence is mounting that making the market one's religion is a false faith, because under the pretense of bringing happiness, it actually causes suffering. That is the nature of idolatry: people think they're doing the right thing, when in fact they're destroying themselves and others.

One final objection needs to be surfaced: have American believers made peace with the *priority* of market values in America? Some undoubtedly have, but Loy also believes that traditional religions provide strong resources to challenge the religion of the market. Buddhism, for instance, "teaches renunciation and generosity. . . . To see and accept that everything goes away—including ourselves—is necessary in order to live serenely. Only someone whose identity is not tied to acquisition and consumption can truly renounce the world. The sign of renunciation is generosity, which is deeply honored in Buddhism as in all the major religions."[13] Indeed, that greed can make one happy is a delusion also critiqued by Hinduism, Judaism, Islam, and Christianity—to mention only the four largest streams of human religiosity in the world. In Hinduism, texts like the *Bhagavad Gita* clearly teach that attachment to the material consequences of action—whether success or failure—blocks the true bliss of living. Similarly, the Jewish prophets, as we shall soon see in some detail, insisted above all upon "justice" in economic exchange and clearly condemned exploitative financial arrangements. Islam, which encourages the acquisition of material wealth, also institutionalizes charity and the redistribution of resources in one of its five pillars of faith—*zakat*. And, finally, greed has not, to my knowledge, been rehabilitated from its ranking as one of the seven deadly sins in traditional Christianity. Indeed, many early Christians continued the Jewish prophets' prohibition of lending money at interest, and some communities practiced a communal lifestyle in which property was shared in common. Despite these strong foundations, however, people of faith throughout the modern world have often demonstrated easy accommodation between their religions and the delusion of greed.

As Loy suggests, however, it is a peculiarly weak form of faith—not true to the depths of each tradition—that accommodates itself so easily to the priority of market values.[14] The causes and catalysts for such accommodation are complex, but trips to the mall won't help. For if places as well as events shape the contours of piety, then clearly a trip to the mall can have an impact upon the content of one's faith. Personally, I have rarely left a mall inspired to be a more generous and caring person. I *have* left a mall and been unable to locate my car because my mind was so addled by the range of choices that had confronted me within the labyrinth of desire that I forgot where I had parked. The bottom line is this, if I may be forgiven the market cliché, and the following mixed metaphors: shopping malls are temples of trade, churches of consumption, synagogues of excess, or mosques of the market.

Shopping Malls as Sacred Places

Thankfully, I'm not the only one to see shopping malls as sacred places. Ira G. Zepp, a professor of religious studies at Western Maryland College, has suggested in a brief book, *The New Religious Image of Urban America*, that any large shopping center functions "interchangeably and simultaneously [as] a ceremonial center, an alternative community, a carnival, and a secular cathedral."[15] More specifically, Zepp contends that malls "as we experience them cannot be reduced to commercial and financial enterprises. They are far more than places of business." It is this "more" about malls that Zepp finds particularly interesting. People don't just visit malls to shop, he points out. Pilgrims go to malls to hang out, to exercise, to pray, even to get married. This latter function should not be surprising, since malls are designed to be like temples. Zepp quotes approvingly James Rouse, an architect responsible for over sixty malls, including many of the earliest and most famous in the United States. According to Rouse, "it is in the marketplace that all people come together—rich and poor, old and young, black and white. It is the democratic, unifying, universal place which gives spirit and personality to the city."[16] Such faith in the "spirit" and "unifying" potential of the marketplace led Rouse to design malls in ways that drew upon common symbols from the Protestant faith he practiced his entire life. According to Rouse, businesspeople were the clergy of a new religion that transcended the parochial boundaries of creed and cult. The shopping mall, then, was to be the cathedral in this new religion, the sacred space for a "universal" faith with a distinct spirit.[17]

Just how successful Rouse was in realizing his dream can be verified easily enough. Visit a mall, as I did at Southlake Mall in Merrillville, Indiana, one afternoon with a group of students, and observe and ask questions. Expect resistance. You'll be trampling on some folks' sacred compulsions, sort of like violating the taboo against swearing in church or talking about religion at a private party. If you want to be legitimate, make your first stop the management offices. You will probably not get any further. My students, typically not concerned with either ritual or legitimacy, simply started interviewing people with my video camera: "So," they asked, "do you think the mall is a sacred place?" They made it through about a dozen interviews with bewildered or amused shopper/pilgrims before the security guards found them and shut them down. "You can't ask people questions in here," the guards said. Indeed, questions might make people think about why they are there, thereby disrupting the process of disorientation and reorientation by means of which the place induces us to buy. People expect a mall to be a public place. Of course, it's not. It's a privately owned enterprise that can establish its own rules about who is in, who is not, and on what terms.

Malls communicate the "spirit" of the market through a common formula. They *disorient* us, by using natural and religious symbols and spatial patterns in an enclosed indoor setting, and then *reorient* us toward one or another of the purveyors of goods. During my young adulthood, I would get a headache after more than a half-hour in a mall. Without some critical distance from the place, my brain couldn't take the constant stimuli that sought to persuade me that my salvation depended upon this or that acquisition. Surely, the mall is a sensual feast, if not an assault. For within the labyrinth of the typical mall, we experience water, light, trees, words, food, music, and bodies, the combined effect of which is to make us feel entranced, dazed, disoriented, and, finally, lacking something. Thus vulnerable, the soul can sell itself to the nearest, if not always the lowest, bidder. To feel lost is the customary, indeed intended, feeling. Fully 40 percent of visitors to the mall do not intend to purchase anything. Only 10 percent get out without lighter purses or wallets.[18]

Water, for instance, is used in almost every mall to prepare one to "go with the flow" of shopping. Water dissolves boundaries and is a widespread religious symbol—as we shall see in chapter 7. Among the religious meanings of water, of course, is purification: malls use fountains, waterfalls, and reflecting pools symbolically to cleanse shoppers of any filthiness all the lucre involved in the place might suggest. Zepp points out that at many malls you might bathe symbolically in a fountain, be refreshed by the sound of a mock waterfall, or even be baptized symbolically beside mini-flowers of water—as I pointed out to my students at Southlake Mall. In short, water initiates the visitor into an experience that is designed to be "more" than a shopping trip. As Zepp argues, "mall developers have attempted ingeniously to satisfy [the] human longing to be near water. . . . We consider water a gift."[19] But of course, this "gift" is one we will, ordinarily, feel compelled to pay for. Furthermore, we will be happy to do so, for the water in malls is "safe" water, controlled water. There is never a need for an ark in a mall. Water in malls has no utilitarian purpose—it's not necessary. It does have a poetic, and a political, function, and more than one pilgrim has gotten soaked in the process.

Just as malls use water to appear to be something "more" than an ordinary place, so too do malls abound with light, yet another vital religious symbol, as shown in chapter 8. Light of many kinds is featured in shopping malls, but each light is strategically placed to draw the senses in and toward one attraction or another. Neon light is used to beckon with its peculiar glow, especially in the signs above the entries to mall attractions, casting an aura that entices with its soft yet vibrant colors. Natural light is also a prominent feature of most mall designs. At the center of most malls, as Zepp notes: "You can usually find . . . a huge skylight or a colorful and often circular series of lamps shedding such bright light . . . that you know you are in a space set apart."[20] Light, of course, is our primary experience of energy. Thus, Zepp concludes, "malls, at their centers, strive to be places of vitality and energy."[21] That they succeed admirably in drawing visitors like moths to a candle is evident in the fact that the largest one, the "Mall of America," welcomes 35 to 40 million guests annually. That's some serious energy.

Along with water and light, the powerful symbols of the tree and vegetation are commonly employed in mall design. Growing things are held sacred in almost every religion, and many traditions have stories or myths about trees of life or gardens of human delight—as is detailed in chapter 10. The inclusion of growing things in shopping malls is, again, more than a utilitarian decision by mall developers to help keep interior air clean. For, significantly, none of the trees in the mall ever die. The trees in malls are all evergreens, even if they are deciduous. Life—abundant, even eternal—is the message. Malls thus play upon the human desire to experience growth and new life, even while juxtaposing such symbolism with profit-making that clearly tries to sap (sorry) as much life from visitors as possible. Still, the symbolism is powerful and effective: life is growth, offers this gospel, in exactly the terms that we want it. This is the Garden of Eden without the fall; the resurrection without the cross; spring and summer without fall or winter. That this growth in fact comes at a price is constantly masked or obscured by the clever design that entices us to imagine that we're inhabiting a garden of free delight. The constantly green trees whisper to us just that message, if we only have ears to hear: "Don't count the cost."

More directly, malls advertise themselves in words that promise us unity, devotion, love, happiness, and other phenomena that were once the benefits of traditional religious practices. Zepp catalogs dozens of advertising slogans and catchphrases that clarify the point. He admits being surprised by the use of religious language in advertising, and in fact, most of us rarely pay attention to the words used in malls. We're too busy being disoriented or distracted by the water, light, trees, or music. Yet the words are there, with unmistakable religious meanings when we start to think about them. Thus the mall offers community: "You're a part of us," one intimates. And the mall promises us devotion. It's a place "devoted to eating, shopping, and the pursuit of happiness," offers another. The words cascade together in a barrage of religious meanings: "You are going to *love* the experience." "We want to touch your life!" "We can identify with all your needs!"[22] Really? Of course not. There is no "we" there. But clothed in such promises, and covered up by soothing music, the naked reality of the mall as a place to turn a profit is concealed, and we are enticed to partake in the sacred rites. The mall cloaks its profit-driven purpose in a poetics of promise.

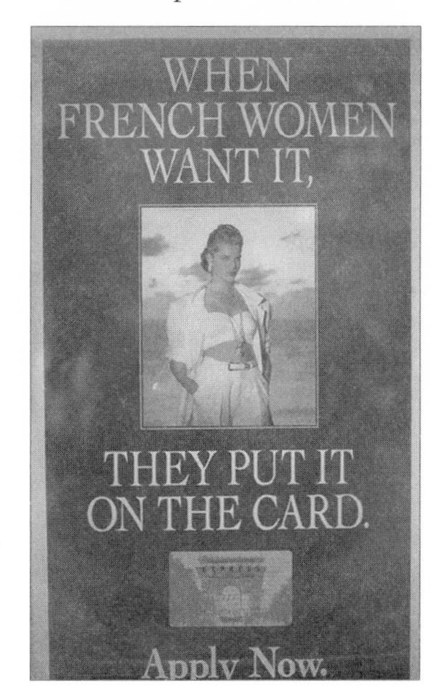

Now, I move here into an area that risks offending some readers, but it seems obvious to me that until very recently malls primarily targeted women, and their bodies, with their messages of salvation. Like other images that encourage consumption—notably those on television—malls are filled with mannequins, posters, and other props that promote an image of an ideal female body—always young, always slim, and always "beautiful," in a stereotypical kind of way. Such images, of course, seek to reduce the identity of women to their desires for the commodities that can help them "match" the ideal. As the poster in one shop window put it, "When French women want it, they put it on The Card." This is a fascinating assertion. Of course women, and not only French ones, "want it." But if what they want can be put "on the card," or charged on a piece of plastic, then the body becomes nothing more than a naked place on which to hang commodities, or "it." In the mall, the body then becomes nothing more than a whirl of atoms: a place without soul, consciousness, or orientation. All places are equal; desire has no bounds, as long as "it" can be put on "the card." Thus vacated, the body can be possessed—so to speak—by any number of spirits of the place, attached to any number of illusions that guarantee the body some "it"—something "new" or "improved" or "bigger" or "better" or "more." People have often been possessed by such promises.

Men, of course, experience the consequences of this system differently—but in no less damaging ways. "Real" men, for instance, are supposed to disdain the mall. Many have confided in me, after reading drafts of this chapter or hearing me speak about it: "I hate the mall, too. I guess it's a guy thing." As I've reflected on this comment, it amuses me and makes me sad. As it happens, I don't hate malls, and in fact I have learned to enjoy them quite a bit—while simply recognizing them for what they are. As I've put it before, malls have lots of cool stuff, and the best ones have manifold delights for the senses. We can smell perfumes and colognes, eat lunch, a snack, or an entire dinner, listen to music or scan books for hours on end, and revel in displays of human craftsmanship, ingenuity, and diversity. My sons, and many young people, have taught me to appreciate my experience of the mall without having to buy into the sacred promises. When guys tell me, then, that they "hate the mall, too," it suggests that men can't take pleasure in the carnivalesque atmosphere of the mall or in the sensual or aesthetic pleasures the places convey. And the fact is that most men in America aren't terribly attuned to this level of experience. By being unable to appreciate the obvious delights of such a place, men ironically "buy into" the flip side of the gender stereotypes that oppress women, although men's bodies, too, increasingly are subject to pressures to conform to stereotypical ideals of beauty.

I'm glad, then, that my children and other young people have taught me how to appreciate malls without getting a headache in them. In fact, I can even admire inveterate mall pilgrims, especially the numerous senior citizens who exercise in them, or who otherwise find malls sanctuaries of civility in an otherwise uncivil society.[23] I've come to understand, in fact, that malls may be functioning better as "churches" than are many buildings bearing the name. As Ira Zepp concludes: "The shopping mall, open almost every day from 10 A.M. to 9 P.M. . . . is a more inclusive and egalitarian center [than] most churches."[24] That he is right is a sign of just how disoriented believers in God have become in America. If churches aren't connecting people to true happiness, how can we blame people for seeking happiness in a place that promises it to them accompanied by powerful experiences of water, light, trees, and bodies? Zepp again: "Malls are contemporary versions of that age-old combination of commerce and community. They will continue to fill the void created by our social institutions' failure in providing centers of ritual and meaning."[25] Malls have become sacred places because traditional churches, synagogues, temples, and mosques have failed.

Finally, however, even though traditional religious communities often fail to fulfill their own promises, I also have to say a gentle but clear "no" to the promises of the mall. For the success of the mall's offer of salvation depends upon my coming to feel a fabricated sense that somehow I lack something that only the mall, as a cathedral of the market, can provide. And, frankly, the most serious absences in my life have not been due to my failure to acquire a particular commodity, but can be traced directly to my own poor choices or uncertain will. Sin, to use an old-fashioned word for that lack, is a little deeper than my failure to acquire a wide-screen TV, and surely human suffering is more serious than not having the latest style of tennis shoes. Still, we all can get trapped in the false logic, because we do not want to have to confront our deepest personal, moral, or political failings. It's much easier to have to "confront" only the absences that the images of the mall make us feel. Indeed, malls exist to mask true absences, deny them, or make us forget them. All the mall can give us are very finite experiences of consuming whatever commodity happens to strike our current fancy, in exchange for our cash. The promises of "unity" and "happiness" and "love" are lies. This stairway to heaven is, then, really nothing new in history; it's as old as humanity. It's the same system rejected in the *Bhagavad Gita,* the same system that the Buddha saw through as he sat under the Bo tree, and the same system that Luther protested in the Reformation, in which people were offered salvation for dropping a few coins in an indulgence coffer. But today the system is packaged in such a way that souls continue to climb this stairway to heaven, when it is really an escalator, leading nowhere.

True Shopping? Pilgrimage to the Mall of America

If there is a religion of the market, and if malls are sacred places, then the Mall of America outside Minneapolis, Minnesota, is surely the holy of holies. In August 2001, with the help of some research funds from the Association of Theological Schools, I embarked upon a pilgrimage to this self-described "Mother of all malls."[26] I took along with me, as my "research associates," my wife, Lisa, and our children—Justin (15), Nathan (13), and Rheanne (8). After a fitful night's sleep at an area hotel (well equipped for pilgrims), by 9:30 A.M. we had piled into our family truckster van for the short drive to the holy place. Predictably, we got lost on the expressway system, but eventually we found our way into the mall's south parking lot. I expressed delight at finding a parking place almost directly in front of the main entrance to the huge, brown, windowless building. It was a Monday, and the mall was just opening. As I stepped out into the sunny August morning, I couldn't help but exclaim, "God, it's ugly," as I snapped a few pictures.

I had acquired a map of the mall interior the night before and had plotted what I thought would be a good strategy for a one-day visit. We had eaten only the hotel's meager "continental" breakfast, so our first destination was to be a "food court." As I interpreted the map, this meant we would have to ascend two stories. On the way, my research team seemed prone to wander—especially as we passed the "Lego Imagination Center." I, however, was ruthless in my self-appointed role as pilgrimage director. We purchased nothing. Now clearly on a mission, we ascended the two long escalators to the South Food Court. "Where are we going?" Nathan complained. "I want to go to Camp Snoopy!" cried Rheanne. I was stunned—not only by the energy with which my children had suddenly been possessed, but also by the noisiness of the place. Only one other time in my life have I been so taken aback by unexpected sound—and that was on our honeymoon visit to Niagara Falls. The roar of the Mall of America, however, was neither the rhythmic crash of water on rock nor the soothing sound of a river rushing by. I heard music, of course, but also machines indoors—a roller coaster rattling over its rails, arcade games beeping, and the muffled thunder of thousands of voices murmuring. It was a cacophony, and my children's level of energy and discourse quickly adjusted to match. We found the food court at last and promptly scattered to various vendors to order whatever "convenience foods" happened to suit our moods. We even began to eat at separate tables, although eventually I gathered us all together around a table near the balcony railing that looked out over "Camp Snoopy," the indoor amusement park that is the mall's most notable architectural feature.

The view we "enjoyed" is hard to describe. Across the expanse of the indoor park, which was filled with natural light from a translucent dome, we could watch the "Knott's Camp Snoopy" Ferris wheel gently spinning riders up and around. Trees were everywhere on the floor of the park—all of them (apparently) growing—as part of the "largest indoor planting" in the world, over thirty thousand green things.[27] Advertising was ubiquitous. Huge cereal boxes for products of General Foods, one of the mall's corporate sponsors, adorned the far wall. A gigantic soda spigot and Pepsi cup, probably twenty feet long, was hanging from the rafters just above us. Neon lights glittered and beckoned. And the noise was ceaseless: the roller coaster rattled, the flumes of the log ride splashed just below us, and various musics competed with our conversation for attention. Garish colors were everywhere: pinks, purples, oranges, and greens—all just one shade short of fluorescent. It was a bewildering display for which the cliché "assault on the senses" is not inaccurate. I snapped nearly an entire roll of photographs in the thirty minutes or so that we spent at the food court. Most of the photos tried, and failed, to convey the weird combinations of phenomena the place communicated.

Eventually, of course, the children were ready to move on. The night before, as I scanned the mall's map, our first destination after breakfast became clear to me. From my research, I had learned that a number of couples every year exchanged marriage vows at the mall. This struck me at the time as odd, and I wanted to find the scene of these crimes, if possible. From the map's list of more than five hundred possible attractions or vendors, I noted that site number E345 bore the promising name: "Chapel of Love Wedding Chapel." So, I told the kids and Lisa that we were heading for the mall's wedding chapel. The complaints from Nathan and Rheanne erupted almost immediately, but I proceeded undeterred. Lisa seemed willing to be a good sport, and Justin looked at me knowingly.

Three days before had been Lisa's and my nineteenth wedding anniversary, but we had been unable to celebrate it because Lisa had to work in Pennsylvania while I vacationed in Wisconsin with the kids. She flew into Minneapolis the night before our pilgrimage. In any event, it had been hard for us to be apart on our anniversary, because the last two years had been the most difficult of our partnership. This difficulty was due largely to the damage that lingered following what is euphemistically known as the "male midlife crisis." While in Wisconsin prior to our pilgrimage to the mall, I had purchased (with advice from the kids) an antique diamond ring for Lisa from my cousin, Jim Martin, who now owns the jewelry business formerly run by my late uncle Herb. On our upcoming family vacation (we would spend two weeks together after our mall visit), I had intended to find the right moment to give Lisa the gift. Depending upon what we encountered at the chapel, I thought that maybe it would be the appropriate venue to surprise my wife. Justin had intuited my intention. The ring was in its case in my pocket.

As we approached the chapel, I stifled a laugh. "There it is," I announced: "The Chapel o' Love!" The sanctuary appeared to be just another store. The entrance to it was shared with the mall's "Bridal Shoppe," where one could, presumably, rent or

purchase everything one would need for the "perfect" wedding. It was strange. The clerk working the store was on the phone. I walked toward her, stood right in front of her, and waited for her to look up or otherwise acknowledge our presence. While I waited, the children wandered into the "chapel" proper, divided from the store by a single partition. The clerk never did make eye contact. So, I grabbed Lisa's hand, and we followed the children into the chapel. "Come here," I said, as we walked toward the front of the little room, where a couple of large, white, plastic pillars, wrapped in fake ivy, formed a quasi-gazebo. All of the kids now seemed aware of the purpose for our visit. Nate and Rheanne gathered in the first "pew." Justin lurked near the back. I faced Lisa, knelt down, and asked—tears in my eyes: "Would you be my partner for the rest of my life?" By now, Lisa was crying, too. "I love you," I said, as I opened the case and slipped the ring onto her finger. It fit perfectly. Nate snapped a picture (appropriately soft-focused), and eventually I stood up and Lisa hugged me tightly. I looked my partner in the eyes, and we shared a smile, while the kids laughed and played around us. It was only several hours later that Lisa sidled up to me as we stood outside a coffee shop in one of the mall corridors and said: "Yes." When I looked in her eyes, puzzled by the one-word address, she went on: "I was so surprised that I didn't say anything," she remembered. "But the answer is yes."

The event was meaningful, but both the potential and the shortcomings of the "Chapel of Love" as a sanctuary come into relief through our brief recommitment ritual there. On the one hand, the mall can provide a "free" space, where even the most intimate and human behaviors can be celebrated and remembered, although of course most users of the space need to pay for it. Nevertheless, we cried there. Some people whose vows would not be recognized by church or state, or those who for whatever reason resent ecclesiastical or political power, could celebrate a commitment at the Mall of America in the eyes of family and friends. On the other hand, without the narrative here, the ceremony between Lisa and me would have been only a private family confession and promise—made in the anonymous and vast expanse of the Mall of America. The clerk on the phone had no clue what had transpired as we walked away, arm in arm, wiping away the tears of both sadness and joy.

Simply put, the "Chapel of Love" is a tacky excuse for a religious shrine, surrounded as it is with the cacophony of the market, and adjacent as it is to a crass and impersonal "Bridal Shoppe." The pillars were plastic. In the chapel, Lisa and I created a moment of tenderness that recognized human frailty and commitment. But the moment was a more or less spontaneous creation, in contrast to the spirit of the place, which ordinarily operates according to strict market values: you get what you pay for. Geographer Jon Goss helps explain, in an excellent study of the mall, that the task for pilgrims is not only to wake up to the world outside of consumption but also to "awaken to the potential of the dream inside of which we shop, and so to reveal the traces of ideals of collectively meaningful life that are so vulnerable to forgetting."[28] The problem with the mall is that it actively encourages us *to forget any ideals of collectively meaningful life beyond those that the market creates.* The mall creates no enduring community, rests upon no tradition, and promotes no values beyond those determined by corporations to whom consumers are all but anonymous units or marks. We are "united" by the place only in the hierarchy determined by our ability to consume. It is no coincidence that this hierarchy—where the rich get more and the poor get the door—also dominates American political life. The Mall of America thus accurately replicates a fragmented vision of our collective future, driven by an illusion of limitless and constantly shifting "loves." Lasting commitment is contrary to the mall's spirit. Our brief ceremony at the Chapel of Love felt like an act of civil disobedience. It was surely a trespass.

The rest of our pilgrimage naturally oriented us in the way the mall intends. Namely, we enjoyed a few hours of expensive diversion through thrill-seeking and shopping. We spent most of our time at Camp Snoopy, where we dropped some money on daily passes for the various amusements, such as the log ride, bumper cars, and roller coaster. At lunch, after about three hours of "fun," it was eight-year-old Rheanne who offered the most succinct and accurate observation about the spirit of the place. She did so in a way that belied the optimistic promise of James Rouse and other designers about the mall as a secular cathedral and that revealed the basic logic of the place as a warehouse to produce profit. As we sat at a table together in the North Food Court, Rheanne simply blurted out: "I want to buy something."

She repeated the phrase several times. "I want to buy something!" she bawled, nearly melting down emotionally in the process. The object didn't matter; our nice, usually civil and polite young daughter wanted to *buy something!* I naturally concluded she'd been possessed.

Steven L. Shepherd, writing in the *Humanist,* describes this process of possession quite accurately. "The malls," Shepherd writes, "are temples of our culture, and going to the mall is in truth an initiation rite . . . part of the relentless and powerful seduction of our children by that portion of our culture that accords human beings no more value than the contents of their wallets. It is part of the initiation into a life of wanting that can never be sated, of material desires that will never be satisfied, of slaving to buy and to have, of a life predicated upon unhappiness and discontent."[29] Rheanne's exorcism was accomplished simply: we fed her. The reader can draw the conclusion.

Basically, the mall "works" by shifting our attention from a basic need to the limitless desires for commodities. Geographer Goss puts a more technical spin on this process, but the point gains in clarity: "The modern megamall is a dreamhouse of the collectivity, where fantasies of authentic life are displaced onto commodities. . . . The shopping mall brings together the archetypes of the 'good world' with the world of goods, presenting the world of commodities apparently innocent of the commodification of the world."[30] Theologically speaking, in other words, the mall gives us an idol as a replacement for some real presence. The mall clothes God in some tacky clothes, obscuring the source and goal of authentic life, and the location of goodness, truth, and beauty, in objects that advertisers want to sell to us. It's not that God can't be found at the mall. It's rather that the way God is presented there confuses and befuddles pilgrims about what is truly satisfying in life. As Goss puts it, at the Mall of America, visitors invariably experience "the enchantment of objects."[31]

This process of enchantment proceeds as the mall mobilizes and activates our desires, attaching them not to objects or relations that satisfy, and that might be freely available, such as the commitment between partners, but instead to commodities that meet desires that are created by the mall or its tenants. Desire shifts, most dramatically, from sociability to possession, from relations with real people to the acquisition of objects. Goss again: "The Mall incorporates distant places and times associated with the imagined possibility of authenticity, but its visual and verbal rhetoric displaces desire from its 'natural object' . . . onto commodities, which then stand as souvenirs of the dreaming experience."[32] Rheanne wanted to "buy something" to remember her dream time at the mall, but under the influence of hunger, her desire became so intense that it threatened to consume her. In fact, Rheanne also claimed, shortly after entering the mall: "I want to live here." Such a dream would, inevitably, be deferred. The best she could hope for was a token, a sign, a memento of her experience in the American Garden of Eden.

My daughter was deluded. Given that she was eight years old at the time, and that she is in all likelihood blessed or cursed with having to live with me for the next ten years, I expect she'll grow out of it. At times, furthermore, the system of symbols at the

mall reveals its own contradictions, such as in a T-shirt I noticed at one of the Mall of America gift stores. The shirt was bright red, and contained three silk-screened slogans on its chest. The first, at the top, was a large set of capital letters, spelling "WHASSSSUP?!" The second, smallest sign, in the center of the shirt, was the corporate logo of the Mall of America—a red, white, and blue "wave" over a star. The third sign was another set of smaller capital letters, all in white, that read: "TRUE SHOPPING." Now, this is a fascinating piece of clothing that I can't imagine anyone would wear. The big "whassssup" on the T-shirt was borrowed from a popular television commercial for beer, aired in the late nineties, in which a bunch of guys greet one another with the phrase, uttered in guttural and generally drunken tones. The logo, of course, is self-explanatory, although I find significant that it was the smallest of the signs on the souvenir—as if the corporate character of the place was the least significant fact about it. But the bottom sign is the one that is most interesting to me: "TRUE SHOPPING." What does this mean? The only sense I can make of that sign is that it is an answer to the question posed at the top of the T-shirt, and a description of what supposedly goes on at the Mall of America. The Mall of America was promising me truth.

Needless to say, I didn't buy it. As Goss concludes, the big lie of the mall is that "images of the good life . . . live in goods."[33] But of course there is no "life" in this T-shirt, and there is no truth in the mall. Goods don't "live," and shopping isn't a proposition that can be determined to be either true or false. Shopping is an economic exchange. This is obviously the case *unless a merchant tries to make it more so, and unless a consumer buys such a truth*. In the case of this T-shirt, that exchange would cost the buyer $14.95. Now, I guess that's not a bad price for truth, although at the Swarthmore Goodwill I buy far more clever and attractive T-shirts for $2.95 that I would not, furthermore, be embarrassed to wear in public. In any event, when merchants and consumers collude to imagine that shopping might be "true," both have succumbed to a falsehood. The T-shirt thus offers an unwitting testimony to the contradictions of the place. There is no "true shopping" going on at the mall, only the befuddling of pilgrims who imagine that they might live in a fantasy world of limitless commodities and amusements, while they go through life clueless enough to wear a guttural "whassssup" on their chests. For there is one last fact that readers need to know: we couldn't find a "Chapel of Death" at the Mall of America. Merchants may indeed want you to "shop till you drop," but if you really do drop, you can be sure you'll be transported elsewhere.

We completed our pilgrimage to the Mall of America with a complete circumambulation of the space, and walked out into the sunshine after only five hours. It felt to me like a liberation. We'd spent a little over a hundred dollars.[34] As far as the rituals of affliction and sacrifices often associated with pilgrimages go, this was pretty easy.[35] Now, in the interest of full disclosure, I have to admit that I have a more complicated economic relationship with this behemoth in Bloomington than has been apparent so far. More specifically, I've actually (albeit unwittingly) shared in the profits of the place—to the tune of far more than a hundred dollars. The construction and success of the Mall of America helped make possible dramatic growth in my retirement portfolio, which I held while I was an undergraduate teacher through TIAA-CREF, the Teacher's Insurance and Annuity Association/College Retirement Equity Fund. TIAA-CREF, I learned after the fact, is (or was) heavily invested in the Mall of America. When I left college teaching, I withdrew those funds and invested them in real estate by purchasing the home in which we now live, about which you will read more in chapter 5. That I did so just before the market tanked was a matter of sheer luck: I needed the money for a down payment (and I'm still paying the taxes).

Still, I'm grateful that the success of the Mall of America has "trickled down" to me. But I also know that not everyone has shared equitably in those sprinkles of blessings, and my gratitude does not entail that I buy into all of the mall's promises—most of which strike me as pretty "Mickey Mouse" these days. Among the most egregious of these promises is one I discovered from Macy's, an anchor store in the Mall of America. It invited pilgrims to shop at Macy's, because "Macy's Means More: More Vision, More Real, More Mix, More New, More You."[36] Now, I don't know about you, but I surely don't need any more of me, and most of us who can afford to shop at the mall don't really need much more of anything. Of course, more vision would be nice, but I doubt if Macy's is really selling that. I also doubt that I'll ever return to the Mall of America. I could do so, but I don't anticipate visiting Minneapolis anytime soon, and I'm sure there are far more interesting places in Minnesota that I wouldn't want to miss. All in all, I'm sure I'll make visits to the malls nearby our home, led more often than not by my children. But after my pilgrimage, I am more convinced than ever that there are sacred places not controlled by corporations, that don't fuel greed, where I can experience grace, passion, vision, beauty, and truth for far less cash than I'd spend on shopping. In fact, some of these places are so close to me that I often take them for granted. And as for Mickey Mouse—he's the topic of the next chapter.

4

Worshiping the Golden Mouse

Walt Disney World and American Civil Religion

> The LORD said to Moses [on Mt. Sinai]: "Go down at once! Your people . . . have acted perversely; they . . . have cast for themselves [in gold] an image of a calf, and have worshiped it and sacrificed to it."
>
> Exodus 32:7–8

I was well into my teenage years when I made my first pilgrimage to the Magic Kingdom of Florida's Walt Disney World (WDW). It was the spring of 1975, and the trip to a Disney theme park was the culmination of a lifelong dream. My earliest memories include sitting on the couch in the den of the small Wisconsin home in which I grew up, staring intently at "Darlene" (I think her name was), from the *Mickey Mouse Club* television show. I was maybe four. Truth be told, "Darlene" was my first love. My mom always wondered why there were drool marks on the television, until one day she caught me in the act of kissing the image of the nubile young girl as it flickered on the black-and-white screen.

My dream of meeting Darlene was, alas, deferred until our family could afford it, by which time I was seventeen. And was I ready! I gleefully helped load up our maroon and wood-paneled 1969 Ford LTD Country Squire station wagon—a car I called with grudging affection "The Tank" during my college years. For our trip to Orlando, we also borrowed a Sears car-top carrier, into which we stuffed some of the luggage that we couldn't squeeze around the seven intrepid pilgrims who were packed into the vehicle. For the duration of the roughly 2,718-mile round-trip, "The Tank" was filled with sleeping bags, pillows, food, books, luggage, my two younger brothers, Andy and Dave, my elderly Aunt Gertie and Uncle Lawrence, my mom, my dad, and me. I'm surprised we didn't bring along our German schnauzer, Willy. Maybe we did.

Anyway, it took the seven of us three days to make the trip from Wisconsin to Orlando. My memories of the journey are hazy; some of them are no doubt repressed. Eventually we arrived, but oddly I remember very little from my first visit to the Magic Kingdom. The "Mad Tea Party," whose whirling cups are featured in many postcards and Disney advertisements, I do recall as a huge disappointment. First of all, "Darlene" wasn't there. More important, though, the ride provided less of a rush than the "Tilt-A-Whirl" I rode every summer at Wisconsin county fairs. The line was also a whole lot longer. Another memory I've held onto, probably because we snapped a picture, is that my parents purchased Uncle Lawrence a silly fishing hat with mouse ears that he wore to keep the sun off of his balding head. We still worried that he and Aunt Gertie might suffer heat stroke.

In the interest of preserving Gertie's and Lawrence's health, we left the park before dinner. My brother Andy and I expressed dismay (to put it nicely), because we had been unable to ride "Space Mountain," the most recent and adventuresome ride in the Magic Kingdom. The lines, of course, had been too long. Upon returning to our hotel, however, we quickly found our way to the outdoor pool. There I had the good fortune to meet two young women from Rocky River, Ohio, as I recall, one of whom was a reasonable enough approximation of "Darlene" to revive my earlier Disney-inspired lust, only now in the concentrated form known only to adolescent boys. In the brief conversation we had, I suggested to "Darlene," who looked simply lovely in her bikini, that we meet again at the pool later that night. After dinner, however, my Mom offered to take Andy and me back to the Magic Kingdom so we could ride Space Mountain. Andy immediately agreed, but I was now faced with a dilemma. I anguished over it for about five seconds and then decided to stay at the hotel and wait for my date at the pool. As it turned out, I was stuck in fantasyland, anyway. Nevertheless, this episode can foreshadow everything I have to say about Walt Disney World. My hope for a rendezvous with flesh and blood was more powerful than my dream to experience a ride in Tomorrowland. I never have ridden Space Mountain. I'm sure I would have enjoyed it. I would have enjoyed talking with "Darlene" more.

The point of this brief account of my adolescent pilgrimage to Walt Disney World is to suggest that I understand from experience the allure that draws tens of millions of visitors to this spectacular site every year. At the same time, however, I hope my experience also suggests that Walt Disney World might not be quite the sacred place it sells itself as. That it is a pilgrimage site is a contention supported by a rapidly growing body of literature.[1] Probably the best of these books is Stephen M. Fjellman's *Vinyl Leaves*. Fjellman, a professor of anthropology at Florida International University, simply states that Walt Disney World is "the major middle-class pilgrimage center in the United States." Developing that thought a bit more fully, Fjellman suggests that the Disney theme parks have been so successful because they offer "an antidote to everyday life." In our everyday lives, Fjellman explains, middle-class folk have experienced the industrialization, specialization, and mobility of contemporary society as fragmenting and confusing. At the same time, we have come to depend upon those same forces of technological and media sophistication for economic survival.[2] In such a situation, Fjellman goes on, "what we buy at WDW is not just fun and souvenirs but also a welcome civility on a human scale."[3] In other words, just as pilgrims to the mall shop to fulfill a dream, so do pilgrims to Walt Disney World "wish upon a star" that is at some level very real. In a world filled with inescapable incivility, where people feel threatened by an overwhelming amount of information, a nostalgic desire to "rediscover one's inner child" or the utopian wish to "go to a place where you always feel good" cannot be glibly dismissed. Even the most simple "vacation" to Walt Disney World, then, incarnates a desire for a more compassionate world where we can be *free* from the pressures to perform, produce, choose, and consume that come with life in a complex service economy.

But ironically, and sometimes pathetically, the "freedom" pilgrims find at Walt Disney World is, of course, a commodity itself.[4] Walt Disney World is a 27,000-acre or 24-square-mile product. Fjellman's explanation is again helpful: "Unlike many holy places, which become so through the unanticipated quirks of history, Walt Disney World is an *intended* shrine. It was built by a corporation for corporate purposes, and it has, as intended, transcended that corporation by assimilating and even inventing key symbols of the version of the United States it presents."[5] In the terms we shall develop more fully throughout this chapter, Walt Disney World is a pilgrimage site in what scholars have called "the American civil religion." In truly spectacular fashion, at Walt Disney World the Walt Disney Company compresses and commodifies selected "American" values of "innocence" and "progress," casting them into a golden mouse, if you will. It then sells these "values" back to its millions of customers, who increasingly come from around the entire globe to worship them. It is a small world, after all.

A Mickey Mouse Mecca

Italian writer Umberto Eco, in an essay entitled "Travels in Hyperreality," once proposed that Disneyland was America's Sistine Chapel.[6] To Eco, Disney's designers devoted such attention to detail, and visitors to the park displayed such intense devotion, that an analogy between the Anaheim theme park and one of Christianity's most famous pilgrimage sites made sense. At the time Eco proposed this analogy, in the early 1980s, he was right to locate the sacred place of this peculiarly American cult in California. But since the development of Florida's Walt Disney World in 1972, and its dramatic expansion ever since, Orlando has become the undisputed center of this original form of American national devotion. Furthermore, few Americans have ever visited, and many have never heard of, the Sistine Chapel. In light of recent world events, a Middle Eastern analogy might be more appropriate. Walt Disney World, then, might aptly be called a "Mickey Mouse Mecca."[7]

An analogy between Walt Disney World and the city to which all Muslims are duty bound to undertake a pilgrimage makes sense because most parents in America also can feel compelled to take their children to the Magic Kingdom. One difference, of course, is that the *hajj* to Mecca can be fulfilled in a once-in-a-lifetime journey, whereas many pilgrims to Mickey's Mecca seem compelled to go back again and again. Pilgrims to the authentic Mecca also are fully aware that what they are doing has religious significance. There are some clear guidelines to keep the function of this ancient ritual oriented toward the worship of Allah, the beneficent and the merciful, and there are structures in place to orient the pilgrimage toward the unity of God's people and compassion for the suffering. Many pilgrims to Mickey's Mecca, on the other hand, do not appear to be quite so conscious of what they are up to and consequently wind up suffering themselves.

Consider, for example, Joe and Shirley Gireoux of Jacksonville, Florida. The Gireouxs, with their daughter Jennifer, faithfully pilgrimaged to WDW three to five days each month for *eleven years,* according to a 1992 newspaper story that I happened to run across. These pilgrimages cost the Gireouxs roughly $455 per year in season passes and an average of $175 per day for food and lodging at Disney resorts. The Gireouxs thus spent a total of between $6,300 and $10,500 *per year* on trips to Walt Disney World, which means that over an eleven-year span they contributed between $69,300 and $115,500 to the Disney corporate coffers, without accounting for inflation. That's more than many people of faith donate to religious congregations in a lifetime. Souvenirs for the Gireoux family alone racked up bills of $10,000. Jennifer was only fifty-five *hours* old (that's barely two days) when she first visited the Magic Kingdom. She had never, according to the newspaper report, worn anything that was not Disney-issue or slept on anything but Disney sheets. Jennifer's dad himself owned thirty-five pairs of matched Disney shorts and shirts, which meant he could clothe himself in Disney-wear for over a month without doing laundry. Jennifer's mom, Shirley, vowed to continue the pilgrimages even when she lost her job, because Walt Disney World "is a happy place, a fun place, where you always feel good." The couple had to sell some Disney stock to pay their utility bills, but their devotion to the shrine had not failed: "Disney is timeless and ageless," Joe claimed.[8] Now, I don't know if the Gireouxs practiced any *other* religion than this one, but that this behavior is worthy of the word *devotion* seems pretty clear to me.

My last visit to the Magic Kingdom was in 1992, when I was accompanied by my wife, Lisa, and our two sons, Justin and Nathan, then five and three, respectively. My experience at the theme park as a parent suggests that the Gireouxs are only extreme versions of the normal devotion that draws people by the millions to this pilgrimage site. Our day began with a visit to one of Orlando's time-share resorts, where for sitting through a ninety-minute spiel and saying "no" about four hundred times, we acquired half-price tickets to the Magic Kingdom. On the way to the presentation, I began to videotape a family "docudrama" to remember the day. As we walked from the van to the time-share offices, I intoned on the soundtrack, in cynical fashion: "Well, here we are on our way to a sales pitch—surely an appropriate way to prepare for the biggest sales pitch of them all: Walt Disney World." While Lisa and I endured capitalist purgatory to earn an easier path to Disney heaven, Nathan and Justin spent ninety minutes in a "play area." By the time we emerged, tickets in hand, the boys were aching to be unleashed on the Magic Kingdom.

After driving the short distance to the sacred place, we parked the minivan and took the tram to the "Main Gate." Our first stop, once we had strolled down "Main Street, USA," was the ride called "The Pirates of the Caribbean." As we stood in line, the song from the ride, piped through speakers, initially triggered fond memories from my adolescent pilgrimage, when we also visited the site. As the tune repeated itself, however, I began to realize how barbaric (if not racist) the tune was. Now, I suppose there were dark-skinned Caribbean pirates who did in fact "hijack," "burn up cities," "pillage," and "maim," while drinking lots of rum and chasing wenches, as the song puts it. But I wasn't sure I wanted my children to "ooh" and "aah" at the animatronic robots who extolled such virtues. Nevertheless, we were already halfway through the line, and I didn't feel as if I could turn back. My "swashbuckling" boys loved the ride.

Our next stop was the "Haunted Mansion," a spooky-looking Victorian-style "home" chosen as a destination by Justin, who at that age often dressed himself as a "ghostbuster." Along the way, my cynical voice-over in the family docudrama began to give way to muted appreciation of the park's cleanliness and attention to detail. My footage from the Haunted Mansion, for instance, revealed what was in effect a six-minute meditation on the Disney view of death. We approached the ride through a "cemetery," where the camera panned to focus on particular headstones. One read: "In memory of our patriarch, dear departed Grandpa Marc." Another, nearby, offered: "Master Gracey, laid to rest, no mourning please at his request, Farewell." (Both stones, I later learned, provided symbolic immortality to two of the "imagineers" who helped design the ride—Marc Davis, a Disney art director, and Yale Gracey, a Disney designer.)[9]

Such whimsical insider jokes were of course lost on all of us at the time, but the video suggests clearly that we thoroughly enjoyed the ride, which was about a five-minute trolley excursion through the darkened "mansion." We shrieked in delight as models of skeletons popped out of coffins and as spectral "ghosts" were made to "sit" next to us, through special visual effects, in the little cart in which we rode through

the attraction. Along with the visual effects came a wide range of sounds—thunder crashing, hinges creaking, a heart beating, and the song written specifically for the ride, "Grim Grinning Ghosts." The song invites riders, I noted while listening to the video, to join the ghoulish ranks. Naturally, I had missed these lyrics during the ride. I had been so distracted by the robots and other special effects that my verbal reasoning was free to be possessed, so to speak, by whatever messages Disney wanted to insert. And the song is unmistakably—I noted after the fact—an invitation for every rider in the Haunted Mansion to join the ranks of the living dead. That this invitation is extended "for a token fee" is also likely to escape all but the most keenly aware riders. Nevertheless, I have come to believe that this invitation is in fact the key to the "magic" of the entire park in miniature.

The Haunted Mansion subtly brings riders into contact with their mortality. The ride then provides them with a symbolic "escape" from death as they exit the dark tunnel of the ride into the bright Florida sunshine. This interpretation of the ride meshes well with what a Disney designer himself offered about the Disney "magic." "What we do here," explained Walter Hency, "is to throw a challenge at you—not a real menace, but a pseudo-menace, a theatricalized menace—and we allow you to win."[10] It's like, I suppose, a "theatricalized" version of a second birth. And exactly as intended, once our family emerged from the tunnel of the Haunted Mansion, we were all, in company with the Gireouxs and the millions of others who visit Orlando, converts. My cynical video counter-commentary was over. I'd been reborn into Mickey-love.

We stayed at the Magic Kingdom the entire day, through dinner, and up to closing. Our visit ended, as all of the tour guides suggested, with the "Main Street Electrical Parade." This event (since modified) was quintessentially American—complete with flags and bands and all the trappings of the high holy days of the American civil religion. By the time this show began, we had walked for miles, stood in line for hours, experienced maybe a dozen different attractions, and spent a small fortune on food, drink, and souvenirs. We were tired and ready to be amused. It was a pleasantly cool evening, so we had bought sweatshirts for the boys. We queued up with the growing crowds to a place on the curb, grabbed a seat, and the parade began.

A deep, soothing male voice welcomed us to the "greatest parade on Earth," and music began to play over loudspeakers hidden in the buildings behind us. One by one the floats of the parade passed, with lights gleaming images we had never seen before, but which still seemed familiar. They were recognizable, yet alien; warm, yet dangerous. And light was the key theme throughout, borrowed from the imagery in every religion on the globe, and of course from nature, but now presented in such a dazzling spectacle that our senses could not possibly encompass it all. So we were disoriented. We searched for some meaning in the chaos of bodies, sound, and light, as strange image after strange image turned the corner and struck us.

And then there was one body, any body, but probably a young woman, waving to us from a circle of light, up on a pedestal. And then there was another body—Cinderella! She smiled and waved to us from her carriage, safe now from poverty and abuse, since we know how the story ends—she's a princess! I joined the pilgrims around me in devotion, a Ph.D. in religious studies reduced to uttering simple "oohs" and "aahs" as the fairy-tale figures passed me by. I could scarcely think, and even more, I didn't want to. And then the music crescendoed, timpani rolled, snares rattled, trumpets blared, horns declared—all electronically recorded and synthesized—that something special approached. We were bombarded by the fanfare and disoriented again, but anticipated an arrival. And, then, there he was—shrouded in a golden halo, the icon of all Disney icons, the image around which all this spectacle was centered. "There he is," I exclaimed to my boys: "It's Mickey!" And we all worshiped in delight.

Now, if this system of symbols that I experienced so powerfully in 1992 was only a one-day phenomenon, a mindless vacation, then it could be dismissed (as my students continually encourage me to do) as "harmless entertainment" and even "innocent fun." But the Disney "gospel" carries over into the real world, and even more, it *reflects* and *compresses* the real world. And that world, in America, is one where too often we worship spectacle, technology, and "innocence," while at the same time we ignore and deny our own penchant for violence and tolerate crushing poverty among millions. That violence and poverty take an especially high toll in the lives of children and youth makes the assertion of "innocence" on the part of the corporate owners of the Magic Kingdom all the more contradictory and tragic. The Magic Kingdom, then, not only provides visitors with an illusion of a second birth, enabling us to be reborn into the small world of Mickey-love. It also compresses and repackages, for a token fee, the prevailing myths of the American civil religion, through which many U.S. citizens, and increasing numbers of people around the globe, get distracted from doing anything substantive about the systemic causes of poverty and suffering.

The "Magic" Unveiled: Selling Denials of Death

The idea of a "civil religion" goes back to the eighteenth-century French philosopher Jean-Jacques Rousseau, but in the United States, the idea was popularized in 1968 by sociologist Robert N. Bellah. He argued in an influential article, and in a later series of books, that there "exists alongside of and rather clearly differentiated from the churches an elaborate and well-institutionalized civil religion in America."[11] Scholars since Bellah have contested his definition, but that he identified something significant was recognized by almost everyone.[12] Bellah and other scholars have since located the civil religion in the rhetoric of political campaigns, presidential speeches, and inaugurations, and from the annual cycle of nation-related commemorations and holidays, such as Memorial Day, Veterans Day, and the Fourth of July. Along with these national events and rituals that convey religious meaning, some scholars have pointed to particular institutions or places as bearers of the civil religion. Public schools, the legal system, the media, national shrines and monuments, and secular voluntary societies have all been implicated as venues of ritual behavior and as conveying particular values and ideals consonant with national identity.[13]

It is, however, in the realm of ideas, symbols, or language that the slipperiest features of the civil religion appear. Princeton historian John F. Wilson has identified several symbols that characterize what he called American "public religion." Two are particularly significant for our purposes. According to Wilson, the national religion of the United States depends, first, upon the idea of an optimistic, millennial expectation that America has a special destiny to promote *progress* in the world. Second, argues Wilson, the civil religion represents America as a new land, a place marked by *innocence*, in contrast to old-world corruption. These ideas or symbols, Wilson suggests, do not constitute a "specific, positive religion within American society," but rather provide "mythic elements within the culture amounting to a religious sanction" for national policies and practices.[14] We will attend in the section that follows to the theme of "innocence" at Walt Disney World and then turn to the theme of "progress" in the last section of this chapter.

The best place to find the theme of "innocence" at work at Walt Disney World is in the ride that is at the heart of both Disneyland and Walt Disney World, namely, "It's a Small World." The ride is a five-minute "boat" trip (it seems longer) through yet another mechanized tunnel. Brightly colored animatronic robots dressed in "native" apparel "sing" in various languages the song the ride made famous. And they sing it again, and again, and again, at high decibels. The robots are all designed to look like children and supposedly represent over one hundred different cultures from around the world—although the facial features of the figures are largely from a similar mold. Each "room" on the ride represents a different region. Western Europe comes first, followed by Asia, Africa, Latin America, and the Pacific. In a final, eclectic room, all the robots wear white. This last room, described by one critic as a "Disney

United Nations," almost brought tears to my eyes on my second trip through it, in 1992, as my sons sat beside me on the ride. The reason I experienced such an emotional tug here is clear enough, as Fjellman explains: "This room suggests—not without reason—that children don't have much interest in competition, strife, and war. Even in its homogenized sameness, the white room presents a salutary fantasy, a kind of harmonious world community as white Californians might imagine it."[15] I have always disliked strife, and like most people with children, I enjoyed the dream expressed by the ride that my offspring might grow up to inhabit a peaceful world. But of course the ride does nothing, in fact, to bring that dream to realization—and probably works to thwart it.

The lyrics of the song made famous by the ride ostensibly plant the rider in the real world of children, which is "a world of laughter, a world of tears." One ordinary devotee describes the ride and its song well, in language worth attending to in some detail. She writes to recommend the ride to potential pilgrims:

> This most charming boat ride through the countries of the world sets the mood for a visit to Walt Disney World. Especially if you're a first-time visitor, going straight to *It's a Small World* and having it be your first attraction will give you the glow you'll appreciate for the rest of your stay in the parks. . . . It is timeless. A beautiful ride in its simplicity, there is one word of caution: the theme song . . . will stick in your brain. . . . Hint: If you are still in the Magic Kingdom and really need to flush the song out of your mind, try Diamond Horseshoe Saloon.[16]

This is a fascinating commentary. I find especially interesting the language of this devotee about the effect of the ride on a pilgrim's "mood." According to anthropologist Clifford Geertz, religions work especially on the level of mood, where symbols can effect "lasting moods and motivations in people."[17] There appears, however, a contradiction in the narrative of this devotee about what It's a Small World does to a rider's moods and motivations. On the one hand, she claims that the ride produces a lasting "glow." On the other hand, she suggests that the song at the center of the ride is so insipid that one experiences the need to "flush" it out of one's head. I have to admit I find more believable the latter claim, although I doubt that there's enough liquid in the Diamond Horseshoe Saloon to do the trick.

Most intriguing of all, though, is this pilgrim's claim that the ride is "timeless." This is, of course, a slight exaggeration. This ride was built in 1972. So what does it mean to claim that It's a Small World is timeless? What we have here, I believe, is an "adult" interpretation of the ride, indicating a desire to connect with some place beyond the ordinary limits of time. As we age, the lure of the timeless seems somehow to increase. Of course, most young people don't share this concern. In fact, I have found that young people generally find the ride annoying. I barely remembered it from my first trip to the park as an adolescent in 1974, although of course the song I could sing by heart. And for some reason on our visit to the park in 1992, I videotaped the entire thing. It's fair to say that it loses something in translation. The lights look cheap. The robots seem, well, robotic. And the song becomes a lyrical version of the Chinese water torture. When we watched it at home several years after the trip my sons actually screamed for me to "FAST FORWARD!" well before we were halfway through it.

With our wits about us, then, we can recognize the promise constructed for our consumption by the Walt Disney Company in this ride as superficial, sentimental, and banal. No one really believes that war will end if we simply learn to say "hello" and "goodbye" in all the languages of the world. But by the time we emerge ("reborn") from the tunnel, our brains have been so bombarded with images of light and sound that we *want* to believe it. Our dream of a world of peace for our children has been captured, and commodified, and our emotional energy has been attached to the Disney version of global cultures. We feel joy at having "moved" from a world of tears and fears to a world where "a smile means friendship to everyone." Of course, we have actually moved only through a tunnel built on a former Florida swamp, and a smile won't get you very far in a world of nuclear and biological weapons. But we have paid dearly to enjoy this ride, and if we have to take on a timeless glow to do so, then so be it.

All in all, then, It's a Small World is anything but simple and "charming." It is, however, the most sacred of all the sacred places at Walt Disney World, because it is the most focused ride in the park. There the Disney gospel is compressed to its most succinct. As we discovered in chapter 2, sacred places often function as "focusing lenses." In sacred places, our attention is directed to the values and ideals that the culture represented at the sacred place holds most dear. In a sacred place everything might mean something; nothing is accidental, everything is contained within a controlled world of meaning.[18] And nothing happens by accident on this ride, or on most of the Disney attractions. Disney critic Henry A. Giroux, a professor of Education at Pennsylvania State University, draws out the significance:

> In the popular mind, Walt Disney, the man and the company, has become synonymous with the notion of childhood innocence. . . . [In fact, however, none of the Disney attractions is really] about the power of the imagination. . . . On the contrary, Disney offers a fantasy world grounded in a promotional culture and bought at the expense of citizens' sense of agency and resistance, as the past is purged of its subversive elements and translated into a nostalgic celebration of entrepreneurship and technological progress.[19]

Walt Disney World and the Walt Disney Company do not, then, at It's A Small World or in any of Disney's other for-profit products, value or protect the "innocence" of children. It exploits them. It's a Small World, in fact, turns children into robots. No wonder kids dislike it. Robots, having no unpredictable imaginations of their own, do what they are programmed to do. Real children can't (or shouldn't) be programmed.

But of course most children in the world are spared the ride, because it costs too much. And more to the point: millions of children will never have the opportunity to exercise their imaginations, not only because Disney has captured them, but because the real world isn't yet small enough for us to find a way to keep children from starving. Even healthy children simply don't have much of a voice in how things run, and Walt Disney World does little to help us understand how to change that injustice. In fact, by hoarding profits, under the guise of creating a place "where kids are king," as one advertising slogan had it, Disney actively *prevents* children from reaching fulfillment. In 1997, Disney CEO Michael Eisner set a corporate record by cashing in $570 million in stock options. Imagine what that money could do in an inner-city school district—or in several. In 2000, Disney revenues totaled $25 billion dollars, leaving a profit of $1.9 billion, according to a summary in *Forbes* magazine.[20] And what does the world have to show for this profit? Personally, I'll begin to believe again in Disney's promises when they make the Magic Kingdom a nonprofit enterprise. Surely they could afford it, and I have no doubt that the revenues from the theme park, if turned over, say, to the Children's Defense Fund, could indeed end lots of the "fears" and "tears" of the children of the world. Until that glorious day, however, of which I hold slim hope of seeing, we will continue to witness at Walt Disney World religion at its worst—as masking, as opiate, as disorienting, and as a huge corporate con job.

Now, of course, to critique Walt Disney World through one ride dominated by an insipid song may seem too easy. Fortunately, literary scholar Jason Isaac Mauro has offered an interesting critique of the Magic Kingdom attraction known as "Splash Mountain" that parallels my own sense of the place. On the surface, Splash Mountain is an innocent enough "log ride." I remember it vaguely from my first family visit to the park in 1974, but I don't recall riding it on any of my other visits. Splash Mountain, like It's a Small World, is a mechanized ride on a river of water. Once again, you go into a tunnel, then come out. This ride, however, is not a gentle float "through the countries of the world" but is rather an adventuresome roller-coaster trip through a bit of "Americana." It is also, according to Mauro, a ride that deals "invisible blows" to children by masking the systemic racial violence of America's past in a way that makes children (and all riders) complicit in its perpetuation."[21]

The ride is based loosely on a tale of Br'er Rabbit, Joel Chandler Harris's "The Wonderful Tar-Baby," as filtered through the Disney film *Song of the South*. The *original* story of Br'er Rabbit was, of course, a slave tale. In it, a rabbit, known to be wily and tricky, eventually gets trapped by its aggression toward a black "tar-baby." The symbolism does not take much deciphering. In the context of slavery, whites (the rabbit calls himself in the slave tale a representative of "'spectubble folks") elude justice for a while. Eventually, however, the whites, like Br'er Rabbit, get trapped by their own violence. Indeed, in the original story, the rabbit may, or may not, be eaten by the red (we can presume) Br'er Fox, who "lay low" while the rabbit entangled himself in the tar-baby. The original tale of Br'er Rabbit, then, is an African-American prophetic tale of subversion that points out the inevitable accounting likely to follow from the violence of slavery. That this prophecy came true in the war that Abraham Lincoln called a "judgment" on the United States for slavery makes the story all the more powerful. The tale of Br'er Rabbit, then, was originally a tale of subversion—a story about the violent consequences of racism.[22]

But this is not the meaning of the story that Disney's ride conveys. On Walt Disney World's Splash Mountain, there is no slavery, no black, no white, no tar-baby—no context for the story at all. The ride becomes an individualized experience of "adventure," surrounded by a "cute" animal story. Br'er Rabbit even escapes in the Disney version of the tale. Indeed, the rider *becomes* the wily rabbit. After surviving the big drop at the end of the ride, the visitor passes under a sign that says "Welcome Home Br'er Rabbit." The rider is then ushered into a Mississippi steamboat scene of the Old South, where the characters all "welcome" the rider home, while singing "Zip-A-Dee-Doo-Dah." Mauro explains: At the end of the ride "we are welcomed into the antebellum South. . . . We are relieved and grateful for this welcome [having just survived a big drop], yet this overpowering relief . . . blinds us to the troubling and brutal implications of the narrative world into which we are uttered."[23] That world was a world built on the backs of slaves, for the benefit of a few plantation owners. Disney's version of the tale of Br'er Rabbit completely reverses the subversive meaning of the slave tale. At Walt Disney World, visitors don't face justice for racism. They escape intact.

The crucial logic behind the Disney "magic" is again coming to the surface. Mauro puts it well: "I am certain," he argues, "that Disney World maintains its position as the Mecca of vacationers because its competitors . . . have misconstrued the real power of Disney's rides. . . . Disney provides for each of its rides a narrative frame, a fiction, that houses our terror within a salvational vital lie."[24] Mauro's language of a "vital lie" here is particular; it refers to a Pulitzer Prize-winning book by Ernst Becker entitled *The Denial of Death*.[25] According to Becker, humans have a psychological need to avoid facing our own mortality, and in order to do so will construct, or acquire, a "vital lie." People are usually unconscious of how this "vital lie" works to gain them symbolic immortality or salvation. That's why it's called denial. But we have seen this process of denial at work now in three different rides from the Magic Kingdom. In the first, the Haunted Mansion, the "vital lie" is that Disney provides a theatricalized second birth for riders by bringing them beyond a dark tunnel filled with "Grim Grinning Ghosts" and into the Florida sunshine. A second version of the same "vital lie" became evident at "It's a Small World." Here, one is "reborn" into "innocence" through yet another dark tunnel, where one is promised repeatedly that "it's a small world, after all," and that Disney (like you) cares about the children of the world and wants them healed of "tears" and "fears." The third example, as unearthed by Mauro, is both more dramatic and more obviously a lie. The quick drop at the end of Splash Mountain, after yet a third tunnel experience, produces an adrenaline rush that inevitably triggers a biological reminder of our mortality. But then we are "saved" by being ushered into the "heaven" of the Old South.

Needless to say, for all but a privileged few, the systemic violence that was the slavery of the Old South was no heaven. Just as some slave owners shrewdly used religion to keep slaves in line, so too does Disney use religion to keep its riders riding. Indeed, the success of the entire park depends upon riders "buying into" the false stories, usually by being blissfully unconscious of what they're doing. The ironies are ample. Riders build Walt Disney World in the same way that slaves built the South. No riders, no park. And the Disney owners, like the plantation holders of the Old South, profit by depending upon the passive and mindless acceptance by patrons of the vital lies they sell us. Disney sells the largely white, middle-class, and Christian people who visit the park a reassuring fiction that we are among the plantation owners, when in fact we are its slaves. This is truly remarkable. Mauro concludes: "The most pernicious violence at work in Splash Mountain is not in the screaming fall . . . but in the thick, sweet atmosphere of the community that surrounds us after that fall, a community whose violence is silent, pleasant, invisible, and deadly."[26] The most vicious violence, indeed, is the kind that its victims don't recognize as such. And it is exactly this kind of violence being dealt to children, and their parents, through the vital lies of a place ruthless for profit, but where kids are supposed to be king.[27]

"Magic" as Control: The Inevitable Failure of Corporate Reassurance

The Walt Disney Company claims for itself the word "magic."[28] This is not surprising, because according to some anthropologists, magic was indeed the earliest form of religion. For this reason, many devotees of contemporary paganism or witchcraft continue to designate their craft as "magic."[29] But the "magic" of Walt Disney World shares little in common with the localized, earth-centered worship of early or neo-pagans. It shares much with the banal modern hucksterism of carnival shows. That the Disney "magic" in fact depends upon very careful corporate control is evident above all in the way Disney treats nature. We will explore in the remaining pages of this chapter several ways Disney represents the natural world in its Orlando theme parks. These ways of representing nature are all, ostensibly, examples of "progress." Given what we discovered in the previous section about Disney's claim to represent "innocence," one ought to begin with a healthy dose of skepticism about the veracity of that claim. The version of "progress" reinforced by the sacred place of Walt Disney World may benefit some devotees of the American civil religion, but it doesn't do much for ordinary pilgrims, and its impact upon the planet Earth, on which we all depend, has yet to be measured.[30]

"Nature" abounds at Walt Disney World in ways that are often aesthetically pleasing. The park is beautifully landscaped, in a stereotypical kind of way. Surely, visitors can experience comfort, even luxury, at Disney establishments, as Disney advertisements are only too ready to point out.[31] Orlando itself, of course, is almost always sunny and warm, if not hot—which makes standing in lines for hours both possible and an exercise in losing water weight. Air-conditioning is available at enough sites to keep people cooled, and hats, drinks, and other ways to control the unwanted effects of the elements are amply available—for a price—throughout the parks. "Nature" is also present throughout the Disney acreage in the forms of water, earth, trees, even fire—but the contact between pilgrim and elements is carefully controlled. No one can go too close to the water—except in a carefully supervised "water park" or on a contrived "ride." The earth doesn't trespass its careful boundaries, and if it does it's swept up by one of the many young staff members who traverse the park on a regular basis. Such cleanliness was among the features of the parks that impressed me on my first visit, as I observed the uniformed sanitation crew members who cheerily (so far as I could tell) spent their eight-hour days sweeping litter into little steel dustbins. This cleanliness is not, of course, an accident, and neither is the cheeriness. Both are requirements at the parks. Dirt is as unwelcome as death, disease, and dissent, and the absence of dirt is as much a part of the message of denial as the narratives connected with every ride. At Walt Disney World, we get "nature" as we seem to want it in America—tamed and clean and tidy.[32]

This desire for controlled nature is understandable, since left to its own devices the natural world is not exactly tame, and in fact is utterly indifferent to human well-being. Nevertheless, humans are, of course, animals, and thus as Henry David Thoreau long ago suggested, from time to time "we need the tonic of wildness."[33] Conveniently, then, the Walt Disney Company has, in the name of "progress," packaged some of it for us behind fences and containers. The most overt example of this Disney control of nature can be found at Disney's "Animal Kingdom," which opened in April 1998. We visited in November. The occasion was the annual meeting of the largest professional society of college professors in my field, the American Academy of Religion. The juxtaposition of five thousand tweedy professors with characters in Goofy costumes made for a strange blend. Anyway, a former student of mine was working as an undergraduate intern at Walt Disney World, and she arranged for our family to spend a day at Animal Kingdom for free. Our experience there was dreadful.

Originally, the park was going to be called "Wild Animal Kingdom," but after visiting the park, I understand why they changed the name.[34] Basically, there was little that was wild about the place. In fact, we didn't see many *animals* (other than humans) at Animal Kingdom. Our day began typically, standing in line for a water ride. There I discovered a speaker hidden in a plant that was piping in the sound of chirping birds. Real birds, I suppose, would be too messy. At the center of the park stands "The Tree of Life," evoking, of course, the supposedly Edenic quality of life at Walt Disney World. But this "tree" is a fourteen-story monstrosity. According to one advertisement, the tree features "translucent" leaves. I thought they were plastic. As I looked at it, I wondered aloud to my wife and children how many real living green things had been killed to make way for this dubiously named "icon." Most disappointing of all to us was the pathetic exhibit of "pride rock," taken from the Disney movie *The Lion King*. We circled this exhibit in a tram, where we hoped, naively, to see lions running across the one-hundred-acre Disney-created savannah, or perhaps tearing into an antelope carcass. What we saw (far in the distance) was a mangy-looking cat, who struck a very un-Simba-like pose as he lay draped, limbs drooping, across a "rock." Even Rheanne, barely five years old, acknowledged that she "felt sorry" for the sickly looking "king of the jungle." I thought he looked depressed.

Indeed, all the animals at the Animal Kingdom, like the animals in most zoos, seemed rather less than thrilled about their captivity. Disney tries, of course, to spin the park as an "environmentalist" learning center and as a boon to its residents. But when thirty-one animals died within the first few months of the park's opening, Disney had to deal with an investigation by the United States Department of Agriculture. The USDA exonerated the park, of course, and Disney crowed that the deaths were "fewer than would have occurred in the wild." I doubt, however, that the two West African crown cranes run over by Disney tour trucks felt like the park promoted "progress."[35] Indeed, as I observed the listless animals, I couldn't help but think of "It's a Small World." I saw the old Disney "magic" at work once again. Just as Disney packaged the voices of children in robots and sold them back to guests, so does Disney's Animal Kingdom buy or breed animals, repackage them, and sell them back to us in a controlled setting. But of course, just as packaged innocence isn't really innocent, neither is controlled wildness truly wild. Is it progress? Most of Walt Disney World currently stands on what was once a teeming swamp. For many people, the removal of this swamp no doubt constituted an improvement. But progress, like beauty, depends upon the eye of the beholder. The few animals (roughly a thousand) who get to live in the Disney park may indeed have it "easy" compared to creatures in the wild, but what about the millions of wild creatures who originally inhabited the swamp? And, finally, even humans might have reason to wonder what "progress" is being wrought by the burgeoning number of attractions in the Orlando area like "Animal Kingdom." Anyone who had to sit, as we did, for two hours in a traffic jam on International Drive in an effort to travel a mile and a half, might be forgiven for wondering whether "progress" is really such an ideal.

Come to think of it, our student-intern benefactor was not looking or sounding all that healthy, either. She was by nature a cheerful and kind person. She had been lured to spend a semester in Orlando by the promise of understanding the Disney corporate "magic," since she was a business major. In fact, she wound up paying her tuition to work as a counter clerk at one of the fast-food outlets peppered throughout the Disney parks. She also paid to live in a Disney-owned apartment with three other girls and struggled to get enough sleep because of the intense partying that went on among the other workers. Most of these "workers" were also student interns paying to wear silly costumes and look happy while cleaning up trash or flipping burgers. I doubt that many of them learned much about how to tap into the Disney corporate mystique, although apparently they did learn how to work another kind of tap. I understand, however, why they sought relief from their containment in one tranquilizer or another. They were getting an education into the "magic" of corporate exploitation. Maybe it was worth it, but it sure seemed to be depressing for my student.

Speaking of depression, every human animal who visits Walt Disney World has multiple experiences of being controlled in the interest of corporate "progress." On all of my visits to the Disney parks, at least, I spent the largest amount of my time standing in lines. Through these lines, the Walt Disney Company, quite obviously, controls our bodies. We are herded to the attractions through what has always looked to me like the meandering pens through which cattle are led to the slaughter at a stockyard. On one visit, to Lisa's utter chagrin, I made this point while standing in line by starting to "moo" under my breath. A few of the people around us started to laugh, but I kept it up for a while until people began looking at me strangely. I was trampling on their ritual process. Soon enough, anyway, some character or distraction came along, as if by grace, to take our minds off the heat and the proximity of the other sweating pilgrims. But of course there was nothing amazing or miraculous about the character's arrival; their schedules and interactions are closely scripted to ensure maximum exposure to guests, and to control for maximum customer satisfaction.[36]

Walt Disney World is a pilgrimage site with childlike innocence and the unpredictable grace of nature as its intended meaning, then, but in fact, the "grace" is sold to us in a way that controls nature in the interest of American corporate "progress." William F. Van Wert helps us to explain, in a dense set of observations:

> In the overall condensed master narrative of Disney World, we are given the illusion of being [immortal] creatures by avoiding all consciousness (struggle), all ambiguities and complications (when consciousness is always complication), by repressing all vital and potentially shameful moments in American history (words like "war" and "slavery" are not mentioned), and by suppressing names and dates (anything that might be remembered, altogether). . . . Temporality ceases to be: no relationality, no causality, no vicissitudes, no ethnicity, no cultural difference, and no death, which is perhaps the culminating feature of the master's mastery. . . . [WDW is] an invitation to ride passively into the future with nothing to do but be swarmed with progress fed to us by big corporations, whose motives are never questioned.[37]

Walt Disney World, in short, is a corporate product, for corporate purposes, dominated by corporate propaganda, that is sold to visitors as a sacred place where they can experience "innocence" and "progress."

Among the Disney parks, EPCOT—the Experimental Prototype Community of Tomorrow—is where the themes of progress and control are most evident. At EPCOT, not only nature but entire cultures—human natures, if you will—are packaged and sold to us as commodities. I have visited EPCOT only once, in 1994, and it was not a pleasant experience. I had been told to expect that I'd "learn something" at the park, that it was the most "intellectual" of the Disney attractions. In fact, the didactic elements at EPCOT were indeed clear to me throughout my stay. They were so clear, in fact, that I found myself offering to my children a continual counter-commentary to

what I sensed was corporate propaganda. And this time I was never converted. The boys pretty much found the place "boring," and it did not help our experience that Rheanne (about two) bawled loudly almost the whole time we were there. I suspected that she was trying to tell us what she thought of the park, although the fact that she was teething probably had more to do with it.

The origins of EPCOT reveal distortions at the root of the place. Originally, when he envisioned a companion to the Magic Kingdom, Walt Disney intended to build an "Experimental Prototype Community of Tomorrow," a real city in which twenty thousand people would live.[38] But when Disney died without completing his dream, the leaders of the corporation concluded that Walt's utopia was probably going to prove an unprofitable one. So, they transformed the vision of EPCOT into a massive "world's fair." They did so by turning to some of the largest corporations in the United States to help them fund it. Today, the park has two sections. The first, the "World's Showcase," invites visitors to "experience" displaced relics and items from eleven countries around the globe. According to one awed pilgrim, these exhibits represent the eleven cultures "at least as splendidly as the countries themselves."[39] Indeed, why bother to travel to the real places? It's no doubt safer and cleaner at EPCOT, and one doesn't need to bother to learn foreign languages, negotiate foreign currencies, or deal with cultural differences. I experienced most of the pavilions of the "World Showcase" as very large commodity shops. I learned little and had no interest in purchasing trinkets to display my "global sophistication" to others when I returned home from the park. Admittedly, the food wasn't bad, although it was overpriced.

The Disney gospel of American corporate progress is clearest, however, in the second section of EPCOT, called "Future World." Ironically, "Future World" had to me a dated feel—as if the future was a lot like the technology of ten years ago. In any event, all of the primary exhibits at "Future World" are funded and controlled by major U.S. corporations. Kraft Foods, for instance, one of the major supporters of agribusiness and corporate farming around the globe, tried to persuade us that they truly care about "The Land," the title of their exhibit. Exxon, the oil industry giant, sought to reassure us that they care about the "Universe of Energy." And General Motors suggested at their exhibit that no current options—no matter how environmentally desirable—can surpass the "good ol' reliable internal combustion engine," conveniently on display in an automobile showroom where the cars oddly had no price tags. It is, however, American Telephone and Telegraph's "Spaceship Earth" that provides both the most recognizable icon of EPCOT and the clearest example of the corporate control of the place.

"Spaceship Earth" is a ride contained inside the huge golf-ball-like dome at the entrance to the park.[40] That this dome is also a variant of the corporate logo of American Telephone and Telegraph is no accident. The ride inside the dome purports to introduce the rider to the "history" of communication. Like most Disney rides, this one renders the pilgrim passive by forcing him or her to sit throughout the exhibit in a moving vehicle. Then, room by room, the vehicle traverses exhibits that purport to represent key turning points in the development of communications technology. First up are the cave paintings of Lascaux, although one never learns that they are located in Lascaux, when they were painted, or for what purposes (they're in France, date from perhaps 15,000 B.C.E., and probably served ritual purposes). A little later, the rider sees the sixteenth-century printing press of Gutenberg at work, probably cranking out copies of Luther's German Bible or some other Reformation tract. One never knows, however, because one never learns Gutenberg's name, when he built his press, or where. At the end of the five-minute ride, the characteristic Disney "magic" again appears. The cart in which pilgrims are conveyed suddenly spins around 180 degrees, and the rider is then dragged backward up a steep incline. At the top of the incline, which is yet another dark tunnel, the cars turn around again quickly, and the rider blinks at a brilliant and stunning display of laser lights and strobes. This is, again, a disorienting experience intended to foreshadow death and resurrection, a journey from the past to an unknown future. But whatever fear we might have is immediately dispelled by the soothing *basso profundo* voice of the patriarch of television news, Walter Cronkite, who narrates the ride. Cronkite's message is simple, and is to reassure us, in the words of William F. Van Wert, that "whatever challenges the future holds in store for us, AT&T will be there to bring us the Information Age and beyond."[41]

Such reassurance, however, has a short half-life and more than a few strings attached. Notably, we had to pay to experience this bit of corporate propaganda, and we have to pay for whatever services we require from AT&T once we leave the park. The cost of Disney's denials of death just keeps on mounting. Even more, someday this ride will close, and AT&T will fold—just as surely as the telegraph has been rendered obsolete. Many of the rides at EPCOT, in fact, have already met such a fate. Others have had to experience dramatic revision. The future, oddly, keeps changing, and "Future World" has a hard time keeping up. The "Experimental Prototype Community of Tomorrow" is thus neither an experiment, nor a prototype, nor a community, and it has very little to say about tomorrow. EPCOT is, in the words of William Arnal, "simultaneously a manifestation of and a propagandistic ode to American capitalism"[42] More specifically, it is a sacred place in the American civil religion, dedicated to an illusion of "progress."

Now, given the scope of the Disney enterprises, and the budget Disney dedicates to generating devotees, I know that persuading readers to discover better ways to spend their time and money than with Disney products may be an almost impossible task. I have shared drafts of this chapter with hundreds of middle-class folk—mostly with young people in high school and college, but also with adults—and these early readers of this chapter have very often turned my critique back on me. The Valparaiso University undergraduates who first read this material with me, for instance, would routinely show up for the class session in which we were going to discuss Disney wearing Mickey T-shirts, Minnie sweatshirts, mouse-eared hats, Goofy slippers, and Dopey pajamas. My feeble words didn't stand a chance against people who wrapped themselves so tightly in sacred garb. I've had this experience time and again: dissing Disney will all but get you crucified.

So, while I have no doubt that many of my closest friends and their families will continue to join the millions who make pilgrimages to Orlando, I have little desire anymore to accompany them. I've lost my faith in Mickey. The Disney myths of "innocence" and "progress" too easily deny the facts of suffering and death, not to mention the facts of the parks themselves, to persuade me. I no longer want to put my trust in a place that promises me the "magic" of amazing grace, but where everything in fact is carefully controlled. Indeed, the implications of this devotion to control are somewhat chilling. For when we worship a corporation image, we give up on the challenge of clothing power in a way that is truly life-giving, and that can inspire risking oneself in love for something more than a golden mouse. Progress as "control" leaves little room for spontaneity, dissonance, dispute, or difference—all features that might be vital to a democratic society, and features that might flow from an authentic theology of grace.

For the truly amazing thing about grace is that it can't be packaged or purchased. Grace is free, or it isn't grace, and nothing's free at Walt Disney World. Furthermore, I am absolutely certain that every pilgrim who is tempted to shell out some money to experience some Disney "magic" could in fact find something far more fun and rewarding to do in exchange for their cash. There are ample places of grace where one can have needs met and desires satisfied in ways that Walt Disney World can't possibly match. For Mickey-love is, in the final analysis, a weak substitute for love that trusts in the real Power that spins the universe, courses through our veins, and draws us out of our narrow national myths and toward one another in the fragile but profound enterprise of living. When we let a corporation cast a mouse in the divine mantle, we're left with nothing for our own imaginations to control but a few private possessions. And there are troubling implications from that form of devotion, too, as we shall discover in the next two chapters.

5

Private Possessions

American Domestic Religion and the Suburban Household

I grew up in a slightly poorer but otherwise reasonable facsimile of the Cleaver household, made famous in the early television situation comedy *Leave It to Beaver.* Now, the Cleavers have become synonymous with an oppressive variety of American domesticity, but that was not at all my experience. Up until I was nearly six, I was an only child, and the attention lavished on me made the world a very comfortable place. My father was a benevolent young man, whose arrival home from work in the evenings I would await eagerly by the door. When he walked in, he'd pick me up in his strong arms and give me a "whisker rub," as I giggled in delight. My mom was a skilled seamstress, cook, and young housewife, who prepared us hot breakfasts every morning and delicious dinners in the evening. During the day I would "help" her clean around the house, and at night she sang me to sleep with lullabies and folk songs. Such early memories make my sense of home serene.

Once my brother Andy was born, in 1964, I had to share the attention of my parents, but I also had someone to play with. On winter mornings, as soon as Andy could walk, we'd huddle together in front of the furnace register in the living room, arguing over who was "hogging" the heat but savoring the smell of bacon and eggs or pancakes that wafted to us from the kitchen. I also enjoyed teaching Andy to play sports. In spring and summer it was baseball in the backyard or in the fields near our house. In the fall we played football in the street. And in the winter we played basketball after scraping the snow off the driveway and adjusting for an all-but-frozen ball. Each game featured, of course, Andy and me as the team's star players. Even today, in our middle age, when Andy and I get together we'll often shoot hoops or throw a baseball around together, now often joined by our youngest brother, Dave.

I have known, in other words, some of the comforts of home. In what follows, I want to treat those pleasures gently, while also raising some questions about how they've evolved. For the single-family home is widely advertised as "the American dream," and on one level the dream has surely come true. Comfortable shelter is a basic human need, and many Americans now have very comfortable shelters. But on another level, as any homeowner knows, this dream can become a nightmare. Comfortable shelter has increasingly given way in modern America to an obsessive preoccupation with luxury, security, and a never-ending supply of "home improvement" commodities.[1] When one considers that some of the first families of North America lived in tepees as large as your average sport utility vehicle, the size of many homes in the United States today is just a little boggling.

New homes built in the year 2000 across the United States averaged 2,265 square feet of finished living area. That makes them well over twice as large as the typical

983-square-foot home built in 1950.[2] Most of these big houses, furthermore, were located in suburbs. Over 70 percent of mortgages approved in 2000 were for suburban homes.[3] These facts trigger some obvious questions. Why have so many people decided to live in suburbs when this makes necessary a daily commute, sometimes of several hours, to work? And why have homes expanded so dramatically in size and amenities, making my morning experience of brotherly bonding before a furnace

register highly unnecessary? What's behind the big suburban home boom? These questions have many answers, but before suggesting one I must confess: I live in the suburbs. But I also sometimes wonder whether we suburbanites actually own our homes, or whether our homes own us.

I didn't get to be blessed, or cursed, as a suburban homeowner overnight. The town where I grew up had no suburbs, but when I was sixteen (in 1974) my parents sold our little bungalow and moved into a new three-bedroom ranch in a development located exactly three blocks from our former home. My parents still live in that house, of which I remember being so proud that I brought all my friends over to see it. After Lisa and I married, for nearly ten years we rented a variety of apartments and townhouses, until, in 1992, we purchased our own three-bedroom ranch in Valparaiso. I felt like I'd finally arrived, although I quickly discovered that I needed to develop more handyman skills. Then, in July of 2000, we moved from "Valpo" to Media, Pennsylvania, where we purchased a two-story "garrison colonial" in the Swarthmore school district, located fifteen miles west of downtown Philadelphia. That home has four bedrooms, an office, a family room, a living room, a dining room, and a screened-in-porch off the kitchen that is delightful in spring and fall.

All in all, the 2,500 square feet or so provides more than enough space for the five of us and a couple of dogs.

I'm hardly able with integrity, then, to point the finger at owning a home in the suburbs alone as some sort of spiritual problem. The problem with the suburban home arises when the home becomes more than a habitation or more than a place for mutually fulfilling relations between family members, neighbors, and the larger civil society. And I believe it is easy enough to show that, over the course of the twentieth century, American homes have functioned less to promote the nurture of Cleaver family values than to satisfy an unconscious need on the part of people for some kind of sacred place.[4] As the market and nation gradually carve up space between them and sell us places to orient our devotion, we're left with the simple comforts of home. Owning a house, again, is not the problem; I wish more people could afford to do so. The problem is that many of the practices related to home-owning are serving spiritual purposes that distract people from true joy, that divert our energies into banalities, and that blind people to the suffering of others. Put most bluntly, the predominant idol in modern America is the single-family suburban home.

American Domestic Religion

According to historian of religions Peter Gardella, Americans devote themselves not only to the many traditional religions dotting the contemporary cultural landscape, but also to a "domestic religion." Like the "religion of the market" and the "civil religion" profiled in the previous two chapters, the "domestic religion" of Americans draws the private devotion of countless millions. Gardella writes:

> Ask people what they mean by religion and they usually mention God, rules for moral behavior, and whatever happens in their churches, synagogues, and temples. But behind those beliefs, codes, and forms of worship lie the rituals and values they live by at home: the holiday things that absolutely have to be done; the kinds of success for which no sacrifice or effort would be too much; the sports events that connect with the whole struggle of life; the songs that stand for ardent love, sadness, and joy; the television shows that express exactly how life is, or should be; and the foods and drinks that can yield the last happiness of old age. This is the realm of domestic religion.[5]

A religion, Gardella summarizes simply, is "a system of nonrational commitments that hold life together." Domestic religion, then, includes the private, nonrational commitments of Americans; those "ideas, words, names, places, actions, symbols, and stories" that give shape to their domestic worlds.[6]

For instance, Gardella argues that "success means what salvation once meant" to most Americans. He writes: "Millions who practice no organized religion (and millions who do) call themselves to regular internal judgments on the basis of their standards for success. . . . To conclude that one has succeeded in life offers the only consolation in facing death that many will accept." Many Americans, furthermore, interpret "success" in primarily economic terms. How much one produces and how much one can consume become the meters by which the quality of a life is measured. Gardella candidly reveals how his own ambition focused on the production of books and how for many years he felt inadequate because he had not published enough. "How easy it is," he concludes, "for Christians to think that success equals righteousness. . . . The mind, as Martin Luther said, is a busy workshop making idols, and success can be one of the strongest."[7] Among the most obvious markers of "success," of course, is a big home in the suburbs.

Gardella also shares with readers how he has gained a degree of distance from simple worship of success. He writes: "religions can also teach how to let go of success. The first two noble truths of the Buddha—that all is suffering and that suffering stems from attachment—show how every success opens new chances for failure. . . . How cunningly good things lead to more desire. To think in terms of success and failure will cause suffering in itself, increasing the delusion that the world divides between subject and object, winner and loser, and that some people could occupy only one side."[8] Gardella narrates further stories from his own experience to point out the ambivalence of judging life in these terms. Many of his "successes" brought with them what appeared, as their flip side, to be "failures." He published a book that sold well, for instance, but suffered a bad review in the *New York Times.* He earned tenure as a college teacher, but didn't get promoted to full professor. Readers, most likely, could supply examples of their own. Some of them might have to do with the size, or some other feature, of their homes.

Throughout his delightful little book, Gardella traces how apparently "non-religious" phenomena carry special significance in the domestic religion. Eating food, for instance, especially at sacred times like Thanksgiving, can take on the trappings of domestic ritual. "The Thanksgiving turkey has become almost a sacramental food," Gardella points out, "the totem animal of our national identity."[9] Sports, similarly, draw millions into ecstatic identification with "heroes" or "stars," as families gather around a flickering screen dressed in sacred garb to praise and lament the course of the ritual proceedings. "Football players," suggests Gardella, for one example, "impersonate gods, larger than life and almost invulnerable in helmets and pads, following totems drawn from myth and legend: Giants, Eagles, 49ers, Cowboys."[10] In each chapter, Gardella describes another way in which private devotions take on public significance: drinking and drug use, sex and love, even ordinary physical exercise can take on religious significance when such practices orient people's lives, drive their commitments, and organize their experience. The domestic religion, in sum, is "a mixture of many religious traditions under certain social conditions, a fact of life to be described and analyzed."[11] Like any religion, this one has its strengths and weaknesses. Like any religion, this one has its sacred places. Preeminent among the sacred places of the American domestic religion, then, is the single-family, suburban home, with an "immaculately" clean interior and a carefully "manicured" lawn.

The Demons of Tidiness and Toro

So—we turn to the topics of domestic sanitation and lawn care. Some time ago, anthropologist Mary Douglas commented on the religious significance of tidiness in her now classic work *Purity and Danger.* The basic argument of the book is that purification rituals and practices—and categorizations of purity more generally—stem from the human social need to order the dangerous chaos unmediated experience offers.[12] Living is simply not a very tidy process, and dying is even less so. So, we do whatever we can, including spending billions each year on cleaning products of one kind or another, to keep untidy death away from us. Visit any supermarket in the United States, and you will encounter a bewildering array of products designed to satisfy the obsessive rage of Americans to keep a clean house—far beyond what most of the world imagines as "clean," and far beyond what is necessary for personal hygiene.[13]

To some degree, of course, homes have probably always been sacred places, and people have always tried to keep dirt out of them. Ancient Romans, for instance, had gods of the household, and Christians for centuries have used rituals to consecrate homes as abodes of the divine. Closer to home, historian of religions Colleen McDannell has unearthed a wide range of ways American Christians in the nineteenth and early twentieth centuries turned their dwellings into sanctuaries. For example, Horace Bushnell, a leading nineteenth-century Protestant theologian, argued in 1847 that "the house, having a domestic Spirit, should become the church of childhood, [and] the table and hearth a holy rite." Later in the same century, Victorian architects followed Bushnell's lead and designed homes with Gothic Revival spires and gables to resemble churches. Individuals soon caught on and decorated their dwellings to display their "parlor piety," where prayers, songs, and artwork (the family Bible is the most prominent example) could turn the home into a sacred space. In the twentieth century, McDannell argues, social and cultural changes "weakened the common assumption of the sacred character of the home."[14] More accurately, however, people continue to treat their homes as sacred places, but in private, shorn from the symbols and communal assumptions of a traditional religion, and translated into idiosyncratic devotions sold to them by clever advertisers and shrewd manufacturers.

Between the producers and consumers of cleaning products and kitchen gadgets, in other words, people in the modern world have created new forms of worship and devotion without even knowing it.[15] We may think we're just buying a product called "Mr. Clean" when we need a little extra "muscle" to remove that stain from the tile grout, but in fact we're buying the "purity" that will "save" us from germs, from disease, from death. It's an interesting development. At least with traditional religions, you know you're getting sold a product you have to take on faith—whether its heaven, or nirvana, or whatever. Traditional religions are also quite up-front about the reality of suffering in the world, and they do much to remedy it. But the marketers of our domestic religious practices, ironically, lead us to think that *we're* actually *choosing* to spend hours with scrubbing bubbles (or inhaling fumes that let us do it quicker) and that through such choices we'll be "saved" from dirt. Most folks, of course, prefer not to think about why they are so obsessed with domestic sanitation. Students complain about this to me all the time. They "just *like*" a house that "looks nice." Or, more strongly and defensively, they indignantly turn my critique of an American obsession back on me: "What's *wrong* with wanting things *clean?* Do you prefer to live in a pigsty?" Of course I don't. Our house is almost always cluttered, but it's not unsanitary. The corners of some rooms occasionally feature dog-hair dust-bunnies, but these don't appear to pose much of a health risk, since we don't seem to get sick any more often than most folks. Not surprisingly, however, the Soap and Detergent Association takes the side of my students. In a recent survey they found that fully two-thirds of Americans engage "in the ritual of spring cleaning." Women ages 35–54 are the most likely devotees, followed by men aged 18–24 (perhaps the only time of the year they clean?), followed by men aged 55–64. The number one reason all these people engage in this ritual (thereby making me feel guilty as one hopelessly impure)? "It just needs to be done."[16] Religions need no further justification.

We're not talking here, then, about the necessary commitment to sanitation that every household needs to practice. I hassle my kinds constantly to clean their rooms, wash their hands, and flush the toilet. Indoor plumbing is a wonderful thing. We are talking about a fixation on domestic sanitation; possession by the demon of Tidiness. Chances are you know someone possessed by this demon. Chances are you know someone otherwise "normal," who has spent his or her life more or less dedicated to scrubbing, buffing, mopping, vacuuming, and dusting, not as a task, but as *devotion*. Perhaps out of homage to Tidiness, she has sacrificed time with her own children. Perhaps because of his worship of Tidiness, he has neglected attention to his spouse. In any case, for such folks, cleanliness is truly next to godliness; it is the very fabric in which they wrap the divine. Devotees of this demon may lack ancient kosher laws about creating sacred space, but they have nevertheless managed to turn every day into the night before Sabbath. This demon has ruined marriages, and this demon ruins lives (or at least lungs) every day. For, as Douglas writes, "Whenever a strict pattern of purity is imposed on our lives it is either highly uncomfortable or it leads into contradiction, or it leads to hypocrisy. That which is negated is not thereby removed."[17] Cleanliness may indeed be next to godliness, then, but the god you're likely to meet in a rage for tidiness is a naked demon who demands purity and who will suck away days of your life and drain money from your wallet. Humanity, as Jesus once said about the Sabbath, is not meant for cleaning, even if cleaning is necessary for humanity. We won't solve the problem of our mortality through our devotion to a clean house—no matter how tidy we make it. And we may in fact be doing damage to ourselves and to others. According to one EPA report, the toxic chemicals found in typical home cleaning products are three times more likely to cause cancer than is outdoor air pollution.[18]

Nevertheless, we worship undeterred. To verify how far such devotion can go, short of an actual pilgrimage to the home cleaning section of your local hardware store, you might want to visit "Mr. Clean's Home on the Web."[19] There you can be asked the all-important question: "Guess whose wipes run rings around the competition?" The answer, of course, is that Mr. Clean's do, because they are "thicker, bigger," are "lemon scented," and "cut grease, grime, fingerprints, and dirt from countertops, appliances, stovetops, tables, high chairs, microwaves, toasters, coffeemakers, refrigerators, painted wood, doorknobs, phones, and garbage cans." That last one puzzles me. By the looks of the product on the web page (I've never seen them in stores), it would take just about the entire package to clean a garbage can. But I suppose that's the idea. The more you clean, the more the manufacturer—Procter and Gamble—stands to earn in profit. Mr. Clean Wipe-Ups are also disposable, of course, which means that they will add to the clutter of landfills threatening to use up every available inch of nonresidential space in the United States. That part isn't in the ad, naturally.

Or you may want to visit the "Stain Buster" web page—conveniently (and with more than a little implied sexism) located when I first searched at goodhousekeeping.women.com. There you will discover that "whether you had a little spill or are just a plain old slob, there's nothing more frustrating than a stubborn stain. But if you think that stain will be impossible to get out, think again. The Good Housekeeping Institute's Stain Buster tool just might do the trick."[20] The Stain Buster tool is in reality an electronic list that describes how to remove almost every imaginable type of stain—from skunk odors to grease to wine to vomit. I suppose it might someday come in handy. But the implications of the prose on the web page strike me as little short of barbaric. In it, a woman (clearly the target of the ad) is faced with a choice. Either she suffers from "a little spill," or she is "a plain old slob." Such options! In either case, however, it's obvious that "there's nothing more frustrating than a stubborn stain." Really now. I can imagine, just off the top of my head, about seventy million more frustrating things than some grease on a T-shirt. The most stunning thing to realize about the exaggerated rhetoric in ads like this is that they are not pushing a specific product, but an entire worldview. Good Housekeeping isn't selling anything here but a mentality—a mind-set in which women are defined by their purity and by the purity of their homes, by their will and ability to overcome either "a little stain" or (God forbid) being "a plain old slob."

Similar pages can be found easily, and in multiple forms, indicating both the depth and breadth of this devotion. Go ahead and visit "Barefoot Lass's Stain Removal Tips!" Or "Zippygirl's Messie Page." Or "Your Kitchen, Germ Warfare."[21] Most painful, to me, were the hundreds of "testimonials" on these pages. They were almost universally written by women, who asked, cried, and pleaded for help to remove the stain that threatened (if their panicked prose could be trusted and was not in fact a fiction concocted by the advertisers) to all but keep them from salvation. This mentality is a prison. It seeks to enlist people to a set of commitments and acts of devotion that exploit the time and resources of women for commercial purposes. I thought we were beyond this.

We're not, of course, because this mentality represents not only a "normal" psychological quirk of the obsessive type, but a spiritual problem—a necessarily futile and never-ending attempt to maintain order against the chaos of dirt and death. The depth of the damage this problem causes to human spirits can be clarified, perhaps, by a brief quote from Albert Schweitzer—the famous Christian missionary, musician, and medical doctor. In the midst of developing his philosophy of "reverence for life," it dawned on Schweitzer that the problem with human beings is not generally a *lack* of reverence. The problem, rather, is that people shift reverence for life onto dead objects that can't bear such weight. And when reverence then goes unrequited, as it is likely to do when directed toward a marble kitchen countertop, something inside people dies. The specific quote is one I cite repeatedly for students: "The real tragedy of life," Schweitzer suggested, "is what dies inside a person while still living."[22]

I suspect many people living in suburban America know the experience of this tragedy. For something happens to us here that makes us settle for small dreams. There was a time, and there are places still, where people can visit one another without regard for the spotlessness of their domicile. The people mattered more than the place, or rather, the place was a setting for sociability, not a sign of status. Today, though, at least in most of the households I know, we exhaust ourselves prior to family visits in hours of cleaning frenzy, and it's even worse if friends are coming. Strangers, alas, don't often get in the door. This shriveled practice of hospitality is exactly the kind of tragedy that Schweitzer lamented. We get stuck on the tiny dream of a spotless kitchen, when a slightly messier one might free us really to attend to the people who inhabited or visited it.

The causes for such shrinking of human dreams are manifold. One is advertising. Another is the failure of traditional religions to communicate a deeper and more fulfilling vision of life. But whatever the causes, all too often I see people I know give up on their big dreams—for love, for happiness, for creativity—and settle instead for small dreams like a clean house, or a trip to Walt Disney World, or a shopping spree at the mall. We may no longer, in other words, create sacred space in the privacy of our own homes by decorating our houses with religious kitsch. But we surely display our private pieties for all to see through the righteous icon of a spotless kitchen or the ordered uniformity of a manicured lawn.

This latter demon's name is Toro, or perhaps Lawn-Boy, which is what it turns every one of its devotees into. Max Weber and R. H. Tawney understood long ago that just as Protestants created the capitalist spirit of acquisition to prove their status as children of grace, so would capitalism change Protestantism into a private religion of eccentric signs. Weber and Tawney could not possibly have perceived how far this mutual influence would proceed.[23] The fetish of the American ChemLawn (wrap your brain around just what that name is telling you) is a stunning example of the privatization of religion, and an amazing incident of the human capacity to locate or clothe God in the most ludicrous forms. This is truly strange. Grown men (usually), otherwise professional and competent, spend lonely hours mowing, thatching, watering, weeding, feeding, seeding, edging, and even making certain that the mower pattern on a freshly cut lawn is perfectly symmetrical. Alternatively, they spend thousands of dollars to have others do those things for them. The devotion to the image is the same in any event. I have been mildly possessed by this god, I confess. I have spent hours on my knees in devotion—pulling dandelions; perfectly pretty dandelions (my daughter loves them), hearty and resilient dandelions. Why did I do it?

Turfgrass is not native to North America. It is an English transplant, and it is not well suited to American soils and climates. Yet English barons used it, and nineteenth-century American "barons" wanted it too. Chemical manufacturers, recognizing a potential buffer against the unstable market for agricultural fertilizers and pesticides, exploited the desire. And now we live with the artificial ideal of a lawn made up of millions of one-inch blades of identical little plants, dependent upon ten times the fertilizers farmers use, and spilling millions of pounds of pesticides and herbicides into our soil and water every year.[24] Why do we do it?

Pat Armstrong, a Chicago landscape architect, suggests one reason. Lawns, she contends, have become ceremonial farms for the modern American male, a way for office and factory workers to "get back to the land." She explains: "There are a lot of men who really enjoy riding around on the lawn tractor on Saturday morning. It may be something that goes back to their primeval feelings about being on the land, but it has been so distorted and contorted by our modern lives—they tend a piece of land that they don't do anything with." Herbert Bormann, a Yale University professor and coauthor of the book *Redesigning the American Lawn*, sees the change as a recent one. Up until World War II, most Americans lived with what Bormann calls a "freedom lawn," which was a "motley assortment of grasses, clover, plantains and any other mowable species that shared the space." After 1950, however, desires shifted to the current rage for an "industrial lawn," with its uniform, chemically dependent, and environmentally unsound turfgrass.[25]

In fact, the American war against crabgrass has even deeper roots, so to speak. Historian Virginia Scott Jenkins traces some of them in a delightful book with the revealing title: *The Lawn: A History of an American Obsession*.[26] In it, Jenkins notes that modern lawn care depends upon the narrative of a "war of man against nature." From their first steps on North American soil, native Europeans had a hard time with the "wilderness" and sought to domesticate, control, and conquer it.[27] Now that the frontier is officially closed, the rhetoric of the battle against nature has been manipulated by chemical companies to target male aggression on the lowly dandelion. In an earlier era, ads for lawn care products characteristically exploited the motifs of war. "It's time to take up arms against the weeds," read one. "Your best bet," it continued, "is wholesale slaughter by chemical warfare."[28] Such language was more popular in the Cold War than today, but even now the metaphor of conquest and control is evident. The most widely used domestic product's very name betrays the mentality: Turf-Builder with Plus 2 Weed Control.[29] As Jenkins summarizes, "American front lawns are a symbol of man's control of, or superiority over, his environment."[30] If we clothe ourselves to hide our animality, we dominate dandelions to hide our kinship with the fragile grasses.

We grow and tend grass to "get back to the land," then, and kill weeds to demonstrate that we can dominate nature, but we also "manicure" (the metaphor is significant) our lawns to display our superiority, like birds preen their bodies, to our neighbors. Every summer Saturday in our Valparaiso neighborhood was a virtual lawn mower derby. Dads (and a few moms) would "start their engines" and then ride or walk behind their prized machines, competing in displays of domestic piety. Sometimes they would even be accompanied by their children, to whom they would be teaching the sacred lore of lawn care. Advertising, again, gives us a clue into the motive for the madness. For instance, the "Savage Lawn Mowing Company" (I did *not* make that up) suggested in 1947 that with the help of their product, an American's yard could be "the envy of the neighborhood."[31] In identical language, the Worcester Lawn Mower Company advertised to competition-minded consumers in 1953 that by buying their product their lawn would also become "the envy of the neighborhood."[32] Call it turfgrass envy. Such imitative rivalry is nothing new, of course. People have always competed with one another over one object or another. What is new, however, is how this competition has been created by specialized industries, as well as how the practices of this peculiar form of piety demand the owning of a home. Chemical, lawn care, and real estate industries, in this case, use advertising to create or escalate desire, and then manipulate the desire so that it is linked to the particular product they have to offer.

And so the devotion proceeds, despite the fact that products used as herbicides and pesticides in creating the perfect lawn have repeatedly proven to be unsafe to human beings and other mammals. The most famous, of course, is DDT—an insecticide widely used in yards and on farms in the immediate post–World War II era. Cheap, effective, and thought to be relatively nontoxic to mammals, DDT was banned in 1972 after researchers identified a link between the chemical and rapidly diminishing numbers of large carnivorous birds across the United States. Chemical companies resisted the ban, arguing in what now appears to be somewhat exaggerated rhetoric that the ban would mark "the end of all human progress" and would bring "disease, epidemics, starvation, misery, and suffering."[33] Since the ban, however, the number of bald eagles has increased tenfold, from fewer than five hundred pairs across the United States to over five thousand. The number

of peregrine falcons has also increased from 39 breeding pairs to 993, and the number of ospreys and brown pelicans has also increased dramatically.[34]

More recently, debate between environmentalists and lawn care companies has focused on 2,4-D, a herbicide developed in the early 1940s, released to the public in 1944, and widely used until very recently. Jenkins reports that in the early 1990s, 2,4-D was used in more than a thousand weed-killing products, despite having been widely suspected to be a carcinogen and having been linked chemically to the active ingredient in the notorious defoliant used in the Vietnam War—Agent Orange.[35] Many lawn care companies today, including the largest—TruGreen ChemLawn—have discontinued use of 2,4-D. TruGreen ChemLawn nevertheless felt compelled on its web page to dismiss as "controversial" the findings of an article in the *Journal of the National Cancer Institute* that linked 2,4-D to a doubled rate of risk for malignant lymphoma in dogs whose lawns had been treated with the chemical.[36] Yet another group of chemicals used in lawn care products, known as organophosphates and including well-known names such as Abate, diazinon, and malathion, have been linked to neurological disorders, muscle weakness, and heart disorders in mammals.[37]

When I tried to discover on their web page the chemicals used by TruGreen ChemLawn, however, I had to travel through four layers of links from their main page and still couldn't find specifics. I did, however, find some interesting information on their "Frequently Asked Questions" page. The last question was, I thought, particularly telling. "How toxic are your products?" it asked. The answer began: "TruGreen ChemLawn does not manufacture the products that we use in lawn care." Call me suspicious, but does that answer the question? It does, of course, set up a very large hedge against a lawsuit. The "answer" to the question of toxicity then went on to list a range of incomprehensible (to me) numbers about one test conducted on "rodents" of the "oral acute toxicity" (that would be when you ate a bowl of their product) of the "twelve combinations of materials most regularly used by TruGreen ChemLawn." Finally, the author (a ChemLawn employee) concluded that the test demonstrated that the mixtures were "practically non-toxic."[38]

Nevertheless, I continue to see little white "stay off" signs posted from time to time on lawns throughout my neighborhood. Despite the protestation of the companies that these are "not warning signs" but only to reassure "customers and their neighbors" to take "whatever precautions they feel are necessary," I'm not buying it, literally or figuratively.[39] My backyard is a delightful and motley mix of clovers, broadleaf plants, and weeds whose names are unknown to me but that blossom with little purple and yellow flowers in spring. In my front yard the previous owner installed a Zoysia lawn, which is a seed variety resistant to both drought and weeds. I got lucky, I guess. Both front and back yards will be, for as long as I own the house, pesticide- and herbicide-free.[40] I keep the lawn mowed, mulch the clippings, and have planted several roses and other flowering perennials in a flower and rock bed in the front, and a variety of herbs (all legal) in back. The neighbors seem happy—although if they're worried about my lawn, they need to get a life. I expect that I'll take a financial hit for having a "substandard" lawn when it comes time to sell the house, but I also suspect that I might just save almost as much as I'd spend on chemicals or a lawn service over the years. In any event, applying chemicals whose "practically non-toxic" character has been "verified" by the company whose interest it is to sell me the product no matter how toxic it is, does not seem to warrant the risks to myself, to my family, or to the environment. Such an application becomes even more impossible to justify when I recall that the very ideal of a "good" lawn is largely the fabrication of corporations seeking to dig into my pockets. Does this make me "righteous"? Hardly. It's one small choice I can make to help preserve the beauty I see around me in the environment.

Safety and expense aside, then, I simply see little purpose, and much folly, in the typical American quest for a "perfect" lawn. A writer for *Life* magazine caught the spirit well in 1969 when he claimed that lawn mowing was the "one act by which America judges the moral fitness of her citizens." The tongue-in-cheek article continued:

> Let a man drink or default, cheat on his taxes or cheat on his wife, and the community will find forgiveness in its heart. But let him fail to keep his front lawn mowed, and to be seen doing it, and those hearts will turn to stone. For the American front lawn is a holy place, constantly worshiped but never used. Only its high priest, the American husband, may set foot on it, and then only to perform the sacred rites: mowing with a mower, edging with an edger, sprinkling with a hose, and rooting with a rooter to purify the temple of profane weeds.[41]

Why we do it, then, *is* finally a matter of theology. We seek to control what space we own when we lack common symbols to orient us to the truly amazing gifts of grace, or when places have been co-opted by corporations or agents of the state. In the absence of a coherent, publicly agreed-upon way to clothe God, we turn to the idiosyncratic and private for salvation. We buy into myths that hold up for us some advertised ideal, and we enact rites that help us to maintain control in what appears to us to be a truly chaotic time.

American lawn care, like rituals of domestic sanitation, reveals a vestige of ancient religions, as the journalist Dennis Rodkin has pointed out:

> The ancient Greeks told the story of a mortal who so angered the gods that he was sentenced to spend eternity performing a futile and hopeless chore. Sisyphus spent each day pushing an enormous boulder uphill, only to watch it roll back down each night. No matter how hard Sisyphus worked on any day, he still had the very same job ahead of him the next day. This, to the Greeks, was hell. Modern Americans who do the same kind of never-finished, perpetually frustrating work, call it lawn care. The difference between Sisyphus and us is that upon reaching the top of the mountain each afternoon, Sisyphus didn't shove the boulder back down the slope. It wasn't his fault that the job was never complete. We, on the other hand, keep the endless cycle going on our own![42]

The myth of progress over the ancients is durable, but doubtful. We find new ways to create hells for ourselves all the time.

The Public Shame of Private Theologies

Jesus, or at least the author of the Gospel of Luke, knew that people faced temptations to do hellish things all the time. While there were of course no lawn mowers in ancient Palestine, the root of the peculiar evils under discussion in this chapter were more than evident. Thus, near the middle of the Gospel of Luke, Jesus says to his audience (the lawn care experts and domestic sanitation engineers of his time): "Take care! Be on your guard against all kinds of greed; for one's life does not consist in the abundance of possessions." This passage clarifies nicely for us that greed takes many forms, from a passion for the mall's commodities, to a quest for the perfect Disney vacation, to the dream of an immaculate lawn and home. Characteristically, however, Jesus does not dwell on the negative. Rather, he illustrates his aphorism—his warning to avoid something that harms us, with a story. "The land of a rich man produced abundantly," the story begins.

> And [the rich man] thought to himself, "What should I do, for I have no place to store my crops?" Then he said, "I will do this: I will pull down my barns and build larger ones, and there I will store all my grain and my goods. And I will say to my soul, 'Soul, you have ample goods laid up for many years; relax, eat, drink, be merry.'" But God said to him, "You fool! This very night your life is being demanded of you. And the things you have prepared, whose will they be?" So it is with those who store up treasures for themselves but are not rich toward God.
>
> Luke 12:15–21

Greed kills, in whatever form it takes.

To return to Jesus' story, however, what I find most interesting in it is not primarily the critique of greed but its last line, where Jesus clarifies greed's opposite. The opposite of greed, Jesus asserts, is being "rich toward God." What does this mean? The teacher from Nazareth turns to his disciples and followers to explain:

> Do not worry about your life, what you will eat, or about your body, what you will wear. For life is more than food, and the body more than clothing. Consider the ravens: they neither sow nor reap, they have neither storehouse nor barn, and yet God feeds them. . . . And can any of you by worrying add a single hour to your span of life? If then you are not able to do so small a thing as that, why do you worry about the rest? Consider the lilies, how they grow: they neither toil nor spin; yet I tell you, even Solomon in all his glory was not clothed like one of these. But if God so clothes the grass of the field, which is alive today and tomorrow is thrown into the oven, how much more will God clothe you! . . . And do not keep striving for what you are to eat and what you are to drink, and do not keep worrying. . . . Do not be afraid, little flock, for it is [God's] good pleasure to give you the kingdom. Sell your possessions and give alms. Make purses for yourselves that do not wear out, an unfailing treasure in heaven, where no thief comes near and no moth destroys. For where your treasure is, there will your heart be also.
>
> Luke 12:22–34

This famous passage clinches the whole: when we clothe or locate God badly, we invariably suffer the heartaches of fear, worry, boredom, and disappointment. People seek grace through a place, but greed turns the place that they anticipate possessing into an agent that possesses them.

Let me say it one more time: cleaning isn't inherently evil, and neither is owning a home or caring for one's yard. Under the right circumstances, in fact, cleaning can almost be an ecstatic experience. For instance, for three summers I was the "Spiritual Advisor" to the staff of a Lutheran summer camp in Northern Michigan. On certain nights, I'd help out the kitchen staff as we cleaned up the dining hall and food prep areas after dinner. Led by the chef, Kurt Harvey, those occasions of cleaning became dances of delight. We'd turn the music up, loudly, and twelve to fifteen people would move together in an unchoreographed but careful set of movements—whirling, spinning, bending, and reaching. All we were doing was cleaning, but in the moment, and through communal goodwill, it became something more. Sometimes I'd stop, stand back, watch, listen, and grin. It was beautiful, because it was done in the service of hospitality: we were cleaning as a community of friends to prepare a place for our guests, not to display our private status to them but to extend the boundaries of the community by preparing for our common meals.

I've also experienced a foretaste of heaven while mowing my lawn. For most of my life, I've had walk-behind mowers, and when you mow a yard with skill behind one of those machines there is a certain repetition that borders on ritual. One leg moves after the other; you turn corners or end rows with the same motions; and your arms and hands push and release the mower with movements that are best effected by following similar patterns. If all is going well, you can get into a "zone" with such motions: a mindless mindfulness that heightens one's appreciation for everything. Your rate of respiration increases, oxygen flows through your veins, and endorphins flood your brain. You begin to notice the smell of the freshly cut grass, the clear blue of the sky, and the bright greens of the trees around you. The most anxiety-producing problems may come to mind—financial, filial, or otherwise—and then they go away, just like in a meditation session. Worry evaporates, as transient as the problems themselves are likely to be under the perspective of eternity.

Now, what distinguishes such rare moments of transcendence through cleaning and lawn care from the normal obsessions that turn the home into a private possession is how we participate in the place. In each case, the private fixation that signified obsession was missing. I experienced from the place and the events in it a connection to another that allowed me to participate fully in the place without being overwhelmed by it or without losing the specificity of the place. Such connections in which we participate, in which we are fully incarnate, if you will, are what the Christian tradition has meant when it has spoken about "eternal life" and are what Jesus meant when he spoke about being "rich toward God." People who seek the "treasures" of the mall, Walt Disney World, and the suburban home may be seeking a little slice of heaven. But it is precisely because we have to pay for such places that makes our full participation in them unlikely. In my stream of the

Christian tradition—Lutheranism—this "you get what you paid for" mentality is called "works-righteousness," and it is well understood as the biggest obstacle to salvation (although, in practice, Lutherans are no better at avoiding it than most). The works-righteousness path to heaven contrasts, of course, with the path of grace—in which a way is prepared for one already, and all one has to do is participate and the promise is fulfilled! This is amazing, as the most popular hymn in America puts it: "I once was lost, but now am found, was blind, but now I see." Grace takes people lost in the possession of possessions and helps them find themselves, others, and the world—by letting them participate in whatever place they might happen to be. And that's a little taste of heaven.

Of course, many people have trouble believing this because they have a hard time believing in heaven, which they define as "life after death." We've seen, in the last three chapters, how people cling to the places of the mall, Walt Disney World, and the home because they fear dying and seek some way to control life. This fear is understandable, and it is this fear that turns people into frantic seekers of the salvation of success. But heaven can be understood not only as a private place to which one hopes to go *after* dying, but also (and perhaps even primarily) as a vision of what is good for life here—as a vision of the public good. It is conceivable, then, that whatever goodness, truth, and beauty one experiences in this life may in fact extend eternally through the same patterns, connections, and participation. Eternal life begins with this life, in other words, and heaven is as much here as there, and here can even *include* the mall, Walt Disney World, and the home. Nothing is beyond redemption. A brief excursion into the history of heaven will help us clarify this final point of the chapter.

In a carefully researched volume, Colleen McDannell and Bernhard Lang have sketched a wide variety of ways that Christians have imagined heaven over the centuries. Basically, they suggest, there are two: an "anthropocentric" view of heaven and a "theocentric" one. In the first, people imagine heaven as a place of other people—for instance, as a place to see friends and family again. In the second, people imagine heaven as a place to be with God. The authors further argue that contemporary "Christians still accept heaven as an article of faith, [but] their vigor in defining the nature of eternal life has much diminished."[43] In other words, even people who claim to believe strongly in heaven now doubt it. The reasons for this doubt are not difficult to discern: there's no empirical evidence, and there's been plenty of skepticism in the age of science and technology.

In fact, however, McDannell and Lang may miss that between the two models of an anthropocentric and a theocentric heaven is a deeper metaphor on which both depend. Both a heaven with people and a heaven with God are, rather clearly, still imagined by people as *places*. The predominant models of heaven depend upon a metaphor of place; when we clothe ourselves, or God, in heaven we put ourselves, or God, in place. This insight extends in two directions. The first is that the place of heaven is, somehow, continuous with other places. Even if heaven is a "supernatural" place, we cannot conceive of it other than in continuity with places we know through our material senses. It has always been a central affirmation of orthodox Christianity, furthermore, that eternal life entails the resurrection of the *body*—and the body is, needless to say, a material place. McDannell and Lang suggest that such a material view of heaven was briefly popular in the Middle Ages, when a few writers understood heaven as a garden, but I believe the seed (so to speak) of this way to clothe God in place is found in any orthodox view of eternal life.[44] Secondly, the place of heaven is somehow continuous with community. Even if one "goes" to heaven as an individual, one is not there alone. Again, McDannell and Lang suggest that the idea of a "heavenly city" was a peculiarly medieval notion, but such a substrate can also be found more broadly—from Scripture, through Augustine, to the present (a conception more fully developed in chapter 12). These two different features of participation, then—in nature and in community—distinguish any place of grace from a place of possession and distinguish, furthermore, an experience of any place based on works-righteousness from an experience based on grace. One *can,* in other words, find heaven at the mall, with Mickey, or at home. But many times we do not, because we are blinded from the grace of such places by our desires to possess them.

The way such blinding works is described well in Kristin Hahn's *In Search of Grace: A Religious Outsider's Journey across America's Landscape of Faith*. Hahn grew up in an "a-religious" family, and after schooling, she worked for twelve years as a Hollywood screenwriter. At the age of 29, she set out on a quest that took her across the continent visiting religious communities, searching, as she puts it, for "grace." Hahn explains the absence that inspired her search for presence—or rather for the hyper-presence that required her to find some space. Of growing up with her mom, she recalls: "Like many Americans, purchasing had become our religion, a practice of accumulation we believed would make us feel whole." And as an adult:

> I perfected the art of distraction, doing all the multitasking things we do that keep us from seeing clearly what is right in front of us, or confronting what lurks just below the surface of ourselves. Like many . . . overstimulated, overworked, but adequately fed, clothed, and sheltered Americans—I had developed a host of remedies to quiet my acutely preoccupied mind, soothe my exhaustion and anxiety, and submerge the inconvenient feelings I didn't have time for. I had my aura, chart, palm, and coffee grounds read; I was acupunctured, acupressured, and hypnotically regressed; I was depolarized, magnetized, and analyzed. . . . But I grew tired of hiring people to make me feel better.[45]

That puts well the frantic and possessed character of private theologies, and how they can blind a soul to the public tranquility that follows from experiencing a place of grace.

Two final implications are necessary to draw out. The first is that from a grace-filled perspective, work assumes its rightful place as a human activity. Lutherans call this vocation. Works are the fabric out of which a life is woven, not the bridge over which heaven is achieved. Whatever one does for a living or for a hobby is a "calling" from God inviting participation in life, not a path to get beyond one's body into some never-never land of perfect control. The second implication is more sobering. If there is a heaven, so too is there a hell—as any home owner who has sat through a mortgage closing can surely attest. These hells are, of course, primarily of our own design, and we can tell they are hell because through them we become depressed, anxious, and ashamed. By their fruits you shall know a sacred place. These hells that masquerade as heavens offer us only fragments of community without coherence, a fabric of living torn and tattered in a frantic effort to control life. The Russian writer Fyodor Dostoyevsky put it well: "Hell is the suffering of being unable to love." When we cling to a private love, I have learned, we may end up with no love at all. Love is a gift, not a private possession.

And that is, finally, what Jesus meant when he said that the opposite of greed was to be "rich toward God." In this phrase, there are no outrageous promises of something more, something bigger, or something better. Jesus doesn't promise us some heaven "out there," as a reward for our sacrifice here. No, in fact, the heaven is right here all along, in continuity with the gifts of incredible beauty right in front of us, *in* the ordinary ravens and lilies and dandelions of everyday life. For when we receive all of these "treasures" as gifts, they no longer can possess us. Then they are given to our "hearts" to enjoy and to share with all. When we do so, faith and hope and joy flow through us, rather than being greedily hoarded in the storehouse of the psyche. Being "rich toward God," in short, means being grateful for whatever we have been given, and being freed to work for the common good.

All in all, then, the problem with the sacred places of the mall, Walt Disney World, and the suburban home is that they leave people lonely and ungrateful. They are sacred places whose power depends on private control—and private control is a banal and limited kind of power. When something that deserves to be a public trust, available to all, is turned into a private affair, people suffer. That's the shame of it all. This happens first of all on the level of language—in the ways we clothe God—for our private languages for sacred power can have bad consequences for our personal lives. But theologies also have political implications, and the public shame of private theologies is that they can motivate people to do damage to an entire culture—indeed, to the entire world. We will witness, in the next chapter, just such a process at work in the rise of the Third Reich in Germany. And we may also get a glimpse of how private devotion to the mall, to Walt Disney World, and to big suburban homes may be leading public America down a similar, terrifying path of the violence of banality.

6

God Naked

The Violence of Banality and the Crisis of Affordable Housing in America

> [Then the soldiers] crucified him, and divided his clothes among them, casting lots to decide what each should take.
>
> Mark 15:24

In the ancient world, as in ours, clothes mattered. To be clothed was to be a participant in public life, and the style of one's garments signified one's social status. Prophets, kings, priests, artisans, prostitutes, warriors, and slaves all had distinct colors and fashions of clothing. To be naked was to be nothing—or very nearly such. Only infants were naturally naked, but losers in a battle or political prisoners could also be stripped of their clothes as a way to add to the humiliation of their punishments. To be naked was to be shamed, unnecessary, disgraced—as Jesus was when he was on the cross, while soldiers cast lots for his garments.[1]

Jesus' nakedness on the cross is attested in all four of the Gospels and is one of those tidbits of information that can perplex interpreters. On the one hand, the Romans were well practiced in the art of humiliation, so it is likely that the Gospel reports are historically accurate—and that soldiers did actually barter for this "criminal's" clothing. On the other hand, this detail rather clearly—and in John, explicitly—links Jesus to the lament of Psalm 22, traditionally ascribed to David. This detail might thus serve to "cover" (or perhaps dis-cover) Jesus in the garb of

Israel's greatest king. For our purposes, though, the point holds more theological than historical interest. If God was incarnate in Jesus—as orthodox Christianity has always asserted—then at some point God was stripped bare, and soldiers cast lots for God's clothing. God was naked.

That this nakedness was not natural, but an act of violence, is also theologically significant. Soldiers were supposedly among the civilized members of Roman society. They were provided distinctive uniforms, with tunics, armor, helmets, swords, and shields. Yet the Gospels record that the soldiers who crucified Jesus were so driven by greed that they disregarded the fact of the death whose cause they had become and instead threw their attention to a few pieces of fabric. They played games over his clothing while Jesus suffered.

Now, this is not only a story about ancient times. The first section of this chapter suggests that violence is an ongoing human problem with some specific causes. Developing the theory of Stanford Professor René Girard, I'll suggest further that violence in America is often hidden—not at all the typical crime and punishment that makes it on the nightly news. Indeed, through Girard's influential logic, we will see that violence is hidden especially by religious myths and rituals that "legitimize" the punishment or sacrifice of a victim. Religions create scapegoats, and scapegoats solidify the social order by uniting all against one—either through overt violence or through ignoring victims' suffering, attending instead to some distraction.

The second section of the chapter will then go on to show how this process worked in Nazi Germany, where ordinary citizens became willing executioners in the service of a "sacred place" called the Third Reich. Genocide was "legitimized" in Nazi Germany through fabrics of myths and webs of rituals that were brilliantly analyzed by Hannah Arendt as she observed the trial of Nazi Party leader Adolf Eichmann in the early 1960s. Arendt called what she saw the "banality of evil," but that phrase misses a bit how the banalities made evil not only acceptable but attractive to perpetrators. Hence, we will speak of the violence of banality—a phrase by which we intend to signal both that people can be drawn to violence, and that banality violates people. Violence, suffering, and genocide were rendered banal *as well as* a greedily sought religious duty by the Nazis—just as the soldiers long ago in ancient Rome apparently rendered reasonable their duty to murder a single Jew as they cast lots for his clothing.

In the final section of the chapter, then, we turn toward home. Here we examine the crisis of affordable housing that exposes many to the brutal elements of nature or market in America. The numbers are numbing, so to give them some life I also narrate two stories. One describes the failure of Christians to attend to the suffering of the poor, and how distractions and a single-minded sense of duty can produce violence. Another describes a solution—a way out of the violence of banality through participation in a project that attends to suffering and subverts the numbness and calculating duty of banality. It is a sad fact that among the victims of the crisis of affordable housing in America are children. They are the ones now naked, as Jesus once was, ignored and victimized while we gamble over God's clothing.

The Desire to Acquire

For several years, I have been studying and teaching the complex works of René Girard,[2] whose 1972 volume *Violence and the Sacred* constituted a breakthrough in the history of religions. Briefly, Girard argues that violence stems from a certain way of human desiring and manifests itself in some peculiar forms of social interaction. Violence, for Girard, is not only physical assault but also the entire process that produces or causes aggression—the lies, misunderstandings, misperceptions, and ideologies that *justify* or *mask* the creation of enemies and the violation of others.

Violence stems, Girard argues more specifically, from a particular form of desire, which he usually calls "mimetic desire" or, sometimes, "acquisitive mimesis." These phrases convey in shorthand a simple truth: People learn what is worthwhile in any civilization by imitating others. As children, we act without thinking to try to acquire the same objects and practices as the people around us. This is how we learn language, for instance, and it is also how we learn to grasp objects—such as a toy. To stay with this example, any parent can attest that a child's mimetic desire for a toy—imitated, say, from an older sibling who already possessed it—might produce competition for the object and might lead to violence. According to Girard, though, this childish pattern of "mimetic desire" also carries over into adulthood and, in fact, characterizes much human action. People imitate one another's desires without even thinking about whether those desires are really worth having. Obviously, as more and more people imitate increasingly abstract desires (for land, shelter, sexual partners, prestige, power, and so forth), rivalry escalates. Completely unbridled rivalry—and the violence it might breed—is an obvious threat to any social order, however, and a means to curtail the escalation of mimetic desire must be found.

Here, Girard suggests, religions play the key role. Myths (sacred stories and symbols) and rituals (sacred practices, places, and times) are the key manifestations of religion. Myths and rituals both direct attention *away* from the source and objects of some desires (e.g., food, shelter, community, intimacy, and so forth) and direct attention toward "the sacred," toward substitute objects that can be multiplied and consumed, if not "scapegoated" and "sacrificed," in Girard's favorite terms for the process. Religions thus exist, argues Girard, to *create* and *multiply* desires but then to channel those desires into "suitable" sacred paths or toward suitable scapegoats. Violence is the inevitable, if unfortunate, by-product. Something must be negated, consumed, expunged, sacrificed, or killed, to keep the escalating desire created by religions from producing social chaos. But because religions operate for those within the system as something other than human creations (they are simply "revealed" or "true" or "normal"), the violence inherent in demarcating suitable objects to sacrifice or to consume is hidden, masked, and obscured. Religions "work," in short, because they redirect desire away from the most basic objects of need (over which competition could escalate endlessly) and toward artificial constructs that are expendable and whose consumption or sacrifice unites the many against a few scapegoats. They work, indeed, but they also must be constantly repeated, because they restrain violence *with* violence. Religions are thus both the best hedge against and the fuel that inspires violence. For the first time, perhaps, Girard has given us a way to understand this paradox.

Consequently, Girard's thought has proven remarkably provocative in the academy, inspiring a global organization to study his thought—the Colloquium on Violence and Religion—and producing comparisons of Girard to such pivotal thinkers as Freud and Marx. Most recently, Girard has turned his attention to the Bible, where the warnings of the prophets, especially, and the Gospels and Epistles about Jesus, in particular, often seem to mesh well with his theoretical perspectives, which he developed initially on the basis of classical and medieval literary texts. In any event, among the most famous biblical texts Girard draws upon is one from the first letter to Timothy that rather clearly, in this translation by St. Augustine, highlights the dangers in the desire to acquire:

> Those who wish to become rich fall into temptation and into a snare, and into many foolish and harmful desires, which plunge men into death and destruction. For acquisitiveness is the root of all evils; and those who have this as their aim have strayed away from the faith and have entangled themselves in many sorrows.[3]

This is Girard's point: The desire to acquire can do damage to both individuals and society.

For this very reason, two of the commandments of the Hebrew Decalogue focus on mimetic desire. They prohibit "coveting": "You shall not covet your neighbor's house; you shall not covet your neighbor's wife, or male or female slave, or ox, or donkey, or anything that belongs to your neighbor" (Exod. 20:17). The repetition is significant. By its nature, desire can be imitated by attachment to the "fruits" of desire—the objects whose acquisition confirms the existence of desire. Desire doubles itself. Consequently, the commandments prohibit greed twice. Desire for one's own basic needs—for shelter, intimacy, and productive labor—is affirmed. But imitative desire, coveting, or greed, is prohibited, because it both harms the individual who covets and threatens the peace of the social order.

St. Augustine, with characteristic insight, saw the contradiction inherent in the desire to acquire:

> The only things which evil people count as evil are those which do *not* make people evil; and they are not ashamed that when surrounded by the "good things" which they approve, they *themselves* are evil, who approve those "goods"; and they are more disgusted by a bad house than by a bad life, as if a human's highest good was to have all one's possessions good—except one's self.[4]

The desire to acquire, in other words, leads the self to lose itself—no small accomplishment—as well as to violate another. When one imitates the desires of another, one's own authentic desires wither, get lost, or are distorted. In such circumstances, even the most inhumane behaviors become possible, perhaps even "normal" or "necessary," no matter how brutal and violent. As Girard has argued, under the sway of mimetic desire, as in the thoughtless behavior of a mob, even genocide is possible. When the crowd chooses a scapegoat, slaughter soon follows. Most chilling of all, of course, is when this process is given the sanction of religious authority—when myths and rituals justify as "normal" the depiction of another person or group as scapegoats and then justify their sacrifice for the sake of expedience, or purity, or order.

Many observers, following the logic to this point, will readily jettison all organized religions as violent—and imagine that they will then be righteous. Needless to say, the process through which imitative desire leads to violence is more complex than this, and in modern society the operation of "religion" is more complicated than just membership in an institution. I have tried to clarify the layers of violence through what I call the "violence iceberg," as summarized in the illustration below:

Most people, when they use the word *violence,* use it to refer only to the most overt acts of physical violence, such as street crime. But violence is also produced through

social structures and systems. Some of this violence is legitimized as institutional control. Police, prisons, and the military are all examples. Some systemic violence, however, may be unintended, as in the structures of economic life that perpetuate inequities in education, housing, and health care. People suffer from these inequities as surely as they do from a gunshot. And, finally, as anyone who has experienced a situation of abuse knows, verbal violence can do deep damage to a human being. People suffer when they are described in ways that demean, diminish or destroy, as in racist or sexist stereotypes. And people suffer when they are silenced or ignored. Such demeaning or ignoring is the basic level of violence upon which all of the rest are built. Every specific act of aggression by a human being depends upon a world-view—on language, motives, and metaphors, or the absence of these—that sanction the aggression in any given situation. And among the ways that cultural violence is sanctioned, I have come to believe, is through what some scholars have begun to call "weak" or "thin" religions.[5] Not all religion—as Girard typically argues—but only some forms of religion promote violence.

This construct is controversial. For many years, in order to appear objective, scholars drawn to the scientific study of religion refused to differentiate between constructive and destructive manifestations of religion. Many still do. Needless to say, I'm not one of them. I believe that the material studied by students of religion simply isn't the same as the material studied by, say, geologists, and that therefore a somewhat different method is necessary. I also happen to believe, however, that a differentiation between a strong and a weak manifestation of religion can be made as scientifically as a geologist determines whether a landform is a volcano or a glacial moraine, and with about the same amount of intellectual effort. Weak religion, then, is volcanic. Strong religion is moraine-like. More seriously, in propositions I would be willing to defend: A religion is weak when it depends upon a significant level of illiteracy, ignorance, or self-deception on the part of a devotee; when it manifests in its theology and practice the desire to acquire; and when it involves the devotee in actions that contradict the fundamental tenets of enduring religious traditions, such as love, compassion, grace, and the Golden Rule.

There are, of course, within the enduring religious traditions of the world ample examples of weak religion, both among individuals and as entire movements. Within Christianity, for instance, fundamentalism of the variety practiced by Timothy McVeigh—the bomber of the Murrah Federal Building in Oklahoma City—can be described as a weak version of the faith.[6] McVeigh's peculiar beliefs, shared by many Christian "identity" groups, depended upon an anti-intellectual interpretation of the Bible that imposed upon it all kinds of ignorant "science." Similarly, McVeigh's religion manifested the desire to acquire power—as evident in his scapegoating of the federal government. Finally, he rather obviously managed to justify violence against innocents, including children—in contradiction of the central Christian teaching of love. Within Islam, for another example, militant Islamists such as Osama bin Laden can also be characterized as devotees of a weak religion. Bin Laden's violent faith depended upon an ignorant interpretation of Arab history and a highly selective reading of the Qur'an. It also manifested the desire to acquire, not only in its scapegoating of Jews and Americans but also through the efforts of the Taliban and similar movements to control the behavior of women in the interest of purity. Such a version of Islam, finally, contradicts the intellectual integrity and complexity of a long and rich tradition, and contradicts also the teachings of unity and mercy at the core of the faith. Beyond these two obvious examples, however, are three that seem to me widespread in the United States, with far and away the most victims to their credit. They are, in short, those peculiarly modern religious hybrids that draw the devotion of people to malls, to Mickey, and to the home.

As we have seen in the three previous chapters, the motives that draw people to these typically American sacred places often elude the devotees themselves. People often do not know that what they do at these places has spiritual implications. That's the first mark of a weak religion. Second, as we have also seen, devotion to the mall, to Mickey, and to the suburban home contradicts the fundamental teaching of all traditional religions against greed. The desire to acquire is evident in the interchange between mall developers and consumers, between Disney's CEO and the average pilgrim, and between chemical companies and the typical lawnboy. Everybody in every case is after something; nobody seems grateful for anything. That's the second mark of a weak religion. Finally, as we have also seen, people suffer for their devotion to the mall, to Mickey, and to home. Such dis-ease, if you will, contradicts the foundation of enduring religions, namely that our purpose is to find happiness, to live in peace, and to die after a meaningful life. An obvious question now appears: How can I possibly compare putting herbicide on my lawn with the damage done by Osama bin Laden? Put differently: If weak religions produce dramatic violence, then where are the victims of Mickey Mouse? One last try: If the mall is such a lousy sacred place, then where are the burned-out buildings destroyed by devotion to it? Before we can answer those contemporary questions, though, we need to turn to a historical example of weak religion at work, evident in the twisted effort to make a "sacred place" known as the Third Reich.

The Violence of Banality

Now, it might seem to be a long leap indeed from the green grass of home to the gas chambers of Auschwitz. In fact, however, the route from one to the other is well mapped and, unfortunately, all too well traveled. To support this harsh judgment we will need briefly to turn to Hannah Arendt's classic study on the Nazi mind and culture, entitled *Eichmann in Jerusalem: A Report on the Banality of Evil*. Adolf Eichmann was a midlevel Nazi Party member and an SS officer. He worked in the Hitler regime throughout its time in power, but escaped to Argentina shortly after the war ended, where he lived until 1960. In that year, he was captured and brought to Jerusalem, where he stood trial for his role in the Holocaust. Arendt, at the time a professor of sociology at Wesleyan University, was sent to Jerusalem to report on the trial by the *New Yorker* magazine. *Eichmann in Jerusalem* was the book that she produced to pull her various journalistic reports together. It was first published in 1963.

In this book, Arendt argued, contrary to popular desire and expectation, that Eichmann was not a sadistic and perverse "monster" but rather "terribly and terrifyingly normal."[7] Eichmann "fervently believed in . . . success," wrote Arendt," and success was "the chief standard of 'good society' as he knew it."[8] Eichmann's earliest "success" as a Nazi was to organize the "forced emigration" of Jews from Austria in 1938. He took the job when it was offered to him primarily because he figured it would further his career—a goal most people could understand. And further his career it did, primarily because Eichmann bragged about his "success" in Austria. Bragging, of course, is again hardly a vice unique to Nazis. Even Eichmann's significant role in planning and carrying out the genocide of European Jews—a responsibility given to him after he had been promoted, Arendt described as part of a pattern of "ubiquitous complicity" common throughout Germany.[9] Throughout his defense, Arendt noted, Eichmann refused to acknowledge guilt, even after he reported being physically sickened and "weak-kneed" when he saw the results of his organizational skills firsthand on a visit to the death camps. "This was the way things were," Arendt summarized Eichmann's point of view. "This was the new law of the land, based on the Führer's order; whatever [Eichmann] did he did, as far as he could see, as a law-abiding citizen. He did his *duty*."[10] The motives that moved Eichmann to do what he did, in short, were a little ambition, a tendency to brag, and a strong sense of duty—hardly overt marks of a murderer.

Something had happened in Nazi Germany, Arendt struggled to point out, that turned the consciences of "normal" people away from the customary human taboo against killing and toward the acceptance of genocide. Beyond Eichmann's own willing ignorance of what he was doing, Arendt suggested at least three more causes. First, she argued, the Nazis developed various language strategies to "normalize" killing. One was exaggeration. By appealing to his "duty," for instance, Eichmann appealed to something supposedly "higher" than his person, which made whatever private discomfort he experienced possible to endure. Such exaggeration—again hardly a dramatic vice, but only a little trick with language—helped make even the most horrible acts palatable to the perpetrators. Arendt writes, now extending the pattern beyond one individual: "What stuck in the minds of these men who had become murderers was simply the notion of being involved in something historic, grandiose, unique ("a great task that occurs once in two thousand years"), which must therefore be difficult. . . . 'What horrible things I had to watch in the pursuance of my duties, how heavily the task weighed upon my shoulders!'"[11] Along with exaggeration came euphemism. The systematic gassings and shootings of Jews, gypsies, homosexuals, and others were the "final solution" or "special treatment," and deportation was a "change of residence" or "resettlement." Both linguistic moves—exaggeration and euphemism—are moves characteristic of myth—and of advertising. Myth, again, substitutes for direct description a "sacred language," and advertising, obviously, tries to persuade consumers with words to buy a product to which the words refer. Both can be rigidly enforced by rules of dogma. In Nazi Germany, indeed, the use of the euphemistic terms for murder was as carefully regulated as any dogma. For Eichmann, such dogmatic clichés became the only language he knew. "Officialese became his language," Arendt contends, "because he was genuinely incapable of uttering a single sentence that was not a cliché. . . . The longer one listened to him, the more obvious it became that his inability to speak was closely connected with an inability to *think*, namely, to think from the standpoint of someone else."[12]

Arendt also discovered during Eichmann's trial that along with "language rules," the Nazis developed diversionary practices, or masking rituals, to divert attention from the horror of what they were doing and to create loyalty among the masses. It was all carefully controlled. Thus, on a visit to the death camp Treblinka, Eichmann was surprised to discover that it looked "exactly like an ordinary [train] station anywhere in Germany—the same buildings, signs, clocks, installations; it was a perfect imitation."[13] Inside the camp, too, everything ran according to carefully orchestrated rituals. Eichmann tried to keep his distance. "I kept myself back," he reported about his visit to Treblinka, "as far as I could, I did not draw near to see all that. Still, I saw how a column of naked Jews filed into a large hall to be gassed. There they were killed, as I was told, by something called cyanic acid."[14] Briefly, after this trip, Eichmann tried within the confines of his office to redirect some shipments of Jews away from Treblinka and toward Theresienstadt—the one camp Germans opened to the Red Cross. But within weeks, Eichmann returned to doing his duty without question. The turning point was when he attended a conference with high-ranking Nazi officials, where he wined and dined with them. Afterward, he reported: "I sensed a kind of Pontius Pilate feeling, for I felt free of all guilt." Simple, ordinary rituals, such as eating, drinking, smoking, and observing other Nazis in support of the newly declared "final solution," put to rest whatever pangs of conscience Eichmann may have once had. Arendt summarizes: "The most potent factor in the soothing of his own conscience was the simple fact that he could see no one, no one at all, who actually was against the Final Solution."[15] Having lost his mind in the blur of language rules, Eichmann lost his conscience in the masking rituals and close company of Nazi culture.

The third step by which "normal" Germans slid into genocide was by eliciting the support of some of their victims. At this, apparently, Eichmann was an "expert." Arendt reports: "Wherever Jews lived, there were recognized Jewish leaders, and this leadership, almost without exception, cooperated in one way or another, for one reason or another, with the Nazis."[16] And because Eichmann enlisted Jewish support to help him ship Jews to their death, he could honestly tell himself, and the judges in his trial: "With the killing of Jews I had nothing to do. I never killed a Jew."[17] Of course, he was involved in killing six million, as a key agent in the organization of genocide throughout its operation. But Arendt's point was, and mine is, less to place blame than to understand. And Arendt's point—and here she and Girard are in complete agreement—was that the fall into violence in Nazi Germany was contagious even for the victims, even as it was utterly and completely preventable. She explains: "Evil in the Third Reich had lost the quality by which most people recognize it—the quality of temptation."[18] Had people recognized that they had a choice to make (and a small number continued to make good ones throughout the war), they might have paused before joining in the "ubiquitous complicity" with which the world let the Holocaust happen. Eichmann put it well, describing his own entry into the Nazi party: "[I was] swallowed up . . . against all expectations and without previous decision. It happened so quickly and suddenly."[19] Violence is contagious, the result, primarily, of the mimetic desires that keep one from thinking, and of weak religions that play on one's ignorance, ambition, and ingratitude.

Arendt draws the conclusion, linking Eichmann to the millions like him and shifting, interestingly, from the past tense to the present:

> The trouble with Eichmann was precisely that so many were like him, and that the many were neither perverted nor sadistic, that they were, and still are, terribly and terrifyingly normal. From the viewpoint of our legal institutions and of our moral standards of judgment, this normality was [and is] much more terrifying than all the atrocities put together, for it implied [implies] . . . that this new type of criminal . . . commits his crimes under circumstances that make it well-nigh impossible for him to know or to feel that he is doing wrong.[20]

Lies become truth, illusions become reality, and murder becomes success. This was and is the banality of evil—the fact that temptation is most attractive when it disappears as temptation and becomes, even, virtue. A little ambition, a little bragging, a little sense of duty, a little exaggeration, a little euphemism, a little wine and food, and the victims begin to fall. Eichmann, Arendt was trying to alert us, was more like us than not. He was "an average, 'normal' person," who through a series of apparently small, thoughtless decisions, became so "perfectly incapable of telling right from wrong" that he implicated himself in the murder of over six million people.[21]

Now, what does this have to do with American sacred places? Eichmann and the Nazis generally had developed for themselves a weak religion. "The Third Reich," rather obviously, referred to a place that was to be the sacred ground of an Aryan kingdom. This new sacred place functioned to draw the devotion of millions of ordinary Germans, who then willingly killed and died for it. They did so because through the very mechanisms by which Eichmann was drawn into the regime, it had become "normal" for them to do so. Under the sway of powerful propaganda, and facing suffering of whose reality they were dimly, or starkly, aware, German citizens let their own consciences and, for most of them, their Christianity be violated by a banal new set of language rules and practices. "God" was now dressed in the Nazi state, incarnate in the person of Adolf Hitler, and reinforced by death squads. But such clothing, as tacky and terrible as it was, could only briefly disguise the fact that the living God, the God of Abraham, of Jesus, and of Muhammad, the only God worth worshiping, was—as we saw Elie Wiesel put it so powerfully in chapter 1—hanging on a gallows. In other words, that is the violence of banality: it discovers or strips God naked, forcing us to look, or to avert our eyes in shame. And it is not, alas, a phenomenon observed only in the Germany of 1939–1945.

The Crisis of Affordable Housing in America

There are, in fact, many examples to which I could turn to demonstrate how the violence of banality operates at present in America. The question remains exactly as it was: if weak religions produce such dramatic violence, then where are the victims of Mickey Mouse? Where are the burned-out buildings destroyed by devotion to the mall? Where, to add one last dash of rhetoric, are the six million victims of banal devotion to the suburban home? It is currently fashionable in America to claim victim status, and I do not want to contribute to the blurring of distinctions that leads wealthy Christians in America to imagine themselves as a persecuted minority. The victims of American banality, though, are indeed all around us—suffering far more subtly than in Nazi Germany, but suffering nonetheless. Among those victims are some who live in relative economic and social privilege, whose consciences still fire, but at strange times, and who fail even to see the suffering in the world, or its causes, about which we could actually do some good. And among the victims, most obviously, are the poor. These latter victims of life in modern America are constantly forced to relocate from one expensive shack to another. They have little to eat because they spend more than half of their income on housing costs. And they often wind up behind barbed wire and steel gates in prisons, because we see them as expendable. The crisis of affordable housing in the United States is a convenient place to focus our final reflections on sacred places, for in this crisis the various scapegoats of America's weak religions—the various people we ignore and try to silence—coalesce.

We'll take up the first group of "victims" first. In January of 2001, during my first year of seminary teaching, I accompanied a group of eighteen students on a work trip to Johns Island, South Carolina. We were there as part of the "multicultural" requirements that all seminarians have to fulfill. I was enlisted, without quite knowing what I was getting into, when the usual faculty adviser for the trip went on sabbatical.

For a while, it was unclear whether we had raised enough money for the trip, and I had started to think about alternative "multicultural" experiences for the students. Once it was clear the trip was on, however, I resolved to enjoy it, learn what I could, and do some hard work. My father, who had fled farming out of hatred for its labors, had taught me little about home building or remodeling. I had, however, been given a circular saw by my wife for our first wedding anniversary (she is not much of a romantic), and I had learned over the years to enjoy being a hack carpenter. Indeed, I had learned to like building projects enough that I helped to found a campus chapter of Habitat for Humanity at Valparaiso University and had worked with students to build two houses from the ground up.

Johns Island is one of the "Sea Islands" off the coast of Charleston, inhabited until very recently almost entirely by the descendants of former slaves who spoke a peculiar dialect of English-Creole called Gullah. The novels of Pat Conroy, and particularly *The Water Is Wide*, give a good glimpse of the culture from the not-too-distant past.[22] In any event, we were on the island to assist in the rehabilitation of homes and had brought with us money to pay for supplies, food, and lodging. We would stay for a week.

Being new to the seminary community, I wasn't familiar with most of the students who were with me, and because the itinerary for the trip had been uncertain, we had organized only a few get-acquainted and planning meetings. Still, we arrived in time to watch the Super Bowl as a group, and a good spirit quickly developed. When we were introduced to the variety of projects available to us on Monday morning, I decided quickly that I could handle the rehab of the kitchen of one home, the "Mack" house, named for the family who was living in it. The kitchen needed work; in fact, I had never seen more dire living circumstances. The ten-by-ten-foot kitchen had no running water, one electrical outlet, two small windows, and a floor with large, visibly rotted holes in several spots. On my first walk across the floor, my left leg pushed through the floorboards and found the sand below. The entire house was maybe six hundred square feet, and it was propped up on cinder blocks and leaning badly. The family had raised seven children in it, although now only the husband and wife remained.

Over the next three days, we scraped off numerous layers of tile, ripped up the floorboards, installed some new joists, and laid down a new plywood floor, which we eventually tiled. I was, I discovered to my chagrin, among the most qualified carpenters on the trip. Meanwhile, others at the project were trying to get the well pump outside working, or fixing screens, or adding some wiring, or painting. Another crew had begun work on a second house, but after two days decided that it was too dilapidated to salvage, so they joined us at the Mack home. A third crew was engaged in various odd jobs around the island—wood chopping and delivery, drywalling, and so forth.

By Wednesday night we were all tired, and I had experienced a frustrating day of work. After a nice dinner, though, the students led a beautiful Eucharist service in which everyone was able to speak about the good in their day. As we "shared the peace" with each other prior to communion, the sense of group unity was palpable, and I was no longer tired. After the worship ended, everyone jumped in cars and vans to go to the local bar for a few beers (these were Lutherans, after all) or sodas. It seemed a nice way to unwind, and it helped maintain the group spirit built in worship for a few more hours.

I felt great at work the next day. We made real progress on the Mack house, and I returned to our shelter with a deep sense of joy. Seven of us had talked in my van during the drive home about the contrast between the house lived in by the Macks and the "luxury homes" in the new developments going in across the island. These developments were often named, without any apparent sense of shame, "Plantations." The conversation ranged across theology, politics, economics, land use, psychology, and more. It was for conversations like these that the seminary mandated such a trip by seminarians. We were learning about the structures and systems that created a society in which a family could live in a shack with no running water and holes in the kitchen floor—while others built luxury homes on Plantations whose land had recently been owned by the former slaves.

Shortly after arriving at our place of lodging, however, I was confronted by one of the student leaders, who said to me in an earnest and somewhat menacing voice: "We need to talk." I was filthy, and it was time to eat. I was also anxious that one of us make a trip to the local hardware store to exchange the well pump, which wasn't working, for a stronger one to try out first thing the next morning—our last full day of work. I really wanted to provide the Macks with running water. The student, however, would not be dissuaded. "We *need* to talk," he told me, and I promised him we could do so after our meal. During dinner I sensed a strange tension in the group. Shortly after dinner, I discovered why.

Not everyone had experienced our joy in work that day. Three or four were feeling "left out," either because they had not yet worked at the Mack house or because they had not worked there enough. For the next two hours, I sat and listened to a group of privileged, middle-class white people bicker with one another about what appeared to me to be petty resentments. I was seething with anger. When I finally spoke, I said bluntly that we were missing the point of the whole trip and that I was angry. We were there to work, I said, and whatever work we happened to do, or were capable of doing, we should do with joy. We were privileged, and here we were complaining like plantation owners about *our* "plight" when there were people without running water down the street.

My remarks were, shall we say, not well taken by some in the group. For articulating my anger, especially, I came under attack. People had clearly expected or desired something, and they felt that they weren't getting it, and I was going to hear about it. My anger turned to incredulity. I couldn't believe what I was hearing and seeing. Here we were, in the midst of abject poverty, and people were complaining about what I came to describe, derisively, as a lack of contact with "the natives." I was feeling like our mission trip had turned into a goddamned visit to a zoo (the language is appropriate here if anywhere). After two hours of bickering, it was simply announced (as had been planned) that we would now worship together. I couldn't do it. I sat there—still in my filthy work clothes—and cried. I suppose I should have left. The singing stung my ears, and the Scripture readings and prayers stank with hypocrisy. The warm community of the night before had disintegrated completely in my eyes.

The whole incident was, as I have reflected on it with many of the participants since, a rather dramatic encounter with banality. To the credit of one student in the group, it was described, in fact, as "evil" in the worship that night. We had all blinded ourselves to the suffering around us, both inside and outside the group. By fixating on what we thought we were supposed to accomplish or "get out of" the week—our mimetic desire, if you will—we wound up harming each other. I never did get to talk about the joy I had felt that day or to reiterate some of the conversation we had shared on the drive home. I had been too locked into the "duty" of my righteous cause to acknowledge the pain the students were articulating to me. Others in the group were too locked into the expectations and assumptions they had brought with them to attend to the suffering around them. In any event, we had managed to self-destruct within four days. The last two days of the trip were tense, and we never did get the well pump working. The Macks, however, took everything in stride and seemed happy with a functional kitchen floor, some new electrical outlets, a little fresh paint, and a new front door and screens. When I said to the homeowner, with false bravado (knowing absolutely nothing about well pumps), "We'll get that pump working," he replied with a line whose assertion of dignity, competence, and resignation at my blind arrogance I'll never forget: "Yes," he said, "*we* will." And, eventually, they did.

I tell this story now to illustrate from personal experience, or perhaps through a confession, how our various myths and rituals, our various efforts to justify ourselves and control the realization of our desires, can produce victims. I do not imagine myself as a victim here—I brought on whatever suffering I experienced through my own insensitivity. But I can recognize how other people among us, for complex reasons unique to each person but also consistent across the culture, suffered as victims. Our desires were not the problem, just as the desire for a decent home is not evil. The problem developed when we lost sight of the commonly shared but personally unique desires that led us to make the trip to Johns Island in the first place, and instead, imitated desires (or expectations or assumptions) about what we "thought" (without really thinking) others were experiencing. The suffering followed as surely as the violent words. Each person on the trip at least had to suffer through that two-hour session of mutual condemnation. The work surely suffered. And the Macks' suffering, like the suffering of so many in poverty, went on unabated, as it would no matter how much we had accomplished in a week. We had exhibited the characteristic failing of people in privilege. We had found a way to avoid doing the good we wanted to do and did instead the evil we had hoped to avoid—"victimizing" ourselves in the process and perpetuating the systemic victimization of others. You will know a true spirit, Jesus taught, by what it produces—by its fruits. On this trip, for me, the yield was initially sparse. I have tried to continue to learn from it.

Fortunately, the process of applying people of privilege to social problems can also work the other way around, and we can be freed from our own obsessions to attend to suffering with compassion. As I mentioned earlier, I helped to found at Valparaiso University a campus chapter of Habitat for Humanity. Habitat, as is well known, is a Christian housing ministry dedicated to working with people in need to build simple, decent housing. The overall goal of Habitat is an ambitious one: to eliminate poverty housing from the face of the globe. "No more shacks!" is the rallying cry of Habitat's founder, Millard Fuller, and in twenty-five years the organization he and his wife, Linda, founded has been responsible for the construction of more than one hundred thousand solid, simple homes around the world.[23]

I began to participate in Habitat partly for self-interested reasons. I started the campus chapter as a way to involve undergraduates in "service learning," for which I received a few small grants. I had always encouraged students to take theology to "the streets," but I had lacked one project or organization to which I could send all of my students. So, for convenience as much as anything, I created my own. Once the chapter was up and running, I worked, usually, on Saturdays, often only in the mornings, and attended meetings on Tuesday and Sunday nights. I also required students in one of my upper-division classes to work one to three hours a week with Habitat, on committees, in fund-raising, or at a work site. Most preferred to do less and spent a few days of the semester in meetings or out at the site. It did not consume any of us.

It did, however, connect us with something subversive, freeing, and often filled with joy. Within a little less than a year, the campus chapter was student-led and student-run, largely independent of my administrative skills (which are minimal). Things took off when a few of the most assertive leaders wrote a grant proposal, and to the surprise of us all, we received $17,500, with a promise of the same amount in matching funds. A typical Habitat house, we were told, cost $35,000. So, we built a house over a two-year period. Then we built another, over another two years.

We learned by trial and error. Students hounded city officials for permits, harassed contractors for donations, and "supervised" work days on the construction site when they themselves were only sophomores or juniors who happened to be majoring in engineering. We inscribed two-by-fours with Scripture verses, stuck cement trucks in the mud, played basketball with the partner families in benefit games, laughed over silly jokes, and cried over construction mishaps. One Saturday morning, as I was climbing into the truck of Rick Blossom—the contractor who also volunteered his time each Saturday—I mentioned to him how much I enjoyed our common work. He concurred, and we went on to talk about how the satisfaction from this job was actually enhanced because we didn't get paid. By volunteering, we were able to work for the sheer delight of the labor and for the common good. Because we worked freely, without constraint, we worked happily. We both acknowledged being grateful, not only for what we could "give back" through our work but also for what we gained from it.

In fact, I'm still grateful for the experience. For by the time I left Valpo, a single mom and her son, Jane and Jake, owned a nice three-bedroom ranch home with monthly payments under $300. They had previously been living in an attic apartment with rotted steps and windows and with one electrical outlet, paying $475 a month in rent. And a family of six—Isidro, Janet, and their four children—owned a four-bedroom, two-story house with a big backyard for the children to run in. They had previously lived in a two-bedroom apartment with a rotting bathroom floor. Both Habitat houses were solidly built, with four nails for every one that was required.

Habitat, as is well known, works within the market economy to redistribute resources. Homes are built with volunteer labor and at no profit. The houses are sold to partner families, who help with the construction process, at the market value of the construction supplies, through a no-interest mortgage. Thus, a house that is appraised for $85,000, and that would normally cost a family $900 a month at 9 percent interest and taxes, sells through Habitat for $35,000, which at 0 percent interest costs a family under $300 a month. A family who had lived in poverty housing now has a home they helped to build, which they own, and on which they pay taxes. One of Habitat's mottos, "love in action," demonstrates how capitalism can be made cooperative. Within a microcosm, the work of Habitat is truly subversive. The very agencies that usually profit from the housing market—real estate brokers, contractors, banks, and building supply companies—must be persuaded to undercut their own profits in the interest of the public good. Fuller calls this subversive system "the economics of Jesus." It takes the pyramid scheme—one of the grossest forms of capitalist acquisitiveness—and turns it into a Christian ministry. For the monthly mortgage payments of Habitat homeowners go into a revolving "fund for humanity," which is then used to purchase more land and supplies. The more homes Habitat builds, the more homes Habitat can build.

The history and functioning of Habitat is remarkable, perhaps the greatest Christian grassroots movement since the civil rights era. Habitat's story is even more astonishing when the origins of the movement are understood. It began from failure, out of a crisis in "the American dream." Millard Fuller was, in his first career, a lawyer. He founded a direct-mail business and made millions. He owned several huge homes, luxury cars, thousands of acres of real estate, horses, and a high-powered career. And then one night in 1965 his wife, Linda, announced to him that she no longer loved him, that she had been having an extramarital affair, and that she was leaving him. Fuller agonized. He was, in the words of the official historian of Habitat, "the image of failure dressed up as success."[24] Eventually, the Fullers met in New York City and reconciled, with one condition: they would give up their money and start a new life. They joined a Christian community—Koinonia Farm, near Americus, Georgia. There the idea that became Habitat for Humanity in 1976 sprouted. The Fullers now live in a modest home in Americus, and Millard and Linda—while traveling around the globe speaking on behalf of affordable housing—have stayed married, raised their three children, and now enjoy grandchildren as well. He writes: "Our physical needs are being met, and our greatest joy is in helping others meet their basic needs rather than piling up more and more for ourselves. We think it is a better way to live."[25]

Indeed it is, and when more follow their example, if not in radical life change at least in restraint, the crisis of affordable housing in the U.S. will end. Fuller explains:

> One of the big impediments to solving the problem [of poverty housing] is that too few talented and wealthy people have a developed "theology of enough." They keep striving, struggling, and scrambling for more and more things for themselves and are too short-sighted and immature spiritually to see the futility of that type of grasping lifestyle. . . . The only truly safe investment one can make in life is what is given away. . . . True riches come from a life of service. There are sufficient resources in the

world for the needs of everybody, but not enough for the greed of even a significant minority.[26]

Greed is the root of the violence of banality.

That the housing crisis produces victims is a reality for anyone with eyes to see. People like the Macks—families—are the victims of corporate and individual greed as they inhabit rotting apartments, leaning shacks, wind-swept trailers, and flimsy cardboard boxes all over the richest nation on earth. Their number can only be estimated. Harvard University's Joint Center for Housing Studies reported in "The State of the Nation's Housing, 2000" that roughly 5.4 million low-income renters and 4.3 million homeowners paid more than 50 percent of their incomes to cover housing costs. At the same time, the number of homes available to very poor households fell by 8.6 percent over three years, while the number of units for extremely poor households—those with incomes less than 30 percent of area median—dropped by a rate of 16 percent. Public and subsidized housing, similarly, is vanishing across America. Some 1.3 million citizens—half of whom are families with children, and another third of whom are elderly—live in public housing. Nevertheless, at the end of 1999 over 27,600 public housing units had been torn down, and only 7,273 units had been built or rehabbed. It is impossible, of course, to count the number of homeless, since the number varies from day to day. But at least two million people, by a modest estimate, faced homelessness at some time in 1999. Their average age, according to some sources, was nine.[27]

What do these numbing numbers tell us? My rough math skills put the number of people victimized by the housing crisis in contemporary America at roughly thirteen million, over twice the number of victims of the Holocaust. That does not take into account, of course, the numbers in prison or the numbers dying because of lack of health care. The poor die young. They daily face toxins of the biological or social variety. We may not build gas chambers, but we do let trash incinerators and chemical plants locate in their neighborhoods, which kill them just as surely.[28] We may not gun down the poor, but we let them gun down each other, and then we imprison behind barbed wire those who try to escape through the only market they see open to them—the drug trade that fuels middle- and upper-class habits. The crisis of affordable housing in America, in other words, overlaps and interweaves with the other social problems facing American culture—in economics, in health care, and in violence. And all of these crises connect with our banal desires for commodities, for spectacle, and for luxury. Through the weak, mimetic faiths of the civil religion, the market, and the domestic sphere, we create scapegoats who suffer on our behalf, while we cast lots for God's clothing, distancing ourselves from our neighbor in need, pausing only occasionally to gaze on the suffering. This is what some scholars call "the pornography of suffering."[29] I call it God naked, discovered in a homeless child.

So, if you really need to take that unnecessary trip to the mall, or to Walt Disney World, or to the local ChemLawn distributor, then go ahead, but I'm not going with you. I'll resist at least those temptations, now that I can see them as such. I'm sure there are plenty of others to which I'll succumb. I also do not have a million, like the Fullers do, to give away to start a ministry, and you probably don't either. But we can all gain greater awareness into the way we live, and why, and such awareness is the beginning of a confession—like the one the Fullers had to face—and out of which can come a better, more grateful way to live. That's been the goal of part 1. I know it has not always been pleasant. But unexamined attachments, couched in language, have driven many of us into patterns of banal living that damage us and others. It's hard to say that gracefully.

Fortunately, there are also other religious paths out there that do not lead us thoughtlessly to imitate our neighbor's desires and into complicity with violence. And, most of all, we are fortunate that we do not live in a society in which death squads will force us to clothe God in weak ways. We can make choices about such things. Indeed, as I shall try to show in part 2, we can find delight, compassion, and solutions for our suffering when we take comfort in a God clothed not in commodities, spectacles, or success, but in the more modest gifts of life that we too often take for granted—in water, light, earth, trees, bodies, and cities.

Part 2

God's Clothing

7

Living Waters

"We have not taken enough account of the nature images in the Bible."

Lutheran theologian Joseph Sittler, *Gravity and Grace*

I am haunted by waters." Norman Maclean saved those words for the last line of *A River Runs through It*, but in the film Robert Redford moved them up to the beginning, because they offer the theme of the whole: "Eventually, all things merge into one, and a river runs through it. The river was cut by the world's great flood and runs over rocks from the basement of time. On some of the rocks are timeless raindrops. Under the rocks are the words, and the words are theirs. I am haunted by waters."[1]

I know what he means. When I was nineteen, I worked at a boys camp in North Carolina for the summer. It was a beautiful place—just south of Asheville, with a mountain lake all its own, streams running here and there, and tall pines and birches stretching to the high, blue sky. On one of my days off, I decided with a friend, Dave, to hike up nearby Looking Glass Rock—a granite outcropping of about 3,900 feet in the Pisgah National Forest.

A river runs through the Pisgah and around Looking Glass Rock. At the time, the only way to access the steep trail to the summit was to cross a fast-moving torrent that rushed down off the mountain. And the only way to cross this river was on a cable bridge—two thick steel cables strung across the stream, one for your feet and one for your hands—that were anchored into trees on either side of the river's banks. As we inched across the cables, the river rushed by well below our feet.

We hiked for maybe twenty minutes, until arriving at a good clearing in the woods at the base of the mountain, where we set up camp. We would undertake the big ascent in the morning. The clearing was about twenty-five feet from a little bubbling brook, crystal clear and ice cold, into which we wedged the steaks we had brought for dinner and a six-pack of beer—minus a can apiece. We stretched the tarp we had brought with us between two trees and settled under it. It was about four o'clock, and as we popped open a beer and started to talk, it began to rain.

Now, Dave could ramble, not that I've ever had trouble carrying a conversation, so he and I went on about God, our loves, and our futures, without paying much attention to the rain that continued to fall—cascade, actually—around us. We drank our beers slowly, and when I finished mine I decided to make a run for the little creek to grab another. As I left the shelter of the tarp, I noticed that there were little creeks running all around me. And when I reached the spot where we had lodged the beer and steaks, they were nowhere to be found. In fact, the "little creek"—it had been shin-deep—was now running in a river that would have been up past my waist had I decided to wade into it. Given the speed it was moving, and the slipperiness of the mud and rocks around me, however, I would not have chosen to do that.

I ran back to Dave and reported breathlessly, "C'mon, man. The beer's gone! We've got to get out of here!" He nodded as he looked around. But before we left, Dave snapped a picture, holding a Kodak Instamatic out at arm's length, as the two of us huddled under the tarp. My eyes may not have shown it, but I was terrified.

Then we ran—or more accurately slipped—down the trail, which was itself a little creek now, toward the river. The tarp we dragged behind us, like a tail; it caught between Dave's legs, and he fell hard. He winced and limped, but we felt compelled to run—everything else around us seemed to be moving fast, so we followed the flow. We had no thought of climbing Looking Glass Rock. We ran for our lives, as we raced against the flash flood we were sure was coming, against the storm raging all around us, and against whatever spirit of the place we had offended.

When we finally made it to the cable bridge over the river, the grey, swirling, and roaring water lapped at our feet as we inched across. We never did climb Looking Glass Rock. In fact, I recently learned that the road to the trail we were on has often been closed due to flash floods. When I told this story to my children one night, as we sat at the table together after dinner, Rheanne, four years old, said: "Daddy, I don't want to go to that place."

Waters can haunt us, then, but places with water also draw us irresistibly. After all, we need water. There is no substitute for it. The thesaurus lists no other way to say it. Our bodies are mostly water, as is the surface of the earth. We drink water, wash with water, clean with water, bathe in water, swim in water, sweat water, and are born in water. Water takes endless shapes and forms. "There is mist, dew, droplet, rain, torrent; rivulet, brook, creek, river, whirlpool; there is lake and most of all the boundless depths of the sea. . . . Water produces power, cleanliness, life; it can be evaporated, frozen, changed."[2] Water teems with life.

Hence, religious folk widely incorporate waters as sacred places in their symbolic systems. There are sacred rivers, like the liquid *shakti,* or female energy, of the Ganges, or the faithful wife Oya, otherwise known as the River Niger. There are sacred lakes, like Texcoco, "our mother great water" to the Aztecs, and on whose Western shore was built the imperial city of Tenochtitlán. And there are the waters of creation. In Africa, Asia, the Americas, Europe, and the Middle East, are found stories of waters that preceded humans, preceded life, and from which life came.[3] The Bible practically drips. Water or "waters" appear 694 times in 620 verses, as seas, rivers, and streams, in wells, cisterns, jars, bodies, and more.

It is therefore not surprising that Christians have, in practice if not in theology, made wide use of water. Thus, in Roman Catholicism, ordinary water becomes holy water in three forms: as part of Sunday Mass, as used in baptism, and for consecrating churches. Similarly in the Eastern Orthodox churches, ordinary water is sacramentally transformed into holy water, especially at a river on Epiphany Sunday, and can be utilized for any number of purposes—including consecrating one's home.[4] And Christians of all varieties make pilgrimages—in name or in effect—to the waters of Lourdes, to sacred wells, or at least to their neighborhood beaches or backyard hot tubs.[5] If Protestants like me have removed water from our liturgies and churches, with the exception of baptism, we have not ceased to behave recreationally in ways that indicate our devotion to and fascination with waters.

Theologically speaking, at last, I will develop three liquid fashions for God. First, waters represent our biological origin and a sensual delight—a collective and personal Eden, suggesting that a God clothed in water is a generative and delightful source. Second, from a God clothed in living water we can learn to dissolve our petty attachments in the flow of the infinite or a flood of justice and change. And, finally, a God who wears a fabric of living water promises a rebirth of compassion, like a river flowing through us, uniting all and baptizing everything in its path. As God's clothing, living water reveals life flowing between cosmos and chaos, hinting at delight, threatening dissolution, and orienting us to the hope of eternal life. If, then, we take water as a basic metaphor for God's presence, God is source and joy, God is just—in the sense of desiring fulfillment for all—and God is One.

The Waters of Eden

As narrated in Tanakh, which Christians call the Old Testament, creation is a very wet process. The very first verses of Genesis describe not creation from nothing, but creation from deep (the Hebrew word is *tehom*) waters: "In the beginning when God created the heavens and the earth, the earth was a formless void and darkness covered the face of the deep, while a wind from God swept over the face of the waters"(Gen. 1:1–2). It is not at all surprising that the Hebrews would imagine creation in this way, because watery cosmogonies were common throughout their neighbors in the ancient Near East. For instance, in five different creation stories from ancient Sumeria, Enki—who was the personification of underground springwater—"fertilizes earth by means of rivers and canals, causing life (including human life and cities) to rise along their banks." Enki was in fact a rather lusty deity. He created through sexual intercourse—a mythic pattern not uncommon in the history of religions. Along with Sumeria, Egypt also had a watery creation tale. According to one scholar, "the time before creation was imagined [by Egyptians] as one of limitless waters (personified as Nun), the primeval flood, and total darkness."[6] Finally, in the Babylonian *Enuma Elish,* often called "the standard Mesopotamian creation account," creation begins with the mingling of fresh waters, personified as Apsu, with salt waters, personified as Tiamat."[7]

Like their neighbors, then, the people of Israel imagined creation beginning in water. They also borrowed another plotline from their neighbors: in some texts, the waters represent chaos that God must defeat in a battle. Thus in Psalm 74, God is remembered for vanquishing the waters and the monsters they contain:

> Yet God my King is from of old,
> working salvation in the earth.
> You divided the sea by your might;
> you broke the heads of the dragons in the waters.
> You crushed the heads of Leviathan. . . .
>
> 12–14a

The same violent theme is found in Psalm 104, a very early Hebrew creation account:

> At your rebuke [the waters] flee;
> at the sound of your thunder they take to flight. . . .
> You set a boundary that they may not pass,
> so that they might not again cover the earth.
>
> 7, 9

In these biblical visions of creation, God orders the cosmos by vanquishing the primordial waters; creation is order over chaos. The waters must be kept in their place.

But of course the experience of the Jews has not been as neat and tidy as these accounts relate. God did not always vanquish enemies. And a watery chaos might be preferable to an oppressive order. Thus, in the two creation accounts from Genesis, it is not the opposition between land and water, or a conflict between order and chaos, but their symbiosis and alternation that is the primary theme. In the first creation story, of Genesis 1, God (here named Elohim) simply arranges the waters, like a person tries on clothing.[8] The process is a gentle one, accomplished by words, not war. It reads:

> And God said, "Let there be a dome in the midst of the waters, and let it separate the waters from the waters." So God made the dome and separated the waters that were under the dome from the waters that were above the dome. And it was so. God called the dome Sky. And there was evening and there was morning, the second day.
>
> And God said, "Let the waters under the sky be gathered together into one place, and let the dry land appear." And it was so.
>
> vv. 6–9

Here, in the featured first poetic account of creation, God and the waters of chaos are closely related. Surely there is no violence in the story. God simply gathers the waters together, assembling them, gently speaking into existence their formation.

In the second Genesis creation account, which begins at 2:4, the primeval waters are in the form of a "stream that would rise from the earth, and water the whole face of the ground." From this primeval soup, God (here named Yahweh) immediately creates humanity (not, as in Genesis 1, as the culmination of a six-day process) and places the earthling (which is approximately what "Adam" means) into a garden. And the garden, significantly, is described by its relation to waters:

> A river flows out of Eden to water the garden, and from there it divides and becomes four branches. The name of the first is Pishon; it is the one that flows around the whole land of Havilah, where there is gold. . . . The name of the second river is Gihon; it is the one that flows around the whole land of Cush. The name of the third river is Tigris, which flows east of Assyria. And the fourth river is the Euphrates.
>
> vv. 10–14

These rivers are described dispassionately; they do not contain a hint of threat because of sea monsters, lusty gods, or chaos. They are simply the waters of Eden—the waters of the place of delight, which is roughly what the word *Eden* means.[9]

So, the two prominent creation accounts at the beginning of Genesis significantly temper the association of waters with evil chaos that was common in the ancient Near East. This is in fact the genius of the Hebrew texts. Waters do not personify gods, like the lust-driven Enki. Waters therefore do not need to be worshiped through some sort of ritual repetition of the dripping cosmogony—as apparently happened in some ancient Near Eastern temple prostitution cults. But waters are *close* to God and even participate in the very process of creation itself. If temple prostitution is unnecessary, then neither is it necessary to *avoid* the waters of sex in order to be holy. What Catherine Keller has cleverly called "tehomophobia," or "the fear of the deep," has been a persistent and unfortunate feature of many Christian theologies.[10] And surely there is no warrant in the creation stories for humans to dominate, pollute, or destroy the waters. Waters are our origin, and they surely can bring chaos, but the mastery of God in creation in no way legitimizes conquest of them. In fact, the waters of creation provide people with orient in Eden, and God arranges them with care in creation by gathering them together in rivers, lakes, streams, and so forth, where an ordered chaos, or a soluble solidity, develops.

Not surprisingly, then, given this realistic assessment of our origins and the place of waters in them, the Hebrew Bible often celebrates waters and remembers them for the delight they can bring to human beings. This should hardly be surprising when it is recalled that the people of Israel lived in a more or less desert climate. Archaeological evidence provides ample testimony to the creativity that the peoples of the ancient Near East used to collect and preserve waters—pots, jars, pitchers, flasks, cisterns, fountains, and wells are among the common finds of biblical archaeologists. But the *theological* significance of the Bible's high regard for water has hardly been explored.[11] The sharing of water was a key, if not essential, expression of hospitality in the biblical world.[12] A gift of water was like the gift of life itself.

Truly, manifold associations of water—including the erotic—are celebrated in the Hebrew Bible. There is an entire book, in fact, to celebrate the watery chaos that is human lovemaking. Thus, the male figure in the Song of Songs, traditionally Solomon, describes his lover as "a fountain," whose "channel is an orchard of pomegranates, with all choicest fruits . . . a garden fountain, a well of living water, and flowing streams from Lebanon."

His lover replies:

> Awake, O north wind, and come, O south wind!
> Blow upon my garden, that its fragrance may be wafted abroad.
> Let my beloved come to his garden, and eat its choicest fruits.

And the man responds:

> I come to my garden, my sister, my bride;
> I gather my myrrh with my spice,
> I eat my honeycomb with my honey,
> I drink my wine with my milk.
> Eat, friends, drink, and be drunk with love.
>
> 4:12–5:1

Here, waters—streams of Lebanon, a garden fountain, living waters—merge with wine and honey in a sweet liquidity that is celebrated with all the passion—even unto drunkenness—that humans can muster. My students, less attuned to poetry than literal description, took to calling this text "The Oral Sex Song."

In any event, the Hebrew Bible celebrates waters as hinting at our origins and intimating delight. We, of course, still experience this conjunction today, not only in the waters of sex but also in the experience of birthing. None of us can be present at the creation of the world. We can, however, understand why the writers of the

Hebrew Bible valued water in the way they do, when we reflect on the experience of giving birth; the creation of new human life. God is clothed as living water in the birth of a child.

Each of our children was born under unusual circumstances. Eventually, I'll tell all three stories, but Justin, now 16, was the firstborn, and his arrival was an experience I will never forget. On September 1, 1985, two and a half months before she was due, Lisa went into the hospital in labor. Various treatments alone could not get her contractions stopped, so for the next six weeks she was flat on her back at Michael Reese Hospital on Chicago's south side. I was in my second year of graduate school at the University of Chicago Divinity School and had no income to speak of. With the help of a wonderful church (Ascension Lutheran in Riverside), understanding faculty, a part-time job I took to make ends meet, supportive friends and family, and eventually public aid, we got by.

On Monday, October 17, the morning after she had been released from the hospital, I received a call in Hyde Park, where I was working. "Jon," Lisa said, "my water broke. This is it." It was still a month early, but I climbed into our 1973 Plymouth Duster and rattled up the Dan Ryan and out the Stevenson Expressway to MacNeal Hospital in Berwyn.

When I arrived, the medical staff asked me if I wanted to go into the delivery room. I replied with an enthusiastic, "Sure!" In fact, I wasn't quite sure what I was agreeing to do, since we had been unable to complete a "birthing" class for which we had registered prior to Lisa's hospitalization. Lisa's labor was to prove difficult. It lasted six hours, and by the end of it I was exhausted, despite the fact that my contribution—typical for males in such a situation—was to sit next to Lisa and offer moral support. I had never experienced such chaos.

I remember very vividly, near the end, the doctor calling, "Get me an internal monitor!" I heard fear in his voice and could only sit and listen, feeling rising anxiety myself, as with each contraction the beeps indicating Justin's heartbeat grew farther apart and fainter. "We've got to get him," I heard the doctor say, although by this time I was in a fog, holding Lisa's hand, sweating, and breathing hard. The monitor's beeps grew even fainter. I was terrified. And then all of a sudden there he was, all five pounds and ten ounces of him, with the umbilical cord wrapped around his neck, bruised and battered, slippery and wet but alive and breathing and HERE!

I know I gasped when I first saw him, and exhaled forcibly. I half-laughed and half-cried, overcome with joy and relief. The waters welled up in my eyes. I had never before been so frightened and never before felt such exultation.

For the longest time, after they whisked Justin away to the nursery, I sat on the stool next to the delivery table and held Lisa's hand. I couldn't move. I was in shock, I'm sure, and Lisa had drifted off from medication shortly after the birth. For a long time I simply sat there in silence, holding her hand, with the blood and water all around me.

Eventually, a nurse woke me from my reverie. She stood in the door of the delivery room and said, "Mr. Pahl, you can go see your son now." My son. Slowly, unsteadily, I slid off the stool and followed her down a long corridor.

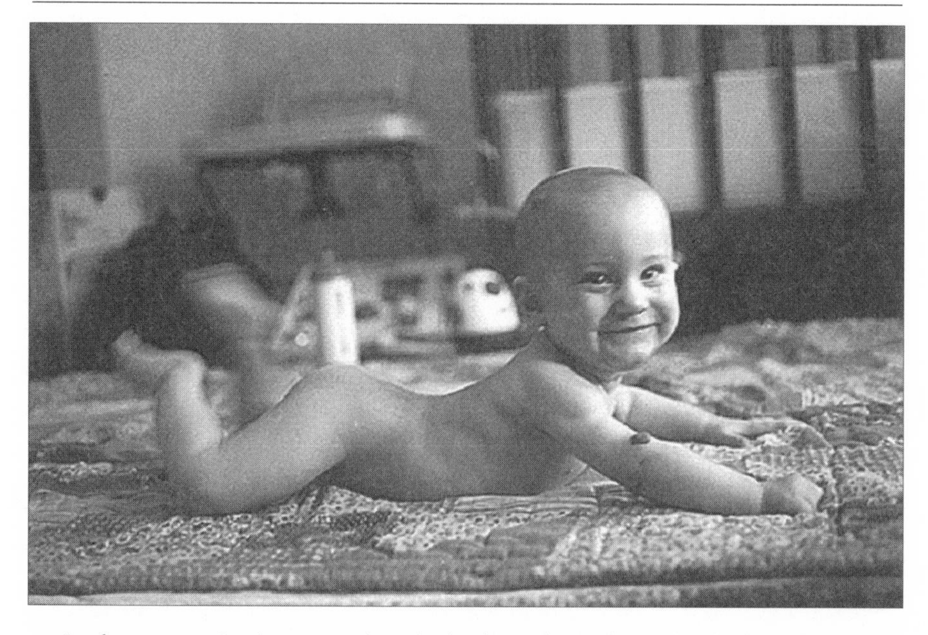

In the nursery, Justin was under a little clear plastic thing that looked like a cake pan. "It helps him breathe," the nurse told me. I bent down to his level, and looked through the side of the layette. He was awake! Little blue eyes met mine, and we stared at one another for minutes that could have stretched into days as far as I was concerned. "It's very unusual for them to be awake," the nurse told me. I barely heard her. Justin and I just kept staring at each other, blinking through my tears and through his watery new eyes, seeing the world anew, in the first hour of birth, a new creation, from water, through the chaos, and alive. My son.

This experience of new life has helped me to understand why the biblical writers chose to clothe God in waters and how waters signify the gracious source of all life. In fact, this fabric for the divine is among the many stunning metaphors used by the author of the Gospel of John to depict Jesus. The scene is early in his ministry, and Jesus is in the Samaritan city of Sychar, sitting by a well—no small aquatic symbol itself. He's tired after walking all morning. It's about noon. The narrative continues:

> A Samaritan woman came to draw water, and Jesus said to her, "Give me a drink." (His disciples had gone to the city to buy food.) The Samaritan woman said to him, "How is it that you, a Jew, ask a drink of me, a woman of Samaria?" (Jews do not share things in common with Samaritans.) Jesus answered her, "If you knew the gift of God, and who it is that is saying to you, 'Give me a drink,' you would have asked him, and he would have given you living water." The woman said to him, "Sir, you have no bucket, and the well is deep. Where do you get that living water? Are you greater than our ancestor Jacob, who gave us the well, and with his sons and his flocks drank from it?" Jesus said to her, "Everyone who drinks of this water will be thirsty again, but those who drink of the water that I will give them will never be thirsty. The water

> that I will give will become in them a spring of water gushing up to eternal life."The woman said to him,"Sir, give me this water, so that I may never be thirsty or have to keep coming here to draw water."
>
> John 4:7–15

The dialogue goes on for several more verses, making it the longest single conversation between Jesus and an individual in the Scriptures. It is an important and provocative narrative, with many layers of meaning.

For our purposes, however, the key is its water-language. Drawing upon the imagery of the Song of Songs, the author of John here depicts Jesus engaged in a teasing erotic conversation with a woman at a well. To John's audience, the erotic elements in this narrative would have been obvious and shocking. Rabbis were not to talk with *any* women in public, and this woman was at the well around noon because she was unwelcome among the respectable women, who would have drawn their water in the cool of the early morning. Indeed, we learn later in the story, she had been married five times and was presently living with a man to whom she was not married. There's an erotic undertone to the story that would not have been missed by John's intended readers.

And then there is Jesus' promise—to give a woman "living water;" a "spring of water" that would gush up in her "to eternal life." This imagery is, again, clearly drawn from the Song of Songs, but what does it mean in this context? A little later in the Gospel, Jesus uses similar imagery to describe believers: "Let anyone who is thirsty come to me," he proclaims, "and let the one who believes in me drink. As the scripture has said, 'Out of the believer's heart shall flow rivers of living water'" (7: 37–38). This is a stunning assertion: living water flows from a person. But the author of John has an even more specific connection to make. Throughout the Gospel of John, Jesus commits the "sin" of blasphemy by identifying himself in "I am" phrases that should properly be used only of God. "I am the bread of life," Jesus proclaims, identifying himself with the gift of manna from heaven given to the people of Israel as they wandered in the wilderness (6:35). "I am the way, and the truth, and the life," Jesus proclaims at another point (14:6), in a rich, and scandalous, triad. And finally, "I am the good shepherd," Jesus proclaims, in a metaphor drawn from a description of the Lord in Psalm 23 (10:11). And thus, it is significant that at the end of his dialogue with the woman at the well, she suggests that only the Messiah could fulfill the promises Jesus has made. He replies, simply: "I am he, the one who is speaking to you" (4:26). In other words, Jesus is *himself* the gift of living water—as the rest of the Gospel, and especially the crucifixion, makes clear. Jesus is the living water—the delight of life, the joy of desiring for the woman at the well, and for all believers.

These associations in the Gospel of John constitute what scholars have come to call a "high" christology, where Jesus is identified with metaphors that properly refer to God. That such associations were blasphemous in John's context should not be missed. Indeed, in the very first verses of the Gospel, John mixes a dizzying blend of metaphors to identify Jesus not only as Messiah, but as one with the Creator of the universe. Jesus was there right along with the primeval waters. Jesus is *tehom,* the deep river of life flowing from a believing heart, and Jesus is the living water that gushes up to delight a person with eternal life.

These associations have become conventional in many Christian circles; their eye-opening value has often been effaced by recurrent usage. But they do identify a shocking truth. The very fabric of the divine is found in waters. Our biological source is also our spiritual delight. After all, water constitutes three-fourths of our bodies and nearly the same proportion of the earth's surface. All the living participate in the living waters. We share in the same source and can experience the same delight. I know that was true of my experience of Justin's birth, and I suspect that such an experience of delight in the living waters of another is about as close as any of us can get to the place of Eden.

The Flood of Justice

My experience of Justin's birth was a delight, but it was also terrifying, and any theology that clothes God in waters must account for that terror. Between the ages of about twenty and twenty-three, I had a recurring nightmare. I was in a car, driving fast at night on an unfamiliar country highway. It was raining. I would come over the crest of a hill and see two yellow, blinking lights in the distance. I would also see a reflection in front of me in the dark; lights shimmering back at me, undifferentiated and uncertain in their meaning. As I came closer to the warning lights, I would see a bridge—one of those old steel-frame bridges that look as if they're about to let go of the road and wash away downstream at any time. Trees lined the roadway, there was no moon and no streetlight, and as I sped along, my headlights bounced off the wet blacktop; in fact, everything seemed a black glass surface reflecting light here and there in weird ways. But I kept cruising along, sometimes even speeding up, until I noticed that the warning lights were in front of the bridge and were attached to barriers indicating that the bridge was out and the river had risen high. "High waters," read the sign, illuminated in orange and white, and then I saw the swirling, eddying flow, up over the banks of the river, submerging trees, crawling toward me. Too late, I would apply the brakes and start to skid, slipping toward the swirling waters that had risen way over the banks, across the road, blocking my path and threatening in a second to engulf me in their slow but angry flow.

I started having these dreams *after* my experience at Looking Glass Rock, so I think I understand their genesis. But there was another set of complex events that contributed to their recurring. Just before going to work at the camp in North Carolina, I received at my home in Wisconsin a letter from a girl I had dated in college. We had fallen in love, and the letter was long. Near the end of it, she wrote: "You had an amazing year. You got straight A's. You played lead alto in the jazz band. Your team won the freshman intramural tournament in basketball. You were in Hamlet. You pledged a fraternity. And you got me pregnant."

I thought that last line was a joke—probability was with me—so I didn't panic. I wrote back, not too anxious, but wanting to verify the fact. I told no one. Within a day, though, I noticed that things were really tense around the house, especially in my relations with my parents, and I wasn't clear why. The anxiety level kept rising, until one night I blurted out after dinner: "What's going on around here?" The facts then came out: my parents had found out about my premarital sexual experimentation.

For the next six hours, at least, I sat in our family room with my mother and father and we argued, talked, yelled, and cried. "We didn't raise you like that!" is one line that I remember hearing. Most generally, though, I recall, if not the actual words, then the sentiment, "What if she IS pregnant? What will everyone think?"

I was a first child, and I had always trusted my parents—they were and are wonderful people. I could never keep much from them, and I was a lousy liar, in part because I had had little reason to practice the art. It wasn't that I was perfect—far from it in fact—but I liked approval and thereby generally followed conventions. My parents also took pride in my accomplishments and successes, and I was happy to share them with them. But that night my trust in the trustworthiness of the world took a shaking. I experienced accusation and condemnation that threatened to overwhelm me.

That talk took its toll. By the end of the summer, I had broken up with my girlfriend (she wasn't pregnant—it was all a joke) and taken a vow of celibacy. The next semester at college I took a class, "Marriage, Sex, and the Family," and wrote a paper entitled "The Call to Commitment," arguing from the biblical record for chastity until marriage. And I dated only women who were "safe," that is, who shared my now reinvigorated commitment to chastity prior to marriage. For a year, it worked.

And then, one night during the fall of my junior year, I met a beautiful young woman, and we danced, talked, and enjoyed each other's company until about two in the morning, when I walked her home. The next night we met again and sat quietly before a fireplace. She told me about herself. I told her about what my parents had done. It was the first time I had told anyone. We cried together. And we kissed. After that, we spent every night for the next week together, and one night, alone in my room, we made love. After, I cried. She didn't understand, and I didn't understand, but from that point on my vow was over. We fell in love, so I thought, moved in together the next year, even got engaged, although we fought more or less constantly and were plagued by jealousy. It lasted a little over a year, and by the time it ended I was a mental mess. I barely graduated from college, took two F's my senior year, and spent as much time as possible tranquilized. And that's when the dreams began. They did not end until three years later, after I had met my wife, Lisa, and we, together with a psychiatrist, reenacted the scene from that night in my family room, in which I had been engulfed in a flood of "justice."

In the Hebrew Bible, waters often symbolize danger—and especially the threats of violence and infidelity. Perhaps the most famous water story in the world, in fact, is the flood of justice in Genesis 6–8, involving Noah, his family, animals, and an ark. As with the creation accounts, this story was borrowed by the people of Israel from their neighbors. At least three accounts of a world flood are found in Mesopotamian texts. But the Hebrews turned their neighbors' myth into a theological and moral tale: "Now the earth was corrupt in God's sight, and the earth was filled with violence. And God saw that the earth was corrupt; for all flesh had corrupted its ways upon the earth. And God said to Noah, 'I have determined to make an end of all flesh, for the earth is filled with violence because of them; now I am going to destroy them along with the earth'" (6:11–13). After commanding Noah to build an ark for his family and two of each animal, the Lord causes the waters to rise until the entire earth is flooded, and everything—birds, domestic animals, wild animals, all swarming creatures, and all human beings—die (6:11–7:24).

This is a terrifying tale. It is also a true story—although not in the sense that we have to try to figure out how there might have been enough water in the world to flood the entire earth. The truth of Noah's story does not depend on some kind of superstitious belief in God's power to control nature—as if we had to drop everything we know about meteorology, geology, and geography at the theological door. Rather, the flood account is a true story because it reveals the way our own violence, desires, ambitions, and limited attachments will destroy us. That point is abundantly clear from the previous passage: It is *violence* that is the corruption that causes chaos. There is a logic to the tale that reveals how the waters of justice will roll down as the consequence of our own attachment to limited aims, to private possessions, rather than to the God clothed in living waters, in whose image we are made.

Thus the story of Noah ends with a covenant—a new creation—that entails people's commitment to law, not as a set of rules, but as a way that brings fulfillment. In the Hebrew Bible, the covenant frees waters to flow once again within their banks of righteousness, harmony, and justice. Thus, after the waters have subsided, God blesses Noah and his sons and tells them, "Be fruitful and multiply and fill the Earth." Obviously, the issue here is not sex. Rather, the central message of the flood is that the shedding of blood through *violence* will produce violence, therefore do not heedlessly shed and consume blood: "Whoever sheds the blood of a human, by a human shall that person's blood be shed; for in his own image God made humankind." (9:6) Whatever one thinks of this quid pro quo—and I do not believe it legitimizes capital punishment—it does clarify clearly the cyclic quality of violence. The tense is not an imperative "thou shalt kill one who kills." The tense points to the future and establishes cause: whoever kills a human shall meet a similar fate. Violence perpetuates itself. Like God, humans are clothed in living waters; but those waters are contained within bounds that can be violated, and once violated, the violence will likely spread.

We will return again later to the flood story, but water is also terrifying in the Bible for another of its manifestations—as "bad" water, or poison. This aspect appears in Numbers 5:11–31, where a husband who suspects his wife of adultery is commanded to bring her before a priest, who will:

> take holy water in an earthen vessel, and take some of the dust that is on the floor of the tabernacle and put it into the water. . . .Then the priest shall make her take an oath, saying, "If no man has lain with you . . . be immune to this water of bitterness that brings the curse. But if you have gone astray while under your husband's authority, if you have defiled yourself and some man other than your husband has had intercourse with you . . . now may this water that brings the curse enter your bowels and make your womb discharge, your uterus drop!" And the woman shall say, "Amen. Amen.". . . He shall make the woman drink the water. . . .This is the law in cases of jealousy, when a wife, while under her husband's authority, goes astray and defiles herself, or when a spirit of jealousy comes on a man and he is jealous of his wife; then he shall set the woman before the LORD, and the priest shall apply this entire law to her.

Now, here the danger of waters is obvious—the waters can be poison and can render barren, or even kill.

This text surely seems a harsh judgment on women for adultery, or even the suspicion of adultery. Men, of course, had no such threat of judgment for extramarital sex (although as is well known that David ran into problems for his dalliance with Bathsheba—see 2 Samuel 11–12). But even this curse on a woman suspected of adultery could be a rather elaborate ruse. It was a ritual curse designed as much to ease the troubled mind of a jealous husband as to produce any drastic consequences. The water used, after all, was "holy" water, thereby pure and clean, and it was mixed with "dust" from the tabernacle; the Holy of Holies where only the High Priest could walk. Thus, the chances for this "water of bitterness" to actually cause illness resulting in childlessness were slim to none, with the exception perhaps among women whose consciences were truly guilty. In most cases, however, the "waters" of justice are turned back on the jealous husband, who is basically being told in this ritual: trust your wife, get over your jealousy, why are you troubling God with this matter?

A similar curse involving poisoned water for infidelity appears in Jeremiah, but now the curse has been extended to *all* of the people. The prophets frequently used the image of adultery to describe what happened when Israel worshiped false gods and to warn people of the violent consequences idolatry brings. Hosea developed such imagery most fully, but Jeremiah put the warning (after the fact) in particularly vivid language:

> Who is wise enough to understand this? . . .Why is the land ruined and laid waste like a wilderness, so that no one passes through? And the LORD says: Because they have forsaken my law that I set before them, and have not obeyed my voice, or walked in accordance with it, but have stubbornly followed their own hearts and have gone after the Baals. . . . Therefore thus says the LORD of hosts, the God of Israel: I am feeding this people with wormwood, and giving them poisonous water to drink. I will scatter them among nations that neither they nor their ancestors have known; and I will send the sword after them, until I have consumed them.
>
> 9:12–16

Again, this terrifying vision of God serving people "poisoned waters" seems harsh, even vindictive. The point, however, is similar to the point of the flood story: falsehood brings violence, which is then returned upon itself. Furthermore, as with the curse against a woman suspected of adultery, there is an antidote. This antidote, interestingly, is also water: the waters of repentance, of justice, of tears. Jeremiah goes on: "Thus says the Lord of Hosts: Consider, and call for the mourning women to come; send for the skilled women to come; let them quickly raise a dirge over us, so that our eyes may run down with tears, and our eyelids flow with water" (17–18). Humans are, after all, the only mammals who cry. The flood of justice can purify from within.

But the flood of justice is also a social, and cultural, command. Responsibility is collective as well as personal. Pious individual practice is not enough. The prophets of the Hebrew Bible consistently condemned complacency and called for greater justice on the part of people and communities. Amos put it most clearly, speaking for God: "Because you trample on the poor, and take from them levies of grain, you have built houses of hewn stone, but you shall not live in them; you have planted pleasant vineyards, but you shall not drink their wine" (5:11). Without justice, there will be no flow for anyone. Indeed, no amount of piety will replace the absence of justice. Amos has God say, "I hate, I despise your festivals, and I take no delight in your solemn assemblies. . . . But let justice roll down like waters, and righteousness like an everflowing stream" (5:21, 24). Complacent worship unconcerned about justice brings its own consequences, just as injustice itself inspires its own vengeance.

So, the God clothed in living waters wants us to find the flow of justice—not as retribution—but as fulfillment for all flesh. Indeed, the whole point of the flood story, the curses against adultery (individual or collective), and the prophetic call to justice is to heighten our responsibility to live without initiating violence; to give us the freedom to care for the waters of creation—in all forms. They are, after all, stories narrated for a purpose. Their intent is to motivate us to behave a certain way. Thus the flood story concludes with a promise. God will not again destroy all living flesh with a flood, and the rainbow will be the sign of this covenant. "When I bring clouds over the earth and the bow is seen in the clouds, I will remember my covenant that is between me and you and every living creature of all flesh; and the waters shall never again become a flood to destroy all flesh" (Gen. 9:14–15). God does not desire violence and will not inflict it upon us. The treaty—for that is what a covenant was in the ancient world—stipulates that the flow of justice is now up to us. *We* create the conditions in which we either live in peace and harmony or live with bloodshed or violence. God is clothed in the promise of justice. But we—made in the image of that promise—can choose to clothe ourselves in justice as well or to live with the natural consequences of our own callous greed.

At root, then, God clothed as the flood of justice reveals the truth, and prospect, of change. Among the prophetic literature, the account that best highlights the way God promises change is Jonah. Jonah is commanded by God to call the people of the Assyrian city of Nineveh, no friends of Israel—to repentance. Instead, Jonah flees "from the presence of God" on a boat headed in the other direction. A storm comes up, and Jonah is thrown overboard, where he finds himself in the belly of a sea monster (1:1–17). We are back in the realm of Genesis, or even Psalm 104—the primeval waters of creation have now engulfed a living soul.

Ironically, however, the chaotic waters bring Jonah closer to God. He prays: "I called to the LORD out of my distress, and he answered me; out of the belly of Sheol I cried, and you heard my voice. You cast me into the deep, into the heart of the seas, and the flood surrounded me; all your waves and your billows passed over me" (2:1–3). Jonah realizes, but only partially, that he is *now* in God's presence. So he continues, "The waters closed in over me; the deep surrounded me; weeds were wrapped around my head . . . yet you brought up my life from the Pit, O LORD my God" (2:5–6). He is *in* the belly of the sea monster when he says this. By the end of his prayer, the not-too-bright prophet gets the point: "Deliverance belongs to the LORD!" (2:9). And after Jonah has spent three days and three nights in the fish, the fish spits him up on the dry land.

Then comes the command again: "Get up, go to Nineveh, that great city, and proclaim to it the message that I tell you" (3:2). This time Jonah goes. He proclaims the impending overthrow of Nineveh, and to his surprise, the people repent. The king of Nineveh proclaims: "All shall turn from their evil ways and from the violence that is in their hands. Who knows? God may relent and change his mind; he may turn from his fierce anger, so that we do not perish" (8b–9). Surprisingly, at least to Jonah, God does change, the people are saved, and violence is avoided. The story ends with the prophet, apparently having forgotten his experience in the waters, pouting and sitting outside the city in anger, baking in the sun. As for Nineveh, in the last verse of the text God asks Jonah, "And should I not be concerned about Nineveh, that great city, in which there are more than a hundred and twenty thousand persons who do not know their right hand from their left?" (4:11).

This is a great story, although it is liable to bog readers down in all kinds of wild speculation about what kind of "fish" could eat a man whole. But among the Jewish people, the point has been kept clear: The tale is read on the Day of Atonement. Jonah's story is a story of change. Jonah represents all people, and how it sometimes takes us awhile, even through some trials and tribulations—to get the message of grace. Nineveh changes (for the better). Jonah changes (but not enough). Even God changes. Truly, the closest Jonah comes to God is within the belly of the sea monster. Jonah prays from the deep; it is from underneath the waters that Jonah is no longer fleeing from the presence of God. Only by going through the waters does Jonah find, or is given, the motivation to be the agent to turn Nineveh from its violent course. Waters can do that. They change everything in their path. Justice, by definition, demands change. Fulfillment for all flesh does not imply a static state.

So, when I reflect back on the flood of justice I experienced that summer night of my nineteenth year in a family room in Wisconsin, the most realistic assessment I can make of the situation is that it changed us. My folks meant well but were too attached to the conventions of society regarding sexuality to let me grow up. As a result, they tried to control change, and we all got caught up in the violence that ensued. For my part, I now can recognize how I had violated their hopes and dreams for me, more by sneaking around than anything else. I also discovered that we seldom can control the consequences of our actions. Life is unpredictable, and every action has implications and ramifications that extend far into the future, affecting places and people we don't intend. We were all, in short, like the people of Nineveh—we didn't know our right hands from our left, and as a result, we did violence.

But I hope we aren't like Jonah, left sulking in the sun. I know I learned from this event—even though it took me years to do so, as the reader will discover more fully in chapter 10. I learned to distinguish the living God from my parents; *their* justice wasn't too just. My naive trust in them—or my idolatry of them, if you will—needed to be shaken. And I think my parents learned from this event, too. They learned to recognize that they couldn't control the changes that one of their offspring went through, after a certain point. It's true in family after family—my two younger brothers had a much easier time in this matter than I did, not because my parents were more lax, but because they had learned that there were more important changes going in my brothers' lives that needed their attention and love. We were all unaware of just how attached we were to cultural conventions and to various efforts to save ourselves. As God says to Jeremiah: "My people have committed two evils: they have forsaken me, the fountain of living water, and dug out cisterns for themselves, cracked cisterns that can hold no water"(2:13). Complacency, on the one hand, and excessive attachment to partial and flawed goods, on the other, leads to injustice that will invariably need to be changed.

So, when young people ask me about premarital sex, I tell them about my experience. I tell them that sex is beautiful, great, a glorious gift of God. I tell them I take delight in the pleasure of my body, and in sharing pleasure with my wife, and that I understand committed and honest sexual expression as a most enjoyable aspect of being human. But I also tell them that sex is dangerous. Actual living waters, after all, don't just give us life and delight. Sometimes—like at Looking Glass Rock, or in any other flood of justice—they can threaten us or even kill us. The living waters of God's clothing reveal not only our origin and delight but a glimpse of the truth that we can get too attached to things. We can grow obsessed with conventions, ourselves, another human being. When we do, if we're lucky, we will be swept up in justice that "flows down like water, and righteousness like an overflowing stream." The living water in which God is clothed can dissolve our petty attachments in an infinite flood of change.

Clothed with Compassion

The sacrament of baptism is the most prominent way Christians incorporate water in their symbolic system. As the rite of initiation, baptism includes both of the associations with water already discussed—the delight in origins and the dissolution of petty attachments in the command of justice. Baptism is a new birth and a washing away of sin. But it is also more. According to the apostle Paul, in the waters of baptism we "put on" Christ, as we put on a piece of clothing. Indeed, Paul makes the metaphor explicit: "As many of you as were baptized into Christ have clothed yourselves with Christ. There is no longer Jew or Greek, there is no longer slave or free, there is no longer male and female; for all of you are one in Christ Jesus" (Gal. 3:27–28). Paul wrote these words to a community struggling to understand its calling, beset by disunity, and losing sight of God's promise. Paul did so because the metaphor of God clothed in living waters, in whom we could be clothed in baptism, promises to unite us, indeed all things, into one, with a river running through it. In baptism, when we are dribbled or doused with or dunked in waters, as an infant or as an adult, we wear God.

But wearing God is hardly a call, as it unfortunately is often interpreted, primarily to a life of individual purity and moral obedience—for instance, to celibacy. Quite the opposite is the case, in fact. We are baptized not to avoid, but to engage in new ways with, the world. If the old ways of the world focus on worrying about and hoarding possessions—including our own self-righteousness—the new ways of a person clothed in Christ focus on practicing compassion, on living a life risked in love. The example of such a life, of course, is found for Christians in the person of Jesus of Nazareth.

Jesus' life, so far as scholars have been able to reconstruct it from the historical record, was marked by the practice and teaching of compassion. Marcus Borg, a biblical scholar who also has a gift of writing for a popular audience, suggests that for Jesus, "compassion was the central quality of God and the central moral quality of a life centered in God. These two aspects of compassion are combined most clearly and compactly in a single verse: 'Be compassionate as God is compassionate'" (Luke 6:36). Borg goes on to note that in Hebrew, the word *compassion:*

> is the plural of a noun that in its singular form means "womb." In the Hebrew Bible, *compassion* is both a feeling and a way of being that flows out of that feeling. . . . Compassion . . . means feeling the feelings of somebody else in a visceral way, at a level somewhere below the level of the head; most commonly compassion is associated with feeling the suffering of somebody else and being moved by that suffering to do something.[13]

In short, to "be clothed" in Jesus by baptism is to be clothed in his passion. *Compassion* literally means "to feel passion with."

And for what was Jesus passionate? What do the garments of Christ suggest we are to "put on" through the living waters of baptism? Obviously, a fundamental characteristic of waters is that they flow. And this reality is also true of people, at our most fully human. Mihaly Csikszentmihalyi, in a best-selling study of human psychology, determined that it was an experience he called "flow" that was the optimal experience commonly shared by people at their best. On the basis of hundreds of interviews, he determined that at love, work, and play, we are at our truest when we are "in the zone," when we feel "compassion" with others, when we "flow." This experience can be found on a sporting field or at a symphony, in an office or at a construction site, in celebration or in service. Flow happens whenever we are so fully engaged by our surroundings and circumstances that we lose the self-consciousness that accompanies much of everyday living. Paradoxically, by losing self-consciousness, we also find our truest self *in the process.*[14] This psychological phenomenon is paralleled spiritually by the freedom the Gospel writers found through identifying with Jesus' death on a cross. Thus, Mark has Jesus teach: "If any want to become my followers, let them deny themselves and take up their cross and follow me. For those who want to save their life will lose it, and those who want to lose their life for my sake, and for the sake of the gospel, will save it" (Mark 8:34–35). This is not an injunction to masochism. It is a promise that when we "give up" *attachment* to self we will find the gracious flow of our deepest self. When we love, we live. And when we live, we are clothed in the living waters in which Christ himself was clothed—compassion for all the living.

This is true freedom, where chaos and order, depth and surface, coexist. Such freedom is not only a psychological reality. The story of the exodus is a famous example of how the flow of freedom is political as well as personal. Thus, on Passover, the Israelites paint their lintels with the liquid blood of a lamb. On the way to the promised land, they pass through the sea. And when they come to the land, it is flowing with milk and honey. Anyone in slavery knows that the passage to freedom must go through the waters: through trust in another, compassion with another. The old slave spiritual puts it well: "I looked over Jordan, and what did I see, coming for to carry me home, a band of angels, watching over me... Swing low, sweet chariot." We are at home in freedom; clothed in waters that flow unheeded within their banks and that sweep us into participation in community. As Borg puts it, "compassion for Jesus was political. He directly and repeatedly challenged the sociopolitical paradigm of his social world and advocated instead what might be called a *politics of compassion.*"[15] A God clothed in living waters wants us, beginning in baptism, to find such flow that brings personal and political fulfillment.

This is not a magic trick. It is a metaphor that motivates—an invitation to comfort as well as challenge. A second characteristic of the waters in which we are "clothed" through baptism, then, is conveyed in the beautiful words of Psalm 23:

> The LORD is my shepherd, I shall not want.
> He makes me lie down in green pastures;
> he leads me beside still waters; he restores my soul. . . .
> Even though I walk through the darkest valley,
> I fear no evil, for you are with me. . . .
> You prepare a table before me in the presence of my enemies;
> you anoint my head with oil; my cup overflows.

> Surely goodness and mercy shall follow me all the days of my life,
> and I shall dwell in the house of the LORD my whole life long.

Waters restore. Green pastures revive. A meal around a table brings overflowing goodness and mercy—even in the company of our enemies! For Christians, these truths are not only communicated in the images of this psalm, but are also conveyed in the life of Jesus, the good shepherd, as he calms the waters of storms, walks on them, and incarnates mercy in his own message that we must love our enemies (see Mark 4:35; 6:45; Matt. 14:22). Being clothed with still waters in baptism invites us into a calm confidence to face our deepest fears and to invite even our enemies to the table.

This is a literal as well as a metaphorical truth. People seek waters to calm their souls. We saw in previous chapters how mall designers almost always include water in some form, and how even Walt Disney World carefully uses water to create a sense of serenity among its guests. Such symbolism is also increasingly common in suburban homes. One year for Christmas, for instance, my son Nathan gave me a small, bubbling fountain. Knowing my love for water, my son thoughtfully purchased me a calming reminder. It now graces my office but for a time was in our foyer, where it welcomed guests with the soothing sound of water trickling over polished stones. Many suburban homes have also recently included miniponds among their landscaping options, in an interesting trend, and of course swimming pools and hot tubs have long been desired commodities in home design. Gentle waters have the potential to heal, and people want to be near them. The Christian sacrament of baptism, where we are clothed with Christ, initiates us into a community where such a way of peace is open to us—for free.

Finally, being clothed in Christ through baptism gives us hope for the healing of the nations and that we will all be united someday. I have often thought that the problem with the "Holy Land" of the Middle East is that there just isn't enough water to go around, and that if the people there could be brought to the waters—or the waters brought to them—they might find peace. It is not at all surprising to me that the only lasting peace in the recent past of the region was created at Camp David—a place lush with greens and blues. Not surprisingly, the biblical prophets' own dream of a peaceful world emphasized the presence of water. In his last vision, for instance, the prophet Ezekiel saw a river running from the temple, first ankle-deep, then knee-deep, then too deep to cross. The river ran out into the world and brought life wherever it flowed. What was stagnant became fresh. Every living creature flourished. And "on the banks . . . of the river, there will grow all kinds of trees for food. Their leaves will not wither nor their fruit fail, but they will bear fresh fruit every month, because the water for them flows from the sanctuary. Their fruit will be for food, and their leaves for healing"(47:12). This is the river of life, these are the waters of Eden, again bringing delight to people.

And at the end of the writings about Christ, in fact in the last chapter of the Bible, the writer of Revelation sees the same image:

> Then the angel showed me the river of the water of life, bright as crystal, flowing from the throne of God and of the Lamb through the middle of the street of the city. On either side of the river is the tree of life with its twelve kinds of fruit, producing its fruit each month; and the leaves of the tree are for the healing of the nations. Nothing accursed will be found there any more
>
> 22:1–3

Clothed in living waters, God offers us the hope that even warring nations will be healed, and that no one will be left behind.[16] Theologian Barbara R. Rossing summarizes well the scope of this vision: "When we glimpse in every river the river of life . . . we [can] see ourselves as citizens of a holy city, as stewards and 'priests' of Earth's water and trees. . . . The New Jerusalem is a city where life and its essentials are given 'without money,' as a gift, even to those who cannot pay for them."[17] The sacred places of waters, and a God clothed in them, point us to our origin and delight, to the fulfillment of justice, and to the prospect of unity in compassion.

Now, all these metaphors can seem to remove us from the actual world of water, and that is not at all my intention. Having grown up in the lush Midwest, where lakes and streams were a matter of everyday confluence with my experience, I feared that when I moved to Philadelphia in the year 2000 I would leave behind lushness in exchange for the dryness of concrete. In fact, I've never lived wetter. Within a five-minute walk of our house is an old-fashioned swimming hole, ten feet deep, formed by an ancient dam, complete with bluegills, rock bass, and a rope swing hanging from a tree. The water body is Crum Creek, a meandering stream that winds its way through Philly's western suburbs toward the Delaware River and from there to the Atlantic Ocean. Shortly after moving to the area we discovered the swimming hole on a hike through the park in which it's located. The park is seldom visited, no doubt because it is bisected at several points by a major interstate highway, up a hundred feet or so on several impressive bridges.

Anyway, within a year I had arranged to test and report on the water quality in Crum Creek for the local watershed association. After my first test, I found the water surprisingly clean—not laden with either nitrogen or phosphates, and suitably oxygenated to support even trout. So, I dove in. Urban legends (and probably, from time to time, fact) about bacteria and parasites scare all but a few foolhardy teenagers away from the swimming hole, and I think it may be illegal to swim there. But on more than one hot summer day each year, I'll pack my suit and towel in a bag and take my chances on a dip in a wild run of water less than five minutes from my house. Often Justin, Nathan, and Rheanne will accompany me. They like to help with the chemical testing, but they haven't yet joined me in a swim—although they do wade with me from time to time. They're afraid the water's polluted. My children have never lived in a world where water is naturally clean. My modest hope in lifting up the Bible's own way of clothing God as living waters, then, is that perhaps such a close association between the sacred and the source of all life on earth will motivate us to care for this vital substance that courses through our veins as well as covers the surface of the earth. Maybe then our children's children will not grow up with the fears my children suffer.

8

The Light of the World

When I had journeyed half of our life's way,
I found myself within a shadowed forest,
for I had lost the path that does not stray.

Dante, *Inferno*

Despite the Church's curse,
there is no one so lost that the eternal love cannot return—
as long as hope shows something green.

Dante, *Purgatorio*

The glory of the One who moves all things
permeates the universe and glows
in one part more and in another less.

Dante, *Paradiso*

A few summers ago, I was officially inducted into the "Polar Bear Club" at Camp Arcadia, near Traverse City, on the coast of Lake Michigan. It was a cold July morning, with a hazy sky, when the six of us emerged, shivering, from the inn where we had slept the night before. The sun was just starting to rise in the east behind us as we faced the huge lake, towels wrapped around our shoulders to keep us warm. Everything was a uniform blue-gray. There was no horizon. The lake simply blurred into the sky; one long, wide, deep, and broad expanse. It was impossible to tell where the water ended and the heavens began. The six of us had, until days before, been strangers. Gradually, we shed the towels and tiptoed down the beach toward the waters. As I stood at the edge of the glasslike surface, I asked my companions, "Can I just walk on it instead?" They laughed, and one of them, Jeff, answered, "If you can, do it!" I tried, and sank, and after a few steps dove in. It was cold. My heart stopped. My lips turned blue. But when I came up out of the waters, I saw a huge, faint rainbow, arching from south to north across the whole sky. You couldn't see it from the shore. It was visible, and then only barely, from water that was waist-deep. "Look," I said, breathlessly, "a rainbow." And the six of us, days before strangers, now friends, stood in the water in awe, having been initiated through the water into the Polar Bear Club. We shivered together in joy, sharing the beauty of God's promise, clothed in red, orange, yellow, green, blue, and gray—living water reflecting the light of a new day.

Rainbows, sunrises, and sunsets are extraordinary light shows that are appreciated by almost everyone for their beauty. But even ordinary light deserves appreciation, because it is the primary way we experience the energy without which we cannot live. Without light, we have no warmth, no plants, no photosynthesis, no oxygen, no animals, no day, no night. Every morning the sun rises, and every afternoon it sets, and more often than not we don't notice. We take for granted something none of us created but upon which we all depend. We are warmed by light and see by it. We are healed by light and made joyful by its presence. Light radiates, shines, reflects, glows, beams, gleams, glitters, sparkles, and burns. Light is a hierophany—a fabric of the sacred—that appears in every place and for all people.

Hence, religious folk widely incorporate places of light as sacred space in their symbolic systems.[1] The sun, stars, moon, sky, and fire—along with lights of many metaphorical or spiritual varieties—have been revered, feared, and personified throughout history. Ancient Egyptians worshiped the sun as Ra and left a magnificent text in the pharaoh Akhenaten's *Great Hymn to the Aten*—the sun disk.[2] In India, the god Agni personifies the sacrificial fire and is venerated throughout Vedic literature.[3] All across Asia and around the globe Buddhists remember Siddhartha Gautama as "the Enlightened One." The Hebrew psalmist exclaimed of God that "in Your light we see light." And among the cultures directly influencing Christian thought and practice, the ancient Romans celebrated the birthday of Sol Invictus (the Unconquered Sun) on December 25, and Anglo-Saxon tribes celebrated spring rites to honor their female sun-deity, Eostra, from whom we derive our word *Easter.*[4] Not surprisingly, then, early Christians made ready use of light imagery. The Nicene Creed—perhaps the benchmark of Christian orthodoxy down through the ages—affirms that Jesus was "light from light, true God from true God."

When we see God clothed in light, then, we can recognize, first, that God is like energy; a predictable and pervasive gift that warms and frees with its beauty. Clothed in the movement of the sun, the light of the world alternates with the darkness as day completes night, sustaining life and strengthening us through its power. Second, as the fire of God's love, places of light transfigure us, refining whatever is impure, and carrying us upward like incense. The fire of God's passion can blind and consume, but the light of conscience also illumines for us the path of justice. Finally, places of light promise wisdom, vision, and insight that will shine with all the colors of the rainbow, a wisdom as broad and wide as the spectrum. Through light, we can glimpse an enlightenment that will never dim. Light is the clothing of resurrection, the fabric out of which new life is woven. As the clothing of God, in short, the light of the world reveals God to be an ever-present and gracious energy, a refiner who will change us with fires of passion, and Wisdom who will display for us the glory of all the colors of the spectrum.

The Energy of Grace

Writing in the tenth century, Symeon—a Christian monk on Mount Athos in Greece—developed a mystical theology in which light played a central role. According to Symeon, "Let no one deceive you! God is light, and to those who have entered into union with Him He imparts of His own brightness to the extent that they have been purified." To identify the self so directly with God's light not surprisingly landed Symeon in some trouble with church authorities. Still, he persisted: "The light envelops me and appears to me like a star, and is incomprehensible to all. It is radiant like the sun, and I perceive all creation encompassed by it." Symeon recognized that he was here dealing with "symbols and preliminaries" and that the essence of the light was "immaterial," but Symeon also found in these "symbols" vitality and strength: "I conversed with this Light," he claimed. "The Light itself knows it; it scattered whatever mist there was in my soul and cast out every earthly care. It expelled from me all material denseness and bodily heaviness that made my members to be sluggish and numb. What an awesome marvel!" Light "invigorated and strengthened" Symeon. He even claimed to be so enveloped by this light that it was as if light replaced the "garment" of his body.[5]

These themes were developed and refined in the fourteenth century by another Eastern theologian, Gregory Palamas. For Gregory, the light that Symeon described was one of the "energies" of God. "This light is not the essence of God," wrote Gregory, "for that is inaccessible and incommunicable." Rather, the light is an *energeia* of God (literally an "action" or "operation") by means of which God is manifest to believers, indeed, even is infused into believers: "Natural energy is the power which manifests every essence . . . for the being which participates in an essence will also surely participate in the power which naturally manifests that essence."[6] Through the light, which manifests God's energies, we participate in God's own power.

Indeed, for Gregory, nothing less than the grace of God is manifest through the *energeia* of light, which clothes believers in divine and beautiful garments:

> The divine manifestations, even if symbolic, remain unknowable by reason of their transcendence. . . . So, when the saints contemplate this divine light . . . then they behold the garment of their deification, their mind being glorified and filled by the grace of the Word, beautiful beyond measure . . . just as the divinity of the Word on the mountain [of transfiguration] glorified with divine light the body conjoined to it. . . . [Thus are

> believers] initiated into [God], for [God] is . . . deifying light: They truly draw near to God, and enjoy direct participation in His divinizing rays.[7]

For Christians in the East—Greece, Russia, and so forth—salvation does not mean "rescue," as it often has for Christians in the West. In the East, to be saved is to become divine. The classical formulation has it: "God became human, so humans can become divine." This Eastern emphasis on salvation as "divinization" is evident in this passage of Gregory's, where light metaphorically represents the energy of God's grace. God, clothed in light, clothes us in light.

Of course, Gregory's theology raised questions among authorities, too, but it does have ample biblical warrant. Perhaps the most famous association between God and light is in Exodus 3, where Moses encounters God through a burning bush. The context of the story is important. The Hebrews are suffering as slaves in Egypt, and Moses, on a shepherding expedition, senses the "angel of the Lord" present to him "in a flame of fire out of a bush." Moses looks closer at the bush, and notices that although it is "blazing" it is not burned up. He moves closer, and then God speaks, first calling Moses' name, and then saying, "Come no closer! Remove the sandals from your feet, for the place on which you are standing is holy ground" (v. 5). This is the first time this phrase—"holy ground"—is used in the Bible, and it is used in connection with a place of fire and light. Fire was obviously a prominent way in which people experienced light prior to the discovery of electricity.

As the story in Exodus continues, though, God indicates to Moses through the voice from the fire that the "misery" of Moses' people is manifest and that God is committed to being their deliverer. "I have come down [God is clearly a sky god] to deliver them from the Egyptians, and to bring them up out of that land to a good and broad land, a land flowing with milk and honey" (v. 8). When Moses asks God's name, God reveals only that "I AM WHO I AM." The Hebrew name here revealed, Yahweh, highlights the essential hiddenness of God. We can know only God's clothing—not God's essence. But the point is clear—God speaks from the energy of fire, and Moses listens.

And the work God promises from the burning bush is to liberate the Hebrews from slavery. God's grace—manifest in light—frees. Indeed, this symbolism of light has worked in history again and again to liberate the oppressed. Martin Luther, writing in the sixteenth century for Christians suffering under the strictures of feudalism and an imperial church, helped motivate his followers by reminding them that "the title of light . . . is the best figure or representation of the Divine Majesty; the Holy Scriptures themselves call God 'light.'"[8] Several centuries later, Martin Luther King Jr. invoked a metaphor of light in his famous "Letter from Birmingham Jail" to describe the working of nonviolent direct action: "We who engage in nonviolent direct action are not the creators of tension," King asserted. "We merely . . . bring it out in the open, where it can be seen and dealt with. Like a boil that can never be cured so long as it is covered up but must be opened with all its ugliness to the natural medicines of air and light, injustice must be exposed, with all the tension its exposure creates, to the light of human conscience."[9] Then, when TV cameras caught bigots hurling rocks and racial epithets at peaceful marchers, the ugliness of racism was made manifest to the light of human reason and compassion. Images of light also empowered the oppressed to endure in their struggle, as they sang "This Little Light of Mine" and other freedom songs from jail. Indeed, in the exodus story itself God returns—after the people have fled Egypt and are wandering in the wilderness—to lead them as a pillar of fire by night, an image to which the prophets return again and again.[10] God clothed in light first exposes injustice and then lights the way to liberation by "pointing out the way of justice and mercy." Both are aspects of God's grace, manifest in light, as an energy that changes things.

As Luther pointed out, the Bible explicitly describes God "wrapped in light as with a garment"(Ps. 104:2). This imagery from the Psalms inspired another influential biblical story in which light "clothes" the divine—namely the account of the transfiguration of Jesus. This story was central to the theology of both Symeon and Gregory. It is substantially the same in all three Synoptic Gospels—Matthew, Mark, and Luke. Here's Mark's version:

> Jesus took with him Peter and James and John, and led them up a high mountain apart, by themselves. And he was transfigured before them, and his clothes became dazzling white [as light, adds Matthew], such as no one on earth could bleach them. And there appeared to them Elijah with Moses, who were talking with Jesus. Then Peter said to Jesus, "Rabbi, it is good for us to be here; let us make three dwellings, one for you, one for Moses, and one for Elijah." He did not know what to say, for they were terrified. Then a cloud overshadowed them, and from the cloud there came a voice, "This is my Son, the Beloved, listen to him!" Suddenly when they looked around, they saw no one with them any more, but only Jesus.
>
> 9:2–8

Here in this hierophany, Jesus—along with the prophets Moses and Elijah—is "clothed in light," just as the psalmist had claimed the Lord was. That was, of course, the point of the story: to identify Jesus with Moses and the prophets, by clothing him in the same light that clothed them—and that clothed God.

In the Gospel of John, written some years later than Mark, the connection between Jesus and light developed further. The famous prologue of the Gospel states the argument of the whole in a dense mixture of metaphors:

> In the beginning was the Word, and the Word was with God, and the Word was God. He was in the beginning with God. All things came into being through him, and without him not one thing came into being. What has come into being in him was life, and the life was the light of all people. The light shines in the darkness, and the darkness did not overcome it.
>
> There was a man sent from God, whose name was John. He came as a witness to testify to the light, so that all might believe through him. He himself was not

> the light, but he came to testify to the light. The true light, which enlightens everyone, was coming into the world.
>
> 1:1–9

John, writing for a different audience than Mark, universalizes the story of Jesus through the metaphor of light. Jesus was the "light of the world," (8:12) who conveys to people "power to become children of God" and from whom all can receive "grace upon grace"(1:12, 16). God's grace, manifest in the light of world, is an energy—a power—available to all.

Now, there is also another theme in John's Gospel related to the imagery of light that has been the source of considerable trouble in history. John dualistically opposes the light to "darkness" and later in his Gospel associates "the darkness" with the enemies of the Jesus movement (see esp. 8:12 and 12:35–36). John drew this dualism in part from within Judaism. In Deuteronomy, for instance, God is clearly a sky god, whose victory over the enemies of Israel is celebrated as the victory of the day over night: "There is none like God . . . who rides through the heavens to your help, majestic through the skies. He subdues the ancient gods, shatters the forces of old; he drove out the enemy before you, and said, "Destroy!"(33:26–27). This is an understandable image but not one that should be applied indiscriminately. When a people are an oppressed and violated minority, as were the people of Israel for whom the Deuteronomist wrote—and probably the Christians for whom John wrote—freedom does indeed mean freedom *over* oppression, light *over* darkness. But this is not the central pattern of the light metaphors in the Bible, nor need it be the central teaching of Christians who worship a God clothed in light. Dualism is a decidedly minority report in the biblical record.

Even John's prologue, it will be recalled, was retelling the story of creation. And in Genesis, there is no dualism between day and night, light and darkness. The text juxtaposes the two: "Then God said, 'Let there be light'; and there was light. And God saw that the light was good; and God separated the light from the darkness. God called the light Day, and the darkness he called Night. And there was evening and there was morning, the first day"(1:3–5). Darkness is the primordial condition—everything came from darkness; light is from darkness. Even after it is created, light has to be separated from the darkness in a distinct operation. And, finally, it is when light and darkness *alternate* that creation is completed. The *movement* from day to night, not the victory of one over the other, is the seven-day pattern that marks the foundation of order in the cosmos. The text could not be clearer on this point: "There was evening and there was morning," the second, third, fourth, and every day since.

So, to be precise, monism—rather than dualism—is the characteristic biblical stance on light and darkness. Not opposition but alternation is the way light and darkness are related. Both are part of the one creation. God is responsible for both, and it is by no means clear that "light" is the only clothing God wears. God *is* clothed in light; we can see the light; hence, we associate the light with God's presence. But beyond the light, the darkness endures, and there is a grace and beauty of darkness all its own. And after all, absence is as much a part of any honest experience of God as is presence, just as night is as fully a part of life as day. Even more: not every light is sweet. Not all fires gently warm or lead to freedom. God's grace is also an energy that burns to refine.

The Refiner's Fire

Light is energy and thus sustains life. But light is also fire. To discuss how God is clothed in purifying fire is to move onto dangerous theological terrain. Great damage has been done with this idea. People have been burned on the basis of metaphors whose sole intent was to warn—to help people avoid violence, rather than to create more victims of it. Any use of the prophetic imagery of fire to legitimize the real use of fire against people (or the planet!) is a horrible travesty of the prophetic intent. For the fire described by the prophets was *not* intended to legitimize the oppression of the powerless by the powerful, as in an inquisition, witch-trials, or the Shoah—to mention only a few of the most heinous examples. Rather, the fire of the prophets' wrath was directed *at* the powerful, on behalf of the poor and powerless. The prophetic fire of love sought to purify *limited* human attempts to establish justice and to replace the sacrificial fires of solemn ritual with the all-inclusive love of God, clothed in light.

Undoubtedly the most famous biblical story of judgment by fire is that of Sodom and Gomorrah. The story—often interpreted as condemning homosexuality—in fact is primarily a judgment upon inhospitality, exclusion, and violence. The story is told in Genesis chapters 18 and 19. It begins when Abraham and Lot extend hospitality to strangers who visit them. These strangers are variously described as "men" and "angels," leaving their identity ambivalent. Abraham offers the guests water, washes their feet, and has prepared for them bread, meat, and cheese. Lot, likewise, offers the three lodging in his home and prepares for them a meal. By contrast, the men of Sodom threaten the "angels" with rape and eventually also threaten Lot for harboring these "aliens." It is, in the context of the tale, clearly this contrast between the hospitality of Abraham/Lot and the threat of violence by the men of Sodom that calls forth God's judgment of "sulfur and fire." Rather than welcoming strangers, the people of Sodom seek to violate them. This is a story that contrasts hospitality with violence and that conveys how violence brings its own consequences. The story was addressed, most likely, to the inhospitable members of the tribe of Israel. It also addresses the inhospitable part of us—that part of us that is unwilling to give up our own righteous claims to superiority, and that part of us that is thereby willing to exclude others from full participation in society—women, gays, and strangers among them.

In other words, the story teaches that it's our own limited attachments and fixations that blind and consume us. Thus, the men of Sodom—as they threaten Lot—become "blind" and are unable to find the door of his home (19:11). And Lot's wife—fleeing from Sodom as it is being destroyed—looks back, symbolically indicating attachment to the inhospitable place that had nevertheless been her home—and she turns to a pillar of salt. We're burned, stuck, fixated by the violence of our own limited attachments. The imagery of fire is thus a warning, a call to change.

The prophets use it repeatedly. In the introduction to his work, Isaiah assumes knowledge of Sodom and Gomorrah's inhospitality and compares the limited "fires" of Israel's inhospitable sacrificial worship with the overwhelming fire of God's love:

> Your country lies desolate, your cities are burned with fire. . . . If the LORD of hosts had not left us a few survivors, we would have been like Sodom, and become like Gomorrah. Hear the word of the LORD, you rulers of Sodom! Listen to the teaching of our God, you people of Gomorrah! What to me is the multitude of your sacrifices? says the LORD; I have had enough of burnt offerings of rams and the fat of fed beasts. . . . bringing offerings is futile; incense is an abomination to me. New moon and sabbath and calling of convocation—I cannot endure solemn assemblies with iniquity. Your new moons and your appointed festivals my soul hates . . . your hands are full of blood. Wash yourselves; make yourselves clean; remove the evil of your doings from before my eyes; cease to do evil, learn to do good; seek justice, rescue the oppressed, defend the orphan, plead for the widow.
>
> Isaiah 1:7–17

Clearly—it is the way the poor are treated—the oppressed, children, and women, that has led to the fire. Israel had done plenty to try to "control" the fires—the lights from sacrificial fires burned endlessly; they had sacrificed and worshiped and obeyed all of the liturgical prescriptions. But they were unjust, and the fire that destroyed their cities came as the consequence of their own violence. Isaiah awaited the day when the people changed and learned to seek justice.

Indeed, throughout the prophetic literature, violence and injustice to anyone eventually burns all.[11] In an age when military conquest culminated in the burning of the conquered city, this imagery made perfect sense. When a people were conquered, the reasons for the conquest invariably rebounded back on the people themselves: they had been unprepared, unfaithful, had made enemies, had excluded some "foreigners," had been inhospitable.[12] Whatever the specific cause, it is always internal violence that provokes the fire of God. Ezekiel, for instance, condemned Israel's princes who "devoured human lives," Israel's priests who "[did] violence," Israel's officials who "destroy[ed] lives to get dishonest gain," and Israel's people who "practiced extortion and robbery" and "oppressed the poor and needy." "Therefore," concludes the prophet, "'I have consumed them with the fire of my wrath; I have returned their conduct upon their heads,' says the Lord GOD" (Ezek. 22:23, 26, 27, 29, 31).

Six centuries after Ezekiel wrote, growing out of this prophetic milieu, the authors of the writings about Christ developed the theme of judgment by fire and applied it to their own situation. Indeed, according to them, no prophet condemned humans when they replaced God's universal light with limited human "law" more soundly than did Jesus. Matthew's Gospel has the fullest theology of fire: at least eight times the term is used as judgment against injustice. The theme culminates in chapter 25, where Jesus preaches that on judgment day (it is unclear when this is—present or future) people will be separated from one another, "as a shepherd separates the sheep from the goats" (v. 32). To the sheep, "the king" says: "Come, you that are blessed by my Father, inherit the kingdom prepared for you from the foundation of the world; for I was hungry and you gave me food, I was thirsty and you gave me something to drink, I was a stranger and you welcomed me" (vv. 34–35). The "sheep," in short, were hospitable; they practiced justice. To the "goats," the king says:

> You that are accursed, depart from me into the eternal fire prepared for the devil and his angels; for I was hungry and you gave me no food, I was thirsty and you gave me nothing to drink, I was a stranger and you did not welcome me, naked and you did not give me clothing, sick and in prison and you did not visit me. Then they also will answer, "Lord, when was it that we saw you hungry or thirsty or a stranger or naked or sick or in prison, and did not take care of you?" Then he will answer them, "Truly I tell you, just as you did not do it to one of the least of these, you did not do it to me."
>
> vv. 41–45

Now, what is often overlooked in theological interpretation of this passage (it usually gets "spiritualized" into a vision of life after death) is that it continues the prophetic tradition. From the destruction of Sodom and Gomorrah through Jesus' teaching, the point of fire is to refine and purify—to remove injustice and establish justice.[13] Fire rhetoric inflames. In other words, prophets and biblical writers told stories with fire in them to warn and to encourage a larger vision. They did not intend to legitimize the use of real flames against real flesh. They did intend to motivate their readers to accept strangers, feed the hungry, and heal the sick. Words of fire are a light meant to refine. We survive them and, if we listen, are changed.

The pattern is unmistakable, for it is repeated throughout the Hebrew Bible. In the apocalyptic Book of Daniel, for example, three faithful Jews—Shadrach, Meshach, and Abednego, are accused during the reign of King Nebuchadnezzar of breaking the law that mandated worship of the state gods of Babylon. They "confess" to the crime and are thrown, fully clothed, into an overheated furnace prepared for them. They emerge unscathed—even their clothes are untouched. Here, the "fiery furnace" is a symbol of the trials and temptations of exile, of the tendency of people in a strange land to worship the limited gods of the civil religion rather than the living God who cannot be possessed by nation or tribe. Yet, the author affirms, devotion to the living God can even sustain people through the fire, in a way that will keep them from being consumed (Dan. 3). The prophet Malachi, for a briefer example, explicitly imagines God as a "refiner's fire." The Lord will purify a remnant of the people of Israel, he writes, and will "refine them like gold and silver, until they present offerings to the LORD in righteousness" (Mal. 3). Zephaniah, for yet another example, foresees the day when in the fire of the Lord's passion "all the earth shall be consumed." The point of this fire is to "change the speech of the peoples to a pure speech," so that "all of them may serve [the Lord] with one accord" (3:8–12). Fire rhetoric is intended to refine, to change, to purify. In the writings about Christ, the pattern remains prominent. The apostle Paul is converted from his life of violence by a searing and blinding encounter with the light (Acts 9). He then goes on to imagine faith as a building that must be tested through fire (1 Cor. 3:10–13). And most vividly, at Pentecost, the Spirit of the Lord anoints the apostles with tongues of fire (see Acts 2), and they speak in the languages of the nations. In sum, the language of fire in the Scriptures is metaphorical, presented in extravagant and exaggerated terms, to show us how to end exclusions and to reach "the nations." God's fire refines. God desires that we see the path of justice and follow it. Any other path will consume us with the violent fires of our own limited passions, rather than the refining fire of God's love.

Now, I have experienced this refining fire. It happened when the sun saved our newborn son Nathan. Like his older brother, Justin, Nathan was a little anxious to arrive on earth. Lisa started having regular contractions a month prior to her due date, so she was admitted to the hospital and was required to stay more or less immobile. Three weeks went by. On the morning of May 10, 1988, the physicians—aware of the difficulty of Lisa's first pregnancy, decided to induce labor. We moved Lisa into a birthing room, and the wait began. For a few hours we watched TV, read, and talked. I rubbed Lisa's back when a contraction was particularly intense. Around noon, a nurse stopped in to make a routine check just as Lisa began a prolonged contraction. "I think the baby's coming!" Lisa exclaimed. The nurse, now looking startled, said, "Oh, my God—the head's right here!" She turned to me and yelled, "Go get the doctor! Right away!"

I sprinted out the door and down the hall to my left. When I arrived at the nursing station I said, breathlessly: "The baby's here! You're supposed to come right away!" The staff members looked up and after a moment of hesitation dropped what they were doing and sprinted with me back down the hall. We arrived in the midst of an intense contraction (probably the same one), and by the time everyone took a spot beside the bed, Nathan—the name means "gift" in Hebrew—had arrived in a surprising whoosh!

I remember laughing out loud and grinning from ear to ear at the joy of it all. Nathan cried immediately, and within seconds Lisa was able to snuggle with him—even feed him—at her breast. Nate was a "cone-head" because of his rapid delivery, but he was beautiful. For a while we both cuddled with our new gift. When he fell asleep, we wrapped Nathan in blankets, and the nurse took him to the nursery. Later that day, I stood outside the nursery, looking at our newborn in his layette under the lights, and for some reason I grew worried. I asked at the nurse's station: "Everything's OK?" They assured me it was. Two days later we took him home.

But Nathan's skin had a slight yellow tinge. Upon discharge, the staff told us that Nate's bilirubin count was a little high, but that wasn't unusual for preemies. He'd be fine. I remained anxious. The doctor told us that "light stimulates the liver; put his crib in front of a window with lots of light." We were told to return in two days for another blood test.

The two days passed quickly, and early on Saturday morning, May 14, we returned to the hospital. The staff assured us again that he was fine. But Nate seemed listless to me, and he now looked really yellow. Lisa, a nurse, knew that if the body collected too much bilirubin, seizures and brain damage could occur. So, about every hour after we returned home I kept calling the hospital for lab results. Repeatedly, they weren't in, and no one called us back. I kept worrying.

Finally, in early afternoon, I wrapped Nate—naked but for his diaper—in blankets and took him outside. It was a bright, sunny spring day. I pulled a lawn chair from the garage and sat on the sidewalk in front of our house. The street was busy, and as cars zoomed by I held Nathan up to the sun. I opened up his blankets—it was warm but not hot—so that his little body could absorb as much energy as possible. I'm sure people who drove by thought I was nuts. I held our son in my hands, arms outstretched to the sun, like a shaman from an ancient solar cult offering his newborn to the deity. I prayed he'd be OK, and I worried that he wouldn't.

When the phone call came from the hospital around 3 P.M., the doctor's voice was urgent. "You'll have to bring Nathan into the hospital right away. His count was 19.8 this morning (over 20 is critical). We'll have to put him under the bilirubin light." And so Lisa and I whisked our gift back to the hospital, where for the night he caught some rays. Lisa stayed with him. Gradually the ultraviolet light worked its way through his skin down to his liver, the yellow tinge began to leave him, and he turned a bright, delightful, pink. And thus our son was saved by the sun. The light of the world refined away his impurities, saving him as the gift to us he was, and is. The same happy ending, even if it must be through the refining fire, is God's intent for all the living.

The Color of Wisdom

The light of wisdom is a central motif in the Bible. The Book of Daniel celebrates "those who are wise," who "shall shine like the brightness of the sky" (12:3). In Ecclesiastes, wisdom conveys that everything is vanity, "under the Sun" (1:3). This recurrent phrase in the text indirectly affirms the natural link between "light" and "wisdom," probably as distinct from conventional court wisdom of one variety or another. Even more, the author directly asserts that "light is sweet, and it is pleasant for the eyes to see the sun"(11:7). And in Proverbs, where wisdom is personified (see esp. ch. 8–9), "the path of the righteous is like the light of dawn, which shines brighter and brighter until full day" (4:18).

Naturally, the writings about Christ develop, and intensify, this association between light and Wisdom. Thus the apostle Paul encourages Christians at Rome to "put on the armor of light," which means to "put on the Lord Jesus Christ" (13:12, 14). The author of the letter to the Philippians encouraged believers there to "shine like stars in the world," which meant to live "without murmuring and arguing," and with their eyes set on salvation (2:14–15). The letter to the Hebrews, similarly, describes believers as ones who have been "enlightened, and have tasted the heavenly gift" (6:4). Finally, Paul uses the lights of the sky to help believers make sense out of the idea of the glorious body they will have in the resurrection: "There is one glory of the sun, and another glory of the moon, and another glory of the stars; indeed, star differs from star in glory. So it is with the resurrection of the dead" (1 Cor. 15:41–42).

Developing these intuitive associations between light and Wisdom in manifold ways, Christians throughout the centuries have clothed their churches in light and color. Some churches emphasize muted light; the colors of Wisdom are grays and blacks, with only occasional beams of white, blue, or yellow from a stained glass window high up, or a candle burning beside an altar. Other churches convey the colors of Wisdom as the colors of nature—greens, tans, pinks, brown, white, and yellow. And some churches depict the colors of Wisdom as extravagant, with colors as bright as precious metals and jewels: sapphire blues, gleaming golds, ruby reds. In fact, I often took my undergraduate students on a tour of three such churches in Chicago, to demonstrate how places of light can teach us about the Wisdom of God.

The first church we visited was Fourth Presbyterian Church, located on North Michigan Avenue, or as the ad in the *Chicago Tribune* put it for years, "The John Hancock Tower is across the street from us." Dedicated in 1914, the church was designed by Gothic revivalist Ralph Adams Cram, and it is a study in gray and brown with only limited gleams of color and natural light. The exterior and interior are dominated by the uniform gray Bedford limestone of Indiana, each block depending upon the other in buttresses up to the steep Gothic arches, on which rest the gabled (and pastel-colored) roof ridge, seventy-seven feet above the floor. Height is featured here, and austerity. White oak furniture and beams have aged darker, as the little natural light allowed into the nave through the stained-glass windows mixes with the light from candelabra suspended from the ceiling. Somber, formal, even forbidding, the building reflects its history as the church of the McCormicks and other solid, successful, and persevering Chicago industrialists and businessmen.[14]

The second church we visited was Old Saint Patrick's Roman Catholic church, located on the corner of Adams and Dearborn, on the west edge of the Loop. Dedicated on Christmas Day in 1856, Old Saint Pat's is built in the Romanesque Revival style. The gradually sloping roof and the warmly pastel walls of the nave welcome believers into a communion of saints, many of whom are depicted in delicately shaded windows, in statues, and in a skylight above the main altar that depicts the four evangelists. The windows of the nave, designed by Thomas Augustin O'Shaughnessy in 1912 and crafted in the studios of the Kinsella Art Glass Company, include motifs derived from the *Book of Kells,* an illuminated manuscript (with Celtic roots) produced by Irish monks during the seventh century. Greens, tans, pinks, browns, yellows, and purples are the colors that meet the eye, as do the eyes of St. Patrick and St. Brigid, Mother Cabrini, Catherine Tekakwitha, and others from the history of the church in Ireland, America, and the world, depicted in the statuary and windows. Students invariably "liked" Old St. Pat's better than Fourth Presbyterian, even though most of them were Protestant, and few of them would ever have imagined lighting one of the red votive candles and offering a prayer in a corner shrine, before a statue of the Virgin and the wounded Christ.[15]

Finally, we traveled to the 2200 block of West Superior St., where we visited Sts. Volodymyr and Olha Ukrainian Catholic Church. Students were immediately aware that they were in a different culture as they beheld the golden domes of the Byzantine-style church before them. A bright mural on the west entry to the church depicts the "Baptism of the Ukraine," which occurred, according to tradition, in 988 under the rule of Volodymyr and his grandmother, Olha. Inside the church, a dimly lit narthex reveals a few dramatic icons, as well as heavy golden doors guarding the nave. As these doors were opened, our guide illumined the central chandelier. The golden circle of light with over a hundred bright electric candles blazes, revealing walls covered and circling around us with sky blue, red, green, black, brown, orange, tan, burgundy, yellow, and more colors than one glance can encompass. The walls are covered with icons from floor to ceiling.

In front of us, up a few steps on the gleaming white, brown, and gold marble floor of the chancel, is the hand-carved golden wood of the icon-screen. After letting us catch our breath, the guide explained the meaning of icons—they are a kind of language; each color means something, and the stylized figures are designed to draw attention to the central message they proclaim. Thus, in the dome, we see Christ, the All-Ruler (Pantocrator). All points to this. Descending the walls, we see the events of salvation history—the stories of the Bible—until on the ground level, we find ourselves in the company of our forebears—the saints of the church in the world, in Ukraine, and in America. I have visited the church over a dozen times, and words fail to explain the experience of color and energy that the building conveys.

These churches and their traditions differ dramatically, but all three clothe God in light and color, communicating a theology of refraction. It is hard not to *feel,* as one walks around the stark and yet achingly beautiful grey Gothic edifice of Fourth Presbyterian, the Calvinist themes of God's sovereignty, human depravity, and the perseverance of the saints, among others. In Old Saint Pat's, it is similarly difficult not to *sense* the link between nature and grace in the sacramental labor and joy of the Irish immigrants who built the church as one wanders among the pastel-robed saints and earthy illuminations from the *Book of Kells.* And at Sts. Voldymyr and Olha, one can *see* the Eastern Christian belief that God became a human so that humans can become divine in the vivid spectrum of colors that ascend through level after level of history to the all-ruling Pantocrator in the dome above.

Of course, these are not wholly rational associations; they are intuited, poetically revealed more than intellectually realized by pilgrims. And they are ancient. Light and enlightenment have for ages and across cultures been used by poets to signal the appearance and presence of Wisdom—not only "reason" and "intelligence" but the common sense and goodwill that are able to appreciate a gift when it is offered. It is no coincidence, then, that perhaps the richest Christian account of how God is clothed in all the colors of light, and of how humans perceive this presence, is the poetry of Dante's *Divine Commedia.* As is well known, the three works in the *Commedia* follow the narrator through hell and purgatory to heaven. This journey has many levels, but among them is a movement toward richer and fuller colors and toward bright and intense light. The story begins with *Inferno,* where the narrator (clearly Dante himself) finds himself "within a shadowed forest." Dante descends through levels of hell, passing by and conversing with sinners being punished in ways appropriate to (as consequences of) their sins. He moves continually deeper downward, into "dense and darkened air," then "dense and darkened fog," to the lowest level of hell, a place like "when night falls on our hemisphere." Here Lucifer lies frozen and ugly, flapping batlike wings that send cold and freezing air all around.

Finally freed from this "cave" (paradoxically by climbing through its depths), Dante discovers that

> There is a place below, the limit
> of that cave, its farthest point from Beelzebub,

a place one cannot see: it is discovered
    by ear—there is a sounding stream that flows
along the hollow of a rock eroded
by winding waters, and the slope is easy.
    My guide and I came on that hidden road
to make our way back into the bright world;
and with no care for any rest, we climbed—
    he first, I following—until I saw,
through a round opening, some of those things
of beauty Heaven bears. It was from there
    that we emerged, to see—once more—the stars.[16]

Dante continually has trouble "seeing" in Hell; darkness, fog, and blindness are chief characteristics of the place.

By contrast, the pilgrim's move through purgatory to heaven is a move toward the bright light of the stars. In *Purgatorio,* Dante ascends a mountain initially steep and arduous to climb but which becomes easier, as at each level he purges himself through an act of will of one of the deadly sins—pride, envy, wrath, sloth, avarice, gluttony, and lust. After learning the corresponding virtues—humility, gratitude, gentleness, courage, charity, temperance, and chastity—all forms of love, Dante reaches the summit of the mount, where he experiences earthly paradise, a place filled with "incandescent" light. There he is "pure and prepared to climb unto the stars."[17]

Finally, in *Paradiso,* Dante's vision at the highest level of heaven is one of "'Living Light,' . . . always what It was before—

but through my sight, which as I gazed grew stronger,
that sole appearance, even as I altered,
seemed to be changing. In the deep and bright
essence of that exalted Light, three circles
appeared to me; they had three different colors,
but all of them were of the same dimension;
one circle seemed reflected by the second,
as rainbow is by rainbow, and the third
seemed fire breathed equally by those two circles.

Ravished by the beauty of what he beholds, Dante nevertheless desires to see even more how "our human effigy suited the circle and found place in it," when

my mind was struck by light that flashed
and, with this light, received what it had asked.
Here force failed my high fantasy; but my
desire and will were moved already—like
a wheel revolving uniformly—by
The Love that moves the sun and the other stars.[18]

Here, grace fulfills nature, as revealed light uncovers the love that is the gift of natural light for all life.

So, what is the color of Wisdom? It is the color of the whole spectrum, revealed to us in the common light of the world that calls us to live a life of love. This light was first made apparent to me by my parents, Barbara and Fred Pahl, by my childhood pastor, Henry E. Simon, and by a small (now quite large) church congregation, Faith Lutheran in Appleton, Wisconsin. It was through them that I received my call to ministry. It's a cute story, how it happened.

We played church at my house. It began when I was six. I'd dress up in one of my dad's white dress shirts, which stretched down to my ankles. My mom had an old funky silver cross, which I wore around my neck. I'd stand in the living room, on our olive-green carpet, and my parents would sit on the brown couch. We'd sing a few songs, read a few Bible verses, and then I'd gleefully collect the offering. It was all fun, and we played the game often.

One night, when our pastor and his wife, Dorothy, were over for dinner, someone suggested that we "play church." Everyone agreed, I "robed up," and the congregation entered the nave—our living room. We conducted the brief service (the offering was larger than usual), and afterward, back in the dining room, I asked, "How do you become a pastor?" Henry Simon was a wise man. He did not say to me, "Son, you must wait for a call from God." Instead, he took a page from his pocket calendar and wrote an address on it: "Dr. Walter Stuenkel, President, Concordia College, Milwaukee." He handed me the paper and said, "Write this man a letter asking him for some books on how to be a pastor." That was it.

The next morning—I think it was a Saturday—I remember kneeling on the wood floor of our dining room, the sun streaming in through the southern window, writing a letter to Dr. Stuenkel. I wrote on the paper typical for a second-grader—the kind with two solid lines and a dotted line down the middle so that your letters are straight. The letter read:

> Dear Dr. Stuenkel,
>
> My name is Jon Pahl. I am seven years old, and I think I may want to be a pastor. Could you please send me some books on how to be a pastor?
>
> Thank you very much.

I signed the letter, addressed and stamped an envelope, and put the letter in the mail.

Then I forgot about it, until one Sunday, as our family arrived at church and I was greeted by even warmer smiles than usual. One woman in the congregation came up to me, put her arms around me, and said, "Oh, the little pastor!" I was clueless, until we received our bulletins from the usher and took our seats in our usual pew—up near the front on the right. My dad nudged my mom, and the two of them shared a smile as they read the bulletin. Inside, as they eventually showed me, was "The Concordia College Camera," a bulletin insert from Concordia College, Milwaukee, that was sent to every congregation of the Lutheran Church—Missouri Synod in the states of Wisconsin, Minnesota, Michigan, Illinois, Iowa, and Indiana. My letter had been published! It was printed under the headline, "Never too early to recruit." It had a brief introduction by Dr. Stuenkel, in which he applauded my parents and pastor, and then there was my letter, verbatim, for all the church to see. I couldn't help but grin from ear to ear as I read it, and even now as I think of it I am warmed by the gesture. A few days later, some books arrived from Dr. Stuenkel, primarily a catalog to Concordia College, Milwaukee.

I have been a pastor, in one form or another, ever since. I saw no flash of light, there was no dramatic, blinding insight—but "only" the sunlight from a south window illuminating the laborious writing of a seven-year-old. I saw no direct vision from God but "only" the loving faces of my parents and a minister and the smile of a woman in whose eyes I saw approval and encouragement. I saw no stunning epiphany to show me the way but "only" the gentle light of Wisdom conveyed by many Sunday school teachers, pastors, professors, friends, and loved ones over the years. That is the color of Wisdom: the color of the human eye, the human face, human love—reflecting the light of the sun, which shines on us all. The God clothed in all the colors of light is a God of Energy, a Refiner, who is wise.

9

The Rock of Salvation

The desert world accepts my homage with its customary silence. The grand indifference. As any [one] of sense would want it. If a voice from the clouds suddenly addressed me, speaking my name in trombone tones, or some angel in an aura of blue flame came floating toward me along the canyon rim, I think I would be more embarrassed than frightened—embarrassed by the vulgarity of such display. . . . Only petty minds and trivial souls yearn for supernatural events, incapable of perceiving that everything—everything!—within and around them is pure miracle.

Edward Abbey, *Abbey's Road,*
as cited by Belden Lane, *The Solace of Fierce Landscapes*

It was early June 1989, and I had recently finished my first year of college teaching. I was in Piedmont, South Dakota, outside of Rapid City, in the foothills of the Paha Sapa mountain range. I was there to celebrate the high school graduation of my godson, Rich Krueger. I had spent the beautiful, sunny Saturday morning of the ceremony sitting on the porch of the Krueger house reading. Their house faces south and is at the base of a series of rather significant hills (by my Midwestern standards). Around noon I decided to go hiking. Wearing nothing but a pair of shorts and tennis shoes, I set out across a gravel road toward the hills. As I did, my Uncle Guy pulled out of the driveway in his pick-up truck, tooted his horn, and waved for me to come toward him. As I approached the truck, he leaned across the seat and said through the open window, "Be careful out there—look out for the rattlers.

Don't you want some boots on?" I raised my eyebrows, shrugged my shoulders, and waved him away. He rolled up the window, and I walked off.

Now, I grew up in Wisconsin, where the only poisonous snakes are the ones given the name of "Timber Rattlers" while they play on the local minor league baseball team. So as I crossed a meadow at the base of one hill, I walked *very* gingerly, picking up my feet good and high with each step. Naturally, I made it through the meadow without an encounter (rattlers prefer rocks). I climbed a little gully, found a trail, and headed west toward the afternoon sun. A canopy of arching pine covered the trail, and the scent in the air was fresh, clean, and invigorating. I inhaled deeply and walked faster. After about ten minutes, I reached a place where the trail split, with one branch going directly up the side of the mountain. I took it, climbed for about another ten minutes or so, and then came to a crest where the trail ended. About a hundred yards to my right and up I spotted a large outcropping of rock hanging out like a ledge over a precipice. I decided to go there.

As I (carefully) crawled my way through heavy brush toward the crag of rock, I noticed that a strong wind had recently blown down a path through the trees behind me, so that I could see clear across the Piedmont Valley. The view was stunning; my vision extended probably twenty or thirty miles. When after a little more climbing I arrived on the rock and carefully crawled out to the edge, I had my breath taken away again by what I saw. Well below me, maybe two hundred feet, was a wide, tree-lined gulch—I learned later it was called "Stagebarn Canyon"—that opened up into a U shape that extended probably five miles to another crest to my south. I sat, dangling my feet over the edge of the cliff, and tried to take it all in. I had brought a cigarette and matches with me in my shorts pocket—I smoked at the time. After a few minutes of just sitting on the rock, I lit up and enjoyed the mild nicotine buzz while the smoke wafted in circles around me. It was a peaceful and tranquil moment. I know I paid rapt attention to what was around me. It was beautiful.

And then, in the sky across the gulch a black speck came toward me—a winged one. As it flew closer I saw that it was large, larger than any bird I had ever seen in the wild before, with a wingspan I estimated as wider than my own arms could stretch. The bird flew closer, and I sat on the edge of the cliff in awe, neck craned upward. And then, as the bird flew above me, I saw another come across the gulch. And then another. And another—until, all told, five huge birds circled in the sky above me. I marveled at their flight, watching how they adjusted the tips of their wings like flaps on a plane to catch the slightest hint of a breeze. And as I sat, legs dangling over the edge of the rock, the lead bird sailed closer and closer. I saw its eyes, bright and penetrating, and noticed its extended talons, huge and sharp. I was transfixed, motionless, in awe. The huge bird closed in until it was maybe thirty feet from me, with the other four birds all circling closer and closer, when I noticed the carnivore's sharply hooked beak—open, with a bright red tongue pointing, lashing, hungry.

Finally, I saw my place. I was sure I was lunch. But I was also paralyzed—transfixed by the beautiful terror as my heart began to race. I could not move. I couldn't speak.

I finally managed to clap my hands together once. The lead bird darted up quickly about fifty feet, and then just as quickly descended again, even closer than before. I heard the rush of wings. I clapped my hands again, but now the bird came even closer. My heart was pounding, and I was now sweating. Instinctively, I pulled my knees back up over my head and did a backward somersault away from the edge of the cliff. I rolled two or three turns (completely oblivious now to any threat from rattlesnakes), until I came to rest against a small tree, slightly scratched and with leaves in my hair and on my bare back and chest. I looked up, fearing that I had been followed. But the lead bird had headed back across the gulch, and one by one the other birds flew away as well, leaving me gasping for breath, stunned. I had never before felt hunted. After briefly composing myself, I immediately left the mountain and hurried back down to the porch of the Kruegers' house. It took a long time for my heart to slow down.[1]

Now my encounter at Stagebarn Canyon was likely the closest I will ever get to what many Native American people call a "vision quest." I will interpret this experience in the conclusion to this chapter, but for now it can serve simply to indicate why people through the ages have sought spiritual insight and orientation in visits to rocks, mountains, and other earth forms. I stumbled onto my vision quest. For many other people around the globe, however, places of rock, mountain, and earth have served as intentional places of orient, helped to free them from illusions of grandeur, and given them a sense of participation in something more enduring and solid than the self. Rocks have provided people with gifts that point to permanence, with challenges that tempt human hubris, and with experiences of wonder at the intense delight of life that is only enhanced by its fragility.

In other words, the religions of the world are replete with rocks. For instance, the Yoruba people of Africa say: "Ota oki iku," or "the rock never dies." Indian worshipers of Shiva recall this God of light with a stone *lingam,* or pillar, representing the permanent, penetrating power of the sacred. Muslims circumambulate the stone Ka'ba in Mecca and stoop to kiss the "black stone" embedded in one of its walls, remembering thereby their continuity with Abraham and all founders of the faith back to creation. Rocks and stone, for obvious reasons, form the foundations of many religious practices and sacred places, from megalithic monuments to pyramids, temples, tombstones, *stupas*, stelae, and churches.[2]

In their collective form, of course, rocks form mountains—and mountains have been sacred landforms in religious traditions as far back as the record of human history goes. Hindus learn humility in the shadows of the Himalayas and call the crown of their temples a *sikhara,* which also means "mountain peak" or "crest."[3] Jews recall the gift of Torah to Moses upon Mount Sinai and visit the Temple Mount of Zion to offer prayers.[4] Japanese pilgrims, dressed in white, ascend Mount Fuji, Mount Ontake, or any number of other ranges across their island home. And Lakota Sioux might well be visited by the children of the same vultures who visited me as they undertake vision quests today on the hillock known as Bear Butte—less than thirty miles from Piedmont. Rocks humble humans as well as promise us permanent gifts.

Finally, when rocks erode they turn to earth—and the earth has been treated as sacred in many religious traditions. Many Jews see the land of Israel as a gift to them by God, and they take dwelling upon it as a religious duty.[5] Native Americans have venerated the earth itself as their "mother" or at least as a source of life and sustenance whose significance is not to be treated lightly.[6] And even Christians, through a thinker such as Sallie McFague, whom we met in chapter 1, have wondered whether the earth might be understood as God's body, from which humanity was shaped in creation, and to which humanity returns at death, like dust. In short, clothing God as rock, mountain, and earth might point us to a permanent gift, a challenge and temptation, and the wonder of life.

Permanent Gift

Among the earliest sacred places in the Bible is a stone. The story is told in Genesis, chapter 28. Jacob, son of Isaac, grandson of Abraham, is sent from his ancestral home to seek a wife. We pick up the text as he camps for the night:

> He came to a certain place and stayed there for the night, because the sun had set. Taking one of the stones of the place, he put it under his head and lay down in that place. And he dreamed that there was a ladder set up on the earth, the top of it reaching to heaven; and the angels of God were ascending and descending on it. And the LORD stood beside him and said, "I am the LORD, the God of Abraham your father and the God of Isaac; the land on which you lie I will give to you and to your offspring; and your offspring shall be like the dust of the earth, and you shall spread abroad to the west and to the east and to the north and to the south; and all the families of the earth shall be blessed in you and in your offspring. Know that I am with you and will keep you wherever you go, and will bring you back to this land; for I will not leave you until I have done what I have promised you." Then Jacob woke from his sleep and said, "Surely the LORD is in this place—and I did not know it!" And he was afraid, and said, "How awesome is this place! This is none other than the house of God, and this is the gate of heaven." So Jacob rose early in the morning, and he took the stone that he had put under his head and set it up for a pillar and poured oil on top of it. He called that place Bethel; but the name of the city was Luz at the first. Then Jacob made a vow, saying, "If God will be with me, and will keep me in this way that I go, and will give me bread to eat and clothing to wear, so that I come again to my father's house in peace, then the LORD shall be my God, and this stone, which I have set up for a pillar, shall be God's house; and of all that you give me I will surely give one tenth to you."
>
> Genesis 28:11–22

There are many themes we might draw out of this story. In it, the writer orients the reader through Jacob to basic needs—bread, clothing, ancestors and descendants, land on which to live, and peace between people. The writer also establishes the precedent of tithing, which has had a long history in principle, if not in practice.

Most significant for our purposes, however, is the simple fact that the "house of God" in the story is a stone. The story clothes God in rock.

The metaphor is a frequent one in Scripture. Psalm 18 clarifies both the frequency of the image and one of its meanings. It reads: "I love you, O LORD, my strength. The LORD is my rock, my fortress, and my deliverer, my God my rock in whom I take refuge, my shield, and the horn of my salvation, my stronghold. I call upon the LORD, who is worthy to be praised, so I shall be saved from my enemies" (vv. 1–3). The strength of rock, and its use in building walls and fortresses, makes it a fitting metaphor for the protection people seek from God. The psalm is reprised in 2 Samuel, where the imagery's significance is recalled in vivid terms: "The LORD lives! Blessed be my rock, and exalted be my God, the rock of my salvation . . . who brought me out from my enemies . . . [who] delivered me from the violent" (22:47–49). Indeed, the living rock who protects from violence even gives birth to the people of Israel, who are tempted to forget that the rock is a gift, not a possession: "The Rock . . . is perfect . . . a faithful God, without deceit." Yet God's people forget their source in the living Rock: "You were unmindful of the Rock that bore you, you forgot the God who gave you birth" (Deut. 32:4, 18). Those Christians who seek a safe way to introduce female imagery for God could find no clearer evidence to support the validity of their claims than this verse. God gives birth.

Even the names for God in the Hebrew Bible can lend credibility to earth-centered, female ways to clothe God. The most famous name for God in the Hebrew Bible is Yahweh. Naturally, it is revealed to Moses on a mountain—Mount Horeb. The name "Yahweh," as a variant on the verb *to be,* has no gender referent and, in fact, relativizes all efforts to affix gender or any other attribute to the divine. "I am that I am" or "I will be what I will be" is the name "revealed" (some revelation!) to Moses on the mountain—along with God's promises to be with Israel and to bring the Israelites to freedom. Other Hebrew names for God are even more explicit. "El Elyon," often translated as "God Most High," probably refers to the mountains in which the Canaanite predecessors of the Israelites worshiped. "El Shaddai," translated as "God Almighty" in most English versions, in fact is better rendered "God of the Mountains." Indeed, although the etymology of the term is ambiguous, it may be a female form, and thus could be translated—as one colleague has suggested to me—"God of the rounded breasts." The neighbors of the Israelites, notably the Canaanites, had plentiful ways to clothe the divine in female form, so it should be neither surprising nor shocking, and even should be celebrated, that some of these female images for God are found in the Scripture.

Rocks and mountains provided the biblical writers with excellent metaphors to clothe God, then, but the gift beyond all gifts to the people of Israel was the land. Walter Brueggemann has penned an excellent study of the land in biblical theology that clarifies in a very helpful way the promise, and problems, of grounding a theology (pun intended) in this way. According to Brueggemann, the land carries four meanings in biblical theology: as gift, temptation, task, and threat. We will develop all four eventually, but for now the theme of land as gift is the key. In Deuteronomy, the point is made most clearly. Moses explains to the people that

> the LORD your God is bringing you into a good land, a land with flowing streams, with springs and underground waters welling up in valleys and hills, a land of wheat and barley, of vines and fig trees and pomegranates, a land of olive trees and honey, a land where you may eat bread without scarcity, where you will lack nothing, a land whose stones are iron and from whose hills you may mine copper. You shall eat your fill and bless the LORD your God for the good land that he has given you.
>
> 8:7–10

This "good land" is clearly here a gift—with its bounty and beauty available for all the people. As Brueggemann concludes, "Land is a central, if not the central, theme of biblical faith."[7] *Land* is also, interestingly, a feminine noun in Hebrew.

Not surprisingly, given these manifold metaphors, the first followers of Jesus interpreted him in light of them. At the conclusion of a long series of sayings in Matthew, for instance, the author records Jesus as saying: "Everyone then who hears these words of mine and acts on them will be like a wise man who built his house on rock. The rain fell, the floods came, and the winds blew and beat on that house, but it did not fall, because it had been founded on rock" (Matt. 7:24–25). To Jesus' hearers, steeped as they were in the images of God as rock in the Torah and Prophets, to associate his own teachings with the rock could not have but offended or amazed. And indeed, the apostle Paul had made the association even more explicit well before Matthew wrote. Recalling the wandering of the people in the wilderness, and their salvation by "the rock" that united them, Paul concluded for his followers in Corinth that "the rock was Christ" (1 Cor. 10:4). The image is a favorite of Paul's. Jesus was the "cornerstone" on which the church was built, even though the builders rejected the stone, and people sometimes stumbled over it. Biblical scholar Brueggemann draws the conclusion in the sharpest terms. The Christian faith, he argues, growing as it does out of the Hebrew emphasis on a theology of the land, might be summarized as a dialectic (or tension) between land loss (or law) and land gift (or grace), with the latter always the last word of Jesus.

All in all, then, when Christians clothe God as rock, mountains, and land, we can point to God's presence as permanent gift. These associations should not surprise us. When we build a church, we often use stone. When we promise ourselves to a partner for life, we give a diamond. When we want to remember a loved one's place of burial, we place on the earth a tombstone, made of marble or some other durable mineral. And when we say goodbye to a loved one at a funeral, we remember that we all are "dust, and to dust we must return." Indeed, then, as this last example suggests, there is another set of associations between God and rocks, mountains, and earth that points not only to the gift of God's presence but also to the threat of loss. For if land is a permanent gift, many people also try to make it into a possession. In such cases, we need a reminder that a God who is rock is not ours to possess, but rather a matrix of challenge, temptation, and task.

The Challenge, Temptation, and Task of Being "Landed"

In the summer of 2001 I watched my two sons, aged thirteen and fifteen, scale a 350-foot rock face. We were back in South Dakota, again visiting my Aunt Joan and Uncle Guy and my godson Rich. Rich is a certified rock-climbing instructor, and he had arranged his schedule to meet us at his parents' home. After one day of a few "test" climbs, Rich announced that the boys were ready to tackle a more serious outing (I prudently concluded that my surgically repaired left knee wasn't up to the challenge). The next morning, bright and early, we drove from the Krueger home in Piedmont to the back side of Mount Rushmore, to a rock face whose official name is "The Emancipation Rock Formation," but which is known colloquially as "Washington's Crack."

It was a beautiful morning. After parking the car across the highway from the formation, we hiked with the boys and Rich to the rock face, which was about seventy-five feet up and a quarter of a mile into thick woods. As we stood at the rock face, looking straight up, while Rich arranged the ropes and other "safeties" for the climb, I began to regret that I hadn't volunteered to go along. It didn't look that daunting. But there was equipment only for two, besides Rich, and the boys were enthusiastic about the climb—although they also were just a tad quiet. Soon enough, Rich scaled the face to a ledge about seventy-five feet up and beckoned for the boys to follow. Nate, the younger son, went first, and without a single slip made his way to join Rich. Justin followed and, after a few scary moments, eventually made it to the ledge, where all three guys waved to us with pride. Lisa and I then started back down the rock scrabble to the highway, where, Rich had instructed us, we could sit on a rock in the sun and watch the rest of the climb.

It took about twenty minutes for us to climb down through the woods. When I turned around to look at the boys' progress, my heart dropped. What had not seemed that "daunting" now looked impossible. The boys were tiny white specks on a stark rock face, spiders on a huge rock wall. (The two boys can be seen in this location in the bottom left corner of the photograph.) "What have we done?" I asked Lisa, as she turned to take in the same view. "Oh, my God," she said. "They look so tiny." With binoculars we could see the ropes that held them in place through safeties Rich had placed every six feet or so, but the ropes looked as slender and tenuous as the boys looked vulnerable and fragile.

For the next four hours, Lisa and I sat on a rock across the highway as the boys climbed with Rich. Drivers visiting the Rushmore memorial would stop after spotting the climbers and talk with us. A typical conversation went like this. "Do you know those climbers on the rock? Those are your children? How old are they? You're kidding, right?" We tried to explain that the boys were probably safer than they were in a car, statistically speaking, but most parents weren't buying it. We weren't sure we were. Lisa and I had little choice, however, but to sit there and feel our blood pressures rise as the boys scaled ever higher. The last face or portion of the climb looked particularly difficult to me. The rock bulged outward, meaning the boys would actually have to hang parallel to the ground, to a degree, while pulling themselves upward. "How are they going to do that last section of the climb?" I asked Lisa. We did have walkie-talkies to converse with Rich, and I'm sure our voices sounded more than a little strained at various points. I know I breathed much easier when Rich called us on the radio and announced: "I'm happy to say Justin and Nathan are here with me at the top, and the view is spectacular." Then came the rappel down—which was at least mercifully brief. When the boys were finally back on solid ground, Lisa and I each embraced them both with deep affection and newfound admiration. They had achieved a significant challenge, and I was proud.

This pride, of course, is part of the temptation that goes along with clothing God as land, rock, and mountains. Pride can make one forgetful, mindless, careless. Pride can distort trust, turning it from an honest recognition of one's limits and dependencies to a self-asserted importance or arrogance. The author of Deuteronomy knew this temptation well and reminded the people of Israel: "Take care that you do not forget the LORD your God, by failing to keep his commandments. . . . When you have eaten your fill and have built fine houses . . . then do not exalt yourself, forgetting the LORD your God. . . . Do not say to yourself, 'My power and the might of my own hand have gotten me this wealth'" (8:11–17). Being "landed" brings with it the temptation to forget that land, like life, is a gift. And the land can turn on and devour those who imagine they can possess or conquer it. Rocks can smash into pieces, choke life of sustenance, and pulverize or be pulverized into dust.

The psalmist—who is the most insistent of the biblical writers at clothing God as rock and fortress—is equally clear about the other functions of rock. Vivid and even brutal imagery conveys the danger rocks can bring. For instance, after the Babylonians captured the Israelites and took them into exile—in what was no doubt an unpleasant experience for the Israelites—the biblical writer imagined revenge in some of the most horrific language in any Holy Scripture. "Happy shall they be," the psalm reads, "who take your little ones and dash them against the rock!" (137:9). Rocks can kill as well as protect. Such imagery is, and should be, banned from use in Christian liturgies. But here its function can be clarified. Such a sentence can clarify the temptation that experiences of violation and oppression always bring. Clothing God as rock can be not only a refuge, but a catalyst to revenge. "Their rock is not like our Rock," offers Deuteronomy 32, in the midst of an account of warfare, "our enemies are fools" (v. 31). Rocks can be thrown at each other, just as language for God can be turned to curses. Clothing God as rock is as dangerous as clothing God as flood or fire, then, because such language can perpetuate the cycle of violence that anyone who has ever been in an intense dispute with another knows all too well. "Deliver me, O LORD, from evildoers," prays the psalmist in another place. "Protect me from those who are violent, who plan evil things in their minds and stir up wars continually. . . . When [the violent] are given over to those who shall condemn them, then they shall learn that my words were pleasant. Like a rock that one breaks apart and shatters on the land, so shall their bones be strewn at the mouth of Sheol"(140:1–2; 141:6–7). These unpleasant words point to a truth that ought to promote peace making: human forgetfulness, pride, and violence invariably turn on themselves.

Clothing God as rock thus poses a stumbling block for human arrogance and pretension. The prophet Isaiah describes this feature of clothing God as rock particularly well. In the midst of conflict, some will find the God who might unite all the people in a permanent gift, not a refuge but a barrier to their own ambitions to possess this or that piece of the land. "[God] will become a . . . stone one strikes against; for both houses of Israel he will become a rock one stumbles over—a trap and a snare for the inhabitants of Jerusalem. And many among them shall stumble; they shall fall and be broken; they shall be snared and taken"(8:14–15). The prophet Ezekiel elaborates on the imagery. When a conquering army invaded a city, he explains, the rock walls and towers that fortified the city were first assaulted with battering rams, then breached with a ramp, and finally smashed into pieces. In the worst cases, the stones that built the walls were then carted to the sea and thrown in, rendering their reuse in rebuilding difficult if not impossible (26:1–14). Under siege, of course, the rock fortress in which humans trusted became not only a stumbling block but a death trap—an illusion of security that produced only plunder and destruction. God as rock challenges all illusions of security.

Yet, even in such cases, the last word of the prophets is comfort. The land itself mourns when it is broken. Hosea puts it best:

> Hear the word of the LORD, O people of Israel; for the LORD has an indictment against the inhabitants of the land. There is no faithfulness or loyalty, and no knowledge of God in the land. Swearing, lying, and murder, and stealing and adultery break out; bloodshed follows bloodshed. Therefore the land mourns, and all who live in it languish; together with the wild animals and the birds of the air, even the fish of the sea are perishing.
>
> 4:1–3

In such cases, hope is found not in a rocklike refuge, which becomes a stumbling block and a snare of destruction, but in a more humble form. Consequently, Hosea turns near the end of his book to imagery of birth and gestation to comfort the people. God the rock gives birth to the people, bends down, and feeds them—as mothers throughout the world feed their infants—from her breasts. Therefore, "I will not execute my fierce anger . . . for I am God and no mortal, the Holy One in your midst, and I will not come in wrath"(11:1–9).

Such imagery for God as rock was the matrix out of which the first Christian writers wove their stories about Jesus. As we have seen, for Paul, Jesus becomes the stumbling block. He writes, to a church at Corinth beset by conflict: "We proclaim Christ crucified, a stumbling block to Jews and foolishness to Gentiles, but to those who are the called, both Jews and Greeks, Christ the power of God and the wisdom of God. For God's foolishness is wiser than human wisdom, and God's weakness is stronger than human strength"(1 Cor. 1:23–25). This remarkable passage contains many themes to be lifted up—including Paul's metaphor of Jesus as the wisdom, or *Sophia,* of God—another female image. But most important is Paul's point that clothing God in Jesus as Messiah is not an easy way to clothe God, but a difficult task indeed, in which apparent weakness becomes strength, and foolishness becomes wisdom. The most direct route to power is not always the most enduring and what seems the most obvious way to preserve life might in fact deal death.

To sort out this paradox it will be good to look briefly at another way God is clothed through Jesus, namely as one tempted. In the Gospels of Matthew and Luke, Jesus experiences exactly what every other human undergoes: the temptation to imagine oneself as the possessor of power, rather than to realize life is a gift. Matthew's account reads:

> Then Jesus was led up by the Spirit into the wilderness to be tempted by the devil. He fasted forty days and forty nights, and afterwards he was famished. The tempter came and said to him, "If you are the Son of God, command these stones to become loaves of bread." But he answered, "It is written, 'One does not live by bread alone, but by every word that comes from the mouth of God.'" Then the devil took him to the holy city and placed him on the pinnacle of the temple, saying to him, "If you are the Son of God, throw yourself down; for it is written, 'He will command his angels concerning you,' and 'On their hands they will bear you up, so that you will not dash your foot against a stone.'" Jesus said to him, "Again it is written, 'Do not put the Lord your God to the test.'" Again, the devil took him to a very high mountain and showed him all the kingdoms of the world and their splendor, and he said to him, "All these I will give you, if you will fall down and worship me." Jesus said to him, "Away with you, Satan! for it is written, 'Worship the Lord your God, and serve only him.'" Then the devil left him, and suddenly angels came and waited on him.
>
> 4:1–11

Here, the temptation to Jesus is exactly the temptation the prophets suggested all human beings face—to trust in our own desires to acquire, rather than to be oriented by the gifts of life. The temptation is dizzying. Jesus, isolated and hungry, is taken up higher and higher, offered first food and then all the power in the world, if he will only acknowledge that part of himself that imagines that power is his to possess. But Jesus refuses, resolutely clinging to the rock of the Other. This Other is manifest clearly in the words of Scripture, but of course Satan (the word means "opponent," "accuser," or "obstacle") also quotes those words. Beyond the clothing, though, is the rock on which Jesus rests. And that rock is identified as worship and service of the living God. Worship and service of the living God—manifest in gratitude for all of life as a gift—is the only power worth expressing.

Such a magnanimous vision of God is, of course, why Jesus had to be killed. Only when God is turned into a possession can power be concentrated. And people who point out that true power cannot be possessed will invariably wind up silenced, at best, or smashed against a rock, at worst. Jesus, of course, was crucified on a cross, as a victim of capital punishment. He was put there by a concentrated effort on the part of the authorities of his day—both political and religious. And when he died, the Gospel of Matthew records that "Jesus cried again with a loud voice and breathed his last. At that moment the curtain of the temple was torn in two, from top to bottom. The earth shook, and the rocks were split. . . . Now when the centurion and those with him, who were keeping watch over Jesus, saw the earthquake and what took place, they were terrified and said, "Truly this man was God's Son!"(27: 50–54). This imagery highlights how the veils authorities put over their attempts to possess power—the curtain in the temple by which the Holy of Holies was hidden, or the rocks on which the occupying army of centurions stood—were smashed by the death of this single Jew.

The accounts of Jesus' resurrection continue that theme. After his death, Jesus is wrapped in burial clothes, according to custom, and placed in a stone tomb or cave, which is itself protected by a large rock rolled over its entrance. After the Sabbath passed (or on the third day), the Gospels agree that a woman or women who had followed Jesus during his lifetime traveled to his tomb. There they found a mystery—and the accounts vary widely about what they experienced. The Gospel of John, for our purposes, puts it most directly. The rock is rolled away, and the tomb is empty. All that is left are Jesus' burial clothes—the linen wrappings around his body, and the shroud that had cloaked his head, "rolled up in a place by itself." Much has been made, of course, of this shroud. Most of it has been spurious. But the intention behind its veneration is good. We need, indeed, to attend closely to the ways we shroud God. For such clothing can split rocks, roll away tombstones, and be a stumbling block both to powers and to ordinary people.

Clothing God as rock, then, highlights by way of contrast our own fragility—and the temptations, challenges, and tasks that go with being a finite being. Being "landed" means we have to care for the land—as the only earthlings who have the capacity to do so through language and other political structures. Many Christian ethicists and theologians have in recent years stressed this point: Christianity must become "earthbound," as Larry Rasmussen puts it.[8] Or we must establish a link between "Gaia," the living earth, and God, according to Rosemary Radford Ruether.[9] And perhaps we can even think of the earth as "God's body," as Sallie McFague has suggested.[10] All in all, a

God clothed as rock, mountains, and earth also highlights our place on the land, and points us to the fragility of finitude. Of course, such clothes for God can also point to life, even life eternal, wonderful life that death itself cannot contain.

Wonderful Life

The late Harvard paleontologist Stephen Jay Gould, in a book on a single fossil record—the Burgess Shale in British Columbia—borrowed the title of the famous Frank Capra film to describe what he found revealed in that rock formation. Briefly, Gould synthesized the work of many paleontologists to suggest that the Burgess Shale reveals that it is quite improbable that human intelligence should ever have developed on the planet Earth. One species—one fragile species—survived what was otherwise a decimation more thorough by far than the decimation of the dinosaurs. Most of the animals represented in the record of the Burgess Shale no longer exist. They are extinct, victims of the contingencies of history and their own design. But that one species that survived was a little soft-tissued critter by the name of *Pikaia gracilens,* literally "the grace of Pika." Pika is a mountain located near the Burgess Shale. And *Pikaia gracilens* was a chordate—in fact the world's first known chordate. A chordate, for those who like me struggled with high school biology, is an animal with a stiffened rod along its back. Among human beings, of course, we call this our spinal cord.

Gould draws out the significance of this tiny detail, buried in rock fossils and long hidden in the record of a rock formation in the mountains of British Columbia:

> *Pikaia* is the missing and final link in our story of contingency—the direct connection between Burgess decimation and eventual human evolution. . . . Wind the tape of life back to Burgess times, and let it play again. If *Pikaia* does not survive in the replay, we are wiped out of future history—all of us, from shark to robin to orangutan. And I don't think that any handicapper, given Burgess evidence as known today, would have granted very favorable odds for the persistence of *Pikaia*. And so, if you want to ask the question of the ages—why do humans exist?—a major part of the answer, touching those aspects of the issue that science can treat at all, must be: because *Pikaia* survived the Burgess Shale. This response does not cite a single law of nature. . . . The survival of *Pikaia* was a contingency of "just history." I do not think that any "higher" answer can be given, and I cannot imagine that any resolution could be more fascinating. We are the offspring of history, and must establish our own paths in this most diverse and interesting of conceivable universes—one indifferent to our suffering, and therefore offering us maximal freedom to thrive, or to fail, in our own chosen way.[11]

This is, indeed, one way to read the record; and it is a way that believers in God have not often respected, even though it is, mostly, true.

But Gould himself suggested another path to the same truth, and even other language to interpret the same record, although he is hardly aware of the significance of his own language when he uses it. The paleontologist writes:

> People, as curious primates, dote on concrete objects that can be seen and fondled. God dwells among the details, not in the realm of pure generality. We must tackle and grasp the larger, encompassing themes of our universe, but we make our best approach through small curiosities that rivet our attention—all those pretty pebbles on the shoreline of knowledge. For the ocean of truth washes over the pebbles with every wave, and they rattle and clink with the most wondrous din. . . . The animals of the Burgess Shale are holy objects—in the unconventional sense that this word conveys in some cultures. . . . They are grubby little creatures of a sea floor 530 million years old, but we greet them with awe because they are the Old Ones, and they are trying to tell us something.[12]

The "Old Ones," of course, are not only rocks. They are also the human authors who used metaphors of rocks to reveal to us truth, as they knew it. If *Pikaia gracilens* is a missing link in the story of human evolution, a pebble in the ocean of truth, then, exactly the same must be true of the ways people before us have clothed God in language. Words, in short, can be pebbles of truth, impressing a record of grace and beauty just as surely as the imprint of an ancient chordate in a piece of shale. The universe is indifferent only if we resolve to let it remain so, refusing to clothe indifference in compassion.

Among these ways to clothe God in truth, and which point to the wonder of life, are stories of surprising contingency in the desert. One such story is told in Numbers 20. The people of Israel, having recently been freed from slavery in Egypt, are wandering in the wilderness. They are lost and have no water to drink, and the people are complaining. Their leaders, Moses and Aaron, pray to God, who invites them to gather the people and to command water to come forth from a rock. This seems like an unlikely path to political success, but Moses, undoubtedly perturbed with his people but at a loss for any other way to proceed, gathers the people together. The account goes: "'Listen, you rebels,'" Moses asks them, "shall we bring water for you out of this rock?' Then Moses lifted up his hand and struck the rock twice with his staff; water came out abundantly, and the congregation and their livestock drank" (10–11). This seems like a happy, if surprising, ending. In fact, however, God is not pleased. God had told Moses to command the waters to come forth—and "command" usually implies "using language." Instead, Moses struck the rock, calling his people "rebels" in the process, and claimed that he and Aaron ("we") were the sources of the miracle. For his recourse to violence, and for his arrogance, God prohibits Moses from entering the "Promised Land" along with his "rebels." Moses' shortsighted grab at using God for political power kept him from the long view that would have allowed him to enjoy the fulfillment of his vision among his people. There is, in short, a right way and a wrong way to handle the contingencies of life. Calling people "rebels," running around smashing rocks, and claiming all the glory for oneself is the wrong way. Gently acknowledging grace as the gift it is when it presents itself is better.

A second story that reveals a way to clothe God in the wonders of life—even in fragile crystals of sand—is the story of the Indiana Dunes National Lakeshore. I

studied or taught in Northwest Indiana for sixteen years, and while to many people the area is Chicago's armpit, the National Lakeshore is an undisputed gem in the region. In fact, the story of how "the Dunes" were preserved is a remarkable story of survival in the face of a technological and political onslaught.[13] Steel mills, harbors, and other industries were, in the late nineteenth and early twentieth centuries, mining the sand of the huge dunes on the south shore of Lake Michigan and building smoke-belching factories along its shoreline. A few individuals perceived that without political intervention, the Dunes would soon be gone. In what became an eighty-year struggle, called by one observer "the most savage conservation-industry confrontation in history," at least some of the great dunes of southern Lake Michigan were preserved, first in a state park, and then in a much larger national lakeshore. Consequently, I was able to go sledding in winter down "Mount Baldy," the tallest of the "living" dunes, whose huge sand face moves a few feet inland every year. And I was able to take my students on "pilgrimage" to Mount Tom, where the early preservationists held pageants and parades in hope of preserving what they came to call the "sacred sands."[14] That God dwells among the details of that place makes good sense to me, and I am grateful that some others before me saw the place not only as sand to possess, but as grains of grace whose fragile wonders were worth preserving for future generations. That this sacred place was forged through contest—as David

Chidester, Edward Linenthal, and other historians we encountered in chapter 1 claimed—is clear enough. That it can also function as a place of grace, where the fragility of goodness can be manifest for all to see, should also be clear.

Finally, I want to close this chapter with what many take to be the central vision of a sacred place in Christianity—the hope of heaven. It should be obvious by now—and especially in the earlier discussion of heaven in chapter 5—that I agree with the author of the Gospel of John that God's house has many mansions and that trying to contain God to this or that theological fashion is a bad mistake. Heaven is a minor theme in the Bible, almost an afterthought among the places where the Scripture writers located God. But the vision of heaven in the Book of Revelation is so beautiful, and so illuminating of the deepest human hopes, that it should remain for Christians a goal that can orient life and a grace that can free us from obsessive preoccupation with our own efforts. Of course, this way of clothing God can also be badly abused, when it obscures attention to life here and now and reconciles people to their own victimization as if such suffering were God's will for them.

The vision of heaven comes near the end of the Book of Revelation. We will attend to it in some detail in the last chapter, but for now I want to draw attention only to the wall, streets, and gates of the New Jerusalem, described by the seer in the following terms:

> The wall is built of jasper, while the city itself is pure gold, clear as glass. The foundations of the wall of the city are adorned with every jewel; the first was jasper, the second sapphire, the third agate, the fourth emerald, the fifth onyx, the sixth carnelian, the seventh chrysolite, the eighth beryl, the ninth topaz, the tenth chrysoprase, the eleventh jacinth, the twelfth amethyst. And the twelve gates are twelve pearls, each of the gates is a single pearl, and the street of the city is pure gold, transparent as glass.
>
> 21:18–21

These are, of course, the "pearly gates" of folklore and of many bad jokes. They are also a way of clothing God's presence in beautiful stones—in the red-golden cream of jasper, the deep blues of sapphires, the shimmering blacks and tans of tiger-eye agate, the greens of emeralds, the purples of amethyst, and on and on through all the bejeweled colors the eye can envision. These are pebbles on the ocean of truth, too, pointing us to the wonderful life we have been given here, which we hope is continuous with and a foretaste of the wonders of life to come.

If death is the ultimate problem Christians seek to solve through sacred places of rock, mountain, and earth, then suffering is surely a close second. Stephen Jay Gould suggests that human beings exist in a universe indifferent to our suffering, and on one level that is no doubt true. Christians and other people of faith for too long have imagined ourselves at the center of the universe and consequently have arrogated to ourselves control over the cosmos in ways that have violated it badly.[15] A more humble view is needed, where we understand both our fragile place in the cosmos and our dependence upon other fragile life-forms for existence. Contingency, as Gould suggests, is a reality in the flow of time.

But this reality of contingency is hardly new to Christians and other people of faith. "Time, like an ever-rolling stream, soon bears us all away," goes one of my favorite Isaac Watts hymns. "O God, our help in ages past," it continues, "our hope for years to come. Our shelter from the stormy blast, and our eternal home." If we clothe God as an eternal home or shelter, then, not in some comfortable suburban sense that seeks to deny suffering but that acknowledges our place in it, perhaps the doctrine of heaven can function to steel us for service in the midst of suffering. And maybe, after all, we will then discover that the universe will prove to be not *only* indifferent. Perhaps we will discover that we also play a role in shaping the grand indifference, in ordering the chaos of contingency, in effecting how history turns out. Indeed, with God as our refuge, perhaps the flow of history becomes largely what we make it through the ways we interact with the other places on the planet. When we take our honest place in the scheme of things, in short, perhaps we can experience the other places on the planet not only as being indifferent but perhaps even as places of grace.

Belden C. Lane, a professor of theology at St. Louis University, has made just such an effort with the harshest places on the planet, in a beautiful and dense book entitled, *The Solace of Fierce Landscapes: Exploring Desert and Mountain Spirituality.* Lane readily acknowledges the indifference of the cosmos to human suffering. He wrote the book as a way to respond to the extended suffering of his mother as she died in a nursing facility. Drawing upon the mystical tradition that sees prayer under a threefold typology of purgation, illumination, and union, Lane explains how he finds grace in deserts and mountains that appear, on one level, indifferent to his salvation. In an "austere landscape," he writes:

> I realized more than ever before the healing capacity of fierce terrain. The desert did for me what the nursing home had begun to do for my mother. . . . It invited me out of myself, out of my fears and need for control, out of a self-absorption wary of opening itself to intimacy. The way of purgation involves an entry into what is unnerving, even grotesque in our lives, into what quickly reveals our limits. It seems at first, like most beginnings in the spiritual life, a mistake, a false start. . . . Only through hindsight do we recognize it for the unexpected gift that it is.[16]

This is a God "hidden in the grave-clothes of death," as Lane puts it, a God "unavailable to . . . anxious denial of aging and pain." As Lane sat beside his mother through hours that turned into weeks that became years, observing her twisted body and gaping mouth, he realized that a "broken God" was the one available to him then. The rock was split. Inside its fissure came comfort and even salvation. A broken God alone brought him good news, much like a single chordate species was the link that made the decimation of the Burgess Shale an event of wonder, not only an indifferent ending.

So, as I reflect back on my encounter with five turkey vultures at Stagebarn Canyon, I think of it in terms like these. I think of it now as a gift, a challenge, and a wonder. I love to tell the story to groups. I was so out of place, so naive, that my immediate reaction to this strange encounter was fear. Each time I retell the story, though, I learn from it—not least about the existence and habits of vultures, which, according to one interpreter is a more accurate interpretation of the Hebrew word *nesher*—used for God in Deuteronomy 32—than the more frequent translation, "eagle."[17] And indeed, the more I know about them, the more God as rock-dwelling vulture is an image I can live with.

For these huge birds, with wingspans of up to six feet, are sociable, friendly birds, according to the Turkey Vulture Society—a nonprofit organization whose members study the birds and seek to preserve their habitats. The omnivores also primarily eat plants, for they cannot always find a good carcass to clean up. They live in families or roosts, often in the same place for over a century, usually rock ledges or cliffs. In short, I was in their place—probably the first person to visit in decades, and quite possibly ever, given that no trail ascended to the spot. They were curious. Other observers have noted that the birds like people. In captivity, a turkey vulture will play with its caretaker, bouncing a ball back and forth with its head, following the caretaker around and watching his or her motions, and even playing tug of war with an object, like a pet dog. They are called the "Peace Eagle" by the Cherokee, because they so rarely hunt.[18]

Still, my experience surely brought me into touch with my fragility. I learned that I lived in the same world with turkey vultures, and I wasn't sure I trusted them. I knew they were huge, and that I was in an unfamiliar and dangerous place—quite possibly their roost, or even a nest where a mating pair might have left a couple of eggs. Now, I suppose that if my experience had been part of a formal vision quest, my name might be Jon "Five Vultures" Pahl, with all the ambivalence that such a name would bring. I kind of like it. Some might find it morbid, but I saw firsthand not only the awesome nature of those birds but also their freedom, their beauty, and their stunning ability to soar. The Turkey Vulture Society calls them "the most graceful soaring bird in the world," and I would have to agree. They hold their wings all but silent, in a V shape, without flapping, just "feeling" the air current and making adjustments with their wing tips to soar for hours on end. They communicate with other birds when they find some food and enjoy playing games in the air, like follow the leader, tag, and speed soaring.

Maybe, then, the birds were just playing a wonderful joke on me. I like to imagine that at turkey vulture religious ceremonies they tell the same story I do, and laugh together about the folly of human efforts to imagine ourselves as innately superior to the "beasts" of the forest. They surely proved smarter than I on that sunny Saturday—and I suspect that all of us can benefit from reflecting on the wisdom of these rock-dwelling creatures. For, finally, while we share with the vultures a proximity to death, they face it honestly and even manage to thrive from it. We, too often, deny death in ways that find us clinging to some cliff or another that invariably proves to be no more than the same dust with which we are made. But such indifference of nature to our suffering need not paralyze us. In fact, our awe at the vastness of the cosmos, and our wonder at its fragile beauty, can motivate us to care for the planet better than we have in the past century. Indeed, by clothing God as the wonderful pebbles of *Pikaia gracilens,* in the shifting sands of the Indiana Dunes, or in the ivory gleam of the pearly gates, perhaps we can learn to extend compassion to all who face the decimation of suffering and the despair of death. By clothing God as the stumbling block to pretensions of power, perhaps we can learn to trust in more fragile but enduring forms of political association, rather than to trust in violent force. And by clothing God as the rock of our salvation, we can realize—as Edward Abbey suggests for us in the epigraph to this chapter—that everything points to our one foundation, that everything is a miracle. Everything!

10

The True Vine

Everything is threatened, but meanwhile
everything presents itself:
the trees, that day and night
steadily stand there, amassing
lifetimes and moss, the bushes
eager with buds sharp as green
pencil points. Bark of cedar,
brown braids, bark of fir, deep-creviced,
winter sunlight favoring
here a sapling, there an ancient snag. . . .

Denise Levertov, "In the Woods"

One spring, I began to clean up the yard after a long winter. We were living in Chicago at the time, in a townhouse whose front yard faced a forest preserve and whose backyard was separated by a fence from a golf course. We were surrounded by large, leafy oaks and maples, which seemed determined, I came to believe, to drop all of their leaves in our yard. Although we rented the house, I had not yet done my research on lawn care, so I felt compelled to make the yard look "presentable" for the neighbors. On this particular April morning I had a helper, Justin, who was about three. We trimmed hedges, scattered some grass seed in bare spots, and raked the countless leaves out from under shrubs and bushes.

As we were picking up one pile of leaves to put in the wheelbarrow and cart across the street to the forest preserve, I absentmindedly took one particularly dry leaf between my fingers and crumpled it up. It turned to dust.

This attracted Justin's attention, and he asked me, "Why does that leaf turn to dirt, Daddy?" It was early in the morning, and I was not thinking too clearly. Had I been fully awake, I would have responded very carefully, mindful of the fact that my son had displayed almost from the time he could speak a very high sensitivity to death—perhaps because of his difficult birth. Justin's childhood awareness of death had become, in our family lore, notorious. There were two stories in particular that I should have remembered.

One of them recalled how Lisa had taken Justin to a Wisconsin children's museum whose prize exhibit was a mummified Native American "princess." (It is no longer on display.) As Lisa and Justin approached the exhibit, Lisa noticed our son's eyes darting back and forth repeatedly from the blackened husk of a body to a "painting" of the Indian girl as she had appeared while alive. Lisa reported to me later that her son's scream was positively chilling: "IS THAT WHAT HAPPENS WHEN YOU DIE!?" he bellowed for the entire museum to hear. It took about an hour to calm him down. The other story I should have remembered was about the time that Justin announced, in the line to board a plane to Florida, and in a clear and definitive voice loud enough for everyone to hear: "THIS PLANE IS GOING TO CRASH AND WE'RE ALL GOING TO DIE!" Again, I wasn't there, so I'm not sure what effect this had on flyer morale. We are, however, grateful that as Justin has matured he has shown no more fear of death than your average teenager, which means, basically, little to none.

Anyway, it was an early April morning, and I wasn't thinking clearly when my sensitive son asked me, "Why does that leaf turn to dirt, Daddy?" So, I said, accurately if bluntly: "Well, because it's dead, Justin."

The questions came immediately, in rapid-fire sequence: "Why did it have to die, Dad? Can I turn a leaf to dirt, too? Why do people have to die, Daddy?"

"Oh, no," I thought to myself, now wide awake. Visions of years of therapy bills passed by my eyes as I pondered my next step. Naturally, I took the easy way out, and answered the practical middle question: "Sure you can turn a leaf to dirt, Justin. Here, take this," I said to him as I handed him his own dry leaf, "and crumple it up." He did, it disintegrated in a few seconds, and then my son looked at me with his bright blue eyes and repeated, relentlessly, the other two questions: "Why does a leaf have to die? Why do people have to die, Daddy?"

There was no escape possible. I wasn't a professor yet, but I knew that one effective teaching technique was to turn the question back to the questioner. So, I tried it on my own son. "Wow, that's a really tough question, Justin," I said. "Why does a leaf have to die?"

The boy bailed me out. He smiled up at me and said: "I know, Dad, that's just the way life is, isn't it?" I laughed, and almost cried at the same time. Justin's answer motivated me to try one myself.

"Yeah, I guess so, Justin," I said. "That's just the way life is. It's like this: that leaf dies and turns to dirt, and what grows in the dirt?"

He furrowed his brow for a few seconds and said, not quite having grasped logic yet: "Grass."

"Yes," I replied, "grass grows in the dirt, but so do trees. And what grows on trees?"

He answered immediately, catching on rather quickly if I may say so: "Leaves."

"Right," I said. "So that leaf dies. Out of the death of the old leaf comes the new. It's the same with people. We're here for a while, to live and to work and to love, but then we die so that new people can come along with new ideas."

My son nodded, and then, looking very thoughtful and profound, asked: "Daddy, we're new people, aren't we?" I could only laugh again, and hug him, reassuring him without words that we were, indeed, new people.

The idea of being new people, of course, is one that is presupposed in every conversion, every confession, and every therapy session. It is also an idea that is easily, and frequently, linked to the life-and-death cycle of things like trees, vines, flowers, and grasses. The Christian gospel is hardly the only religious system to assert that we can all be made anew, but for Christians the message is crystal clear: God promises to be with us, as the tree is with the branch, pushing us to new life, new growth, new ways of being. This may be easy to assert; it is much harder to live.

Nevertheless, the metaphor of God as vine, tree, life-growing plant to which we are connected rings the globe among the world's religions. For instance, among the Lakota Sioux, Black Elk, a shaman or medicine man who was also a sometimes convert to Catholicism, recalls seeing near the end of his life a vision of a cosmic tree, atop Harney Peak in South Dakota. He narrated what he saw to Joseph Epes Brown:

> Then I was standing on the highest mountain of them all, and 'round about beneath me was the whole hoop of the world. And while I stood there I saw more than I can tell and I understood more than I saw; for I was seeing in a sacred manner the shapes of all things in the spirit, and the shape of all shapes as they must live together like one being. And I saw the sacred hoop of my people was one of the many hoops that made one circle, wide as daylight and starlight, and in the center grew one mighty flowering tree to shelter all the children of one mother and one father. And I saw that it was holy.[1]

This vision from Black Elk may blend Christian and Lakota imagery, but it points us to a truth, whatever its source. All trees share one thing: they live and they die. All people, of course, share the same thing. Perhaps, then, we can learn something about this matter of living and dying from observing, and even from listening to, the trees—as a way to clothe the God who unites us all.

Among some of my genetic ancestors—the Scandinavian peoples of Northern Europe—appears a vision similar to the one of Black Elk. In a text over a thousand years old, a female prophet is awakened from deep sleep by the great god Odin and declares:

> I remember . . . those who first gave birth to me. I know of nine worlds, nine spheres covered by the tree of the world, That tree set up in wisdom which grows down to the bosom of the earth. An ash I know, Yggdrasil its name, With water white is the

great tree wet; Thence come its dews that fall in the dales, Green by Fate's well does it ever grow.[2]

This cosmic tree, Yggdrasil, is the home of Odin, from which he surveys the whole world. All creatures live in, or off, the tree—squirrels run up and down, goats, eagles, and people all flourish in its branches and are shaded by its leaves.

In a similar fashion, the classic Chinese text *Tao Te Ching* draws upon the changes in the life and death of plants, including trees, to convey the important idea of "stillness," or living in harmony with the Tao, or "the way." "When things (in the plant world) have displayed their luxuriant growth," the meditation begins,

We see each of them return to its root.
This returning to the root is what we call the state of stillness;
And that stillness may be called a reporting that they have fulfilled their appointed end.
The report of that fulfillment is the regular, unchanging rule.
To know that unchanging rule is to be intelligent;
Not to know it leads to wild movements and evil results.
The knowledge of that unchanging rule produces capacity and forbearance,
And that capacity and forbearance lead to a community of feeling with all things.
From this community of feeling with all things comes greatness of character;
And whoever is great of character goes on to be heaven-like.
In that likeness to heaven, one possesses the Tao.[3]

Trees and plants, then, serve as metaphors in religious traditions from around the globe.

The reasons for the centrality of these metaphors are not difficult to discern. Life would not exist without the oxygen made possible by the photosynthesis of green things. We depend on trees and other green plants. We need them. They provide shade to cool us on a sunny day, and wood with which we build shelter. They give us fruits and berries, bread and wine, herbs and spices. They feed our animals, provide fabric for our clothing, and offer up medicines for our bodies.

Consequently, trees and plants play a prominent role in Jewish and Christian Scriptures. Trees are mentioned 300 times, in 252 verses of *Tanakh* and the writings about Christ. The meanings of these verses are many. We will highlight only three. Trees in Scripture and Christian tradition first reveal God as Life-Bearer, as a place of rest and peace in the midst of conflict and violence. The grasses of the field and the vines of the earth mentioned in Scripture also reveal, second, that God as True Vine labors with us as we take each breath of life. God labors with us even through death and suffering, seeking through the fragile fall and winter of life a rebirth free from fear and violence. And, finally, the trees of Scripture and tradition show us God as Greening Power, wrapped in a garment like a lush garden, offering us gifts of life and inviting us to grow greener despite the dusty fact of death.

The Tree of Life: God as Life-Bearer

In the ancient world, a tree meant rest, shade, and peace. After a long, hot ride or walk through a desert, a glimmer of green on the horizon must have been a most welcome sight indeed. One of the very first stories in Scripture—which we studied briefly in chapter 8—highlights this role of trees as places of encampment, rest, and peace for people. Abraham—the patriarch of Judaism, Christianity, and Islam, has taken up abode under a grove of oaks near Mamre—an ancient sacred place in the hill country of Canaan. It is a typical day in Canaan, which means that it is hot. At noon, Abraham "sat at the entrance of his tent" and saw three men approach. Now, in the ancient world, the approach of strangers was an important moment. Practices of hospitality might make friends of the strangers, thus allowing one to keep one's encampment in the shady grove. The failure to extend hospitality, in contrast, could cause conflict and create enemies, and perhaps result in the loss of the green place. In this story, at stake was not only the shade of the oaks at Mamre, but the entire history of God's people.

Fortunately, Abraham extended hospitality to the strangers. The story details the encounter: "When Abraham saw [the three men], he ran from the tent entrance to meet them, and bowed down to the ground. He said, [addressing one of them], 'My lord, if I find favor with you, do not pass by your servant. Let a little water be brought, and wash your feet, and rest yourselves under the tree'" (Gen. 18:2–3). The three visitors assented to Abraham's offer, and Abraham then had his household prepare a meal of bread, tender meat, and milk and curds (cheese) for his guests. As a good host, Abraham then set the food before his guests, and "stood by them under the tree while they ate" (v. 8). This simple practice of hospitality—providing water and food under the shade of a tree—prepared the way for the guests to offer to Abraham the most specific promise yet from God—that his wife Sarah would bear Abraham a son. From the peaceful hospitality experienced under a tree comes the promise of the future of Israel. Under trees, the promises of God begin.

Of course, the oaks at Mamre are not the first trees in the Bible. In the second creation story (Gen. 2:3) in Genesis, trees play perhaps the crucial role. There, trees serve to orient the first human beings. Insofar as the first earthlings live in harmony with the trees, all is well. When, however, the first humans arrogate to themselves a knowledge beyond that of the trees, they find themselves in trouble. The story is a familiar one, but it has often been misunderstood, with tragic consequences.

The earthling (for that is what *Adam* means) has been formed from the dirt, and the earthling's partner has been formed as well. The happy couple is naked and not ashamed. God had spoken to the earthling and said, even before a partner was created, "You may freely eat of every tree of the garden; but of the tree of the knowledge of good and evil you shall not eat, for in the day that you eat of it you shall die" (2:16–17). The point of this statement is simple but often missed. First, it affirms that trees provide food for human beings. Trees meet a human need. They are life-bearers. Second, the prohibition in the statement affirms that a tree can orient human beings to the knowledge of good and evil and the difference between life and death. A tree, in short, was the first "sacred place" in Hebrew Scripture.

Now, the earthling's partner (taken from a rib, as an equal) is wandering through the garden one day, and a talking snake appears and says: "Did God say, 'You shall not eat from any tree in the garden'?" (3.1). The question is highly disorienting—a distortion. Trees now no longer provide as life-bearers; they are simply prohibited. The earthling's partner is bewildered by this imaginative prospect. The orientation has become unclear. Understandably, the partner's reply is confused: "We may eat of the fruit of the trees in the garden; but God said, 'You shall not eat of the fruit of the tree that is in the middle of the garden, nor shall you touch it, or you shall die'" (3:2–3). Again, here the central point is affirmed: trees are life-bearers. But the prohibition has also escalated. Now even to *touch* the tree, the one in the middle of the garden, will bring death. The talking snake replies: "You will not die; for God knows that when you eat of it your eyes will be opened, and you will be like God, knowing good and evil" (3:4–5).

This is, of course, the crucial moment in the story, but a momentum has already developed making the outcome all but inevitable. Desire has developed—and not just any desire, but mimetic desire, or an imitative desire to consume. Humans imagine—consciously entertain—being "like God." The earthling needs to eat, but the prohibition of desire has, through imagination, escalated to the point of making the desire irresistible. Needs have given way to imaginative wants, and in the spiral of imagination all orient is lost. So of course the earthling consumes the fruit of the tree and then gives some to its partner—and the imitation escalates even further. The fruit looked good, and who wouldn't want to be wise, and who can imagine one's own death? Amazingly, as it turns out, the snake was right: "the eyes of both were opened" (3:7).

This text is not, as it is often interpreted, primarily the story of a "fall into sin." It is, first of all, the story of the dawning of self-conscious awareness, which is both a blessing and a curse. People experience this in adolescence, usually. One "wakes up" to oneself, to both the potential and the problems of being an earthling. The second aspect of the story points to the awakening of desire, and desire is also productive of both pleasure and pain. The only aspect of the story that points solely to a fall is when a very particular kind of desire disorients the two characters. This aspect of the story is also repeated in every earthling, in one way or another. At some point in life, we "talk to a snake," some projected or imagined part of ourselves, and it frightens us. Self-consciousness can be scary. In reaction, we seek to be like someone else or to possess something that someone else possesses. We grow envious and greedy. Often, such mimetic desire is triggered by a prohibition—even if it is only an imagined one. That which was perfectly acceptable and normal now becomes a problem. Once this process is under way, it never ceases. The internal dialogue of desire and prohibition goes on endlessly. Just try to stop it. Once we desire to know good and evil, every choice becomes a burden. Once we desire to know good and evil, every encounter becomes a potential seduction by a serpent. Once our eyes are opened, we discover, as did the first earthlings, that we are naked, vulnerable, fragile—in a word, that we die. Clothing ourselves, and clothing God, then becomes all but necessary.

Death was not the consequence of this process; the consequence was (and is) the awareness of death—the knowledge of value and limit. Like the first earthlings, when we become aware of our desires and their flip side—limits and mortality—we will often attempt in the wake of this discovery to patch together some strange clothing to cover things up. For many of us, this awareness manifests itself slowly in an "identity crisis" of some kind, in which as we lose the easy orientation of childhood, and we try out new identities to orient our action in the world. Awakening to choice is a disorienting thing.

The first couple, according to the story, made loincloths of fig leaves—products, of course, from a tree. But these patched-together clothes don't help, and the disorientation just grows deeper. The earthlings hide in the woods, the story continues, and we know it's true, because what adult has not at one time or another hidden a desire or its consequences from another? Imitative desires bring a sense of shame, because they reveal rivalry. We fear that such rivalries might bring conflict and death—as the story intimates—and so we feel shame. We are lost in the forest of desires, without orientation or direction.

The story goes on to describe God, however, out for a walk in the woods. God discovers the first couple hiding. "Who told you that you were naked?" God asks (3:11). The problem, again, is not nakedness, not death itself, but the awareness of nakedness, fragility, and mortality. And this knowledge—manifest at first in the desire to flee, to cover up—invariably manifests itself also in the will to fight. The desire to know good and evil, like the desire to hide one's nakedness, the story suggests, invariably spirals up into violence. The ironies are ample. It is the "best" of human invention—the knowledge of good and evil—that, paradoxically, gets us into the most trouble. When we think we know something, when we make distinctions, everything then falls into place; but precisely by making a distinction, everything falls apart.

The story puts the paradox clearly: the man (the couple didn't *know* their genders before this moment in the story) blames the woman, who blames the serpent, and then all three have the consequences of their actions explained to them by God. The consequences of "knowing good and evil" are the awareness of violence and suffering. The serpent experiences "enmity" with humanity; the woman will experience the pain of labor and suffer under dominion; and the man will experience the pain of labor and suffer under dominion. The message to the man confirms the limits of all: "You are dust, and to dust you shall return" (3:19).

This story is, again, not primarily the story of a "fall" into sin, but rather the story of the ambivalent lot that is human being: glorious knowledge on the one hand, and the potential for radical evil on the other. And it all comes as the fruit of the trees. Really, the story changes nothing. Adam was always an earthling. But the fact that people now know their situation and can choose to act within it makes this tale the perfect setup for the importance of the covenant accounts that follow later in Genesis—as of course the author intended. The earthlings have discovered that they are different from the earth, from the trees, and from each other. This discovery is a great gift; it brings with it the good of desire, but also a great responsibility. For now the couple *knows* they will die, and once our eyes are opened to that fact, we begin to fashion denials of one kind or another. As long as we are unaware of our mortality, our "nakedness," there is no need to "clothe" ourselves. But once aware, we will never again be unclothed without shame, and so, the story suggests, God "made garments of skins for the man and for his wife, and clothed them" (3:21).

Now this is a homey image. It seems like a rather "nice" thing for God to have done for the man and woman. Despite blaming humans and "cursing" them with labor (they can't just eat from trees anymore), God fashions for the couple some clothes that were better tailored than their makeshift fig leaves. In fact, however, this "homey" little image hides yet another consequence of being alienated from the garden. For the clothes are now made, not of fig leaves, but of skins. And skins, of course, demand a victim. For the first couple to have skins, there had to be somewhere a dead animal. So we have, here, the first victims. Because of human shame, and human blame, death comes. Violence escalates.

And as the violence escalates, so does the imitative desire. The story goes on to have God banish the couple from the Garden of Eden, the garden of delight, because they might eat from the tree of life and live forever. Nothing has really changed. It is still a tree that provides orientation, that bears life, and it is still imitative desire—the desire to acquire—that will lead to trouble. Our awareness of desire and its prohibition—good and evil, if you will—leads us to deny even our delight in life itself in all of its manifold splendor. We are, then, banished from "the garden" when we fixate on our imitative desires, when we become aware of our "nakedness," and when we seek to fashion "clothes" for ourselves behind which to hide. The tree of life—a gift to us in the first place—slips from view as we become fixated upon "the knowledge of good and evil" and grow attached to the labor of our desire. Shame, enmity, violence, and death follow from our fixations—and from our "knowledge." Our eyes are opened, and while they still see good, they also see evil, as if good would not be good unless it had a contrast.

And the story thus concludes with Cain and Abel, the first murder. Cain kills Abel because he imitates his desire and envies him. This murder between the first brothers wraps up the point of the whole narrative. From blissful existence among the peaceful trees of life, the garden of delight, where we "can eat freely of all the trees of the garden" comes "civilization"—where we kill. We now know good only in contrast to evil. We now know life only in contrast to death. We now know delight only as the fruit of our labor and desire.

Most commentators on this story—which I have interpreted at length because it is so often and so badly misinterpreted—have missed the significance of the trees. The story has been used to justify misogyny and the subordination of women. It has been used to justify masochistic and antisexual piety—as if God wanted people to suffer. It may be (we have no way to know) that this story depends on a very early substrate of Canaanite piety, where tree worship did orient the people. But the point holds, no matter the historical origin. This story of the first human encounter with trees is the story of our effort to imagine ourselves different from them, with their orienting cycle of life and death. We want to know "good" and "evil," we want to imagine ourselves "like God," and we want to live forever. These are desires that trees don't have. As far as I know—unless we cause them stress—trees don't suffer anxiety. As far as I know, the needs of trees are amply met, and they don't envy one another, despite being clothed in splendor that the boldest human can only imagine. And, of course, trees don't claim to know the difference between good and evil, and yet they do so much good.

Every tree, in short, is a tree of life; all trees clothe God as life-bearer. The tree of life is still standing, living, and growing. The story of the first human couple details vividly the rise of human envy, conflict, enmity, alienation, and violence, as the flip side of the "good" virtues of imagination, will, and desire. These consequences follow because we imagine ourselves different from, and somehow better than, the orienting gift to us of God in the trees of the garden. Trees provide us with the orientation we need to learn the way of God as peaceful life-bearer.

The lessons of the trees as life-bearers are woven throughout Scripture. Psalms, especially, uses the image of a tree to represent the ideal human. In Psalm 1, for instance, David writes:

> Happy are those who do not follow the advice of the wicked, or take the path that sinners tread, or sit in the seat of scoffers;
>
> but their delight is in the law of the LORD, and on his law they meditate day and night.
>
> They are like trees planted by streams of water, which yield their fruit in its season, and their leaves do not wither. In all that they do, they prosper.
>
> vv. 2–3

The same theme recurs in Psalm 92, where the author praises the "righteous [who] flourish like the palm tree, and grow like a cedar in Lebanon. They are planted in the house of the Lord, they flourish in the courts of our God" (vv. 12–13). God the life-bearer hopes for us to flourish.

In Proverbs, God, in the form of Lady Wisdom, is explicitly personified as a tree. The author writes:

> Happy are those who find wisdom, and those who get understanding, for her income is better than silver, and her revenue better than gold. She is more precious than jewels, and nothing you desire can compare with her. Long life is in her right hand; in her left hand are riches and honor. Her ways are ways of pleasantness, and all her paths are peace. She is a tree of life to those who lay hold of her; those who hold her fast are called happy.
>
> Proverbs 3:13–18

Here, wisdom is a manifestation of God's creative grace. God is clothed like a tree of life—her branches (the Hebrew is feminine) cradle us and protect us, and those who stay near her are happy.

Such happiness, then, is our origin and our lot in life, when we listen to the trees. Indeed, any tree can convey this message. Aside from their beauty, their ecological necessity, and their symbolic significance, they have an economic worth that is impressive to consider. The American Forestry Association estimated that the "70 million or so acres of urban tree spaces [in the United States] are worth more than $50 billion. As for a single tree . . . an average 50-year-old city tree would provide $73 worth of air conditioning, $75 worth of erosion and storm water control, $75 in wildlife shelter, and $50 in air pollution control in one year . . . [for a total] over its half-century lifetime at $57,151."[4] Such calculus, of course, puts a value on a life that in fact demeans it. But such a figure might, perhaps, give us pause when we consider the deforestation or degradation of forests around the globe. It might also help provide us with some figures to suggest in negotiations with (or lawsuits against) those corporate and government types who carelessly destroy forests in the interest of "developing" them for private profit. They have had no problem putting a dollar figure on the lives of trees for their own benefit. Such figures have, of course, been way too low. Since the time of the first earthlings, we have turned violence first onto ourselves, then onto each other, and finally onto the trees. It is time to try another way.

Fruitful yet Fragile

Trees die. This fact has caused more than a little consternation at our house. Early in his life our middle child, Nathan, discovered my love for trees and has made them his own project as well. He surprised us, and delighted us, one April when he declared that for his birthday—I believe it was his fifth—he wanted a tree. It was a rather remarkable request for a young boy but one that I was only too happy to grant.

Our first summer in Valparaiso—when Nathan was just an infant—had been extremely hot and dry, and two different stands of birch trees on the west side of our house had died. The next summer, I bought a small chain saw at a local garage sale. The trees came down without too much difficulty and eventually burned well in our fireplace. Their absence left the west side of our house looking pretty empty. Unfortunately, our budget was also empty, since my starting salary at Valparaiso University in 1988 was $18,000. We struggled to buy groceries, much less birch trees.

Nathan's kind request, however, motivated me to go out and buy a six-foot Autumn Purple Ash from a local nursery, and deliver it to him with a big bow around it for his birthday on May 10th. He seemed really happy with it, and the next morning we set out to plant it, right in the spot where one of the stands of birch trees had previously stood. As we were digging the hole for the tree, Nathan and I talked. He's always been a very perceptive child, but even I was surprised when he acknowledged the significance of what we were doing by saying: "Dad, think about it. . . . Someday after you die, I'll be able to come back here to see this tree, and remember that we planted it together." I know the sentence took my breath away with its beauty. Sure, his statement indicated that he expected me to die. I don't think, however, that he was wishing me dead, and his expectation was, in any event, completely accurate. He was, I think, saying something far more gentle. He was saying he'd remember me even after my death and that what he'd remember was the beauty of a May day. The tree we planted together would be the sign of that beauty we had shared.

I wish I could report that the tree was still there, on the corner of Green Acres Drive and Bloomingdale Avenue in Valparaiso, now grown thirty feet tall, with leaves turning a royal purple every fall. I could report that, but it would only be a nice story, and it wouldn't be true. The tree, after one brief summer, died, despite my best efforts at watering it as directed, pruning it, and keeping a close eye out for bugs. The next spring it never budded, and by July I pulled it up by its roots with one hand and threw it out in the field behind our house.

Two years later, we tried again. This time, Nate and I went to the best nursery in town (according to some natives), where the trees were all planted and cultivated from local hybrids. He and I walked up and down the rows of saplings on his birthday, and he eventually settled on a six-foot tall sweetgum tree, a native of Indiana, and a fast grower. We tagged the tree, paid the owner, but waited until the fall for its delivery, because fall is the optimal season for transplanting. Nathan was very patient during his wait, although we did on one occasion take a trip to the nursery to "visit" his tree. When fall arrived, we again worked together on its planting. I reminded Nate what he had said to me as we planted Tree #1, and we enjoyed a laugh over the fact that the tree had died before I did. We both said we hoped this one would do better.

It did, but not much. I worried over that tree—again watering it with care, pruning it, and watching for pests. It budded and grew well the next spring—a good two feet of growth, at least. I was delighted. The next year, too, it came back—although after it grew a bit, I noticed some spidery little webs on it and called the owner of the nursery. He suggested a treatment, which I applied, and for the rest of the summer it did well. Again, however, an Indiana winter did it in. The tree budded in its third spring, but the buds looked sickly, and within a few weeks the few leaves that had blossomed were brown and withered. Nate and I again had learned the lesson. Trees die. We didn't plant another thing until after we moved to Pennsylvania.

Trees die. It's a simple statement, but its significance is not. As objects of religious devotion, trees share the limitation of all living things—they are fragile and finite. In early Canaan and Israel, by most accounts, people worshiped trees, and apparently this practice was quite durable in some locales, because the scribes, priests, and prophets found it necessary to denounce it repeatedly. The author of Deuteronomy, for instance, specifies that for ritual purposes, you "shall not plant any tree as a sacred pole beside the altar that you make for the LORD your God" (16:21). Jeremiah used more graphic imagery to denounce the worship of trees among the people of Israel: "On every high hill and under every green tree you sprawled and played the whore." Jeremiah, writing in a time when the people of Israel were in political turmoil, felt that the worship of trees undermined civic unity. "I planted you as a choice vine," Jeremiah has God speak to the people, "from the purest stock. How then did you turn degenerate and become a wild vine?" (2:20–21). In the wake of violence, a religious system that did not focus attention on the Lord alone (as Jeremiah envisioned the Lord) was a target for denunciation. Worshiping something as fragile and wild as a tree made little sense in the wake of the devastation and burning of trees that followed conquest—which Jeremiah fully expected for his people if they did not change their religious and political lives.

However, the prophets emphasized that though fragile, and not to be worshiped, trees endured and survived even trauma, and therefore were a fitting symbol for God's presence with the people of Israel. Thus Isaiah writes of a terrible destruction when "the Sovereign, the LORD of hosts, will lop the boughs with terrifying power; the tallest trees will be cut down, and the lofty will be brought low. He will hack down the thickets of the forest with an ax, and Lebanon with its majestic trees will fall" (10:33–34). Such destruction gives way in the vision of the prophet, however, to rebirth: "A shoot shall come out from the stump of Jesse, and a branch shall grow out of his roots. The spirit of the LORD shall rest upon him, the spirit of wisdom and understanding, the spirit of counsel and might, the spirit of knowledge and the fear of the LORD. His delight shall be in the fear of the LORD." This "shoot" from the stump of Jesse, now personified, even wears distinctive clothing: "Righteousness shall be the belt around his waist, and faithfulness the belt around his loins." And the rebirth of this tree brings peace: "The wolf shall live with the lamb, the leopard shall lie down with the kid, the calf and the lion [shall live together in peace]. . . . They will not hurt or destroy on all my holy mountain; for the earth will be full of the knowledge of the LORD." (11:1–9). Isaiah here imagines a political order in which oppression by the strong was overcome, and peace prevailed. It is a beautiful image, filled with hope, and it hinges upon the imagery of a fragile shoot growing from a fallen tree.

Christians have often interpreted this text from Isaiah as a "foreshadowing" of Jesus, and on one level this is understandable. The Gospel writers—among the first people to interpret the life of Jesus—were Jews themselves, and therefore used the images from their tradition to make sense of the teacher from Nazareth. But there is no "prediction" of Jesus in Isaiah, as if by magic the prophet "foresaw" the future. Humans don't do that. Inspiration is not magic. And Isaiah's inspiration was context-specific. The Northern Kingdom of Israel fell during Isaiah's time, and he feared that the same would happen to Judah, the Southern Kingdom where he resided. He hoped, however, that a faithful remnant would "save" his people. The context of the text is the Jewish hope for a reign of peace. Isaiah hoped that God and humanity—indeed the whole earth—would be united. He did not intend, as many Christian writers have done, to exclude others from this grand unity, as if there was only one way to peace. Wolves, leopards, and lions would lay down with lambs, kids, and calves. It is a remarkably pluralistic vision.

And it is, interestingly, very much like the vision of Jesus and the first Gospel writers. The Christian use of Isaiah, if done with integrity and without violating the original context, can illumine some of the ways belief in God can promote a deep peace among fragile people. Thus Jesus' relationship with trees highlights, on the one hand, their fragility. In the Gospels, Isaiah's image of the destruction of trees is picked up by both the authors of Mark and Matthew to convey the revolutionary potential of belief in God. Matthew's story is the clearest:

> In the morning, when [Jesus] returned to [Jerusalem], he was hungry. And seeing a fig tree by the side of the road, he went to it and found nothing at all on it but leaves. Then he said to it, "May no fruit ever come from you again!" And the fig tree withered at once. When the disciples saw it, they were amazed, saying, "How did the fig tree wither at once?" Jesus answered them, "Truly I tell you, if you have faith and do not doubt, not only will you do what has been done to the fig tree, but even if you say to this mountain, 'Be lifted up and thrown into the sea,' it will be done."
>
> 21:18–21

These images of trees destroyed and mountains leveled are familiar prophetic images (see also Joel 1:12; Hosea 2:12; Dan. 4; Amos 4). They would have been understood by the Jewish readers of the Gospels as political messages about the radical potential of faith in God. The curses of the prophets about political oppression against Israel were now being uttered and enacted by the person of Jesus. Jesus' cursing of the fig tree thus occurs in both Gospels on the day after he "cleansed" the temple of its money changers. The spirit of both actions was the same—to critique corrupt political and spiritual power.

Indeed, elsewhere in Matthew, Jesus used the metaphor of trees and fruit to describe how believers can discern good teachers from bad, and good life choices from bad. He says (the passage is similar in Luke):

> Beware of false prophets, who come to you in sheep's clothing but inwardly are ravenous wolves. You will know them by their fruits. Are grapes gathered from thorns, or figs from thistles? In the same way, every good tree bears good fruit, but the bad tree bears bad fruit. A good tree cannot bear bad fruit, nor can a bad tree bear good fruit. Every tree that does not bear good fruit is cut down and thrown into the fire. Thus you will know them by their fruits.
>
> 7:15–20

Here trees are a symbol for the fruitfulness of a life of faith, on the one hand, and the fragility of goodness, on the other.

This paradox of fruitfulness and fragility is incorporated by the author of the Gospel of John in the person of Jesus himself. Jesus teaches:

> I am the true vine, and my Father is the vinegrower. He removes every branch in me that bears no fruit. Every branch that bears fruit he prunes to make it bear more fruit. . . . Abide in me as I abide in you. Just as the branch cannot bear fruit by itself unless it abides in the vine, neither can you unless you abide in me. I am the vine, you are the branches. Those who abide in me and I in them bear much fruit, because apart from me you can do nothing. Whoever does not abide in me is thrown away like a branch and withers; such branches are gathered, thrown into the fire, and burned. If you abide in me, and my words abide in you, ask for whatever you wish, and it will be done for you. My Father is glorified by this, that you bear much fruit and become my disciples. As the Father has loved me, so I have loved you; abide in my love. If you keep my commandments, you will abide in my love. . . . [And] this is my commandment, that you love one another as I have loved you.
>
> 15:1–12

Love is a fragile thing, and one who loves freely often winds up feeling burned, withered, and cut off. Love, unfortunately, is not always returned.

Jesus learned this with his life. Jesus died. The details vary from Gospel to Gospel, as do the interpretations of the event, but the Gospels all convey that Jesus was crucified by the political and religious authorities of his time. Crucifixion, of course, occurred on a tree. The theological significance of that fact did not escape later interpreters of both Tanakh and the Gospels. Thus, for the apostle Paul, a Jew who knew well the prophetic curses against "wild" trees and vines, Jesus' crucifixion on the tree meant that the curse against the "unfruitful" trees—who were often understood by Jews as "the Gentiles" —had been overcome. Through Jesus' death, the promise of God made first to the Jews had now been extended to all people. Thus, Paul wrote in his letter to the congregation at Galatia: "Christ redeemed us from the curse of the law by becoming a curse for us—for it is written, "Cursed is everyone who hangs on a tree"—in order that in Christ Jesus the blessing of Abraham might come to the Gentiles, so that we might receive the promise of the Spirit through faith"(3: 13–14). Paul turned Jesus' death at the hands of the authorities into a critique of the authorities themselves and their unjust use of "the law." Jesus' death, and the community that survived it, showed that the power of capital punishment, the power of state authority, and the power of religious convention could not overwhelm the power of God's love and the love of human beings for God. For Paul, the true vine worked by grace as a gift—not by control.

For Paul, and many interpreters after him, the fragility that Jesus the "true vine" displayed by giving his life on the cross became a model of the fragile power of grace that would prove fruitful even beyond death. Indeed, Jesus' death and the community that survived it provided the root from which a new "shoot" was springing in a fruitful olive tree: "If the root is holy, then the branches are also holy. But if some of the branches were broken off, and you, a wild olive shoot, were grafted in their place to share the rich root of the olive tree . . . remember that it is not you that support the root, but the root that supports you. . . . So do not become proud, but stand in awe"(Rom. 11:16–20). This new community was fragile, but by abiding in the grace of the true vine, it would prove fruitful.

And as history indicates, of course, the fruits of this tree have been plentiful. Christianity grew as an offshoot of Judaism. Because of the grace Jesus displayed—grace that did not fear even death—a remnant from the tree bore fruit and the promise of the prophets was renewed. A movement centered around a "failed" prophet became a movement that reshaped the history of the globe through its message of grace. Thus the last vision in the writings about Christ, which we first saw in chapter 7, imagines again the tree of life from Genesis. The tree has been transplanted in a new Jerusalem, the city of peace, alongside the "river of life," and "the leaves of the tree are for the healing of the nations. Nothing accursed will be found there any more"(Rev. 22:2–3). This vision, as fragile now as then, is yet as potent. Grace bears healing like a tree bears fruit. Both images—one abstract, the other material—point to a God clothed as life-bearer, fruitful but fragile.

Bearing fruit, in short, requires embracing fragility. Trees die. People die. Jesus died. But new trees live. And new people live, too—even in a person who once has been "dead" to life.[5] And for this reason Nathan and I have taken to planting green things again. We're growing herbs—like oregano, thyme, and rosemary—that come back every spring. They're doing well. And we've planted a couple of foot-tall seedlings from the National Arbor Day Foundation, and they've just about tripled their size in a year. I hear that's a pretty good track record for such fragile things.

Greening Power and "the Flesh"

God clothed as tree of life and true vine, then, inherently conveys several meanings. It communicates on the one hand life-bearing fruitfulness, on the other hand, fragility. But underneath both images is yet another that requires rethinking the nature of power. Trees live and die, but they also grow. One Christian thinker has developed this fact about trees and growing things into an understanding of God's power and presence that has fascinating implications. Hildegard of Bingen, a medieval theologian, monastic abbess, artist, songwriter, and reformer, coined a Latin phrase—*viriditas*—to describe the way God's presence produced growth. Hildegard's many works have received considerable scholarly attention in recent years, along with those of many other medieval women writers and mystics, but Hildegard's conception of *viriditas* may be unique for its scope and application. *Viriditas* means "greening power." By it Hildegard meant to "encompass the lush green of life in all of nature's creations as well as the healing powers of the organism, health, and the vitality of the spirit."Viriditas also extended beyond nature to the divine. Thus, she wrote, "There is a power in eternity, and it is green." This color was not literal, of course, but a symbol for the growth potential of all things. Hildegard thought human reason, knowledge, and conscience were all green, because they shared in this "power in eternity."[6] Even more specifically, the grace of Christ brought "lush greenness" to "shriveled and wilted" people and institutions. Indeed, she wrote: "In the beginning all creatures were green and vital; they flourished amidst flowers. Later the green figure itself came down."[7] For Hildegard, the metaphor of Jesus as true vine meant, naturally, that Jesus was *viriditas* incarnate—greening power in the flesh. Greening power came from God, indeed was God.

The theme of greenness, and its underlying message of the nature of true power, is not lacking in Holy Scripture. Among the prophets, Joel offered comfort to the people of Israel in earthy images of *viriditas:* "Do not fear, O soil; be glad and rejoice, for the LORD has done great things! Do not fear, you animals of the field, for the pastures of the wilderness are green; the tree bears its fruit, the fig tree and vine give their full yield. O children of Zion, be glad" (2:21–22). Greening power brings people—and indeed the soil and animals as well—joy, gladness, and overflowing abundance. Hosea makes the link between God and greening power even more explicit: "I am," says the Lord, "like an evergreen cypress; your faithfulness comes from me" (14:8). And of course Jesus himself preached, as Hildegard knew, that he was "the true vine" in which hope always came forth springing green.

This "greening power" in the prophets, in Jesus, and in Hildegard is in direct contrast to what biblical scholar and theologian Walter Wink has called "the domination system." According to Wink, the conventional understanding of power in the world leads people to suppose that power is force, control, and domination. God's way, Wink argues, is rather a "Domination-Free-Order," in which very different patterns of power prevail. If the domination system seeks "power over," God's domination-free order offers "power with." If the domination system seeks power "to *take* life," God's order offers the "power to *give* life." If the domination system claims power "to *control* life," God's order offers the "power to *support and nurture* life." The first model of power is of course the way "the world" understands power—with its militaries and bureaucracies—as force. It was just such a system that killed Jesus. The second model of power, Wink suggests, was evident in the life of Jesus and in the followers who understood—such as Hildegard—that his message was continuous with the prophetic critique of unjust and abusive power that had gone before him.[8]

Wink develops a number of concepts and metaphors used by biblical writers to convey the way the "domination system" works and how it contrasts with "greening power." The most compelling, to my mind, is the Pauline metaphor of "flesh." This term (*sarx* in Greek) is often understood as "body," but to identify it in this way is to misunderstand Paul's intention and to mistake a part of the body for the whole. Paul's term *sarx* refers less to the body than to the attitude toward the body we carry once our "eyes are opened" and we discover our potential for good and evil. The term is intended to isolate or highlight the mimetic, thoughtless, superficial "self" or ego that seeks to preserve its own existence at all costs. The term is found throughout Paul's letters, but its meaning is perhaps clearest in Romans 8: "Those who live according to the flesh set their minds on the things of the flesh, but those who live according to the Spirit set their minds on the things of the Spirit. To set the mind on the flesh is death, but to set the mind on the Spirit is life and peace. . . . But you are not in the flesh; you are in the Spirit, since the Spirit of God dwells in you"(vv. 5–6, 9). The "flesh" here is obviously not the same as the "body," since Paul affirms that the Spirit of God *dwells in* believers. The flesh is the opposite of life. Thus the "works of the flesh" include, for Paul, not only sins "of the body," but idolatry, envy, strife, jealousy, and so forth (see Gal. 5:19–20). The "flesh," then, is death and the fear of it, which produces narrow self-interest and the kind of religious reactions we observed in chapters 3 through 5. You can call those reactions "sins," "idolatry," or the "domination system," but in any event, they are the opposite of the life-giving greening power of the Spirit.

Wink suggests that "flesh" is synonymous with the human experience of alienation. Life "according to the flesh (*kata sarka*)," he writes, "denotes the self externalized and subjugated to the opinions of others. It is the self socialized into a world of inauthentic values, values that lead it away from its own centeredness in God."[9] Such language of "externalization," "subjugation," "alienation," and a loss of "centeredness" expresses the struggle of human beings to articulate what happens when the dawn of consciousness arises and we begin to become a problem to ourselves. We've come full circle to the issues raised earlier in this chapter in our discussion of Genesis 3. A God clothed in greening power reveals to us the glory of a garden, where we have our needs provided for, and where we receive orientation without fear or shame. A God clothed in greening power reveals the fruitful yet fragile path of living and dying well, for others, and for our own fulfillment, out of grace. A God clothed in greening power reveals that the domination system, the way of flesh, can give way to a gentler new life springing as a true vine.

The logic of this fabric for God is the reason Christians display flowers at funerals, weddings, holiday seasons, and other sacred times. I know it is currently customary for many Christians to refuse the purchase of flowers at their funeral and to request instead that money be spent on a donation to a charitable organization. I understand the motive for this request, and will surely honor it when made, but I also think it represents a mistake. Flowers aren't for the dead, of course, but are to console the living. They are reminders, signs of life to help comfort the grieving. Of course this practice can be excessive, and florists will gladly exploit the desire for a sign of greening power at a Christian funeral. But a simple rose—traditionally a symbol of the Messiah—or even the gift to a bereaved one of a living tree, is to me a highly appropriate gift to offer at the death of a fellow believer.

The same impulse to experience and to be reminded of God clothed as greening power is evident in the Christian festival of winter—Christmas. Trees adorn most Christian homes during the season, and while some find this practice offensive and environmentally unsound, it need not be. Most Christmas trees are grown for the purpose they serve, and they are readily recyclable into mulch. Their presence in a home serves as a fitting reminder of greening power, and as their needles start to fall, they also serve to remind us of fragility. The entire cycle of a Christmas tree's life span thus witnesses to a power that is not afraid of death but goes through it to new life, just as the seasons themselves change from winter to spring. Greening things communicate the kind of power God chooses to wield, then, as any honest experience of God's presence reveals: not force, not domination, not coercion, and above all not violence; but persuasion, attraction, mutuality, and love. Indeed, this power, Christians assert, is the only true power. Any other kind of power is illegitimate—or at best a stopgap response to a prior failure of nerve and reason.

Perhaps the best way I can illustrate this power at work is to talk about a wedding—yet another sacred time in which greening power is often invoked. From time to time my undergraduate students asked me to "do" their weddings. I always felt awkward at such requests. I'm not ordained, so the first thing I explained is that—technically—I couldn't. If students were still interested in my presence, perhaps as a reader or a preacher, I explained that a wedding was best conducted in a community setting, like a church, where they could make public their commitments to each other and then count on the support of a community for that commitment afterward. This usually didn't sink in, but I said it anyway. Finally, after a third request, I have on occasion agreed to serve as preacher, and less often as unofficial presider, at a wedding, with a justice of the peace or an ordained pastor witnessing the signing of the marriage license.

Before I preached at weddings, I sat down and interviewed the couple, asking them to relate to me their story, so that I could then weave together a narrative around a chosen biblical verse or reading. This narrative acquainted the congregation with the couple in a way that allows each person in attendance to witness the couple's commitments and, hopefully, to honor them. It also makes for an interesting, often funny and usually touching, homily. Recently, I preached at the wedding of two former students in Kansas City, and the metaphor that surfaced from my interview with them was of their love as a peach tree.

I had grown quite close to the two students—Kirsten and Jaron—over their four years at Valparaiso, so when they asked that there be no mention of God in their service, I understood. Both had grown up in the church, but both had also been repelled by the systemic violence with which they found the church complicit. The service was held in a beautiful outdoor chapel, in a garden, with lots of natural light, flowers, and trees surrounding us through the huge clear windows of the building. As usual, I introduced the couple to the gathered assembly through my homily, which I based on the results of my interview with them and on a reading they had chosen about "walking and talking together on the road of fidelity." I shared how the couple met, one of their worst times together, and one of their best times together—all woven around the ideas of conversation and journeying together. For the final question, I asked Jaron and Kirsten to offer a metaphor or image to describe their loved one. Jaron's metaphor was organic. "Kirsten's sweet," he haltingly began. "She nourishes my soul, and is refreshing," he continued. "After a long day of being away from her, she's a pleasure." And then after a brief, awkward pause he added, softly: "She's my peach."

Kirsten also chose an organic metaphor for her loved one. She first offered an apology: "I'm sure that mine is less poetic than Jaron's, since he was an English major."

I encouraged her to go on. "OK," she said. "Jaron is like a tree. He's strong. And he's beautiful. And he provides excellent shade because he's so tall." After that line, the assembly laughed. I could not resist in the conclusion to the homily drawing out the sympathetic coherence between the two metaphors. I said:

> We are witnesses today to the joining together of a peach and a tree—somehow that seems fitting. . . . Let us then imagine the peach and the tree listening to each other, as they both hear the rustling leaves around them whispering to them the joy and delight of being together. And we can imagine the tree and the peach talking to each other, as branches crack together in the wind and as the young fruit pops forth from a bud into beauty. And we can even imagine the tree and the peach walking together the road called fidelity. The tree can trust the peach for faithful delight and sweetness year after year as she blossoms and matures, and the peach can trust the tree for strength, and support, and shade, year after year, as they learn to grow old together.

Such language clothed the couple in God's grace, without resorting to particularistic language, and invited the congregation to recognize the union of Kirsten and Jaron as also clothed in grace. I hope, of course, that the couple finds a community in which to celebrate their life together. But I hardly thought it was my place to force them to do so to get married. To reject their invitation to me would have confirmed again their conception of the violent "no" the church has often offered to young people. Besides, I also recognize in their appreciation for greening power a kindred spirit to Christianity that I was only too happy to celebrate with them.

At such times of celebration, then—weddings, holidays, and even funerals—we can see human beings at our finest, when greening power is the only power in play. I hope churches will develop and display this power more often, rather than give in to the easy, conventional way of the domination system, or "the flesh." I hope Christians will put greening power into practice in everyday life, for perhaps then others will more readily find God clothed as the life-bearer, as the true vine—and will not hesitate to use the name in public. For whatever one thinks of clothing God in such a way, all human beings share with the green things of the earth their potential for growth, their glory and their fragility, their living and their dying.

11

One Body

For just as the body is one and has many members, and all the members of the body, though many, are one body, so it is with Christ.

1 Corinthians 12:12

In 1985, my maternal grandparents—Ruth and John Olsen—celebrated their fiftieth wedding anniversary. I was by a long shot the most educated person in the family, having wasted (by some accounts) over five years in school beyond college with no appreciable income to show for it. This made me the natural emcee for the celebration to be held in honor of John, aged seventy-five, and Ruth, seventy-one.

Growing up, I had spent a fair amount of time with my grandparents. They lived on and worked a dairy farm near Gillett, Wisconsin, about forty-five miles from my hometown of Appleton, and we visited at least once a month. I'd also spend a week or more living with them during some summers. Then I'd help out on the farm a little and enjoy the incredible meals of fresh milk and cheese, vegetables straight from the garden, free-range chicken or beef, and homemade pies with amazing crusts and delicious fillings. Grandma always served her pies warm, with a dollop of vanilla ice cream slowly melting on top. If it sounds like idyllic living on a small family farm, it was.

I knew my grandparents pretty well, but I'd never heard their story. To remedy that problem before serving as emcee at their anniversary celebration, I sat down with them to conduct a formal interview. I drove up from Chicago to Appleton, they drove down from Gillett, and we chose the quietest room in my parents' house—their bedroom—for the interview. I sat on the foot of the bed and arranged a couple of chairs in front of me, with Grandma on my left and Grandpa on my right, as in the picture above. I started the tape recorder and began to ask questions. It was a little awkward at first, but gradually a sense of their life together began to emerge, and it was simply a delight to hear. I learned about the first time they met, about their first date, and about their mutual love of baseball (I now have Grandpa's glove in my seminary office). I also learned that they went fishing together thousands of times over fifty years, planted fifty different gardens, and went on hundreds of hikes together in the woods. On their hikes they often collected berries for Grandma's jellies and pies, and for Grandpa's wines—elderberry, blackberry, raspberry, boysenberry, wild grape, and on and on. When Grandpa died in 1992 he had cellared dozens of bottles of homemade wine, some of them rather "experimental." My personal favorite was "Pumpkin Raisin Champagne." It sounds horrid, but when we opened it on the Thanksgiving after his death, it had a bright golden color and light effervescence, and was sweet like Asti Spumante. It was a great aperitif. Anyway, as the interview went on I heard the story of their wedding day and a story about each of their five children, and then I asked them: "What's been the secret to the happiness and lasting success of your marriage?" Grandma spoke first, in carefully measured words. She said: "Determination is a lot of it. All in all, it's love, honor, and determination." I noticed that she did not say "obedience," and I told her that I liked her answer.

Grandpa thought about my question for a minute, looked at me intently with his bright blue eyes, and said: "Somebody once said, 'If two people agree perfectly on everything, one of them is unnecessary.'" I laughed at his humor and then listened again as he became earnest and went on: "We don't always agree, but we give each other the opportunity to make some mistakes. If you learn from them, you learn more than from the successes you have. We've emphasized as much as possible the positive. . . . Neither of us is perfect, but I really don't know where I would have found anyone better. All in all, we've gotten along real well." I nodded slowly, loving the opportunity I had found to hear my grandparents express the love for each other that had made them life partners of fifty years. And then Grandpa got a gleam in his eye—a twinkle that I'm sure Grandma recognized well—and he said: "Oh, and it doesn't hurt to have a good love life, either." It was a strange Freudian moment. I was in my parents' bedroom talking to my grandparents about sex. "Oh," I blurted out without thinking, "you had a good love life, did you?" And the couple answered in unison, in words I will never forget, and from which I take great encouragement: "What do you mean, 'had'?"

Our bodies provide us with the most intense and immediate pleasures of life. We delight in the flavors and textures of food through our sense of taste. We enjoy the sounds of harmony and rhythm in music through our hearing and voices. We savor the scents of flowers and perfumes through smell. We see vast vistas and intricate detail in art and nature with our eyes. And from our sense of touch we feel the shiver of delight in a casual caress and the ecstasy of orgasm. Our body, in short, mediates every experience we have. Our body, as Paul affirmed, is a temple of God's spirit (1 Cor. 6:19). Put another way, our bodies are perhaps the central way we clothe God as individuals—incarnating the sacred in the fabric of our own limbs and senses.

Understandably, then, religions have found countless ways to affirm the senses and the body with ritual and myth. Most traditions include some way to "incarnate" or embody the sacred. In Hinduism, for instance, the gods take manifold embodied forms—animals, humans, and various combinations in between. Krishna, for instance, as an incarnation of Vishnu the preserver, is revered as a playful and mischievous child, a passionate musician and lover, and a gracious god whose love for humanity will free us from the cycles of rebirth and suffering. Kali, on the other hand, as an incarnation of Shiva the destroyer, represents a fiercely female embodiment of the sacred; she is represented wearing a necklace of human skulls and with her teeth dripping blood. Ganesha, the god of good fortune, has the head of an elephant, but the rest of his body is human. The list could go on and on through the "three million and more" deities of the Hindus.[1]

Among many Native American traditions, for another example, the sacred is "embodied" in both the earth itself, from which it is often understood that humans emerged, and in particular persons, animals, plants, or representations. For instance, Inktomi the spider is a "trickster" figure in many tales. Tricksters embody both the creative and the destructive features of the sacred, often surprising human beings with their presence. Birds also embody the sacred in many native traditions, and consequently the sacred costumes of tribes often include feathers as objects of adornment and power. And, of course, particular individuals—such as shamans and dancers—are understood as vehicles of both sacred teaching and sacred action in many native rituals and myths.[2]

Other traditions resist locating the sacred in an anthropomorphic representation, but rather locate sacred presence through bodily practices and rituals. Buddhists, most notably, use the practice of meditation or focused breathing to lead a devotee to nirvana, literally "cessation." The idea here is that the body is a vehicle for consciousness, and consciousness tends to fly wildly between mindless and random firings and obsessive and anxiety-inducing fixations. The idea of meditation is to concentrate mindfully on a single thing—breathing—as a way to train attention for mindfulness, on the one hand, and to recognize the futility and transitory character of fixations, on the other. Through the breath, and through other focused bodily practice, we can be freed from slavery to any and all desires.

Even Christians, who have often been misunderstood as anti-body because of the overlay of Platonic dualism on some early Christian theologies, have a rich tradition of affirmation of carnality, once you begin to notice it. Jesus, of course, is the incarnation of God for Christians—the Word become flesh. Christians gather every day around the globe to eat the body and drink the blood of Jesus—an embodied practice whose scandalous overtones were not lost on the first critics of the faith. Christians understand the church itself as the body of Christ. And Christians even hope that their bodies will someday be resurrected, as they affirm Jesus' body was resurrected at Easter—the central holy day of the faith.

Clothing God as a body, then, is in fact a rather conventional theological move, yet it is one with many potential implications and ramifications. We will develop only three. First, clothing God as one body means that the location of God cannot be limited only to human bodies. Our bodies, after all, are the same stuff of all bodies—carbon, hydrogen, oxygen, and so forth. We share the *anima* of animals—the breath or spirit of life with which God is clothed in all living bodies—dogs, cats, cows, birds, fish, and on and on. Secondly, clothing God as one body means God shares not only in the joys and pleasures of our bodies but also in their sufferings and losses. God clothed as a body experiences both the limits and the liberating potential of embodiment. God clothed as one body suffers with us and shares in our healing from suffering. Finally, clothing God as one body means that we all share through each moment, each breath, indeed each place, in the beauty and intricacy of every other living thing. Clothing God as one body helps us to realize the interdependence of all in all.

The *Anima* of Animals

I like all kinds of animals, but I'm primarily a "dog person," in part because my wife, Lisa, is allergic to cats. I've lived with dogs, in fact, since the time I was twelve, and these many years of associations with canines have taught me at least three things about how they might illumine for us some theological insight. First, then, I believe dogs can teach people much about the love of God. Anyone who has ever experienced a friendly greeting from a family pet after an absence (the duration doesn't matter) knows that dogs display affection. Indeed, our current dog, Charlie, can become so overwhelmed by emotion upon our return that he will greet us with what the humorist Dave Barry has called the "wee-wee of joy." This example of dog behavior can clarify, then, my second point about a theology of dogs: their ways are not our ways. They are as different from us as God is different from a typical human being. And, finally, any family that loses a pet to death knows that dogs can teach us vital lessons about the fragility of life. Dogs die. We'll take each point in turn.

Currently, we have two dogs in our household. Cocoa is a lovable and gentle old black Lab for whom we will soon grieve. Charley is a young golden retriever. But the first dog Lisa and I purchased, shortly after we were married, was a German shepherd-mix puppy. At the time, I was working late nights at a local hospital while attending seminary classes during the day, and we were living in a neighborhood with high crime rates. The idea was that a big dog would provide some security for Lisa. She picked out the puppy, but I got to name him. I chose the name "Heidegger."

Now, as many readers will know, Heidegger was also the name of a philosopher who lived and worked in Germany in the early twentieth century. I had read Heidegger's

works with great interest while in seminary, although, truth be told, I primarily liked the name because it ended in "grrr" and therefore sounded like a good name for a dog. I didn't know then that Heidegger (the philosopher, not the dog) had once been a Nazi sympathizer, or I probably wouldn't have used the name. Heidegger, the dog, however, quickly became the best Frisbee-playing canine I have ever seen, including the dogs on television. I could wind up and throw a Frisbee as far and high as I could, and as soon as I began my wind-up Heidegger would sprint away. He could adjust for curved tosses, for wind currents, for trees in his way, and would almost always wind up catching the thing in his mouth by jumping several feet off the ground—all four paws airborne. It was great fun, and we spent hours playing in the fields behind our townhouse in Columbus, and then in the forest preserve meadow across from our house in Chicago. The theological lesson I learned was a simple one that I think even Heidegger the philosopher was starting to figure out in his last, poetically inspired works: God can be found in playful moments with a puppy as well as in serious philosophy. In fact, clothing God in play with a dog might come a whole lot closer to the truth about God than clothing God, as the early Heidegger (the philosopher) tried, as "*Da-sein*" or "Being-There." Or maybe they mean the same thing. Dogs are pretty good at just being-there.

Anyway, Heidegger was the first creature upon whom Lisa and I bestowed mutual affection (in-laws don't count). Raising this puppy was thus helpful preparation, I suppose, for learning to raise children. We made some mistakes. For instance, we heard on a TV show with an animal trainer one night that it was a good idea to have a place to "send" your dog after he did something that you considered misbehavior. The show recommended calling this place "the hole." The animal trainer suggested that you train the dog to go to a small, quiet place, like under the bed, whenever you sent him there with the command: "Get in the hole." This command would separate a pack animal from its pack, so the theory went, and would therefore negatively reinforce the behavior in question. We followed the training perfectly, until Heidegger would crawl under our bed whenever we thought he misbehaved, which, like most puppies, was often. Lisa and I were for a while quite pleased with our "parenting" skills. Our neighbors and friends were also impressed with the way Heidegger would dutifully slink off to our bedroom, tail between his legs, whenever we corrected him. Of course, our satisfaction didn't last long. As Heidegger reached full growth, at about seventy-five pounds, his efforts to fit under the bed rails first became painful efforts at dog contortion and eventually became impossible—although God knows he'd *try*. It was pitiful to watch. So, our grand scheme at Skinnerian behavioral reinforcement ended in failure, and we wound up simply yelling at him, like most dog owners. Fortunately, Heidegger forgave us—and thus conveyed to us the important theological lesson: nothing could separate us from the love of our dog—not height, not depths, not the hole. Paul, of course, claimed the same for God: "Neither death, nor life, nor angels, nor rulers, nor things present, nor things to come, nor powers, nor height, nor depth, nor anything else in all creation, will be able to separate us from the love of God in Christ Jesus our Lord" (Rom. 8:38).

We also made a mistake in assuming that our ways were also the dog's ways. It's an obvious point, I suppose, but dogs simply don't think like us, even though we project onto them all kinds of anthropomorphic characterizations (at Halloween, for instance, we always clothe our dogs in white T-shirts with the word "BOO!" written on the backs in black magic marker). The strangeness of dog logic became apparent to Lisa and me on our first Christmas together with Heidegger in Columbus. Naturally, we bought a tree for our little living room, decorated it with care, and wrapped presents to put underneath it. At night, we'd enjoy the twinkling lights of the tree as we sat on our ratty old couch and snuggled with each other, with the dog curled at our feet. It was sort of a Norman Rockwell or Currier and Ives moment. Well, Heidegger apparently also enjoyed the twinkling lights later at night all by himself, because when we went to load all of the presents in our car prior to traveling to visit our families for the holiday, we discovered that he had tinkled all over them. He had imagined, I guess, that we'd brought the tree inside for his convenience. The theological lesson? Our ways weren't a dog's ways, or rather, a dog's way wasn't our way. Isaiah expressed the same insight about God: "For my thoughts are not your thoughts, nor are your ways my ways, says the LORD" (55:8). The "otherness" of animals can help us to appreciate that God is other than the ways we clothe God in our imaginations.

A final lesson we learned about God and dogs from Heidegger came when we had to give him away. For our move to Chicago, a veterinarian in Columbus had suggested that we tranquilize the dog for the long drive, to keep him from suffering too much anxiety during the trip. So, we did, even though he'd always been a good traveler, and Heidegger crashed on the seat next to me in the U-Haul for the twelve-hour drive. When we arrived in Chicago, where my parents and two younger brothers met us to help us move in, Heidegger woke up, went psycho, and tried to bite my brother Dave. He had never before exhibited aggressive behavior. We think he had a bad trip on doggie downers. He was never the same. Over the next few years, he tried to bite a couple of people—including our aged next-door neighbor, John Tokar, who was convinced ever after that Heidegger was part wolf.

Once Lisa became pregnant with Justin, we both realized that we had to find a new home for our beloved but sociopathic dog. It wasn't easy. He was no longer a puppy, and I felt compelled to tell people that he had developed a mean streak. After newspaper ads produced no "bites," so to speak, I called every shelter in the Chicago area until I finally found one about an hour away that had a "no euthanasia" policy. They promised that they would find Heidegger a suitable home. Lisa by now was in the hospital in premature labor, so I had to go alone. The drive to take the dog there was the longest drive of my life. I cried—no, sobbed—the entire way. Perhaps such behavior indicates how little suffering I had experienced in my life prior to this time, but in any event, the agony and grief I felt at having to give Heidegger up was intense. I remember walking into the shelter with him on his leash, taking it off for the last time, and handing him over to the shelter operator. I hugged him, and said goodbye, and turned to walk out, crying the whole time. To this day, I can remember the pain of that moment. Is there a theological lesson to be learned here about God clothed as one body? Some might say the affection of dog owners for their pets is excessive or misdirected, that we really ought to direct such love to the poor, or to the church, or to God as an abstract "Spirit." I surely don't want to distract attention from the poor, but I do know that Heidegger taught Lisa and me to care for life in ways we hadn't done previously, to be responsible for another, and to grieve. These were lessons I think God understands and would not despise. This was no corporate con job; it was a relationship with a living, embodied being. And who can say that love for an animal is not in fact love returned to the God who promises to be present among the "least and lowest?"

Fortunately, I am not the only Christian these days to be drawing metaphorical and ethical connections between God and animals. Andrew Linzey, for instance, has argued in a series of works that animals deserve reverence, should be treated responsibly, and even have rights that human beings must recognize. Linzey borrows the idea that animals deserve reverence from Albert Schweitzer, who wrote that the principle of reverence for life applied to "all life-forms." Animals—even insects, thus share in the sacred, and fall under our responsibility to "love your neighbor." Of course, this does not mean that we must welcome each mosquito that comes our way to suck our blood. To identify ourselves with animals and to pledge to revere them does not mean that we must masochistically deny our human capacities. Rather, identifying with animals and treating them with reverence means that we can avoid doing thoughtless or malicious injury to them, out of reverence for the presence of God in all things living. For the fact is, as Schweitzer puts it: "I am life which wills to live, in the midst of life which wills to live." If we want to clothe God as living, then all living things share in the oneness of that body of life with which God is clothed.[3]

Linzey develops these three principles regarding animals—reverence, responsibility, and rights—into what he calls a "liberation theology for animals." Jesus, Linzey contends, preached the "moral priority of the weak." "Those who minister to the vulnerable and weak minister to Christ himself," Linzey writes, drawing upon the Gospel of Matthew where Jesus exhorts his followers to feed the hungry, clothe the naked, and visit the imprisoned. Implicit in such specific exhortations is a "generosity paradigm," Linzey suggests, in which the "obligation is always and everywhere on the 'higher' to sacrifice for the 'lower'; for the strong, powerful and rich to give to those who are vulnerable, poor or powerless."[4] And animals, Linzey points out, are among the poorest, most vulnerable, and powerless among us. "Six to nine billion non-human animals are slaughtered in the United States every year," Linzey points out.[5] Animals are experimented on to produce makeup and perfumes. Animals are hunted not for food, but for sport. And, of course, animals are eaten—in contrast to what Linzey suggests is a biblical ideal of vegetarianism.[6] In short, if Christians clothe God when they clothe the poor, Christians also care for God when they care for animals. And by all accounts, animals are often not well cared for in this country. They are treated as commodities, not as living beings. A simple visit to any factory farm will acquaint the reader with the problem. My grandparents, to their credit, once took Lisa and me to a chicken "ranch" where thousands upon thousands of birds were packed in tiny wire cages stacked from floor to ceiling. Things had changed since the time I chased their chickens around the driveway of their farm as a child.

Linzey is joined by an increasing number of voices urging Christians to reconsider animals and how we treat them. For instance, *Good News for Animals? Christian Approaches to Animal Well-Being* collects a wide variety of theological and ethical reflections on the topic. In that collection, L. Shannon Jung contends that disregard for animals has been widespread in both Christianity and Western culture but that such disregard is theologically and morally errant. He writes: "The disembodied spiritualism of [Western] culture has obscured our basic relationship with animals."[7] In short, because we have clothed God in disembodied ways, we have failed to recognize that we share the stuff of our bodies with both domestic and wild beasts. We are animals ourselves. Whatever it means to assert that humans have a "soul," such an assertion cannot be used to deny the obvious fact that we are also animals.

Furthermore, Scripture even goes so far as to identify God as an animal. The prophet Hosea, for instance, used images of animals of predation to convey God's coming judgment on Israel for idolatry. The violence is graphic:

> They forgot me. So I will become a lion to them, like a leopard I will lurk beside the way. I will fall upon them like a bear robbed of her cubs, and will tear open the covering of their heart; there I will devour them like a lion, as a wild animal would mangle them.
>
> 13:6–8

Such terrifying images are, again, warnings to God's people of the catastrophe that would follow as the sure consequence of their own injustice. Not only God's judgment, but also God's compassion could be communicated through animal imagery. God was like a mammalian mother who gave birth to Israel, Hosea suggested, who fed Israel from her breasts, and who enwrapped Israel in strong and warm arms. God's fierceness came from love lost, like a mother bear deprived of her cubs.

Jesus himself, according to the Gospel of Luke, clothed his own care for people in an animal metaphor. "How often," the prophet laments over Jerusalem, "have I desired to gather your children together as a hen gathers her brood under her wings, and you were not willing!" (13:34) God's sadness is here communicated—presuming that Jesus is equated with God in Luke—in the image of a forlorn animal. This imagery in Luke of God as bird had ample precedent in the Hebrew Bible as well. In Exodus 19:4, God is depicted as a soaring eagle, bearing the people of Israel to freedom from the Egyptians: "You have seen . . . how I bore you on eagles' wings and brought you to myself." And in Psalm 17: 8, the author asks God to "hide me in the shadow of your wings," again clothing God as a bird of protection. Finally, the dove—as is well known, has long been a symbol of the Holy Spirit and God's peaceful, protecting, and preserving presence in creation, and Jesus is widely called the Lamb of God. We clothe God as an animal, then, because we know that we share with animals one body—and that God unites us all.

But dogs, at least for me, have a place of privilege in the divine wardrobe. Theologian Stephen Webb, in *On God and Dogs: A Christian Theology of Compassion for Animals,* agrees. He writes:

> Dogs can be merely the repositories of our surplus feelings, all that is alienated during the workday, all of those emotions that could be channeled into social change or into bettering human relations. But good dog relationships . . . do more than this; they offer us more than we could ever find within, take us further than we knew we could go, and make us more than ourselves. . . . Dogs are like a gift, a grace undeserved, that releases us into an economy of abundance, where the economic laws of scarcity and therefore competition no longer apply and where instead we feel ourselves the beneficiaries of a wealth that is actualized only as we give it away, and in giving we see something that we could not see before. . . . [Our relationships with dogs] are graced with the same grace that blesses human society and the same grace that saves us all. This is the grace given to us by God through Jesus Christ, who embodies the pains and hopes of all living creatures and provides for us all.[8]

Some people feel threatened by these associations that link God and animals through grace, as if they somehow erode the special place of humanity in God's eyes. I find it comforting that I share a place of grace with the other animals on the earth. That way, even my own doglike moments in life might not escape the compassion and forgiveness of a God whose love is abundant.

Limits and Liberation

Our bodies not only connect us with the rest of the material world, our bodies also reveal to us our limits, as well as our potential for liberation. Most succinctly: our bodies can feel pain as well as pleasure.

Living with a body can be a painful experience. For me, bodily pain is often concentrated in my left knee, which has experienced four surgeries to repair damage done by sports injuries. But the more telling pain is the sort that I experienced in dealing with an incident that occurred when I was eleven. It is hard to write about it even now. I was in my sleeping bag away from home at a camp in an isolated room late at night. I said, "What are you doing to me?" as I awoke to the presence of an adult in authority over me, who was touching me in a way I honestly did not know how to describe. I did know it was something I did not want him to do.

For almost thirty years I had been unable to process that event, which surfaced in therapy only after a very difficult midlife crisis. The effects of such a buried memory affected in subtle ways almost all of my relationships. From it, I harbored an uneasy mistrust of the basic trust in people I had learned from my loving parents. From it, I developed an inability to say no—especially to those in authority—and I formed a defensive reaction against authority by saying "no" to authority even when authority acted more or less justly. From that violation, I came to suspect that my body wasn't really my own, and I reacted by having uncertain personal boundaries. From that event, and the repression that followed, I became unable to recognize or attend well to my emotions. I was in many ways stuck at eleven. My body continued to grow, but because of a violation of its boundaries, I couldn't understand or in some ways appreciate and enjoy those changes. I was emotionally paralyzed.

My experience is, unfortunately, akin to the experience reported by many people raised within Christianity, even if they did not suffer from any kind of direct trauma. Attention has recently focused on the scandal of pedophilia in the Catholic church, and for obvious reasons I do not in any way want to minimize the scope of that problem. In fact, however, the scandal of pedophilia is part of the much larger scandal of an anti-body theology that has scarred many people—and especially women—in the church. Over the years, many women have come to the realization that their upbringing in the church did not prepare them well to accept the limitations and boundaries that come with being embodied, on the one hand, and the delights of having a body, on the other.[9] Men need to listen to and learn from these women.

Some of them write today as "ecofeminist" theologians. Perhaps the best known of these ecofeminists is Rosemary Radford Ruether. She writes:

> The basic assumption of ecofeminist theology . . . is that the dualism of soul and body must be rejected, as well as the assumptions of the priority and controlling role of male-identified mind over female-identified body. This anthropology is at the heart of the distortion in Western thought of our relations to ourselves, as well as to our fellow earth creatures and the cosmos as a whole.[10]

This anthropology is also grounded in a theology—a refusal to recognize the incarnation of God. When we cannot clothe God as a body, we cannot accept our own embodiment either. According to ecofeminists, until we heal this most basic form of alienation, we will not heal the other oppressions of political, economic, and environmental injustice. My experiences of violation lead me to conclude that the ecofeminists are correct.

Fortunately, the Christian tradition also has another stream of body theology that is not beholden to a body/soul dualism but that honestly acknowledges pain and suffering in order to bring them to the light of healing. Most obvious are the stories of the passion of Jesus—narratives of torture that surface innocent suffering in order to mobilize human compassion. But Jesus not only suffered and died. He also was a healer. This fact can be a real obstacle for contemporary readers, but it also is the key to understanding Christian teaching about the body. It also is the key to understanding my own experiences of trauma. The stories of Jesus' healing are plentiful. Here's the first one in the Gospel of Mark, probably the earliest of the Gospels:

> When Jesus returned to Capernaum after some days, it was reported that he was at home. So many gathered around that there was no longer room for them, not even in front of the door; and he was speaking the word to them. Then some people came, bringing to him a paralyzed man, carried by four of them. And when they could not bring him to Jesus because of the crowd, they removed the roof above him; and after having dug through it, they let down the mat on which the paralytic lay. When Jesus saw their faith, he said to the paralytic, "Son, your sins are forgiven." Now some of the scribes were sitting there, questioning in their hearts, "Why does this fellow speak in this way? It is blasphemy! Who can forgive sins but God alone?" At once Jesus perceived in his spirit that they were discussing these questions among themselves; and he said to them, "Why do you raise such questions in your hearts? Which is easier, to say to the paralytic, 'Your sins are forgiven,' or to say, 'Stand up and take your mat and walk?' But so that you may know that the Son of Man has authority on earth to forgive sins"—he said to the paralytic—"I say to you, stand up, take your mat and go to your home." And he stood up, and immediately took the mat and went out before all of them; so that they were all amazed and glorified God, saying, "We have never seen anything like this!"
>
> 2:1–12

This is a great and true story, but there are ways to interpret it that distort or miss its greatness.

For instance, one might interpret the story through what often is called a "literal" interpretation. Jesus then becomes some kind of "supernaturalistic" doctor; like one of the faith healers on TV. This reading of the text in fact is to distort it badly. From this perspective, the way the people of Capernaum understood "paralysis" is exactly identical to the way we understand it, and "healing" means exactly what we think it means. These assumptions are, of course, false, because they unwittingly impose upon an ancient text modern presuppositions. Hardly a truly "literal" reading, such a reading tries to defend miracles from scientific "attack" but ironically *assumes* that "scientific" truth of the empirical sort (expressed in English, no less) is the only truth. That such interpretations make Christians look stupid to scientists—as in the case of so-called creation science—is only a secondary problem compared to the violence such interpretations do to the texts themselves.

Such interpretations are understandable, however, because there are those who do use science to attack the truth of healing stories. Such people read the stories consciously and solely through the eyes of materialist science and thereby seek to "demythologize" them. This approach to the stories was widespread throughout scholarship in the twentieth century. The stories of Jesus performing miracles were, simply, false. Modern readers might as well skip over them and focus instead on the ethical teachings of Jesus. Truth is determined by describing the mechanical operation of effects by reference to clear and efficient causes. In such a world, miracles simply do not happen. Expecting them to happen reflects a "primitive" or "mythical" worldview that was simply in error. The miracle stories had been made up by the Gospel writers to make Jesus look good, or perhaps they were even staged by Jesus himself. In any event, the miracle stories were myths, and myths might have a symbolic meaning, but they don't refer to something that "really happened." Interestingly, this way of reading the texts—while still influential in many scholarly circles—has also increasingly given ground to a third way that I find very promising.

Most recently, and I believe most accurately, scholars have been abandoning the simple true/false dichotomy of the fundamentalists or materialists and have focused instead on the way that truth and falsehood, like disease and healing, are social constructs that vary from culture to culture and time to time. In other words, we really can't compare what "healing" meant in the ancient world of Jesus to what we understand "healing" to mean today, without first doing a lot of homework. A huge translation enterprise exists to understand the different languages (Greek, Hebrew, Latin, and Aramaic) spoken in Jesus' time and how these languages shaped the reality as experienced by people of the time. Bodies may be bodies, but the bodies in that story are not the bodies of any of us, and neither are the societies represented in that story the societies of any of us. People in different cultures understand their bodies, including modes of disease and healing, in ways that are very different from our understandings—and probably far stranger than we can even imagine.

From this appreciation for the difference between the ancients and us comes this new reading of the miracle stories.[11] This new reading starts with the way an ancient reader might have read the story. Miracle workers were common in the ancient world. The behavior ascribed to Jesus in helping a paralyzed man to walk was not unique. The unique element in the story was that Jesus first forgave the man's sins. This was what made him a "blasphemer." That illness and disease were related somehow to "sin" is something that we do not often suppose today. It is something that people in the ancient world took for granted. And indeed, Jesus "heals" the man in the story, it concludes, to show the authorities that he has the "authority to forgive sins." Because of the association between sin and sickness, people who were diseased often experienced shame in the ancient world. Indeed, this is something that the powerful still try to inflict on the powerless who struggle with disease in our time—as was recently the case with AIDS and continues to be the case with alcoholism and other addictions. But Jesus broke the link between sin and sickness. This is what gives Jesus' healing its power, then and now: Jesus removes shame. He encourages his followers to have faith in him, to approach him, even to dig through a dirt roof and drop down into his midst. That's not how a typical teacher behaves; you'd have to sign up, pay your fees, and wait in line. Jesus could be approached without shame. He forgave sins! This truth in the story is completely independent of whether a physical healing occurred, although with the common expectation of ancients that such healings could happen, it might very well have happened. The body connects not only to "soul" or "mind," then, but also to culture and even to politics. To forgive sins in the ancient world was to free a person to participate in society again.

Such liberation is, needless to say, also needed in the contemporary world. But it begins with the affirmation of the body and its needs. According to theologian James Nelson, the Christian idea of the "incarnation" of God—clothing God in a body—liberates Christians to affirm human bodies free from shame. At the same time, the incarnation also can orient us to bodily awareness and practices that free us from marketed expectations of "beauty." Such marketed ideals do real harm through their production of shame and frantic attempts to control the body, as we observed in the first few chapters of this book.[12] If God is clothed as a body, then any shape, size, color, or appearance of a body is truly beautiful. Nelson joins many Christian writers today calling for a theology of the body and a sexual ethic that affirms the pleasures of the body and the delight of mutuality, without resorting to either repression or frantic promiscuity. He writes: "Sexuality expresses the mystery of our creation as those who need to reach out for the physical and spiritual embrace of others. It expresses God's intention that we find our authentic humanness not in isolation but in relationship. . . . Such theology will understand our sexuality as intrinsic to the divine-human connection."[13] To clothe God as one body, then, is to free our bodies for pleasure. This is a truth so deep we can hardly comprehend it. The Creator, Redeemer, and Sustainer of the universe lives in us, as close to us as our breath, loving us with each blink of our eyes, suffering with us through any trauma, and empowering us to find the pleasure that comes from being a free human being.

So, when I look back at the history of my own body, I have come to terms with the adult I trusted who violated me when I was eleven. I abhor the lack of mutuality in what he did. It was a gross infringement of my bodily integrity, and I would never inflict a similar violation on another. But it happened so long ago that I no longer have any desire for vengeance. I do wish I had been able to name what happened to me at an earlier age. My life and relations with others might then have been much clearer and less confused, and I might have avoided both pain I caused others and pain I experienced because of uncertain bodily boundaries. Yet, I forgive him, as I hope others have forgiven me. I am also happy to report that I am growing emotionally a little every day. Even a thirty-year paralysis can be healed.

One Body

Despite a durable and influential anti-body theology that has harmed many, then, the Christian tradition has also been surprisingly insistent that bodies matter. The apostle Paul, for instance, argued against unbelieving philosophers and theologians that Jesus was truly resurrected in the body, and that such a destiny also awaited all believers. Indeed, for Paul the very community of believers was the body of Christ, one in its integrity, but with diverse members. He develops the famous metaphor in his first letter to the church at Corinth:

> For just as the body is one and has many members, and all the members of the body, though many, are one body, so it is with Christ. For in the one Spirit we were all baptized into one body—Jews or Greeks, slaves or free. . . . Indeed, the body does not consist of one member, but of many. If the foot would say, "Because I am not a hand, I do not belong to the body," that would not make it any less a part of the body. . . . If one member suffers, all suffer together with it; if one member is honored, all rejoice together with it. Now you are the body of Christ and individually members of it.
>
> 12:12–15, 26–27

Paul wrote these words to a church beset by conflict, struggling with jealousy and pride—in short, a church like most.

This affirmation of the unity of the body is most difficult to realize, however, in the face of death. When we lose another to death it becomes difficult to conceive of how we might still be "one body" with them. The case of my grandparents—whom we met in the introduction to this chapter—will serve to illustrate the problem. My grandfather, John Olsen, died in 1990 after a lingering illness. His death was a release from suffering for him and many others—although of course we still missed him and mourned his passing. Grandma, however, faded quickly, in a way that made her absence very difficult to accept. On a trip to South Dakota with my parents in late summer 1992, she suffered from a massive nosebleed and complained of chronic fatigue. Upon her return from the trip and a visit to the doctor, it was diagnosed that she suffered from a very aggressive type of cancer and had only weeks to live. One Friday afternoon in early fall, then, I received a call from my Mom asking me if I could drive up to Wisconsin for the weekend. Grandma wanted to say goodbye to me.

So, I drove the five hours to my home, slept the night in my childhood bed, and the next morning bright and early drove to the hospital in Green Bay. My mom and her sister were already there and greeted me as I came in the door. Grandma was sitting up and smiled as I walked in the room. I reached out to hug her, and held her for a long time in a gentle embrace. She was frail and could no longer speak, but she was still very clearly the same strong woman I had gone fishing with, milked cows with, and helped wash the dishes after dinners. As the day passed we talked—my mom and me and the many guests and family who came in and out of the room bearing gifts and cards and flowers. Grandma slipped in and out of sleep, but when she was awake she nodded and squeezed my hand when I spoke with her. Eventually, as late afternoon arrived, my mom left to go home and make dinner, and the guests stopped coming in, and we were alone. From time to time I would take a little cotton swab, dip it into water, and give it to Grandma to suck on to help keep her mouth from drying out. She had not been able to eat for several days, and my family was debating whether to start tube feedings. I usually just held and rubbed gently her hands. Then, as I thought about all the things those hands had done over the years, I began to cry. Around 5:30 I decided that I'd better get going to make the half-hour drive home for dinner. I planned to be back the next morning, again bright and early, and as I leaned over to whisper that in Grandma's ear, my cheek brushed hers and I noticed that she was crying, too. I brushed her still strawberry blonde hair gently with my fingertips and said quietly, "I love you." I was crying as I left her room.

As I drove over the huge steel bridge across the Fox River heading home, I noticed that I was heading west into the most beautiful sunset I had seen in years. It was a stunning array of pinks and yellows and blues, dramatic and bright orange-red, even the soft strawberry blonde of Grandma's hair. Suddenly then, in an instant, my tears stopped. I felt an amazing and strange sense of peace, even joy, as I crossed over the river and headed onto the expressway for home. It was something unlike anything I had ever experienced before. I have no way to know this, of course, and the feeling was perhaps a mere coincidence of being back in a comfortable setting after an uncomfortable afternoon, but I believe it may have been that exact moment when Grandma died. I do know that she had waited to see me, and that the last words she heard were "I love you." Shortly after I arrived home, in any event, the hospital called to say that my Grandma Ruth had died.

The Christian church has often struggled to convey the meaning of its central doctrine of the resurrection of the body. Often, as we have seen in previous chapters, this doctrine has been spiritualized into a doctrine of "heaven" and has functioned as an opiate for people much like the "Magic Kingdom." Please do not mistake me here. I too profess my faith in "the resurrection of the body" every time I say the creed, and I hope for my life to continue eternally in some form after death. But such future hope for heaven is not the central solace that I draw from the church's teaching on the resurrection. I find that solace, rather, in the meal that I share with fellow believers (and some who might just be seekers) and in the ongoing presence of the community that calls itself "the body of Christ" gathered around a table for a meal. In that meal, we not only clothe God in a body, through bread and wine, but also profess actually to incorporate the body and blood of Christ into our own bodies. It is a scandalous rite, and a shock to polite sensibilities, yet we call it the Eucharist—the thanksgiving—because in it we express gratitude for all the living. An ordinary meal, with ordinary bread and wine, the Eucharist is also, first, a form of resistance to oppressive political orders. When we eat, we join in solidarity to take sustenance for whatever struggles face us. The Eucharist is, second, a re-membering of the community fractured when Jesus died and that is broken any and every time a body is violated or dies. The Eucharist is healing, itself. And finally, the Eucharist is a reincarnating of the body of Christ—and indeed of all bodies—in and among us for the revitalization of the world. When we eat, we take into ourselves the same "stuff" that constituted Christ's body and that constitutes every body in, with, and under bread and wine—the carbon, hydrogen, nitrogen and so forth that weave us all together in one body of the earth.

The Eucharist as resistance is an idea well known in places like Latin America, South Africa, and Eastern Europe, and it was an idea well known by the first Christians. Living in an oppressive political order, the earliest Christians found the power of solidarity in a meal. In fact, I often described the meal in exactly those terms whenever I presided over the table. Although I'm not ordained, for a few years presiding at the table was open to me when I served as a youth minister at a Disciples of Christ congregation in Valparaiso and as a deacon in a little country church in Medaryville, Indiana. I loved to lead these communities in this meal. "This is our solidarity celebration," I would say to the congregation as I broke the bread and lifted up the cup. In resistance to the alienation and isolation of the world, where we clothe God in banal and finally violent places at the beckoning of advertisers, political leaders, and corporations, the Eucharist invites us to a safe place where we eat together from one body in a circle of solidarity. There is nothing banal about this eating of body and drinking of blood—even when the rite is routinized, understood as "only" a symbol, and the people forgetful. Catholic theologian William T. Cavanaugh, writing out of intimate experience of the politically motivated torture and "disappearances" of Christians from Chile in the early 1990s, contends that the Eucharist involves participants in a liturgy of resistance to force, domination, and disappearance. He writes:

> Where torture is an anti-liturgy for the realization of the state's power on the bodies of others, Eucharist is the liturgical realization of Christ's suffering and redemptive

> body in the bodies of His followers. Torture creates fearful and isolated bodies, bodies docile to the purposes of the regime; the Eucharist effects the body of Christ, a body marked by resistance to worldly power. Torture creates victims; Eucharist creates witnesses. . . . Isolation is overcome in the Eucharist by the building of a communal body which resists the state's attempts to disappear it.[14]

The meal of Christians around the table resists, on the one hand, the violence done to bodies in the name of control and power, as in the domination of a civil religion. The meal of Christians around the table also resists, on the other hand, the banal commodification of bodies into consumers or spectators, as in a religion of the market or a domestic religion. The meal frees us to witness to exploitation and violence wherever they occur, out of solidarity with those who live together in love.

The Eucharist, along with being a resistance-meal, is also a meal to remember the body of Christ that is broken whenever and wherever violence occurs. Communion when I was growing up was a fear-filled event. I remember especially the day of my first communion and the anxiety I experienced. Now, however, I have come to understand the meal as a gift of grace that cannot be controlled and that is therefore freely offered to any and all. It is not our "work" that makes the meal efficacious, but the meal itself, body and blood clothed or present as bread and wine. After all, bread and wine are in substance little different from body and blood. They are all mostly water, and share with all matter the energy of the light of the world, the dust of the earth, and the grace of greening power. In the meal, of course, Jesus instructed his followers: "Do this, to remember me." Because of the elements involved, however, the re-membering is not only an intellectual act, but also a physical "putting-back-together" of things that belong that way. By remembering bread and wine as body and blood, we re-member any brokenness anywhere in the world—in our bodies, in the bodies of others, in the body of Christ, and in the body of the earth itself.

Finally, the Eucharist is a meal of reincarnation in and for us, for the revitalization of the world. I have never been particularly drawn to the Hindu idea of reincarnation—of the rebirth of individuals time and again in consequence of particular actions (*karma*). But in the Eucharist the possibility of a distinctively Christian doctrine of "reincarnation" appears. By eating the body and blood of Jesus, we not only take into ourselves the immediate bread and wine prepared that day for our meal, but we also participate in the "body of Christ" constituted by all those witnesses to the resurrection in the past. The meal is an orgy of reincarnations, in short, with people being reborn among and in us in each moment, in each action, in each act of love we perform. In such a meal, we gather around a very large table, where we truly join the communion of the saints—all those who have acted as loving gifts to others over the millennia. At that meal, then, we take into ourselves the elements offered to us that were also offered to them. They are all—Jesus, Mary, Paul, Hildegard and the rest—really present with us in the meal. Such an orgy of reincarnation, of presence in the body, can revitalize us to act as loving agents in the world ourselves.

One of the most delightful changes in the church in recent years is the inclusion of children as recipients of the bread and wine. I think such offering of the elements to even the youngest child is a beautiful sign of the grace of the meal and is a witness to the alternative model of power represented in the Eucharist. Among my treasured memories is the first communion of all three of my children at Washington National Cathedral in the autumn of 1994. I was in Washington, D.C., for a four-month research leave of absence at the time. We usually worshiped at Luther Place Memorial Church (a great, socially aware Lutheran congregation that once served as a stop on the underground railroad and is still riding the peace train), but on this particular Sunday I had taken the family to the cathedral, which we planned to tour in the afternoon. It was my first visit to the place. Our daughter, Rheanne, not quite two, was with us. I had talked with the boys about communing, and they were looking forward to doing so. I was surprised, however, and delighted when as we approached the table, the female presider asked if Rheanne communed, and I immediately nodded in the affirmative. On that day, I believe, Rheanne was linked in resistance and solidarity with all other Christians. On that day, I also believe that it became possible for me to say that Rheanne has even "reincarnated" her Great-grandmother Ruth and her Great-grandpa John—who shared the meal around a table in Gillett, Wisconsin, almost every healthy Sunday of their lives.

This idea of reincarnation through our oneness in the body of Christ may take some explaining, and the best way I can find to do so is to tell you Rheanne's story. Rheanne was born, like the boys, under unusual circumstances. On the night of December 11, 1992, Lisa and I hosted forty theology students and colleagues at our house for the main course of the annual departmental "Christmas Progressive Dinner." Rheanne was due to be born on December 23, and Lisa's pregnancy had been going smoothly this time. We ended the night with dessert over at our good friend Betty DeBerg's house, where, after the students left, the "Young Turks"—Rick and Sarah DeMaris along with Lisa, Betty, and I—sat and had a few drinks and talked. On the way home, Lisa mentioned that she had been having a few contractions, but nothing intense. After we massaged each other's tired feet for a few minutes (a body ritual that provides real comfort to both of us), we fell asleep around midnight.

Around 5:30 Lisa awakened me with a start and said, "Jon, I think this is it. I'm having pretty strong back contractions." Now, I was a veteran of this whole giving-birth thing, so I imagined that I could take at least a little time to attend to my basic physical needs. I had shaved, brushed my teeth, and combed my hair, when I noticed all of the sudden that Lisa was lying on the floor in the kitchen, moaning. I looked at her, she looked at me, and I said, "We'd better get going."

The three-mile trip to the hospital took about two minutes. That whole time, Lisa was in the backseat of our minivan, experiencing one continuous, long contraction. Upon arrival at the emergency room, I ran into the lobby and said, "You have to come right away; my wife's out in the van in severe labor!" I sprinted back to the van to help Lisa slide herself out of it. Eventually—it seemed like an eternity—the nurse appeared with a wheelchair, into which we helped Lisa sit down. As we walked through the double doors into the ER, Lisa suddenly stood up in the wheelchair and exclaimed, "Oh, my God! I can feel the baby coming!" The nurse behind her sensitively replied, "No!" and then grabbed Lisa by the shoulders and tried to push her back down in the chair. I, on the other hand, responding well under pressure, I thought, ran around to the front of the wheelchair and helped pull Lisa through the second set of doors, into the ER lobby. Lisa then stood up, legs apart but feet on the ground in between the wheels of the chair. She was wearing pink sweatpants. She arched her back, let out a cry, and delivered Rheanne in a whoosh of blood and water into the left leg of her sweatpants. I had in the meantime knelt down in front of Lisa. I caught my daughter as she slid down Lisa's leg. It was incredible.

The nurse—it had by now dawned on her that her attempt to prohibit birth had been unsuccessful—had Lisa half-sit and half-stand in the chair, and walk very awkwardly—me holding Rheanne secure in the leg of Lisa's sweatpants—backward through the swinging doors into the first ER cubicle. The nurse then said to Lisa: "Do you think you can climb up on the gurney?" We both looked at her as if she were crazy; in the meantime, with me still kneeling in front of her, we had pulled Lisa's sweatpants down. And there was Rheanne. She was wet, purple, tiny (5 pounds, 4 ounces), and alive. I was the first to hold her. I took her in my hands—she fit in one—and the nurses helped Lisa to get up on the table while I carried the baby. Another nurse had now joined us. She took a little blue bulb to suction out Rheanne's nose, and our baby began to breathe. All the while, I held her in my hands, awed by the beautiful and delicate features of her perfect face, her tiny toes and fingers, and her strawberry blonde hair.

On the way home from the hospital a few hours later (Lisa's mom had providentially paid us a visit, so the boys weren't alone), I pulled up to a stoplight near our house, and the amazing delight of what had just happened to me began to sink in. I raised my hands over my head in a victory celebration, smiled broadly, and let out a loud "Wow!" that I'm sure could have been heard for blocks around me.

That evening, after attending a Valpo basketball game with my boys, I called my Aunt Joanie in South Dakota—another nurse—to tell her the story of Rheanne's arrival. She delighted in the details and then asked about our daughter's name. I told her that we had basically made the name up by combining Rhea—an earth goddess in ancient Greece—with Anne, which means "grace" in old English. Her middle name is Marie, which recalls her great-great-grandmother on my father's side of the family. That name was appropriate since Rheanne was the first Pahl daughter born since Marie's generation, in 1929. And Rheanne proved to be a good name, too, completely apart from its literal meaning. Joanie sounded pleased with the name and asked us if we had named her for my grandmother, her mom. I asked Joanie what she meant, and she said, "Oh, you didn't know? Grandma's full name was Ruthanne."

The delight and significance of these various coincidences does not lie in any one-to-one correspondence between Rheanne and Ruthanne. Rather, the delight of the story lies in the way Rheanne reincarnates features of Ruth while still being herself—her hair color, her name, and her physical strength. Rheanne is also an excellent

athlete, like her grandfather, and she has the same kind of twinkling blue eyes. Now, I know on one level that these correspondences between Rheanne and Ruth and John are just coincidences, mostly genetic legacies. But through story—through the fabric of words—we can recognize them also as something more. We can recognize, as we recognize in the meal through which we profess to be one body, that our ancestors are truly still with us, really present in our bodies. And we can recognize that the Christian doctrine of the resurrection of the body is not primarily about a magical kingdom for the afterlife, but rather is a vision of an inclusive and open city of God here, as in heaven, where love is stronger than death. That is the truth of the doctrine that clothes God as one body: We participate in a living fabric whose threads weave through everything and whose potential to bring peace has barely begun to be explored.

12

Cities of God

> Do not let your hearts be troubled. Believe in God, believe also in me. In my Father's house there are many dwelling places. If it were not so, would I have told you that I go to prepare a place for you? And if I go and prepare a place for you, I will come again and take you to myself, so that where I am, there you may be also.
>
> John 14:1–3

If clothing God as one body is a relatively conventional move theologically, clothing God as a city is not. Yet in practice people have made frequent use of this fabric for the divine. Believers around the globe have often imagined God inhabiting or taking up residence in their particular locales. Rome in Italy, Benares in India, Beijing in China, Mecca in Saudi Arabia, and Jerusalem in Israel are all sacred cities—and the examples could be multiplied through nearly infinite local congregations and communities. Such localizing of God in itself is not a problem: God must be located somewhere. A god of nowhere is no god. The problem arises when these claims to find God in a particular city become exclusive, or become subject to struggles over ownership. Then this clothing for the divine becomes a walled community with closed gates, or a prison, and peaceful cities become places of killing—as the history of Jerusalem reveals all too well.

We will return to this problem of exclusion, ownership, and conflict, in due course. Despite these difficulties, to clothe God as a living city—as a complex human collective that never sleeps—is perhaps the highest revelation of the divine character. It is surely the highest reach of the Christian imagination. Hebrew and Christian Scriptures both include texts that reveal God clothed as an abundant web of human relations, buildings, products, and fabrications—all constructed of natural material but woven together into a living harmony and then expressed in words. Indeed, such a vision of God has captivated any theologian who has ever written about "the city of God." The most famous and important among them, of course, was Saint Augustine.

Nearing the end of his life, Augustine, Bishop of Hippo in North Africa, wrote *The City of God*. It is, as the author himself describes it, "a huge work." He penned it, in part, as an answer to Roman philosophers who blamed Christianity for the sack of Rome by the "barbarian" Alaric in 410. It is also not insignificant that this work appeared near the end of Augustine's long life. But *The City of God* is more than Augustine's reaction to personal and global trauma. It is also the culmination of his lifelong work as a Christian and is a fitting bookend to his much earlier and more personal *Confessions*. If in the earlier work Augustine justified his personal conversion to Christianity, in *The City of God* he justified the conversion of the empire. Throughout, the Bishop of Hippo recognizes the fleeting character of all human endeavors, but struggles mightily against accepting such transience by imposing upon contingency an order that has all the sanction of eternal verity. Augustine wrote the book for the ages—and succeeded.

It was written over a course of twelve years, between 412 and 425. It contains twenty-two "books" that cover two basic topics. In the first ten books, Augustine dismissed those who worshipped the pagan gods for either earthly or eternal happiness. In the next twelve, he contrasts the origin, development, and future of "two cities." On the one hand was "the City of God." On the other was "the city of this world," the "city of humanity," or, as Augustine often referred to it in later chapters, "the city of the Devil." Augustine's initial description of both cities from Book 1 will clarify the rhetorical juxtapositions:

> Here . . . is the fulfillment of my promise, a book in which I have taken upon myself the task of defending the glorious City of God against those who prefer their own gods to the Founder of that City. . . . Therefore I cannot refrain from speaking about the city of this world, a city which aims at dominion, which holds nations in enslavement, but is itself dominated by that very lust of domination.[1]

Augustine repeated often that in any person's experience the two cities merged, mixed, and were confused. Nevertheless, the difference between the two provided the foundation for the most impressive effort of rhetorical juxtaposition in all history.[2] Augustine's work, as I put it in chapter 1, is the most profound work of theology I have ever read.

It is also the most influential, for Augustine's juxtaposition of the two cities has determined the direction of Christian theology from then until now, with consequences that have spilled over into global politics far removed from the humble Episcopal see of Hippo. The most lasting consequence was to drive a bifurcating wedge through "pagan" religious dependencies upon place. Augustine substituted for pagan place-centered spirituality a time-driven longing for eternity. The hinge upon which place and time pivoted was desire, according to Augustine, or love. "We see then that the two cities were created by two kinds of love: the earthly city was created by self-love reaching the point of contempt for God, the Heavenly City by the love of God carried as far as contempt of self."[3] These options were Augustine's own—expressed vividly in his earlier *Confessions,* and now rendered eternal into the two cities. The *material* of longing, however—a body or a city, for instance—was rendered all but immaterial by the juxtaposition. Human cities, like embodied human selves, became not living fabrics where God was clothed but barren stones suitable in the last analysis only for contempt. Surely this was, and is, not the only option. For a variety of reasons, Augustine could not describe human cities as expressions of God's complex character but only as barriers to happiness, where naked human striving etched its scrabbled ascent in futile monuments to domination. *The City of God* was thus the first of many Christian utopias.[4] It solidified the hegemony of an eschatological and ascetic direction to Christian theology that has rarely been challenged since.

The City of God is a rhetorical masterpiece, and its critique of the lust for dominion is unassailable. But Augustine also pushes pilgrims relentlessly in one direction—toward the end times, and away from earth. This bias for time over place is further developed by Augustine through an emphasis on order. He writes:

> The peace of body and soul is the duly ordered life and health of a living creature; peace between mortal man and God is an ordered obedience, in faith, in subjection to an everlasting law; peace between men is an ordered agreement of mind with mind; the peace of a home is the ordered agreement among those who live together about giving and obeying orders; the peace of the Heavenly City is a perfectly ordered and perfectly harmonious fellowship in the enjoyment of God, and a mutual fellowship in God; the peace of the whole universe is the tranquillity of order—and order is the arrangement of things equal and unequal in a pattern which assigns to each its proper position.[5]

For Augustine, the City of God is one where everything is in its place. This does not, of course, correspond to any place on earth, and especially to cities—where energy, movement, freedom, diversity, and surprise prevail.

Given this depiction of heaven as an ordered place, it is thus a little surprising that by the end of his massive book, Augustine presents a much lengthier and more vivid picture of the horrors of hell than he does of the bliss of the saints. Augustine's book 21 on hell is an argument with one point: to prove that flesh can burn eternally and not be consumed, that "there will be living bodies . . . which are destined to burn and feel pain forever, without ever dying."[6] This argument recalls, of course, the prophetic rhetoric of warning about fire. But Augustine presents this rhetoric in such vivid form that it becomes all but a blueprint for people to take it upon themselves to stoke the flames. Augustine's intention, of course, was to juxtapose the flames of hell with the glories of heaven in the interest of helping readers avoid one and seek the other. Such an effort can lead, however, to the ironic effect of making the depiction of evil more vivid than the depiction of goodness. This effect—begun with Augustine—to counterpoise a vivid depiction of "hell on earth" with an eschatological hope of heaven reached perhaps its apex in Milton's *Paradise Lost*. It is dying a long, slow death.[7]

Ironically, then, by the time Augustine gets around to describing the City of God it is a place hardly fit for human habitation. It is even less a place for an incarnate God whose most dramatic display of power was to eat with his surprised followers on the way to Emmaus (see Luke 24). In contrast to his single-minded description of hell in Book 21, Augustine meanders through Book 22, where he talks of heaven. He includes a long excursus on faith healings and miracles that recently occurred around Hippo.[8] He then answers a series of questions—as if writing an ancient advice column—to address the kinds of "bodies" that will inhabit heaven.[9] Yet another two chapters leave heaven altogether to develop a long list of the "evils of humanity," as if the previous chapter had not been convincing enough, and then to develop what Augustine himself calls a "compressed pile of blessings." These blessings are the human "virtues" and "arts," and the beauty of created "nature." But these blessings are, finally, dismissed by Augustine as merely "consolations of mankind under condemnation."[10] At last, in two chapters at the end of the massive tome, Augustine turns to describing "what the saints will be doing in their immortal and spiritual bodies." His conclusion is an anticlimax. "To tell the truth," he begins, "I do not know what will be the nature of that activity, or rather of that rest and leisure."[11]

There is, in other words, little that describes a *city* of God in *The City of God*. At the conclusion of his massive juxtaposition, then, Augustine leaves the reader alone and dying, in a city that is not a city, with a body that is not a body, with a

> nature which is not confined to any space but is everywhere in its wholeness. For we say that God is in heaven and earth . . . but that does not mean that we are to say that he has part of himself in heaven and part in earth. He is wholly in heaven, wholly in earth, and that not at different times but simultaneously; and this cannot be true of a material substance.[12]

The last clause is the jarring one. In it, Augustine limits God, putting God in a place that is no place. He does so because he forgets that his own language is of course made up of material signs. He is caught up in his own rhetoric. The irony is deep. By limiting "God" to "immaterial substances" he is ironically denying both the incarnation and the truth of his own words. If God is not a material substance, nothing that can be said about God can ever convey any truth, since all language is made up of material signs. Ever since Augustine uttered this jarring and tepid conclusion, Christianity has been riddled by a dual tendency to eschatological speculation, on the one hand, and ascetic mortification, on the other. Both tendencies follow Augustine to violate or ignore matter—including real cities—in the interest of some abstract or ideal "substance." Such dualisms—whether of body and soul, matter and spirit, or nature and culture—deny the paradox of the incarnation and set up a dichotomy in its place.

This is particularly unfortunate because Scripture itself presents a far more nuanced and positive picture of human cities than the one Augustine drew. Beginning with Jerusalem, cities were depicted by biblical writers as a way to clothe God as a mother who fed her young. Cities were places of abundance, and Jerusalem was a city that flowed with blessings for her inhabitants. Indeed, Jerusalem was a city for the nations—where even enemies could be reconciled. Such complexity made cities a challenge to human pretensions to ownership or possession of them, and a sure revealer of hypocrisy and corruption—as Jesus apparently made clear to his followers on many occasions. The first Christians were, nevertheless, city dwellers. They were also, however, a small minority—and they thus drew not only upon the positive evaluation of cities in the Hebrew Scriptures, but also upon the stories of Israel in exile to contrast two cities—Babylon and Jerusalem. This ambivalent regard for cities set the stage for Augustine's own juxtaposition. But this early juxtaposition—evident most clearly in the *Apocalypse of John*—was clearly not between *all* human cities and a city of God, since it was addressed in fact to believers in *seven* cities. And even more, the city of God imagined by the apocalyptic writer was a place that *came down* from heaven to earth, not a dematerialized place to which humans were "beamed up." The city of God in the Scripture, like the Son of God in the Gospels, was material: a place where the abundance of creation, and the products of human labor, were gathered and exchanged as garments of God for the children of God. Not a utopia, but a eutopia; a good place, even good places, characterized the city in Christian thought prior to Augustine.

Now, of course, Augustine's bifurcation and elision of the city of humanity from the city of God was a move made for good reason and was not without at least implicit precedent in Scripture. Cities could, and can, be places of violence, destruction, domination, and evil. Early in *The City of God* Augustine calls the divine city as it pilgrimages on earth "a society of aliens," and that description is both an apt one and a key to resolving the problem of conflict over the presence of the sacred in cities. Recalling the themes of exile in the Hebrew Scriptures, and the minority status of the earliest Christians, Augustine highlighted for his readers the tenuous character of any human city and the tendency of people in cities to seek to dominate them. Augustine emphasized these "realistic" aspects of city life not to dwell on the negative, but to open a place for grace. The first half of Augustine's juxtaposition, again, was vivid, and largely accurate. Augustine described well the prideful, greedy, and envious grasping for worldly power that was manifest among both barbarians and Roman citizens, and which has become amply evident among Christians ever since. But at times, the second half of the juxtaposition also glimmered, revealing (as in Scripture it is amply evident) that God works through means, or that grace takes place. These means, furthermore, are not subject to control, since they are places of water, light, earth, bread, wine, and bodies. Grace works, in other words, through the material of cities—through the collective human fabrics of words, buildings, institutions, and processes. To clarify that point is not to diminish the suffering of cities or to posit a "theology of glory."[13] It is rather to recognize suffering honestly and still to have hope. Especially in the early books of *The City of God,* Augustine offers glimpses of a city that would be a graceful and diverse community of strangers whose collective gifts eventually form an abundant circle of friends. Such a city, or cities, would welcome all the living to participate in a community that would be durable because mediated by one who reconciled enemies through a love that transcended narrow love of self. One can observe such processes in any city in the world, of course, implicit in the very human associations, arts, and natural and designed beauty that Augustine dismissed as merely the "consolations of the condemned."

Finally, then, what is only implicit in Augustine's *City of God,* and what can now be made explicit, are the true consolations of places. These cannot be dismissed as only the "consolations of the condemned," unless one is willing to dismiss the incarnation as only an episode in God's revelation to humanity. The actual matter of other people and the world becomes the means through which God works. This means that collective human *senses* take on significance beyond individual perception and ego. We can share places through our senses. As Augustine imagined it, and as most have imagined it since, the city of God is a place of *individual* perception and "sight":

> God will be known to us and visible to us in the sense that he will be spiritually perceived by each one of us in each one of us, perceived in one another, perceived by each in himself; he will be seen in the new heaven and the new earth, in the whole creation as it then will be; he will be seen in every body by means of bodies, wherever the eyes of the spiritual body are directed with their penetrating gaze.[14]

These are, of course, metaphors, but their significance is far-reaching. If a "penetrating" gaze is the primary "sense" in the city of God, then individual perception between subject and object—not relationship between living subjects—is the chief character of that place.[15] But as anyone who lives in a city knows, the individual has to adjust to urban living—the individual must negotiate with or even merge into the flow of traffic with the whole, where one lives by sound at least as much by sight.

Michel de Certeau describes his experiences of "seeing Manhattan from the 110th floor of the World Trade Center" in terms that call to mind, implicitly critique, and ironically verify (given the fate of the towers) Augustine's own:

> A wave of verticals. Its agitation is momentarily arrested by vision. The gigantic mass is immobilized before the eyes. . . . To be lifted to the summit of the World Trade Center is to be lifted out of the city's grasp. One's body is no longer clasped by the streets that turn and return it according to an anonymous law; nor is it possessed, whether as player or played, by the rumble of so many differences. . . . His elevation transfigures him into a voyeur. It puts him at a distance. . . . The exaltation of a scopic and gnostic

> drive: the fiction of knowledge is related to this lust to be a viewpoint and nothing more. . . . The totalizing eye.[16]

If I may paraphrase and apply Certeau for my purposes, his point is that any authentic city of God is first and foremost "lived space," not dead space fixed by sight. Living cities of God then begin "on ground level, with footsteps," where myriad and "intertwined paths give their shape to space. They weave places together." This weaving together of places—the fabric of negotiations that define the very life of cities—is also characteristic of any human collectivity. Any community, and especially cities of God, thus cannot be encompassed by sight alone, cannot be fixed with a "penetrating gaze." After all, even Christians call God not only "Light," but also "Word." Cities of God are fabrics of voices, among other practices. Such practices flow from and through places of grace, in "multiform, resistant, tricky and stubborn procedures that elude discipline," as Certeau puts it.[17] These practices are found not only in the negotiations and mediations necessary to live together in peace, but also in the ever-changing movements, migrations, and music of urban living.

Finally, then, the city—understood in its broadest sense—is the place where the nonviolent gospel of a crucified God finally makes sense. Jesus had to go to Jerusalem to die. To clothe God in a city is to clothe God in suffering, poverty, and pain. Yet it was only in Jerusalem where Jesus could defeat death through practices of love that extended even to strangers and enemies. In the city, we can hear the voices of victims in a way that elicits neither our judgment of them nor resignation to their fate, as Augustine, for complex political and personal reasons, was all too ready to do by the end of his life. In the city, we can hear the sound of suffering in a way that elicits our compassion and that provides us with a community of friends to mobilize to address suffering. And in the city we not only can passively hear the sounds of voices, but can add harmonies and lyrics of our own as gifts of gratitude to the fabric of grace. And that prospect is, as Augustine's work conveys by its sheer massive presence, what makes a city of God so amazing.

Cities of Peace and Plenty

The city of Jerusalem—riddled as it has been by violence—would seem to confirm the worst of Augustine's apocalyptic speculations about the city as a site for domination. Yet Scripture presents the city not only as a place of conflict, but also as a place of peace and plenty. Jerusalem is not only a city of fire, but also a place that is far more fluid. Isaiah's vision is typically ambivalent. It begins with a word of retribution against those who led Israel into exile, against the enemies of the city of God: "Listen, an uproar from the city! A voice from the temple! The voice of the LORD dealing retribution to his enemies!" But the text then goes on with stunningly different imagery:

> Before she was in labor she gave birth; before her pain came upon her she delivered a son. Who has heard of such a thing? Who has seen such things? Shall a land be born in one day? Shall a nation be delivered in one moment? Yet as soon as Zion was in labor she delivered her children. Shall I open the womb and not deliver? says the LORD; shall I, the one who delivers, shut the womb? says your God.
>
> Rejoice with Jerusalem, and be glad for her, all you who love her; rejoice with her in joy, all you who mourn over her—that you may nurse and be satisfied from her consoling breast; that you may drink deeply with delight from her glorious bosom.
>
> For thus says the LORD: I will extend prosperity to her like a river, and the wealth of the nations like an overflowing stream; and you shall nurse and be carried on her arm, and dandled on her knees. As a mother comforts her child, so I will comfort you; you shall be comforted in Jerusalem.
>
> 66:6–12

This is an *earthly* city of God, a maternal image of God's presence and activity that brings joy, comfort, peace, and plenty.

Although Isaiah imagines this city as the enclave of a few—a refuge for the pure—other less exclusive representations of the city of God can be found throughout Scripture. Psalm 87 is one:

> On the holy mount stands the city he founded;
> the LORD loves the gates of Zion more than all the dwellings of Jacob.
> Glorious things are spoken of you, O city of God.
> Among those who know me I mention Rahab and Babylon; Philistia
> too, and Tyre, with Ethiopia—"This one was born there," they say.
>
> And of Zion it shall be said, "This one and that one were born in it";
> for the Most High himself will establish it.
> The LORD records, as he registers the peoples, "This one was born there."
> Singers and dancers alike say, "All my springs are in you."

Each of these images is significant. Rahab was a harlot. Babylon was the city where Israel was exiled. Philistia was the home of Goliath—the enemy of David. This city is a remarkably inclusive place, in short, embracing the nations and their gifts, not excluding them. Not a place only for the pure, a city of God is a place for all peoples.

This inclusive vision of the city was eventually developed among the first Christians. According to the Gospels, Jesus' harshest polemic was addressed to those in power who used that power to exclude others from participation in the city. Jesus called them hypocrites. This is the context for much of the anti-Jewish rhetoric in the Gospels, where Jesus calls the Pharisees and Scribes of Israel snakes and vipers for their narrow vision of the city: "Jerusalem, Jerusalem, the city that kills the prophets and stones those who are sent to it! How often have I desired to gather your children together as a hen gathers her brood under her wings, and you were not willing!"(Matt. 23:37). This is, quite clearly, a critique of the violence of the city. Not a purity that needs defending but an expansiveness that welcomes strangers characterized the earthly city of God in which Jesus walked.

This critique was embodied and enacted in Jesus' crucifixion. The passion stories in the Gospels differ greatly, but their central point is consistent: Jesus died accused of blasphemy and subversion. He was a threat to established power structures because he offered a more inclusive social vision. On the cross, then, Jesus hangs between two criminals. One of these criminals taunts Jesus, but the other comes to Jesus' defense, and Jesus extends to the criminal a word of promise: "Truly I tell you, today you will be with me in Paradise"(Luke 23:43). The city of God is a place where even strangers and criminals are welcome. And then when Jesus dies, a centurion—an enemy of Israel—is converted, praising God and proclaiming Jesus' innocence (in Luke) and his divinity (in Mark and Matthew; see Luke 23:47). The point that these stories intend—that the city of God is a paradise for all people whose progress even violence cannot impede—is confirmed when Jesus appears to his disciples after his resurrection. One example will suffice.

Two disciples are fleeing Jerusalem toward Emmaus, a village. On the way, they encounter a stranger. He talks with the disciples and teaches them, but the disciples do not recognize him. Finally, at dinner, the stranger takes bread and blesses it, and then he is revealed to them for who he is—the Messiah. The outcome of the story is that the disciples immediately return to the city. There, Jesus appears to them again, and this time he stays and eats with them. He then instructs all the disciples to stay in the city, "until you have been clothed with power from on high"(Luke 24:13–49).

This "clothing with power from on high" occurs at Pentecost, where Jesus' followers extend his promise of an inclusive paradise to all people. At Pentecost, the apostles speak in the languages of the known world—to Parthians, Medes, Elamites, Egyptians, and on and on. This story, of course, legitimizes the inclusion of the nations in God's city, extending its boundaries beyond race. The earliest Christians also apparently put this image of the city as a place of plenty for all into practice and shared their goods with one another. "All who believed were together," the story of Pentecost concludes "and had all things in common; they would sell their possessions and goods and distribute the proceeds to all, as any had need"(see Acts 2). This vision of community is hardly a transcendent city beyond the world. It is an economic vision of how life on earth should be, put into practice in a living city.

Finally, the apostle Paul, as is well known, turned from being a persecutor of Christians to being a proselytizer for an inclusive way that even invited Gentiles into the holy confines. In fact, Paul's vision extended beyond the human residents of the city to all of creation, from which the children of God were born, and in which the children of God were embraced:

> Creation waits with eager longing for the revealing of the children of God; for the creation was subjected to futility, not of its own will but by the will of the one who subjected it, in hope that the creation itself will be set free from its bondage to decay

> and will obtain the freedom of the glory of the children of God. We know that the whole creation has been groaning in labor pains until now; and not only the creation, but we ourselves. . . . [Yet] I am convinced that neither death, nor life, nor angels, nor rulers, nor things present, nor things to come, nor powers, nor height, nor depth, nor anything else in all creation, will be able to separate us from the love of God in Christ Jesus our Lord.
>
> Romans 8:19–23, 38–39

This is a vision of a city of God that is not juxtaposed to creation, but is its fulfillment. This city is a place where children flourish.

Of course, many Christians have misinterpreted such an expansive vision as a license to convert and conquer others, in the interest of helping them to realize "fulfillment" and "flourishing." But the use of such force is not the final vision of the city in Revelation—a text to which we have turned again and again. The book is written to the churches in seven cities, and the book itself is divided into seven sections. Such an emphasis on the multitude of places is completely consistent with the bizarre and even excessive imagery throughout the book. Excess and plenty, not ascetic discipline and order, characterizes cities of God. There are, to be sure, ample critiques of cities in the book—but these are directed precisely at the violence, corruption, and injustice of the city—the city "drunk with the blood of the saints and the blood of the witnesses to Jesus" (17:6). Such images crystallize in the image of Babylon—where the people of Israel had once been exiled. Now, though, the referent for this image is abundant to any reader who does a little homework and does not have a vested interest in making profits by scaring readers with apocalyptic scenarios drawn from contemporary politics. Babylon is Rome, a place where "the merchants of the earth have grown rich from the power of her luxury" (18:3). This is the Roman Empire that persecuted the first Christians. It is the violence of Babylon, not its nature as a material place, that calls forth condemnation and serves as the contrast between it and the city of God.[18]

The contrast in the Book of Revelation, then, is not between an "earthly" city and a "heavenly" one, but between two earthly cities—one that is unjust, and one that provides for its people. Thus, the city of God at the end of the book is not a place to which believers are "beamed up," but a place that *comes down* from heaven to earth:

> And I saw the holy city, the new Jerusalem, coming down out of heaven from God, prepared as a bride adorned for her husband. And I heard a loud voice from the throne saying "See, the home of God is among mortals. He will dwell with them as their God; they will be his peoples, and God himself will be with them." . . . I saw no temple in the city, for its temple is the Lord God the Almighty and the Lamb. . . . Its gates will never be shut by day—and there will be no night there.
>
> 21:2–3, 22, 25

A city with open gates is a city with no enemies. This is an extraordinarily pluralistic image of God clothed not as the possession of a powerful few, but taking up residence among all the peoples. And that is Scripture's truest vision of a city of God—as a place on earth as fully as it is in heaven, and as a place of abundance and peace.

A "Society of Aliens" and an Abundance of Friends

Cities have always been repositories not only for people's strongest hopes, but also for their deepest fears. Because of their size and complexity, cities can overwhelm individuals. It is easy to get lost and to wander into areas that frighten and confuse. I had this happen on my first visit to the city of Columbus, Ohio.

Having been raised in a small town, I grew up with all kinds of stereotypes about cities and the people who lived in them. On the one hand, I admired the cosmopolitan opportunities that I knew cities offered and the sophistication that I imagined came with availing oneself of such opportunities. On the other hand, I lived in fear of cities because of the violence in them that I heard about on the news. I grew up during the years of the civil rights movement and the race riots that burned many of America's major cities. Given my limited experience of cultural diversity (as described in chapter 2), my images of the violent city were inevitably wrapped up with images of African Americans. Thus it was to my terror that my car broke down in a predominantly black neighborhood one early Sunday morning in 1979.

I was visiting Columbus to check out Trinity Lutheran Seminary, where I planned to enroll. It was December, and very cold, and I had driven all night from Valparaiso with Lisa—at that time, my girlfriend. Lisa was considering moving to Columbus with me. We broke down about 7 A.M. on Broad Street in front of a dilapidated old hotel with several boarded-up windows. The streets were empty. I got out of the car, Lisa slid over into the driver's seat, and I began to push the car into a gas station across the street from where we had stalled.

As I climbed out of the car, I noticed a green Cadillac Eldorado drive slowly by. The driver of the car turned to look at me, but I didn't think much of it. Then he drove by again, and I noticed that he was African American. To my chagrin, he pulled into a parking lot adjacent to the gas station, got out of his car, and began to walk toward us. He was wearing a full-length fur coat, had pink curlers in his hair, and was wearing alligator shoes. I began to shiver, and not only because of the cold. "Hey, man, you wanna smoke a joint?" he introduced himself. It was a greeting that did not exactly put me at ease. "No, thanks," I replied. "We're just having some car trouble here," I said, hoping he would go away. There was a long silence. "Well," the stranger said, "this station will open up at eleven, and they'll be able to fix you up." "Oh," I said, in a not particularly friendly fashion, although I was grateful for the news. He continued the conversation anyway. "Until then you can come stay warm at my place across the street," the stranger invited, pointing to the hotel. "It's cold out here."

It was very cold, and we knew absolutely no one in the city. I had not even officially applied to the seminary yet. Lisa had by now rolled down her window, and when she heard the invitation, she said, "Yes." She had grown up in Detroit's inner city and was experienced at evaluating the content of one's character regardless of the color of one's skin. "Thank you," Lisa said, getting out of the car and introducing herself—a kindness I finally followed. "It's cold out here." Our host told us his name was Art.

So, we followed Art across the street to the hotel. I was terrified, and still shivering, as we walked in the front door of the hotel, past an old hotel desk—I remember peeling paint and bare lightbulbs—toward Art's little room. We sat on his couch and talked, and gradually felt the warmth from the old iron radiators remove the chill from our bodies. Art had grown up in West Virginia and had moved to the city in search of economic opportunity. He sold shoes and proudly showed us the "Employee of the Month" award that he had earned. He also claimed to have a night job as a "pimp," but I had no way to verify the assertion, and the modesty of his living circumstances made me wonder. He did treat us as a gracious host. After a few hours, he dressed in his Sunday best—including a dazzling hat—and drove us in his Eldorado to the local McDonald's, where he bought us breakfast. Upon our return, the gas station had opened, and we bid Art good-bye, with thanks. Within five minutes we were on the road again.

I have told this story many times, to make various points. To some hearers, I know, the story has reinforced racist stereotypes about the city—although that was the exact opposite of my intention. Many times people would say, in response: "You got lucky." Other times, I suspect, I told the story in a way that absorbed the differences of the city into my own worldview—a linguistic variant on the enterprise that brought Africans to America's shores in the first place. On such occasions, I told the story in a way that communicated that I *felt* I'd gotten lucky—that my fear was somehow justified. Here, I tell the story to thank Art—and to suggest that cities clothe God in a way that can transform a "society of aliens" into an abundance of friends.

The problems arise in cities not when the confusing differences that make people aliens to one another are acknowledged, but when they are ignored in single-minded ambition to control or possess the city as one's own. This is one way to read the biblical story of the tower of Babel. "Now the whole earth had one language and the same words," it begins.

> "Come," [they said to one another,] "let us make bricks, and burn them thoroughly." . . . Then they said, "Come, let us build ourselves a city, and a tower with its top in the heavens, and let us make a name for ourselves; otherwise we shall be scattered abroad upon the face of the whole earth." The LORD came down to see the city and the tower, which mortals had built. And the LORD said, "Look, they are one people, and they have all one language; and this is only the beginning of what they will do; nothing

> that they propose to do will now be impossible for them. Come, let us go down, and confuse their language there, so that they will not understand one another's speech." So the LORD scattered them abroad from there over the face of all the earth, and they left off building the city.
>
> Genesis 11:1, 3–8

The potential meanings of this story are many. To explain the origins of cultural differences is among them. But the heart of the story is a critique of any ambition that seeks to dominate a city. The story affirms the human desire for sociability but condemns seeking "to make a name for" oneself. Early in *The City of God,* before he turned to his individualistic interpretation of heaven, Augustine put it well: human beings, he contended, are "social by nature, quarrelsome by perversion."[19]

It is a perversion of human sociability that establishes a tower of hierarchy in which one controls another, or by means of which one seeks a name for oneself by dominating and controlling any city. This is not to say that mutual consent cannot establish differences in role and responsibility—such is, of course, the political process. In the same way, it is a perversion of theology to imagine that one's fashion for God is the only way to clothe the divine. In a city, everyone is alien to one another, just as a living divine is always beyond the imagining of any human. Just as God cannot be enclosed in one fabric, so a living city cannot be encompassed in one view, one building, or one leader. Better by far a complex society of aliens in which one might find a friend than a totalitarian unity in which one individual or group seeks to make a name for oneself. Art understood this—at least in his life as a shoe salesman and gracious host to two stranded pilgrims, if not in his avocation as a "pimp." Augustine also understood it, at least in the first part of *The City of God:* "The essential context for ambition," he wrote, "is a people corrupted by greed."[20]

The historian of religions Robert Orsi highlights nicely how sociability can be perverted, in a dense meditation on the way cities work:

> The alienness of the city afford[s] the opportunity for the projection and satisfaction of needs and desires otherwise denied in the culture and, conversely, the pivot for articulations of the deepest fears and apprehensions swirling at any moment through the wider society—a focusing lens for the prohibited and the wanted, the unimaginable, the denied and feared. Desire is not necessarily either good or bad, positive or negative . . . [but] when desire is provoked by the distance authorized by race and class, then desire itself becomes implicated in strategies of power and domination; desire so provoked, in order to sustain itself, contributes in turn to the maintenance of distance. Fantasies born of desire for (and fear of) the alien city overwhelm . . . the real lives of city people; the latter [become] figures in other people's dramas and objects of other people's needs.[21]

In such situations, of which the Babel story provides an archetypal case, and my encounter with Art an alternative, regulation, regimentation, supervision, discipline, and order are imposed upon human agency, in place of the scattered, diverse, and spontaneous complexity of a living city. Art defied my conventional expectations and racist fears, just as cities always surprise their inhabitants.

At his more generous moments, Augustine understood this about human cities and then projected this complexity into the very city of God, where humans enjoyed being saved by participation:

> There is such a thing as a bad intermediary, who separates friends; very different is a good intermediary, who reconciles enemies. . . . And that mediator in whom we can participate, and by participation reach our felicity is the uncreated Word of God, by whom all things were created. And yet he is not the Mediator in that he is the Word; for the Word . . . is far removed from mortals. He is the Mediator in that he is man. . . . God himself, the blessed God who is the giver of blessedness, became partaker of our human nature and thus offered us a short cut to participation in his own divine nature.[22]

Any fabric for the divine, any city, is true to the extent that it participates (with humility, Augustine would add) in the larger context of space and time and does not arrogate a "name" for itself. "Created gods are gods not in their own true nature," Augustine concludes, "but by participation in the true God. By aiming at more, a man is diminished, when he elects to be self-sufficient and defects from the one who is really sufficient for him."[23] There are implications of this insight for the relations between nations even today: policies based on reactive self-interest will invariably fail, compared to policies that consider the consequences for the entire global community, over the long haul.

If there is only one living God, then, Augustine at times even recognizes that human beings will need to build many cities of God or clothe God in many fashions:

> While this Heavenly City, therefore, is on pilgrimage in this world, she calls out citizens from all nations and so collects a society of aliens, speaking all languages. She takes no account of [i.e., does not despise] any difference in customs, laws, and institutions, by which earthly peace is achieved and preserved—not that she annuls or abolishes any of those, rather, she maintains them and follows them (for whatever divergences there are among the diverse nations, those institutions have one single aim—earthly peace), provided that no hindrance is presented thereby to the religion which teaches that the one supreme and true God is to be worshipped. Thus even the Heavenly City in her pilgrimage here on earth makes use of the earthly peace and defends and seeks the compromises between human wills in respect of the provisions relevant to the mortal nature of man.[24]

This is a road map for religious liberty and religious pluralism. Insofar as religions themselves—as human constructs—prove themselves to be promoters of peace, they can be welcomed, even revered, by the "Heavenly City in her pilgrimage here on earth."

This "Augustinian" doctrine of the relationship between the two cities is a promising one and is consistent with the inclusive vision of the city that predominates in Scripture. It is a consistent, if minority, theme throughout Augustine's work:

"The way does not belong to one people, but is for all nations."[25] And even nature itself could be included: "All nature's substances are good, because they exist and therefore have their own mode and kind of being, and, in their fashion, a peace and harmony among themselves."[26] In short, it is the justice and peace of any city—not its acceptance of a totalitarian or ideal order—that determines its character as a city of God. "Remove justice," Augustine contended in a famous passage, "and what are kingdoms but gangs of criminals on a large scale?"[27] Along with peace and justice, though, it is especially freedom that marks a city of God. "In the Heavenly City," Augustine concludes, "there will be freedom of will. It will be one and the same freedom in all, and indivisible in the separate individuals. It will be freed from all evil and filled with all good, enjoying unfailingly the delight of eternal joys, forgetting all offences, forgetting all punishments. Yet it will not forget its own liberation, nor be ungrateful to its liberator."[28]

Gratitude, then, as the opposite of greed, determines whether a city is a city of God. And the ways to express gratitude, of course, are ample. For Jesus, according to the Gospel of John, it was to turn strangers into friends. "This is my commandment," Jesus taught, "that you love one another as I have loved you." The content of this commandment is the opposite of any attempt to control another or reduce them to an image of oneself:

> No one has greater love than this, to lay down one's life for one's friends. You are my friends if you do what I command you. I do not call you servants any longer, because the servant does not know what the master is doing; but I have called you friends, because I have made known to you everything that I have heard from the Father. You did not choose me but I chose you. And I appointed you to go and bear fruit, fruit that will last, so that the Father will give you whatever you ask him in my name. I am giving you these commands so that you may love one another.
>
> 15:12–17

Art taught this to me, although it has taken me years to realize it. I supposed him to be an enemy, but he proved to be a friend. He chose us—we surely did not choose him. Yet in choosing us, he showed me that God could even be clothed in the fabrics of the city—in a full-length fur coat, with alligator shoes, and pink curlers in his hair. I was grateful to him back in 1979 for the warm place and the hot food he provided us as utterly gratuitous gifts. I am grateful now for the story that his kindness—which is the expression of love between friends—has allowed me to tell. A city of God is a society of aliens and an abundance of friends.

"A Harmonious Unity in Plurality"

The bifurcation of space that Augustine instituted by juxtaposing the city of humanity with the city of God is still very much with us and can be observed by

an afternoon drive along any major thoroughfare of any large city in the United States. Start, as I have, at the northern boundary of Broad Street near Cheltenham in Philadelphia, and make your way south. You'll pass economic extremes along the way—blocks of crumbling old Victorian homes that now serve as crack houses, a stretch of skyscrapers and monuments to American history and progress, and finally a long block filled by the sports arenas where Philly's professional teams provide circuses to entertain the masses. The same extremes can be observed, for another example, if you began at Lake Shore Drive, and head west along 55th Street on Chicago's South Side. You'll pass by the gentrified Hyde Park and through Washington Park, but then past a row of Chicago Housing Authority projects on to Western Avenue—long known as the dividing line between "white" and "black" Chicago. Eventually, you'll reach Midway Airport—where travelers fly into and out of the city all day and night. What you might miss on such a straight-line shot through any one of America's cities are the city's people—the vernacular landscape, expressed especially in the people's voices.[29]

You will not miss the grid pattern that urban designers imposed upon the landscape, since you will frequently be stopping at intersections along the way. On one level, cities are spatially *ordered* places, as if in fulfillment of Augustine's dream. Orsi explains:

> Grids were imposed on the natural landscapes . . . obliterating the natural contours of the land; topography was transformed into an efficient engine for moving goods and workers across the urban terrain. The gridding had implications as well for the kinds of relationships that might take place in cities. There were no central meeting places on the grid, no places to stop and talk, to congregate. . . . The god of the American city—and this was the singular deity of a decidedly monotheistic faith—was order, and the rituals of this faith were the control and supervision of the streets.[30]

Values of speed, control, efficiency, and order have given us the cityscapes we have today, and they reflect a particularly one-sided vision of human purpose and potential. To discover the alternative, one must get out of one's car and walk a little.

Whenever possible, I have taken trains and/or buses to and from my suburban homes and my city workplaces. I do so for many reasons. I can read and write on trains—and so be more "efficient" with my time. I save natural resources by taking public transportation, and I lessen my contribution to air pollution. I don't have to fight over parking places. It's healthy for me to walk a few blocks to and from stations.

And I enjoy mingling with people—although I of course observe the modesty and commuter etiquette that lowers eyes and avoids staring, no matter how interesting another person might appear to be. Most of all, though, riding trains gives me a chance to slow down and *hear* the city and its people in a way that a quick trip in my car does not.

I've learned to listen to cities in part because I love music. Over the past five years, I have rediscovered my youthful love of the blues by sitting in with gospel choirs as a saxophone soloist. My experience has diverged from when I played in jazz bands directed by and peopled with educated (and mostly white) musicians who read music. Gospel is different. At least in the choirs I've sat in with—both in the Chicago area and in Philadelphia—much of what I contribute is improvisational, and much of what happens is unpredictable. In formal jazz, each tune has a basically similar structure. There's a "head"—a melody and a set of changes that introduce the basic themes of the song. Then there's a space for improvisation—the "body" of the song, which is "opened up" for players to take turns, usually, in solos that are defined by four, eight, twelve or more bar segments, and that are sometimes interrupted by a "bridge" or "chorus." The song then concludes by returning to the head, sometimes with slight variants, but usually recognizable as the song's resolution and conclusion. The vast majority of jazz tunes—and many rock and roll songs as well—follow this pattern.

Gospel songs also sometimes use this pattern, but more often than not there's a less linear and gridlike form to the music. My earliest experience of this process of creation happened with the Valparaiso University Gospel Choir, formerly directed by Judith Erwin Neville. I began sitting in with this choir when some students invited me. I showed up one Tuesday night at rehearsal and asked if I could play along. When the director agreed, for three years after that, until I left the university, I rarely missed a Tuesday or Thursday night practice and seldom missed a worship service where the choir played. I also organized the choir's first tour—to the church my brother David attended in Iowa. I never received a penny for my time and did not think to ask for compensation. I gained far more from my participation in this worship group than any amount of money could have provided.

What I learned from playing with this choir was to listen, and the sounds I heard were sounds of cities. We began each rehearsal with prayer, and then concluded holding hands in a circle where everyone was invited to share with one another a blessing or challenge they were facing. Near the end of my time with the choir, as I struggled with trauma, this circle became very important to me. That circle of prayer became a real "balm in Gilead," as the lyrics of one of the songs we sang put it, borrowing, of course, from the Psalms. I doubt I would have survived without it. In between the prayers, of course, we made music that was unlike any I'd ever made before. I usually had no written notes in front of me, and consequently, I had to listen to participate. It was rarely a linear process, and I never played a song the same way twice. Sometimes we'd begin by learning the end of a song, sometimes the beginning, sometimes the middle. There were occasions when we had never gone completely through a song from beginning to end prior to sharing it in public worship. And yet the music always came together, a "harmonious unity in plurality" that was made all the more enjoyable for the surprise, spontaneity, and complexity of its performance.

This music reflected, historically and in its very structure and form, the sounds of a living city. Robert Orsi again helps us to understand the analogy I'm trying to draw:

> Outsiders have consistently mistaken the vitality and heterogeneity of city streets for disorderliness . . . [but] into every space hollowed out by contempt for the city and its people—the bleak apartments of public housing, streets dwarfed and dominated by massive towers of stone . . . migrants and immigrants have inserted themselves, making themselves present, indeed at times over present, usually on their own terms.[31]

The songs I've played with gospel choirs have been songs of protest, songs of exuberance, songs of praise, songs of resistance, and songs of consolation. They sometimes appeared to outsiders as disorderly, for at times they'd go on and on, repeating choruses over and over, seeking the groove of the Spirit that would lead us to transcend whatever individual limits we brought to the music, or whatever limits were being imposed upon us. They were songs that asserted faith in the midst of mistrust.

Now, it is easy to imagine this faith as passive—as limited to the making of music itself, and not entering into the fray of the city's politics. Nothing, of course, could be further from the truth about such songs. As W. E. B. DuBois noted long ago about the sorrow songs and spirituals—from which contemporary gospel springs—they were "siftings of the centuries," whose messages were "naturally veiled" but in which "breathes a hope—a faith in the ultimate justice of things."[32] This faith takes on flesh in every gospel choir, just as it took on flesh in the practices of active nonviolence that transformed America during the civil rights movement—and can transform cities again. "Faith without works is dead," wrote the author of the New Testament Book of James, and the works of faith are also the fruits of the Spirit active in love. No one understands this more vividly than people living in a city, who hear plenty of rhetoric about peace and progress, but who must take it upon themselves to incarnate it in practices. The sociologist Sharon Zukin explains:

> The very diversity of the population and their need for cultural and economic exchanges create unpredictable spaces of freedom: the markets, restaurant kitchens, designated landmarks, and parades that become both sites and sights of new collective identities. This is the city that people cherish. It is this transcendent narrative of opportunity and self-respect that lends hope to a common public culture. But if entire cities, led by their downtowns, continue to be ghettoized by public rhetoric and private investment, the dream of a common public culture will fall victim to an empty vision.[33]

I was welcomed into a city of God that was no empty vision, through the music of a gospel choir.

What I was participating in by making such music was a "recombination," a "new collective identity" or hybrid that cities around the world are busy creating every day. Somehow, for a brief moment that choir harmonized the saxophone playing of a professor from Wisconsin with the singing of black, white, and Latino students from Los Angeles to New York and the directing of an African Methodist Episcopal Zion minister from Gary, Indiana. Writing it down like that cannot convey, of course, the dynamic of what happened. As Michael W. Harris concludes about the gospel blues in general, "the sources belie the assumptions one would be inclined to make about them."[34] African Americans, like other migrants and immigrants to America's cities, have lived with the dominant Augustinian expectation of the city as a place of order. They have also experienced this order as a totalitarian refusal to recognize them and, sometimes, as a barrier that threatened their very survival. Such an "order" is, of course, disorder, and an ironic denial of the very hope that Augustine at his best intended by clothing God's promise in the metaphor of a city. Yet in worship—and in countless other practices of faith active in love—African Americans and other immigrants and migrating people have improvised to transform their experience of dissonance by adding to it new harmonies and rhythms. Augustine's juxtaposition becomes not a dichotomy, in short, but a lived paradox, a "harmonious unity in plurality."[35]

The challenge before us in the early years of the twenty-first century is to re-create cities so that they reflect this harmonious unity in plurality, not through violence, but through laws and institutions that allow humans to flourish as agents of grace.[36] It is not an impossible dream, and in fact it is one already on its way toward realization across America.[37] As Robert Orsi writes: "The religious idioms improvised in cities respond to [their] dilemmas, offering healing and reorientation by linking the individual both to a larger community and to a shared narrative about the nature of the world."[38] Time and again, cities have been the sites where individual inspiration took root and grew, bearing fruit for peace—as Jesus put it. Time and again the leading edges of human hope emerged not from individual genius but from collective efforts of people living together. Cities are thus among the most promising places of grace, fabrics for God where living can be more than survival and where individuals are more than lonely egos seeking unity with a disembodied God.

For it is, finally, the image of God as one body that also sanctions the plurality of human forms and creation. If God is one, and it is the vocation of human beings to clothe God well, then many fabrics will be needed. We need many cities of God. The only criteria for such fabrics is that they minimize harm, thereby creating spaces for grace to flourish in art, in music, in labor, in religion—in all the threads of human creativity. For nearly two millennia the church has lived with Augustine's rhetoric of juxtaposition that, contrary to its own best intentions, forced believers into grace by dominating their passions with an antimaterial emphasis on order and time, at the expense of place. Augustine's rhetoric of juxtaposition has led us to accept a nature/culture dualism that has impeded the realization of the nonviolent gospel of Christ and the building of cities of God that are as free from oppression and domination as possible.[39] Today—as my analogy with music sought to make clear—people from cities are offering us an alternative, if we will only listen to them. A theology that clothes God not as imposed discipline but as the continual recombining and incarnating of matter and spirit offers us a harmonious unity in plurality, where human justice, peace, and happiness become as possible on earth as in heaven. Such a theology does not deny the human potential for evil and the limits of human finitude. Such a theology, rather, faces evil as the perversion of human sociability it is, and accepts finitude as a natural consequence of animal existence. And such a theology also accepts the beauties of the senses, the goodness of the virtues, and the truth of human creativity—not only as consolations for the condemned, but as continuities that are a foretaste of the feast to come, celebrated in congregations as diverse as the human collectives who create them.

Epilogue

Pilgrims' Process

Salvation by Grace through Place

"We buy the Truth."

Pilgrims at Vanity Fair, in John Bunyan, *Pilgrim's Progress*

"Vanity of vanities," says the Teacher, "vanity of vanities! All is vanity."

Ecclesiastes 1:2

For centuries, Christians have imagined being on a narrow path, fleeing "the city of destruction" for the "city of heaven" by battling against vanity. This itself is vanity. Any obsession with salvation—sacred or secular—is to distrust grace and is likely to result in violence. Driven by a desire to deny death, believers have been blinded to how our "progress" at buying and selling "truth" has destroyed places. This is truly vanity.

Christians, of course, have had plenty of company on this "narrow" path that has left such a broad swath of destruction. From Augustine's Rome to Bunyan's England to Mickey's Mecca, a version of the theological imagination that clothed God as a disembodied agent has let people clothe themselves in vain versions of sacred or secular heaven that have had bad consequences for the earth. Private or parochial ways to clothe God that benefited the purchasing power of a few have paraded as goodness, truth, and beauty available to all. This, too, is vanity—an emperor who thinks he's clothed in splendor but who in fact wears no clothes.

The longer I teach and write, the more I am humbled by the experience. After my first semester of teaching, I remember sitting in the office of my colleague Rick DeMaris, with our mutual friend and colleague Betty DeBerg, sharing a glass of sherry. It had been a long, exhausting semester—the first of full-time teaching for each of us. "You know," I said to my friends, "this semester made me realize how little significance what we do really has in the scope of things." I savored a sip of sherry and went on: "We spent three hours for fourteen weeks with a few eighteen- and nineteen-year-olds. Compared to the other influences in the world—parents, politics, and television, for instance—our puny efforts at cultural critique and nurturing faith don't mean much." Now that I've taught for fifteen years, and written four books, I'm even more deeply convinced of this wisdom. It's all a pilgrim's process. No one can control it.

While I've developed modesty that borders on the cynical, then, I've also come to realize that the shaping of history and culture really is up to us, this side of eternity. This puts me in a predicament. On the one hand, this freedom is an exhilarating prospect: the future is truly open. On the other hand, it's a terrifying reality check: if the future is in our hands, we would seem to be headed for some serious trouble. Historical events and contemporary cultural practices document amply that places can be perverted, ignored, distorted, and destroyed—by the agency of humans acting willingly or ignorantly. This was the discovery in part 1 of this book. In part 2, however, we also tried to sketch a broad way of grace, fashions for God's clothing that might help us to avoid some of that destruction. This, too, in all probability, is vanity.

In this brief epilogue, though, I want to summarize as succinctly as possible the three theological criteria used throughout this study. The first thread in God's clothing, then, is a *poetics of availability,* or how a place works as language. Language is by nature limiting. All images fall short of the glory of God. But some ways to locate God in language are inherently more likely than others to point beyond themselves—to poetically avail a reader (or hearer) of transcendence. Places in nature are preeminent among these potential fabrics for God, by virtue of their widespread availability. Water, light, earth, trees, and bodies are phenomena familiar to all, even if they are not yet flourishing as fully as we'd hope for them. Such places of grace, along with the phenomena of cities, are amply attested as clothing for God in Hebrew and Christian Scriptures, and contrast markedly with the arbitrary limits associated with the places of the mall, Walt Disney World, or a suburban home. Such private places more often than not imprison pilgrims. These places are not evil in themselves, of course, but their consequences can be damaging. Such places—and they are only three examples of many—clothe themselves as something more than ordinary, but pilgrims to them usually wind up with less. The biblical metaphors for God, by contrast, open up living in a way that renders truth, goodness, and beauty available to all, regardless of gender, class, race, or—even—creed. For the central biblical fashions for God can also be found in the rivers of human traditions running around the entire globe. Such metaphors are not specific to any nation. They are (or should be) available to all, possessed by none. They are gifts and thus accord well with the Christian doctrine of creation and the fabric that clothes God as Creator.

I developed, second, a criterion for a theology of place that emphasizes *a politics of necessity,* or how a fabric functions socially. We need places to live. In fact, when we cease to take up space, we're dead, although by way of denying death some people even take up space after they're "gone." This truth is frightening. It is hard to accept that we are transient. To deny this truth we fabricate some clothing for God to wrap ourselves in immortality. Often, these fabrics include words we can use as weapons against those who might remind us of our fragility. We break off a piece of space, or claim to own a particular place, as if this fragment of fabric can buy us a different truth than the transience that is the lot of all the living. Every commodity at a mall, all the adventures of Walt Disney World, and many of the practices undertaken in the privacy of the suburban home serve this death-defying political function. But places we need—like water, earth, and cities—do not share in such denials. Places we need point us instead to our fragility, and even to our mutual interdependence, and perhaps thereby can lead to more fulfilling political arrangements for the human community. Places we need can engage us in practices filled with passion and compassion, rather than in practices riddled with the violence of banality. Gratitude is the essential element here—gratitude for those places we need and that carry us to "flow" both in life and, we can hope, beyond it. The places we isolated in part 2 are only some of many that might function as places of grace, but they take precedence because of their prominence in Scripture and everyday living. We could easily do without the mall, Walt Disney World, or even a suburban home. We cannot do without water, light, earth, trees, bodies, or human societies. A God clothed in such places offers us a salvation that we not only can desire, but that we need, and need has a way of stimulating gratitude. Such a justification by grace through the ordinary gifts of place accords well with the Christian doctrine of salvation and the fabric that clothes God as Redeemer.

Finally, I have developed throughout this book a *rhetoric of participation* as the key to deciding about places. The principle is a simple one and assigns the task of creating the best words and practices by which to clothe God to each pilgrim—where it inevitably resides anyway. The question to guide this task asks, How much does a place or practice invite you to participate fully as a person, using your gifts in the service of justice, peace, and beauty—in short, in the service of the common good? The mall, Walt Disney World, and the suburban home invite guests to participate primarily as consumers, while a few owners reap the profits. Such places fabricate private gods—of the market, of Mickey Mouse, or of tidiness—to provide us an illusion of control or to distract us from suffering. This is vanity. But it is also an ironic accompaniment to a vain interpretation of Christianity that imagines that vanity, surfaces—material places—are somehow less vital than "spiritual" ones. This is to confuse badly the clothing of God with the living God and to deny the central Christian teaching of the incarnation—that God dwells among mortals. And that is truly vanity. The question is not which words have the longest duration in time—although tradition surely has a weight all its own. The question is which words best motivate people to live well. In many versions of Christianity, and in many "Christian" cultures, we have pursued a salvation that's unavailable, from a redeemer who's not necessary, in the interest of profits that satisfy a few. Such a way will, if we are not careful, turn all to less than vanity—indeed, to vapor. By contrast, taking our place as participants in one body alongside a God clothed in the light of the world, or in living cities, can help motivate us to care for the environment and one another. When we locate God not as individuals, but in participation with all the living, we can find the strength to sustain the living for generations to come. Such a principle of participation—that puts into practice our justification by grace through participation in a place—accords well with the Christian doctrine of sanctification and the fabric that clothes God as Sustainer.

Now, I realize fully that for some Christians even these three ways to clothe God—as Creator, Redeemer, and Sustainer—are not adequate replacements for what they imagine to be the Trinitarian "name" of God as "Father, Son, and Spirit." To such readers, I can say, first, that I can and do use these traditional words without hesitation to clothe God—for instance, in the rite of baptism—and take delight in the associations that each offers. But I also know that they, too, are vanity—like all clothing for God, and I know that to try to make them more is to turn them into less. To readers who still remain unconvinced, even after the lengthy arguments of the previous chapters, I can recommend, second, that they return to Scripture itself and read it, with eyes open to the stunning plurality of metaphors for God there contained. And to those still struggling, clinging to some fashion for God's clothing, I can only commend the words of Jesus to those who nailed him to a cross, and then cast lots to determine who would own his garments: "Father, forgive them, for they know not what they do."

Notes

Introduction

1. See especially Martin Marty and Micah Marty, *Places along the Way: Meditations on the Journey of Faith* (Minneapolis: Augsburg Press, 1994).

2. Sidney E. Mead, *The Lively Experiment: The Shaping of Christianity in America* (New York: Harper and Row, 1963), 6.

Chapter 1

1. For a range of definitions and examples, see T. Matthew Ciolek, "Koan Studies Pages," http://www.ciolek.com/WWWVLPages/ZenPages/KoanStudy.html, as cited 2 July 2002.

2. Lawrence Langner, *The Importance of Wearing Clothes* (New York: Hastings House, 1959), 4.

3. Roland Barthes, *The Fashion System*, trans. Matthew Ward and Richard Howard (Berkeley and Los Angeles: University of California Press, 1990 [1967]).

4. Linda B. Arthur, ed., *Religion, Dress and the Body* (New York: Oxford, 1999), 3.

5. Philippe Perrot, *Fashioning the Bourgeoisie: A History of Clothing in the Nineteenth Century,* trans. Richard Bienvenu (Princeton, N.J.: Princeton University Press, 1994 [1981]), 8.

6. Mary Stewart Van Leeuwen, ed., *After Eden: Facing the Challenge of Gender Reconciliation* (Grand Rapids: Eerdmans, 1993), 339.

7. "Coopamerica's Sweatshops.org: Solutions to a Global Problem," at http://www.coopamerica.org/sweatshops/ssjeans.htm, as cited 2 July 2002. This is now at http://www.sweatshops.org/buy/ladders_pants.html, as cited 5 March 2003.

8. Diana Eck, *Darsán: Seeing the Divine Image in India*. 2d ed. rev. and enl. (Chambersburg, Pa: Anima Books, 1985).

9. Among the best discussions of this topic remains Philip S. Watson, *Let God Be God! An Interpretation of the Theology of Martin Luther* (London: Epworth Press, 1947).

10. WA 40II, 329f; 386f, as cited by Paul Althaus, *The Theology of Martin Luther,* trans. Robert C. Schultz (Philadelphia: Fortress Press, 1966), 20.

11. Martin Luther, *The Large Catechism* [1529], in *The Book of Concord: The Confessions of the Evangelical Lutheran Church,* trans. and ed. Theodore G. Tappert et al. (Philadelphia: Fortress, 1959), 365.

12. See, for instance, Mark I. Wallace, *Fragments of the Spirit: Nature, Violence, and the Renewal of Creation* (New York: Continuum, 1996).

13. Sallie McFague, *Models of God: Theology for an Ecological, Nuclear Age* (Philadelphia: Fortress Press, 1987), 34–39.

14. Jean-Luc Marion, *God without Being,* trans. Thomas A. Carlson (Chicago: University of Chicago Press, 1993). I disagree with Marion's solution but agree with his diagnosis, articulated in this catchy phrase.

15. René Girard, *Violence and the Sacred,* trans. Patrick Gregory (Baltimore: Johns Hopkins University Press, 1977).

16. McFague, *Models of God,* 60.

17. Ibid., 68.

18. Daily life is governed by and lived according to rules of market forces, scientific technology, and historically, socially, and psychologically discernible patterns—even among Christians. As people become increasingly aware of the plurality of images and names for God around the globe, furthermore, the potential for any one model of God to dominate all others becomes increasingly unlikely, even if it were desirable. See on this question Diana Eck (*Encountering God: A Spiritual Journey from Bozeman to Banaras* [Cambridge: Harvard University Press, 1993]), who develops a helpful typology of exclusivist, inclusivist (or assimilationist), and pluralist ways of expressing encounters with God. Eck's Pluralism Project at Harvard is mapping the increasing diversity of religious life in the United States.

19. McFague, *Models of God,* 73.

20. Ibid., 77.

21. The line refers to Stevens's poem "Description without Place," delivered at Harvard in 1945. See Alan Filreis, *Wallace Stevens and the Actual World* (Princeton, N.J.: Princeton University Press, 1993).

22. Elie Wiesel, *Night* (New York: Bantam, 1960), 61–62.

23. Hannah Arendt, *Eichmann in Jerusalem: A Report on the Banality of Evil* (New York: Penguin USA, 1994).

24. R. Scott Appleby, *The Ambivalence of the Sacred: Religion, Violence, and Reconciliation* (Lanham, Md.: Rowan and Littlefield, 2000). My next book, tentatively entitled *Violence and the Sacred in America,* will explore four episodes when religion sanctioned violence or motivated resistance to violence in American history, including September 11, 2001.

Chapter 2

1. See, for example, "Where Was God on Sept. 11?" in *Lutheran New Yorker* 13 (fall/winter 2001).

2. Annie Dillard, *Holy the Firm* (New York: Harper and Row, 1977), 44.

3. The titles increase almost daily. Two atlases provide a good overview of more "traditional" sacred places. See James Harpur, *The Atlas of Sacred Places: Meeting Points of Heaven and Earth* (New York: Henry Holt, 1994); and Colin Wilson, *The Atlas of Holy Places and Sacred Sites* (London: DK Publishing, 1996). For more typical explorations of the idea in the context of experimental "spiritualities," see, for example, Marilyn Barrett, *Creating Eden: The Garden as Healing Space* (San Francisco: Harper, 1985); and Denise Linn, *Sacred Space: Clearing and Enhancing the Energy of Your Home* (New York: Ballantine, 1996).

4. See, for selected Christian cases, Victor Turner and Edith Turner, *Image and Pilgrimage in Christian Culture: Anthropological Perspectives* (New York: Columbia University Press, 1978); and for a wider range of examples, see, among many others, Simon Coleman and John Elsner, *Pilgrimage: Past and Present in the World Religions* (Cambridge: Harvard University Press, 1995).

5. The literature here is vast. See in addition to the titles below, Joel P. Brereton, "Sacred Space," in *The Encyclopedia of Religion,* ed. Mircea Eliade. (New York: Macmillan, 1987), 12: 526; and *Sacred Place,* ed. Jean Holm with John Bowker, Themes in Religious Studies Series (London: Pinter, 1994).

6. See, for instance, *The New Age Catalogue: Access to Information and Sources* (New York: Doubleday, 1988).

7. Robert P. Hamma, *Landscapes of the Soul: A Spirituality of Place* (Notre Dame, Ind.: Ave Maria Press, 1999).

8. See the powerful essay by Lynda Sexson, "Home as Eden's Picture Book: The Fiction of Sacred Space," in *The Sacred Place: Witnessing the Holy in the Physical World,* ed. W. Scott Olsen and Scott Cairns (Salt Lake City: University of Utah Press, 1996), 135–52.

9. Mircea Eliade, *The Sacred and the Profane: The Nature of Religion,* trans. Willard R. Trask (New York: Harcourt, Brace, and World, 1958), 20–21.

10. Jonathan Z. Smith, *To Take Place: Toward Theory in Ritual* (Chicago: University of Chicago Press, 1987), 104.

11. David Chidester and Edward T. Linenthal, Introduction to *American Sacred Space* (Bloomington: Indiana University Press, 1995), 5.

12. Ibid., 6–19.

13. For an essay that develops the theme of Christian attachment to place as a way to deal with death, see Douglas Davies, "Christianity," in *Sacred Place,* ed. Jean Holm with John Bowker, Themes in Religious Studies Series (London: Pinter, 1994): 33–61. Interestingly, Monty Python takes up this theme again in an even more direct and cutting way in a daring (and blasphemous) satire of the life of Jesus, dubbed *The Life of Brian.* Between the two films, Monty Python's message is crystal clear, although the evidence in *The Holy Grail* is ample by itself for our purposes.

14. See, for instance, James Reston Jr. *Warriors of God: Richard the Lionheart and Saladin in the Third Crusade* (New York: Doubleday, 2001).

15. On this tripartite foundation for transcendence, see Marjorie Hewitt Suchocki, *The Fall to Violence: Original Sin in Relational Theology* (New York: Continuum, 1994), esp. 36–46.

16. Martha C. Nussbaum, *The Fragility of Goodness: Luck and Ethics in Greek Tragedy and Philosophy* (Cambridge: Cambridge University Press, 1986).

17. Naturally, I have my own definition of a sacred place, which builds upon those of Eliade, Smith, Chidester, and Linenthal, and a few other sources that are noted as appropriate. Sacred places, then, are literal or figurative places that function to *orient, disorient, or reorient* people symbolically. They often operate unconsciously; their function is usually masked, obscured, or mystified. People visit them, but may not be able to explain why, and may resist any functional explanation of their behavior. Nevertheless, because they relate to how people find or make symbolic meaning in a particular culture, sacred places are held in high symbolic value: it is usually taboo to profane or to desecrate them, and people have often sacrificed, fought, killed, or died for them.

Sacred places are connected to sacred times, sacred practices, and sacred persons in a system of symbols—a religion, as Clifford Geertz has argued. Sacred places, like other aspects of religions, direct people's attention to values, practices, and ideas that are deemed important in a particular culture. Sacred places thus have political and economic, as well as symbolic, significance.

Sacred places give human beings a sense of power that comes from participating in something greater than individual existence. They are visited by people for various purposes: to remember significant historical events or persons; to enact rituals that address ultimate questions; to be healed or to otherwise overcome the fear of death and suffering; and to express solidarity with the values of the religious system that claims the place. They can be used by political regimes to legitimize power and by subversive groups to challenge what they perceive to be illegitimate power. They thus can disorient as well as orient, depending upon the status of the pilgrim who participates in the pilgrimage, and the approach of the people who control access to the site.

Sacred places are established by human interpretation; their status is communicated across generations through myths, rituals, and other forms of narrative and practice, such as pilgrimage. They often involve exclusion; entry is refused to outsiders or those deemed impure. Even insiders may find it necessary to perform particular rituals of purification before the place can be entered. A sacred place may lose or gain in status from one generation to the next; new sacred places can also be created by contact with or borrowing from other traditions, or through novel developments within a tradition. Because sacred places often have ancient, if not forgotten, origins, they take on over the course of generations a "life of their own" and may appear to be "given" or "revealed" to human beings.

Of course, people can make any place sacred. But for a place to be sacred in a historically and culturally significant sense, it must be shared. No individual sacred place, furthermore, exists apart from some system of signs that makes it meaningful. Sacred places, like places generally, are always filtered and mediated through language and culture. We may think we are choosing a sacred place because it is "special" to us, but the reason it is "special" to us is likely because we live in a culture where such places are valued and "special" to others. A place is not sacred, in short, until it is articulated as such, and its high symbolic value shared by a people. A place becomes sacred in a historically significant sense when a *group* claims it as such, generally over a long period of time. A place is not sacred, then, if it does not relate to how people are oriented spiritually, culturally, and practically, and if it is not part of a larger symbolic system through which people have dealt with ultimate questions—such as how to live or why we die.

18. The fuller study is published as "A National Shrine to Scapegoating? The Vietnam Veterans Memorial, Washington, DC," *Contagion: Journal of Violence, Mimesis, and Culture* 2 (spring 1995): 165–88. A revised version of the article is forthcoming in my next book, tentatively entitled, *Violence and the Sacred in America*.

19. Jan C. Scruggs and Joel L. Swerdlow, *To Heal a Nation: The Vietnam Veterans Memorial* (New York: Harper and Row, 1985).

20. *The Rhetoric and Poetics of Aristotle,* trans. W. Rhys Roberts (New York: Modern Library, 1984), 223.

21. Aristotle, *The Politics,* trans. T. A. Sinclair, rev. Trevor J. Saunders (New York: Penguin Books, 1984), esp. 57–61.

22. See, for a cogent argument along these lines, Thomas A. Tweed, "On Moving Across: Translocative Religion and the Interpreter's Position," in *Journal of the American Academy of Religion* 70 (June 2002): 263–77.

23. See Edward W. Soja, *Postmetropolis: Critical Studies of Cities and Regions* (London: Blackwell, 2000), 10–11.

24. Ibid., 12.

25. In fact, I had the opportunity to test many of the ideas in this book with a bright and interested group of Jews and Christians, in a six-week course for the Institute for Jewish-Christian Understanding of Muhlenberg College. Thanks to the director, Peter A. Petit, and to all participants for their insights.

26. See my recent *Youth Ministry in Modern America: 1930 to the Present* (Peabody, Mass.: Hendrickson Publishers, 2000), esp. 73–90.

27. And it is precisely here—in this turn to rhetoric—that Augustine, especially in *The City of God,* is our mentor. Augustine studied rhetoric as a youth and used it throughout his career—nowhere more effectively than in *The City of God*. Indeed, Augustine's rhetoric at times could be described as intemperate. As he himself put it: "I am using my most earnest endeavors" to differentiate true from false religion. Among these "earnest" rhetorical endeavors is the use of satire. Especially in part 1 of his work, when he is trying to critique "pagan" spiritualities, Augustine uses the most harsh terms to describe the practices of his opponents. Pagans were blinded by the "worship of inanities," they were marked by "stupidity" and "unconscionable folly." Pagan rituals Augustine did not hesitate to call "ridiculous," "superstitious," and "barbarous folly." All in all, the practices of those Augustine sought to critique in part 1 of *The City of God* demonstrated the behavior of people who had "succumbed to the pressures of the customs and laws" of the time. The satirical tone of Augustine's rhetoric can be seen clearly from the simple sentence: "Stupidity glories in never yielding to the force of truth." See *The City of God,* ed. Henry Bettenson (New York: Pilgrim Press, 1972), 254, 242, et al.

28. Traditionally called, respectively, The Old Testament and The New Testament, the Gospels and Epistles are placed by this naming in proper relationship to their Jewish origin, without sacrificing the central Christian claim that Jesus was Messiah, or Christ.

Chapter 3

1. Like many early malls, Valley Fair has fallen on very hard times, driven into financial difficulty by more "upscale" shopping centers. Current plans include the purchase of the building by a local youth ministry, to provide a safe and secure hangout for young people. For details, see Duke Behnke, "Will Youth Be Served?" *Appleton Post-Crescent,* January 15, 2003, at http://www.wisinfo.com/postcrescent/news/archive/local_7935914.shtml, as cited 16 January 2003.

2. More are being built every year, although they tend to be "upscale" or "designer" malls, targeted at a particular market niche. As many as a thousand current malls are financially troubled, and others have already closed or face redevelopment. See Jonathan Lerner, "The Unmalling of America," *Hemispheres: The Magazine of United Airlines* (January 2002): 48–55.

3. William Kowinski is the most popular writer to identify this religious function of the mall, in his *The Malling of America: An Inside Look at the Great Consumer Paradise* (New York: William Morrow, 1985).

4. Victor Turner and Edith Turner, *Image and Pilgrimage in Christian Culture: Anthropological Perspectives* (New York: Columbia University Press, 1978), 20.

5. See for instance, Jon Anderson, "The Call of the Mall: True Tales of Obsession from Minnesota's 'HugeDale,' " *Chicago Tribune,* 18 October 1992, sec. 12, pp. 1, 10–11.

6. David R. Loy, "The Religion of the Market," *Journal of the American Academy of Religion* 65 (Spring 1996): 275.

7. Ibid., 276.

8. Ibid.

9. Russell H. Conwell, *Acres of Diamonds* (Old Tappan, N.J.: Revell, 1960).

10. Ibid., 20–24, as cited by Material History of American Religion Project, "Acres of Diamonds," at http://www.materialreligion.org/documents/apr97doc.html, as cited 2 July 2002.

11. Loy, "Religion of the Market," 285.

12. Ibid., 286.

13. Ibid., 288.

14. On this matter of "weak" faith, see R. Scott Appleby, *The Ambivalence of the Sacred: Religion, Violence, and Reconciliation* (Lanham, Md.: Rowan and Littlefield, 2000); esp. chapter 6.

15. Ira G. Zepp, *The New Religious Image of Urban America: The Shopping Mall as Ceremonial Center* (Westminster, Md.: Christian Classics: 1986), 15.

16. James Rouse, "The Regional Shopping Center: Its Role in the Community It Serves," unpublished lecture at Harvard Graduate School of Design, April 26, 1963, as cited in Zepp, *New Religious Image,* 31.

17. Scholars have recently turned from disdain for malls to appreciation for their "hip" character or at least have tried to present a more balanced account of the commodification of the world. See, for a relatively tame example, Leigh Eric Schmidt, *Consumer Rites: The Buying and Selling of American Holidays* (Princeton, N.J.: Princeton University Press, 1995). As a historian, Schmidt tries to "put balance before judgment" (p. 7). That this is, in effect, a judgment itself seems to elude Schmidt, although he offers belated "confessions" of his own "slippery positioning" on "ongoing cultural contests" at the end of the work.

18. Zepp, *New Religious Image,* 15.

19. Ibid., 58–9.

20. Ibid., 56.

21. Ibid., 37.

22. Ibid., 12–13, 6–8.

23. See on this theme Witold Rybczynski, *City Life: Urban Expectations in a New World* (New York: Scribner, 1996).

24. Zepp, *New Religious Image,* 80.

25. Ibid., 150.

26. Jon Goss ("Once-upon-a-Time in the Commodity World: An Unofficial Guide to the Mall of America," *Annals of the Association of American Geographers* 89 [March 1999], p. 3) cites this phrase from the Mall of America web page, at www.mallofamerica.com.

27. Goss, 9.

28. Ibid., 8.

29. Steven L. Shepherd, "Mall Culture," in *Humanist* 58 (November/December 1998): 41.

30. Goss, "Once-upon-a-Time in the Commodity World," 18.

31. Ibid., 19.

32. Ibid., 38.

33. Ibid., 4.

34. Of course, just in case an IRS agent happens to be among my readers, I must report that no ATS research funds were spent at Camp Snoopy. The only use I made of ATS funds was to reimburse my travel to and from the mall.

35. See Simon Coleman and John Elsner, *Pilgrimage Past and Present in the World Religions* (Cambridge: Harvard University Press, 1995).

36. *Mall of America: A Guide to Fashion, Food, and Fun*. Mall newspaper/advertising handout, 2 August–15 August 2001, p. 8.

Chapter 4

1. See, among the many other titles listed in notes below: Elizabeth Bell, Lynda Haas, and Laura Sells, eds., *From Mouse to Mermaid: The Politics of Film, Gender, and Culture*. (Bloomington: Indiana University Press, 1995); Susan G. Davis, *Spectacular Nature: Corporate Culture and the Sea World Experience* (Berkeley and Los Angeles: University of California Press, 1997); *Inside the Mouse: Work and Play at Disney World/The Project on Disney* (Durham, N.C.: Duke University Press, 1995); David Lyon, *Jesus in Disneyland: Religion in Postmodern Times* (Malden, Mass.: Blackwell, 2000); Karal Ann Marlin, Canadian Center for Architecture, eds., *Designing Disney's Theme Parks: The Architecture of Reassurance*. (New York: Flammarion, 1997); Arvad E. Raz, *Riding the Black Ship: Japan and Tokyo Disneyland* (Cambridge: Harvard University Press, 1999); Steven Watts, *The Magic Kingdom: Walt Disney and the American Way of Life* (Boston: Houghton Mifflin, 1997). Disney's "management style" has been increasingly marketed to all kinds of businesses in the U.S., and religious groups are increasingly joining the parade. See Bill Capodagli and Lynn Jackson, *The Disney Way: Harnessing the Management Secrets of Disney in Your Company* (New York: McGraw Hill, 1999).

2. For this reason, I prefer to describe our era as "mediated modernity" rather than the currently vogue "postmodernity," which implies that the technological and social foundations of the modern world have been overcome. I find instead that modernity is now distinguished by its mediated character, by new forms of communication. The basic political and social forms of modernity remain unchanged. It is our experience, or the way these phenomena are described to us and the way we describe them to ourselves, that has changed. See on this point the fascinating if somewhat frustrating essay by David Lyon, *Jesus in Disneyland: Religion in Postmodern Times* (Cambridge, England: Polity Press, 2000).

3. Stephen M. Fjellman, *Vinyl Leaves: Walt Disney World and America* (Boulder, Colo.: Westview Press, 1992), 10.

4. Disney generates commodities and controls markets of a breathtaking scope. In 1998, the Disney empire included not just the U.S. theme parks, but also Walt Disney Pictures, Touchstone, Caravan, Miramax and Hollywood Pictures; ABC, ESPN, the Disney Channel, Arts and Entertainment, the History Channel, and Lifetime television networks; nine local TV stations, eleven AM radio stations, ten FM stations; home videos, stage plays, music publishing, and seven daily newspapers; theme parks in Tokyo and Paris, with a new one coming in Hong Kong; computer software, toys, and merchandise; baseball and hockey franchises; hotels, real estate, shopping centers, housing developments, a cruise line, and, of course, clothing. See on this list David L. Ulin, "Mousetrap," review of Carl Hiassen, *Team Rodent: How Disney Devours the World* (New York: Ballantine, 1998), in *Chicago Tribune,* 19 July 1998, sec. 14, p. 3.

5. Fjellman, *Vinyl Leaves,* 11, 21.

6. Umberto Eco, *Travels in Hyperreality,* trans. William Weaver (New York: Harcourt, Brace & Co., 1983), 48.

7. I am aware that this analogy could (should?) be as offensive to Muslim sensibilities as Eco's original analogy could be to Christian ones. I ask, however, the reader's patience as I develop it in a way that I hope will demonstrate my deep respect for the Muslim *hajj,* especially when compared to a Disney pilgrimage. Islam intensifies, after all, the Jewish and Christian condemnation of idolatry that I here seek to surface.

8. Phil Long, "Disneymania Consumes a Family of 4," *Chicago Tribune,* 6 September 1992, sec. 5, p. 2.

9. See Paul "Captain Monorail" Smith, "Tales from the Crypt: Life in the Haunted Mansion," in *Persistence of Vision: Speaking of Characters,* at http://www.disneypov.com/issue09/wdw.html, as cited 12 June 2002.

10. Charlie Haas, "Disneyland Is Good for You," in *New West* 3 (4 December 1978): 18, as cited by Mike Wallace, *Mickey Mouse History and Other Essays on American Memory* (Philadelphia: Temple University Press, 1996), 138.

11. Robert N. Bellah, "Civil Religion in America," in *Daedalus* (winter 1967): 1–21. See also Bellah's *The Broken Covenant: American Civil Religion in Time of Trial* (New York: Seabury, 1975).

12. See, for instance, Donald G. Jones and Russell E. Richey, *American Civil Religion.* (New York: Harper and Row, 1974).

13. See Robert N. Bellah and Phillip E. Hammond, *Varieties of Civil Religion* (New York: Harper and Row, 1980). Bellah's insight spawned a number of studies, not all of them directly utilizing his conceptual framework, but all building upon the idea. See, for instance, Edward Tabor Linenthal, *Sacred Ground: Americans and Their Battlefields* (Urbana: University of Illinois Press, 1991).

14. John F. Wilson, *Public Religion in American Culture.* (New York: Oxford University Press, 1979). Two other ideas are central to the public religion, according to Wilson. These include the idea of America as a refuge for the poor and oppressed, and the idea of America as a land of equal opportunity and liberty. Both are reinforced by Walt Disney World (although also contradicted in practice), but the themes of innocence and progress are clearer and more significant for our purposes.

15. Fjellman, *Vinyl Leaves*, 275.

16. Mary Rolfe, "It's a Small World," at http://www.pansophist.com/fantsmall.htm, as cited12 June 2002.

17. Clifford Geertz, *The Interpretation of Cultures: Selected Essays* (New York: Basic Books, 1973), 90.

18. See also Joel P. Brereton, "Sacred Space," in *The Encyclopedia of Religion,* ed. Mircea Eliade (New York: Macmillan, 1987), 12: 526.

19. Henry A. Giroux, *The Mouse That Roared: Disney and the End of Innocence* (Lanham, Md.: Rowan and Littlefield, 1999), 55.

20. Debra Lau, "Forbes Faces: Michael Eisner," at http://www.forbes.com/2001/01/16/16/faceeisner.html, as cited 12 June 2002. See also Holly Sklar, "CEO Ponzi Scheme," at http://www.inequality.org/ceopayedit2.html, p. 2, as cited 12 June 2002.

21. Jason Mauro, "Disney's Splash Mountain: Death Anxiety, the Tar Baby, and Rituals of Violence," in *Children's Literature Association Quarterly* 22 (1997): 113–17.

22. The story in its original dialect can be found online at University of Virginia, Department of American Studies, "Uncle Remus," at http://xroads.virginia.edu/~UG97/remus/tar-baby.html, as cited on 12 June 2002.

23. Mauro, "Disney's Splash Mountain," 115.

24. Ibid.

25. Ernest Becker, *The Denial of Death* (New York: The Free Press, 1973).

26. Mauro, "Disney's Splash Mountain," 117.

27. On the theme of reassurance, see Marling, *Designing Disney's Theme Parks.*

28. See, for instance, the Walt Disney World web page, which used the word twice in a single sentence, reassuring viewers that "There's plenty of magic throughout our Parks and Resorts during the Walt Disney World® 100 Years of Magic Celebration," at http://disneyworld.disney.go.com/waltdisneyworld/index, as cited 21 January 2003.

29. See Bronislaw Malinowski, *Magic, Science, and Religion* (Boston: Beacon Press, 1948), for an argument linking magic and early religions, and see "The Church and School of Wicca," at www.wicca.org (as cited 12 June 2002) for more recent explorations of "magick."

30. The Magic Kingdom, of course, is only the most concentrated and enduring medium through which this Disney gospel of "innocence" masking greed is communicated. In the same way, similar meanings also appear in Disney's films, as Emory University's Gary Laderman has recently argued. According to Laderman, "death, or the threat of death, is the motor, the driving force that enlivens each [Disney]

narrative." *Snow White and the Seven Dwarfs* (1937), *Pinocchio* (1940), *Bambi* (1942), *Cinderella* (1950), and *Sleeping Beauty* (1959)—to mention only the "classics" —all revolve around pivotal deaths or the threat of death. In *Bambi,* for instance, the plot hinges upon the death of the young fawn's mother, which then leaves Bambi alone in the woods. His father comforts him, from a distance, and tells him, in effect, to grow up and move on. Death must be stoically overcome; grief is unmanly—or unstaglike. So Bambi grows up and, motivated by love for a female fawn, fights his way to the top of the mountain, where he stands at the end of the film at the pinnacle of progress: the new king (taking over for his father) of the forest. This plot is repeated over and over, in film after film, and in ride after ride, until the dominance of the theme of death becomes unmistakable. Like many sacred places, then, the Magic Kingdom finally tries to solve the problem of death for pilgrims. That it must ultimately fail to do so is obvious with a moment of reflection. See Gary Laderman, "The Disney Way of Death," in *Journal of the American Academy of Religion* 68 (March 2000): 39.

31. See, for one example of such inflated rhetoric, "Downtown Disney Resort Area Hotels," at http://www.downtowndisneyhotels.com/hotlspg.html, as cited 21 January 2002.

32. For a fine study of this process of taming and commodifying nature in American theme parks, see Susan G. Davis, *Spectacular Nature: Corporate Culture and the Sea World Experience* (Berkeley and Los Angeles: University of California Press, 1997).

33. Henry David Thoreau, *Walden* (New York: Holt, Rinehart and Winston, 1963), p. 265, as cited in Belden C. Lane, *The Solace of Fierce Landscapes: Exploring Desert and Mountain Spirituality* (New York: Oxford University Press, 1998), 4.

34. See "Park History," at http://www.geocities.com/RainForest/Canopy/1792/history.html, as cited 21 January 2003.

35. See Cory Lancaster, "31 Animals Died at Disney Park," in *Orlando Sentinel*, 14 May 1998, as cited at http://csf.colorado.edu/ecofem/may98/0081.html, on 21 January 2003. See also "Disney Says Animal Deaths Coincidental," at http://www.mndaily.com/daily/1998/04/09ap409c.ap/, as cited on 21 January 2003.

36. See *Inside the Mouse: Work and Play at Disney World,* ed. The Project on Disney (Durham, N.C.: Duke University Press, 1995).

37. William F. Van Wert, "Disney World and Posthistory," in *Cultural Critique* 32 (winter 1995): 188–91.

38. Such a community is now in development in Orlando, under the rather different name of "Celebration."

39. See Mary Rolfe, "Epcot Center," at http://www.pansophist.com/epcot/htm, as cited 12 June 2002.

40. The description here and in the above paragraph follows Fjellman and Van Wert.

41. Van Wert, "Disney World and Posthistory," 202.

42. William Arnal, "The Segregation of Social Desire: 'Religion' and Disney World," in *Journal of the American Academy of Religion* 69 (March 2001): 17. Despite what a reader might have been led to believe to this point, I really don't believe that capitalism is inherently flawed, and I am surely no fan of communism. In fact, I doubt very much that any system other than capitalism would have produced the flourishing of technologies and information we have seen in the past century. Nevertheless, there is surely room for improvement, in the interest of true progress. For the "progress" that is sold to us at EPCOT is only an image of progress, and in fact it promises only more of the same. To become a more effective and humane economic system, then, capitalism needs to be adjusted through two conditions. First, clear and effective checks must exist on the human tendencies to greed and domination. Whether these checks are religious or political doesn't matter, but at present they're not working. After all, the same logic of checks and balances is at the heart of our system of government, and surely the same motivations are at work in the market that come into play in the world of power politics. Unless we develop some of these checks and balances, corporate greed will completely undo democracy. Second, within a capitalist system, personal moral decisions must stem from sources that produce compassion and a sense of commitment to the well-being of all others, as well as to oneself. Capitalism depends upon the goodwill of individuals. But whatever "goodwill" has been evident in the twentieth century did not, often, stem from the deep stores

and sources of human wisdom. Good will arose, instead, from limited interests and resided in recently fabricated and banal stories and practices that were "sold" to people in ways that exploited them and led them to damage themselves, the environment, and others. The preeminent example of this process at work, as we will suggest in the coming chapters, was Nazi Germany. If the problems of the twentieth century could not be solved by a state representing itself as the Third Reich and offering a "final solution," for instance, then neither are the problems of the twenty-first century likely to be solved by technological solutions offered by profit-driven corporations imagining themselves as our saviors. If the problems of the twentieth century were political, the problems of the twenty-first will be religious—and the only way to solve those religious problems is by paying attention to religion. To do so, we need an expanded realm where the not-for-profit wisdom to handle the technologies we have developed can flourish. And we need time, and places, where the true power of the imagination can be free to do its work in ways that build not greed but compassion. That would be true progress. Unfortunately, it is not the kind of progress for which there is currently an exhibit at EPCOT. Needless to say, such time and places do exist, in schools, where the deep traditions of human wisdom can be learned about, and in churches, synagogues, mosques, and temples, where such wisdom of compassion is both taught and practiced. Without balance from streams that motivate people to compassion, or at least charity, capitalism will inevitably devolve into greed-driven destruction.

Chapter 5

1. See for instance, Dave Barry, *Homes and Other Black Holes* (New York: Fawcett Columbine, 1988).

2. See National Association of Home Builders, *Housing Facts, Figures, and Trends* (Washington, D.C.: NAHB, 2001), p. 14. Also available online at www.nahb.com/housing_issues/facts.htm, as cited 13 June 2002.

3. Harvard University Joint Center for Housing Studies, "The State of the Nation's Housing: 2000," http://www.gsd.harvard.edu/jcenter/Research, as cited 28 May 2002. A new study is available at http://www.jchs.harvard.edu/publications/markets/Son2002.pdf.

4. This brackets, for now, the question of how those values fueled the devotion to home. Suffice it to say that whereas once it may have been possible for the "traditional" nuclear family to operate in America in a way that made its relations a matter of comfortably conventional negotiation, more recently, Cleaver family values exist only as an attacked or defended shibboleth. See on this point Stephanie Coontz, *The Way We Never Were: The American Family and the Nostalgia Trap* (New York: Basic Books, 1992).

5. Peter Gardella, *Domestic Religion: Work, Food, Sex, and Other Commitments* (Cleveland: Pilgrim Press, 1999), 8.

6. Ibid., 1, 2.

7. Ibid., 14.

8. Ibid., 114.

9. Ibid., 36.

10. Ibid., 144.

11. Ibid., 45.

12. Mary Douglas, *Purity and Danger: An Analysis of Concepts of Pollution and Taboo* (New York: Penguin, 1966), 15.

13. This is not to deny that cleanliness also has its hygienic functions. On this point, see Nancy Tomes, *The Gospel of Germs: Men, Women, and the Microbe in American Life* (Cambridge: Harvard University Press, 1998).

14. Colleen McDannell, "Parlor Piety: The Home as Sacred Space in Protestant America," in *American Home Life 1880–1930: A Social History of Spaces and Services,* ed. Jessica H. Foy and Thomas J. Schlereth (Knoxville: University of Tennessee Press, 1992), 162–89.

15. See here Suellen Hoy, *Chasing Dirt: The American Pursuit of Cleanliness* (New York: Oxford University Press, 1995) who argues tellingly: "By the 1950s Americans had come to value cleanliness for

personal reasons, but they failed to recognize the connection between how they behaved at home and what they did in public" (173).

16. United States Soap and Detergent Association, "2002 Cleaning Survey," at http://www.cleaning101.com/cleaning/survey02.html, as cited 13 June 2002.

17. Douglas, *Purity and Danger,* 173.

18. See "Shopping for Safer Household Cleaning Products," at http://www.ecomall.com/greenshopping/housecl.htm, as cited 28 May 2002.

19. "Mr. Clean's Home on the Web," at http://www.mrclean.com, as cited 28 May 2002.

20. "StainBuster," as noted in text, is now, as cited 13 April 2003, redirected to http://magazines.ivillage.com/goodhousekeeping/myhome/stainbuster/spc/0,,284550_295273,00.html.

21. The three sites can be found at http://members.tripod.com/~Barefoot_Lass/index-2.html; http://www.mymessyhouse.com/zippymessie.shtml; and http://www.clean-n-brite.com/generic32.html, respectively, as cited on 14 April 2003.

22. I can't remember where I first heard this quotation, which I have modified slightly. The original apparently was uttered by Schweitzer on his deathbed. See James B. Simpson, comp., *Simpson's Contemporary Quotations*, online at http://www.bartleby.com/63/31/5331.html, as cited on 22 January 2003.

23. Max Weber, *The Protestant Ethic and the Spirit of Capitalism,* trans. Talcott Parsons (New York: Scribner, 1958); and R. H. Tawney, *Religion and the Rise of Capitalism* (New York: Harcourt, Brace, 1952).

24. As quoted in Dennis Rodkin, "Lawning America: Our Quest for a Perfect Patch of Earth Is Harming the Earth," *Chicago Tribune,* 2 July 1995, p. 10.

25. Ibid.

26. Virginia Scott Jenkins, *The Lawn: A History of an American Obsession* (Washington, D.C.: Smithsonian Institution Press, 1994).

27. See on this theme, among many others, my first book, *Paradox Lost: Free Will and Political Liberty in American Culture, 1630–1760* (Baltimore: Johns Hopkins University Press, 1992).

28. "Yes, You Can Have a Weed-Free Lawn," in *Changing Times,* July 1955, p. 41, as cited in Jenkins, *The Lawn,* 146.

29. "Scott's Lawn Care," http://www.scottscompany.com/lawncare/lawnCare.cfm, as cited on 27 May 2002.

30. Jenkins, *The Lawn,* 185.

31. Savage Arms Corp, Lawn Mower Division, ad, *House and Garden,* July 1947, 110, as cited in Jenkins, *The Lawn,* 126.

32. Worcester Lawn Mower Co., ad, *Better Homes and Gardens,* May 1953, p. 341, as cited in Jenkins, *The Lawn,* 127.

33. William J. Darby, "A Scientist Looks at *Silent Spring,*" review published by the American Chemical Society, 1962, as cited in Environmental Defense Fund, "25 Years after DDT Ban, Bald Eagles, Osprey Numbers Soar," at http://www.edf.org/pubs/NewsReleases/1997/Jun/e_ddt.html, p. 1, as cited on 27 May 2002. The URL has since changed. Please see http://www.environmentaldefense.org/pressrelease.cfm?contentid=2446.

34. Ibid., p. 2.

35. Jenkins, *The Lawn,* 150–51, 164–66.

36. "Frequently Asked Questions," http://www.trugreenchemlawn.com/ask/health_faq.html, p. 2, as cited on 28 May 2002, .

37. Jenkins, *The Lawn,* 164.

38. "Frequently Asked Questions," 4.

39. Ibid., 1.

40. The resources for someone who wants to avoid a chemically treated lawn are ample. See Warren Schultz, *The Chemical-Free Lawn: The Newest Varieties and Techniques to Grow Lush, Hardy Grass* (New York: Rodale Press, 1989); and Margaret Roach, *The Natural Lawn and Alternatives* (Brooklyn, N.Y.: Brooklyn Botanic Garden, 1993), among many others.

41. William Zinsser, "Electronic Coup de Grass: The Mowing Ethic," *Life,* 22 August 1969, 10.

42. Rodkin, "Lawning America," 10.

43. Colleen McDannell and Bernhard Lang, *Heaven: A History,* 2d ed. (New Haven: Yale University Press, 2001), 307.

44. Ibid., 70.

45. Kristin Hahn, *In Search of Grace: A Religious Outsider's Journey across America's Landscape of Faith* (New York: William Morrow, 2002), 6, xiii–xiv.

Chapter 6

1. See on this matter J. Gamberoni, "Labes/Clothing," in *Theological Dictionary of the Old Testament,* ed. G. Johannes Botterweck and Helmer Ringgren, trans. John T. Willis (Grand Rapids: Eerdmans, 1974–), 7: 461.

2. The best introduction to Girard's work, which also includes a good bibliography, is *The Girard Reader,* ed. James M. Williams (New York: Crossroad, 1996). I have a rather ambivalent relationship with Girardian theory. On the one hand, I admire greatly its analytical insight, as I admire Girard himself as a gentle and intelligent Christian. On the other hand, I disagree with some of the implications drawn from Girard's work, especially his assertion of Christian uniqueness and superiority to other traditions on the matter of violence. I find such a conclusion empirically unwarranted, theoretically unnecessary, and an egregious scapegoating of other religious traditions, which ironically contradicts the theory itself. Christian distinctiveness does not equate with superiority. Consequently, what follows is not, perhaps, "pure" Girardian theory, but rather my interpretation of Girard for the purposes of this book.

3. 1 Timothy 6:6–10. The translation is Augustine's, *The City of God,* trans. Henry Bettenson (New York: Pilgrim, 1972), book 1, ch. 10, 17.

4. Ibid., book 3, ch. 1, 89.

5. See especially R. Scott Appleby, *The Ambivalence of the Sacred: Religion, Violence, and Reconciliation* (Lanham, Md.: Rowan and Littlefield, 2000); and Miroslav Volf, *Exclusion and Embrace: A Theological Exploration of Identity, Otherness and Reconciliation* (Nashville: Abingdon Press, 1996).

6. On McVeigh and other forms of religious terrorism, see Mark Juergensmeyer, *Terror in the Mind of God: The Global Rise of Religious Violence* (Berkeley and Los Angeles: University of California Press, 2000). Juergensmeyer is excellent on "extremist" groups; he is less helpful at sorting out the "ordinary" or "legitimized" religious violence of nation-states and cultures.

7. Hannah Arendt, *Eichmann in Jerusalem: A Report on the Banality of Evil* (New York: Viking, 1963), 253.

8. Ibid., 111.

9. Ibid., 15.

10. Ibid., 120.

11. Ibid., 93.

12. Ibid., 44.

13. Ibid., 85.

14. Ibid., 84.

15. Ibid., 103.

16. Ibid., 111.

17. Ibid., 9.

18. Ibid., 134.

19. Ibid., 29.

20. Ibid., 253.

21. Ibid., 23.

22. See Pat Conroy, *The Water Is Wide* (New York: Bantam, 1972).

23. For more current numbers, see "Habitat for Humanity," at http://www.habitat.org, as cited 3 July 2002.

24. Frye Gaillard, *If I Were a Carpenter: Twenty Years of Habitat for Humanity* (Winston-Salem, N.C.: John F. Blair, 1996), 5.

25. See Millard Fuller, *The Theology of the Hammer* (Macon, Ga.: Smyth and Helwys, 1994), 39.

26. Ibid., 36–37.

27. Harvard University Joint Center for Housing Studies, "Low Income Housing," in *The State of the Nation's Housing: 2000,* at http://www.gsd.harvard.edu/jcenter, as cited 7 January 2002.

28. See, for instance, Mark I. Wallace, "The Wounded Spirit as the Basis for Hope in an Age of Radical Ecology," in *Christianity and Ecology: Seeking the Well-Being of Earth and Humans*, ed. Dieter T. Hessel and Rosemary Radford Ruether (Cambridge: Harvard University Press, 2000), 64, who traces in detail the environmental racism practiced in my own neighborhood of Chester, Pennsylvania.

29. See on this theme the essay by Robert A. Orsi, "Crossing the City Line," in *Gods of the City: Religion and the American Urban Landscape* (Bloomington: Indiana University Press, 1999), about which I will say more in chapter 12. Briefly, however, Orsi's essay draws out how suffering can be used by people of privilege to justify their own purposes—no matter how noble—and that representations of suffering can create a voyeuristic distance that ironically perpetuates it.

Chapter 7

1. Norman Maclean, *A River Runs through It* (Chicago: University of Chicago Press, 1983), 108.

2. Martin E. Marty, *Baptism* (Philadelphia: Fortress Press, 1962), 8.

3. See on these topics *The Encyclopedia of Religion,* ed. Mircea Eliade, 13 vols. (New York: Macmillan, 1987).

4. Peter McKenzie, *The Christians: Their Beliefs and Practices* (Nashville: Abingdon, 1988), 18.

5. Mircea Eliade, *Patterns in Comparative Religion*, trans. Rosemary Sheed (New York: New American Library, 1958), 188–215 collects many examples.

6. Richard J. Clifford, *Creation Accounts in the Ancient Near East and in the Bible*, Catholic Biblical Quarterly Monograph Series, 26 (Washington, D.C.: Catholic Biblical Association, 1994), 32, 102.

7. See Jon D. Levenson, *Creation and the Persistence of Evil: The Jewish Drama of Divine Omnipotence* (San Francisco: Harper and Row, 1988).

8. Interestingly, this theme of water as garment is explicit in Psalm 104, where God "covers the earth with the deep as with a garment," v. 6.

9. The fact that two of the rivers are actual, and two unknown, has led to countless goose chases to determine the "actual" location of Eden. From my perspective, the actual location doesn't matter a whit: what is important is that the waters are not "evil," not "chaos." In fact, the waters provide the people with orientation.

10. Catherine Keller, "No More Sea: The Lost Chaos of the Eschaton," in *Christianity and Ecology: Seeking the Well-Being of Earth and Humans,* ed. Dieter T. Hessel and Rosemary Radford Ruether (Cambridge: Harvard University Press, 2000), 184.

11. Perhaps the two "greatest" Old Testament theologians of a generation ago, Walther Zimmerli and Gerhard von Rad, hardly mention water in their major works. See Zimmerli, *Old Testament Theology in Outline* (Atlanta: John Knox, 1978) and Gerhard von Rad, *Old Testament Theology,* 2 vols., trans. D. M. G. Stalker (New York: Harper and Row, 1962).

12. See the very helpful summary by Phyllis A. Bird, "Water," in *Harper's Bible Dictionary,* ed. Paul J. Achtemeier (San Francisco: Harper and Row, 1985), 1120–21.

13. Marcus J. Borg, *Meeting Jesus Again for the First Time: The Historical Jesus and the Heart of Contemporary Faith* (San Francisco: Harper and Row, 1994), 46–47.

14. Mihaly Csikszentmihalyi, *Flow: The Psychology of Optimal Experience* (New York: Harper and Row, 1990). Csikszentmihalyi describes flow as "the state in which people are so involved in an activity that nothing else seems to matter; the experience itself is so enjoyable that people will do it even at great cost, for the sheer sake of doing it," and "the best moments . . . when a person's body or mind is stretched to its limits in a voluntary effort to accomplish something difficult and worthwhile" (3–5).

15. Borg, *Meeting Jesus,* 49. The currency of this term was obviously applied, or exploited, by the current president of the United States, who promoted his administration under the rubric of "compassionate conservativism." Suffice it to say that I find it hard to locate much compassion in current policies.

16. Diana L. Eck (*Encountering God: A Spiritual Journey from Bozeman to Banaras* [Boston: Beacon Press, 1993], 230) ends her book with these two visions and interprets them to encourage an "imagined community" built upon "interdependence and a wider sense of 'we.'" I agree.

17. Barbara R. Rossing, "River of Life in God's New Jerusalem: An Eschatological Vision for Earth's Future," in *Christianity and Ecology: Seeking the Well-Being of Earth and Humans,* ed. Dieter T. Hessel and Rosemary Radford Ruether (Cambridge: Harvard University Press, 2000), 205, 212.

Chapter 8

1. See Mircea Eliade, *Patterns in Comparative Religion,* trans. Rosemary Sheed (New York: Meridian, 1958), 38–187.

2. See "Hymn to the Aten," in *Sacred Texts of the World: A Universal Anthology,* ed. Ninian Smart and Richard D. Hecht (New York: Crossroad, 1982), 12. See also Jean Rhys Bram, "Sun," in *The Encyclopedia of Religion,* ed. Mircea Eliade (New York: Macmillan, 1988), 14: 132.

3. Thomas J. Hopkins, *The Hindu Religious Tradition* (Belmont, Calif.: Wadsworth, 1971), 14–35.

4. Peter McKenzie, *The Christians: Their Beliefs and Practices* (Nashville: Abingdon, 1988), 21.

5. Saint Symeon the New Theologian, *The Discourses,* trans. C. J. de Catanzaro. Classics of Western Spirituality (New York: Paulist Press, 1980), 202, as cited by William C. Placher, *Readings in the History of Christian Theology, Volume 1: From Its Beginnings to the Eve of the Reformation* (Philadelphia: Westminster, 1988), 93–95.

6. Saint Gregory Palamas, *The Triads,* ed. John Meyendorff, trans. Nicholas Gendle. *Classics of Western Spirituality* (New York: Paulist Press, 1983), 32–34, 47, 64, 93–95, as cited in Placher, *Readings in the History,* 95–99.

7. Ibid.

8. Martin Luther, *Lectures on Genesis,* in *Luther's Works,* ed. Jaroslav Pelikan (St. Louis: Concordia, 1960), 2: 247, as cited in Jaroslav Pelikan, *The Light of the World: A Basic Image in Early Christian Thought* (New York: Harper, 1962), 11.

9. Martin Luther King Jr., "Letter from Birmingham Jail," at *The King Papers Project,* http://www.stanford.edu/group/King/home_new.htm, p. 6, as cited 18 June 2002.

10. This metaphor continues to motivate nonviolent social change. On Latin America, see "Manifesto de la Iglesia metodista in Bolivia," 1970, as cited by Gustavo Guttierez, *A Theology of Liberation,* trans. Sister Caridad Inda and John Eagleson (Maryknoll, N.Y.: Orbis Books, 1973), 116, 155–59; and on South Africa, *The Kairos Document: Challenge to the Church—A Theological Comment on the Political Crisis in South Africa* (Grand Rapids: Eerdmans, 1986).

11. Among the many examples, see Lam. 2; Hosea 8; Joel 1; Amos 1; Obad. 1; Micah 1; Nahum 1; Zeph. 1; Zech. 1.

12. See, for instance, Deut. 4:19; 17:2–5; 2 Kings 21–23; Is. 13, 14; Jer. 10; Amos 5:26.

13. Jesus' teaching (under the influence of apocalypticism and Greek speculation) does intensify the prophetic point by making the fire "eternal," an idea alien to the earliest (and most enduring) strands of Jewish thought and belief.

14. See George Lane and Algimantas Kezys, *Chicago Churches and Synagogues* (Chicago: Loyola University Press, 1981), 130–31; and Marilee Munger Scroggs, *A Light in the City: The Fourth Presbyterian Church of Chicago* (Chicago: Fourth Presbyterian Church, 1990).

15. See Lane and Kezys, *Chicago Churches and Synagogues,* 22–23; and "Welcome to Old St. Patrick's," pamphlet given to visitors, 1992.

16. *The Divine Comedy of Dante Alighieri: Inferno,* trans. Allen Mandelbaum (New York: Bantam, 1982), 3, 149, 285, 311, 317.

17. *The Divine Comedy of Dante Alighieri: Purgatorio,* trans. Allen Mandelbaum (New York: Bantam, 1982).

18. *The Divine Comedy of Dante Alighieri: Paradiso,* trans. Allen Mandelbaum (New York: Bantam, 1982), 303.

Chapter 9

1. See, for more information, the web page of the Turkey Vulture Society, at http://www.accutek.com/vulture/sketches.htm, as cited 20 June 2002.

2. Diana L. Eck, "Mountains," in *The Encyclopedia of Religion,* ed. Mircea Eliade. (New York: Macmillan, 1987), 10: 130.

3. Anuradha Roma Choudhury, "Hinduism," in *Sacred Place,* ed. Jean Holm with John Bowker, Themes in Religious Studies (London: Pinter, 1994), 63.

4. Seth Kunin, "Judaism," in ibid., 124.

5. See among many others, Walter Brueggemann, *The Land: Place as Gift, Promise, and Challenge in Biblical Faith* (Philadelphia: Fortress Press, 1977); and Geoffrey R. Lilburne, *A Sense of Place: A Christian Theology of the Land* (Nashville: Abingdon, 1989).

6. Sam D. Gill, *Mother Earth: An American Story* (Chicago: University of Chicago Press, 1987).

7. Brueggemann, *The Land,* 74.

8. Larry L. Rasmussen, *Earth Community, Earth Ethics* (Maryknoll, N.Y.: Orbis Books, 1996).

9. Rosemary Radford Ruether, *Gaia and God: An Ecofeminist Theology of Earth Healing* (San Francisco: HarperSanFrancisco, 1992).

10. Sallie McFague, *The Body of God: An Ecological Theology* (Minneapolis: Fortress Press, 1993).

11. Stephen Jay Gould, *Wonderful Life: The Burgess Shale and the Nature of History* (New York: Norton, 1989), 322–23.

12. Ibid., 51–52.

13. See, for the full story, J. Ronald Engel, *Sacred Sands: The Struggle for Community in the Indiana Dunes* (Middletown, Conn.: Wesleyan University Press, 1983).

14. Ibid.

15. *Christianity and Ecology: Seeking the Well-being of Earth and Humans,* Religions of the World and Ecology, vol. 3, ed. Dieter T. Hessel and Rosemary Radford Ruether (Cambridge: Harvard University Press, 2000).

16. Belden C. Lane, *The Solace of Fierce Landscapes: Exploring Desert and Mountain Spirituality* (New York: Oxford, 1998), 27, 35.

17. See Daniel Swartz, "Jews, Jewish Texts, and Nature: A Brief History," in *This Sacred Earth: Religion, Nature, Environment,* ed. Roger S. Gottlieb (New York: Routledge, 1996), 88.

18. Bill Kohlmoos, "Some Interesting Information about the Turkey Vulture," at http://www.accutek.com/vulture/facts.htm, as cited 20 June 2002. Kohlmoos is president of the Turkey Vulture Society.

Chapter 10

1. Black Elk, *Black Elk Speaks: Being the Life Story of a Holy Man of the Oglala Sioux, as told to John G. Neihardt* (New York: Pocket Books, 1959 [1932]), 36.

2. Roger Cook, *The Tree of Life: Image for the Cosmos* (London: Thames, 1974).

3. *Tao Te Ching,* 16. For various translations, go to Dao De Jing Translations at http://www.nauticom.net/www/asti/dao_jing.htm, as cited on 27 January 2003.

4. Kenton Miller and Laura Tangley, *Trees of Life: Saving Tropical Forests and Their Biological Wealth* (Boston: Beacon Press, 1991), 6.

5. See on this theme Stephanie Kaza, "House of Wood," in *This Sacred Earth: Religion, Nature, Environment,* ed. Roger S. Gottlieb (New York: Routledge, 1996), 41. Kaza suggests that we attend to "the

tree behind Jesus" as the key to a true "theology of the cross," where suffering is addressed in all of its dimensions. As she puts it, poignantly: "I am weary with wondering how much will be destroyed before we find the tree behind Jesus" (43).

6. Heinrich Schipperges, *Hildegard of Bingen: Healing and the Nature of the Cosmos,* tr. John A. Broadwin (Princeton, N.J.: Markus Wiener, 1997), 66–67.

7. Matthew Fox, "Commentary," *The Illuminations of Hildegard of Bingen* (Santa Fe, N.M.: Bear and Co., 1985), 30–31.

8. Walter Wink, *Engaging the Powers: Discernment and Resistance in a World of Domination* (Philadelphia: Fortress Press, 1992). The "Domination System" is discussed on 13–108.

9. Ibid., 61–62.

Chapter 11

1. For a fascinating exploration of the interface between Hindu and Christian images for God, see Diana L. Eck, *Encountering God: A Spiritual Journey from Bozeman to Banaras* (Boston: Beacon, 1993).

2. See among many others, Sam Gill, *Native American Religions: An Introduction,* The Religious Life of Man Series (Belmont, Calif.: Wadsworth Press, 1982).

3. Andrew Linzey, *Animal Theology* (Urbana: University of Illinois Press, 1995), 4–27.

4. Ibid., 62–72.

5. Ibid., 79.

6. See on this theme the provocative work by Carol J. Adams, *The Sexual Politics of Meat: A Feminist-Vegetarian Critical Theory* (New York: Continuum, 1990). I have not yet been persuaded to forgo meat eating, although I have reduced my consumption of red meat and often share vegetarian meals with my wife, Lisa, who gave up all meat but seafood seven years ago. The arguments of vegetarians are, however, increasingly compelling to me, and vegetarianism has surely been the direction of my eating habits over the past five years.

7. L. Shannon Jung, "Animals in Christian Perspective: Strangers, Friends, or Kin?" in *Good News for Animals? Christian Approaches to Animal Well-Being,* ed. Charles Pinches and Jay B. McDaniel (Maryknoll, N.Y.: Orbis Books, 1993), 47.

8. Stephen H. Webb, *On God and Dogs: A Christian Theology of Compassion for Animals* (New York: Oxford, 1998), 103–4, 126.

9. See, for example, the extraordinary work being done at the Center for the Prevention of Sexual and Domestic Violence, http://www.cpsdv.org/, as cited on 24 June 2002; and Carol J. Adams and Marie M. Fortune, eds., *Violence against Women and Children: A Christian Theological Sourcebook* (New York: Continuum, 1995).

10. Rosemary Radford Ruether, "Ecofeminism: The Challenge to Theology," in *Christianity and Ecology: Seeking the Well-Being of Earth and Humans,* ed. Dieter T. Hessel and Rosemary Radford Ruether (Cambridge: Harvard University Press, 2000), 103.

11. Most interestingly, at the same time that biblical scholars are developing new ways to understand ancient texts and contexts, so too are contemporary anthropologists and scientists suggesting that the world of culture and matter may be far more malleable and less mechanistic than we recently thought. I cannot trace here the fascinating work emerging that studies the relationship between science and religion (especially in physics), or the work of anthropologists into the function of trance, ecstasy, out-of-body, and many other such "paranormal" or "spiritual experiences." Suffice it to say that what physicists suggest about the indeterminacy of the physical universe and what anthropologists suggest about the apparent flexibility in human behavior and experience makes possible new readings of the miracle stories. Such a reading will neither distort the miracles into "supernaturalistic science" nor debunk them as "false mythology." See, for one example, Felicitas Goodman, *Ecstasy, Ritual, and Alternate Reality: Religion in a Pluralistic World* (Bloomington: Indiana University Press, 1988).

12. See on this point Elizabeth Haiken, *Venus Envy: A History of Cosmetic Surgery* (Baltimore: Johns Hopkins University Press, 1997).

13. James B. Nelson, *Body Theology* (Louisville: Westminster/John Knox Press, 1992), 22.

14. William T. Cavanaugh, *Torture and Eucharist: Theology, Politics, and the Body of Christ* (London: Blackwell, 1998), 206.

Chapter 12

1. St. Augustine, *The City of God,* trans. Henry Bettenson (New York: Penguin, 1984), book 1, ch. 1, 5.

2. Patricia L. MacKinnon calls this strategy "antithesis" or "contraposition." See "The Divided Self/ The Divided Civitas," in *The City of God: A Collection of Critical Essays,* ed. Dorothy F. Donnelly (New York: Peter Lang, 1995), 322. I follow Peter Brown in calling the strategy "juxtaposition." See *Augustine of Hippo* (Berkeley and Los Angeles: University of California Press, 1967), esp. 306.

3. St. Augustine, *The City of God,* book 14, ch. 28, 593

4. See on this theme Dorothy F. Donnelly, "Reconsidering the Ideal: *The City of God* and Utopian Speculation," in *The City of God: A Collection of Critical Essays,* ed. Dorothy F. Donnelly (New York: Peter Lang, 1995). Donnelly rejects the label "utopia" for Augustine's work, since she holds that a "true *res publica* cannot, according to Augustine's universal theory of history, be established in the earthly world" (205). This may disqualify Augustine's work for the genre of "utopia" according to literary canons, but by the denotation of the term as "no place," it makes Augustine's work a perfect example. If not a utopia, Augustine's work is surely a dystopia—and of those there are many Christian examples.

5. St. Augustine, *The City of God,* book 19, ch. 13, 870.

6. Ibid., book 21, ch. 5, 973.

7. Ibid., book 22, ch. 22, 1068. The extraordinary success of the "Left Behind" series, by Tim LeHaye and Jerry Jenkins, confirms this trend. See *Left Behind: A Novel of the Earth's Last Days* (Wheaton, Ill.: Tyndale, 1995) and the many sequels and spin offs.

8. Ibid., book 22, ch. 8, 1033–48.

9. Ibid., book 22, chs. 13–21, 1049–65.

10. Ibid., book 22, ch. 22, 1065.

11. Ibid., book 22, ch. 29, 1081.

12. Ibid., 1084.

13. See for clarification of this theme the highly personal, yet historically grounded, meditation of my colleague Timothy J. Wengert, "'Peace, Peace . . . Cross, Cross:' Reflections on How Martin Luther Relates the Theology of the Cross to Suffering," in *Theology Today* 59 (July 2002): 190–205.

14. St. Augustine, *The City of God,* book 22, ch. 29, 1087.

15. See Donnelly ("Reconsidering the Ideal"), who contends accurately that "in *The City of God* the emphasis is on the individual, not on society; it is on the integration of the individual with God, not on an integration with social institutions" (207). This is an odd emphasis indeed for a work with *city* in its title.

16. Michel de Certeau, "Walking in the City," in *The Cultural Studies Reader,* ed. Simon During, 2d ed. (London: Routledge, 1993), 127–28.

17. Ibid., 131.

18. See Wes Howard-Brook and Anthony Gwyther, *Unveiling Empire: Reading Revelation Then and Now* (Maryknoll, N.Y.: Orbis Books, 1999).

19. St. Augustine, *The City of God,* book 12, ch. 28, 508.

20. Ibid., book 1, ch. 31, 42.

21. Robert A. Orsi, "Introduction: Crossing the City Line," in *Gods of the City: Religion and the American Urban Landscape,* ed. Robert A. Orsi (Bloomington: Indiana University Press, 1999), 7, 11.

22. St. Augustine, *The City of God,* book 9, ch. 16, 360–61.

23. Ibid., book 14, ch. 13, 573.

24. Ibid., book 19, ch. 19, 878.

25. Ibid., book 10, ch. 32, 423.

26. Ibid., book 12, ch. 5, 476.

27. Ibid., book 4, ch. 4, 139.

28. Ibid., book 22, ch. 30, 1089.

29. See John Brinckerhoff Jackson, *Discovering the Vernacular Landscape* (New Haven: Yale University Press, 1984).

30. Orsi, "Introduction: Crossing the City Line," 15, 37.

31. Ibid., 48, 41.

32. W. E. B. DuBois, *The Souls of Black Folk* (New York: New American Library, 1969 [1903]), 267–76.

33. Sharon Zukin, *The Cultures of Cities* (London: Blackwell, 1995), 294.

34. Michael W. Harris, *The Rise of Gospel Blues: The Music of Thomas Andrew Dorsey in the Urban Church* (New York: Oxford University Press, 1992), xxi.

35. St. Augustine, *The City of God,* book 12, ch. 28, 508.

36. This will be the topic of my next book, tentatively entitled, *Violence and the Sacred in America.*

37. See Diana L. Eck, *A New Religious America: How a "Christian Country" Has Become the World's Most Religiously Diverse Nation* (San Francisco: Harper Collins, 2001).

38. Orsi, "Introduction: Crossing the City Line," 55.

39. On this dualism, see Shamara Shantu Riley, "Ecology Is a Sistah's Issue Too: The Politics of Emergent Afrocentic Ecowomanism," in *This Sacred Earth: Religion, Nature, Environment,* ed. Roger S. Gottlieb (New York: Routledge, 1996), 347.

Photo Credits

All photos taken by the author, unless otherwise indicated.

Chapter 1

p. 20 Photo of the author, 1976. Rueckl Studios, Appleton, Wisc. Property of the author.

p. 21 Photo of Pahl family leaving for California Amtrak vacation, 1973. Taken by a neighbor.

Chapter 2

p. 44 "Big Bil-Bored," across from North Riverside Park Mall, Harlem Avenue, Chicago suburbs, summer 1987

p. 54 Vietnam Veterans Memorial/Washington Monument, Washington, D.C., November 9, 1994

Chapter 3

p. 71 Water flowers, Southlake Mall, Merrillville, Ind., c. 1990

p.72 Skylight, Southlake Mall, c. 1990

p. 73 Window advertisement, Southlake Mall, c. 1990

p. 76 South entrance, Mall of America, Bloomington, Minn., July 18, 2001

p. 78 The Chapel of Love, Mall of America, July 18, 2001

p. 81 "True Shopping" T-shirt, Mall of America, July 18, 2001

Chapter 4

p. 83 "Cinderella's Castle," Walt Disney World, Orlando, Fla., spring 1992

p. 88 Coffin from "The Haunted Mansion," Walt Disney World, spring 1992

p. 99 Rheanne's Reaction to EPCOT, Walt Disney World, spring 1994

Chapter 5

p. 104 Jon, Andy, and David Pahl, summer 1972. Taken by Fred Pahl.

p. 105 713 Pine Ridge Road, Media, Pa., spring 2002

p. 113 Passing on the rituals, summer 1989

Chapter 6

p. 135 Habitat for Humanity House #3, Valparaiso, Ind., summer 1999

Chapter 7

p. 142 Dave Schreiber and the author, Looking Glass Rock, Pisgah National Forest, summer 1977

p. 148 Justin Pahl, North Riverside, Ill., c. December 1986

p. 160 Crum Creek swimming hole, Smedley Park, Nether Providence, Pa., summer 2001

Chapter 8

p. 173 Nathan Pahl, Yahara Center, Madison, Wisc., winter 1988

p. 174 Fourth Presbyterian Church, Chicago. Courtesy of Micah Marty.

p. 175 Pieta, Old St. Patrick's Catholic church, Chicago, c. 1996

p. 175 Christ, Pantocrator, Sts. Volodymyr and Olha Ukrainian Catholic Church, Chicago, c. 1996

p. 178 Photo of the author, c. 1965. Taken by his father.

Chapter 9

p. 181 Bear Butte, Sturgis, S.D., summer 1987

p. 187 The Emancipation Formation/Washington's Crack, Mount Rushmore, S.D., summer 2001

p. 194 Dune country, near Arcadia, Mich., summer 1998

Chapter 10

p. 199 Muir Woods, California, summer 1996

Chapter 11

p. 219 Ruth and John Olsen, Appleton, Wisc., spring 1985

p. 223 The author and Heidegger, c. 1982

p. 238 Rheanne Pahl, Annandale, Va., December 1993

Chapter 12

p. 239 Luther Place Memorial Church, Washington, D.C., fall 1994.

p. 254 Chicago skyline from the Sears Tower, summer 1995

p. 257 Valparaiso University Gospel Choir, Director Judith Erwin-Neville, 1999

Index